BORN IN BLOOD

Born in Blood investigates one of history's most violent undertakings: the United States of America. People the world over consider violence in the United States as measurably different than that which troubles the rest of the globe, citing reasons including gun culture, the American West, Hollywood, the death penalty, economic inequality, rampant individualism, and more. This compelling examination of American violence explains a political culture of violence from the American Revolution to the Gilded Age, illustrating how physical force, often centered on racial hierarchy, sustained the central tenets of American liberal government. It offers an important story of nationhood, told through the experiences and choices of civilians, Indians, politicians, soldiers, and the enslaved, providing historical context for understanding how violence has shaped the United States from its inception.

Scott Gac is Director of American Studies and Professor of American Studies and History at Trinity College and the author of *Singing for Freedom: The Hutchinson Family Singers and the Nineteenth-Century Culture of Reform* (2007).

BORN IN BLOOD

VIOLENCE AND THE MAKING OF AMERICA

SCOTT GAC

CAMBRIDGE
UNIVERSITY PRESS

CAMBRIDGE
UNIVERSITY PRESS

Shaftesbury Road, Cambridge CB2 8EA, United Kingdom

One Liberty Plaza, 20th Floor, New York, NY 10006, USA

477 Williamstown Road, Port Melbourne, VIC 3207, Australia

314–321, 3rd Floor, Plot 3, Splendor Forum, Jasola District Centre,
New Delhi – 110025, India

103 Penang Road, #05–06/07, Visioncrest Commercial, Singapore 238467

Cambridge University Press is part of Cambridge University Press & Assessment,
a department of the University of Cambridge.

We share the University's mission to contribute to society through the pursuit of
education, learning and research at the highest international levels of excellence.

www.cambridge.org
Information on this title: www.cambridge.org/9781316511886

DOI: 10.1017/9781009053105

First published 2024

Printed in Mexico by Litográfica Ingramex, S.A. de C.V.

A catalogue record for this publication is available from the British Library.

Library of Congress Cataloging-in-Publication Data
Names: Gac, Scott, author.
Title: Born in blood : violence and the making of America / Scott Gac.
Description: Cambridge, United Kingdom; New York, NY, USA: Cambridge University
Press, 2024. | Includes bibliographical references and index.
Identifiers: LCCN 2023026410 (print) | LCCN 2023026411 (ebook) |
ISBN 9781316511886 (hardback) | ISBN 9781009054782 (paperback) |
ISBN 9781009053105 (ebook)
Subjects: LCSH: Violence – United States – History.
Classification: LCC HM1116 .G348 2024 (print) | LCC HM1116 (ebook) |
DDC 303.60973 – dc23/eng/20230804
LC record available at https://lccn.loc.gov/2023026410
LC ebook record available at https://lccn.loc.gov/2023026411

ISBN 978-1-316-51188-6 Hardback

In memory of Edward A. Gac, 1938–2018

A society is always eager to cover misdeeds with a cloak of forgetfulness, but no society can fully repress an ugly past when the ravages persist into the present. America owes a debt of justice which it has only begun to pay.
Dr. Martin Luther King, Jr., 1968

Contents

List of Figures   *page* viii

Introduction: A System of Violence: Liberal Society
in the United States   1

PART I: EARLY MANIFESTATIONS

1   A Revolution Restrained   23
2   Life in the Army of the Continent   50
3   The Code of American Violence   73

PART II: EVOLUTIONS

4   The 1850s: A People's Government and the Politics
of Belligerence   91
5   The United States Greets John Brown   113
6   1860: The Undisputed Election that Sparked Dispute   132
7   Emancipation's Fury   157

PART III: MODERN TRADITIONS

8   To 1877: American Capitalism and the Geography of Violence   191
9   Layering Law and Resistance in the Great Strikes   217
10   Words and Ropes: The Postwar Battles over Racial Order   242
    Epilogue   266

Acknowledgements   270
Notes   274
Index   339

Figures

0.1 "Crispus Attucks, the First Martyr of the American
      Revolution"   *page* 2
1.1 A military flogging   26
1.2 Riding the wooden horse   27
1.3 *Washington Assumes Command*   47
2.1 *Mutiny of the Pennsylvania Line*   64
4.1 "Some Account of Some of the Bloody Deeds of Gen.
      Jackson"   94
4.2 Killing free state supporters in 1858   108
5.1 "Storming of the Engine-House by United States Marines"   119
6.1 "Grand Procession of Wide Awakes at New York"   136
7.1 Robert Smalls and the gun-boat *Planter*   160
8.1 Artillery captured from rebels   201
8.2 Unidentified soldier in Union uniform   202
9.1 Railroad property destroyed by workingmen   232
10.1 Hon. Alonzo J. Ransier   243
10.2 Anti-Black violence in New York City   257

INTRODUCTION

A SYSTEM OF VIOLENCE: LIBERAL SOCIETY IN THE UNITED STATES

On the night of March 5, 1770, a British sentry and a local apprentice traded insults along Boston's King Street. The soldier smacked the working man with his rifle butt and a crowd formed in the man's defense. Soon, after the sentry summoned assistance, nine red-coated soldiers faced an angry mob of several hundred men. "'You lobster,' 'You bloody back,' 'You coward,' 'You dastard,'" shouted members of the throng as they flung spit and threw rocks and ice-laden snow.[1]

Seemingly panicked, the British troops fired their guns. Most of the victims in what soon became known as the Boston Massacre were boys, young workers, and sailors – individuals whose experiences reflected migrations and connections across three continents. Crispus Attucks is the best remembered of those who died on the spot. A child of a Natick Indian and a colonial British African (and himself a former slave), Attucks was only in the city temporarily. He had been set to work a ship headed to North Carolina. Instead, two shots tore through his chest as he leaned on a stick about fifteen feet from the soldiers (Fig. 0.1).[2]

The seaman James Caldwell was also shot twice in the chest. Ropemaker Samuel Gray had his hands in his pockets when he was shot through the head. An apprentice in a wood construction trade, seventeen-year-old Samuel Maverick rushed to King Street out of curiosity; he died slowly from musket shot over the next twenty-four hours. The leatherworker Patrick Carr was more hotheaded as he rushed to the scene. Friends insisted he leave behind a sword that he had tucked in his overcoat. His musket wound took ten days to kill him. Bullets from the nine soldiers' muskets also injured a half-dozen others, including a merchant, a sailor, and apprentices.[3]

As was typical among European militaries, the British soldiers of the 29th Regiment in Boston likewise presented a diverse group from society's margins. Of the six hundred or so fighters in the unit, 33 percent were English, 50 percent were Irish, and a little over 5 percent were Scottish. Notably, Irishmen and Scotsmen appeared alien to those who identified as Englishmen in the eighteenth century. Even more outlandish to many

Fig. 0.1 "Crispus Attucks, the First Martyr of the American Revolution, King (now State) Street, Boston, March 5, 1770." In William Nell, *The Colored Patriots of the American Revolution* (Boston: R. F. Wallcut, 1855). From the Schomburg Center for Research in Black Culture, New York Public Library.

White people in Boston were the seventeen young men marked as "Foreign" in the regiment report. This designation likely indicated Afro-Caribbean drummers, the bulk of whom were "procured" during the British capture of Guadeloupe in the Seven Years' War (1756–1763).[4]

The violence in 1770 in Boston, New England – often portrayed as a uniquely American experience – was thus forged in an eighteenth-century matrix of global markets, colonization, slavery, and imperial force. Colonial Americans hardly stood alone when they questioned why and how the violence of the state touched their lives. But the European worldview they shared focused on hostile regional prejudice. British colonists commonly viewed those in France or Spain (or in French- or Spanish-occupied territories) as enemies, and they viewed Indigenous peoples who allied with the French or Spanish as enemies too. (If the soldiers in the Boston Massacre had "slain a hundred Frenchmen a piece," argued a lawyer in the soldiers' defense, "the English law would have considered it as a commendable action.") Experiencing the world through the lens of such regional affiliation and prejudice, many White colonials of Boston thus failed to connect their plight with that of communities in the West Indies, Africa, South America, and South Asia.[5]

Bostonians focused instead on their local and British experiences to navigate the violence in their city. Patriot physician Joseph Warren marked the Boston Massacre as the "BLOODY CONSEQUENCES OF PLACING AN ARMED FORCE IN A POPULOUS CITY." Indeed, in 1770, the British had stationed enough troops in and around Boston to nearly equal the resident number of adult White males. One in three of all adult men in the city was a soldier. Such figures proved, a Boston committee believed, that the killings resulted from "taxing America," a policy started in 1765 that provided support for the soldiers and included subsequent British political and military abuse. Attorney Robert Treat Paine, when prosecuting the British soldiers involved in the March event, shared a similar sentiment: "The inhabitants, for a long time, had been fully sensible of the evil disposition and abusive behaviour of many of the soldiers towards them."[6]

Most British leaders and their advocates rejected the notion that imperial policy fostered violence. They highlighted unlawful colonist behavior and civil disorder in Boston's streets. A 1770 London pamphlet, *On the Late Unhappy Disturbance in Boston*, complained that "it has been deemed a crime [by Bostonians] to affirm that the authority of the British parliament was supreme in all respects throughout all the dominions of the crown of Great Britain." As to responsibility for the March incident, a letter to former Prime Minister George Grenville left no doubt: "The Townsmen were guilty of several outrages before the military Fired."[7]

The Boston Massacre – and, more broadly, the late British colonial era in North America – highlights a great struggle over the boundaries of violence in society. This struggle shaped institutions and individuals, the subjects of this book. *Born in Blood* is about government force (state violence) and acts of violence by individuals and communities in the United States. It tracks violence as a national tradition, one created by an assortment of persons from the Revolution and Civil War to the Gilded Age. In the following pages, accounts of well-known figures are often featured: Robert E. Lee, for example, whose marines killed and captured members of John Brown's band, and Rutherford B. Hayes, who authorized the domestic use of nearly four thousand troops in 1877. These examples show how state violence can uphold unjust systems – although it does not follow that all uses of state violence are unjust.

Told here, too, are tales of the likes of Rufus Putnam, witness to heartless forms of soldier punishment in upstate New York; Deborah Sampson, who passed as a male soldier in the American Revolution; Robert Smalls, the enslaved man who stole a ship and his freedom from the Confederacy; and Lee Walker, a Black man lynched by White men in

3

Memphis. These individuals navigated the limits and lies of violence in a liberal state. They remind us how people created, tested, resisted, and maintained American violence and its institutional expressions. Men and women in the nation's past built and rebuilt a violent nation.

A focus on the American nation-state is useful, although it is also problematic. Using terms such as *America, American,* or *United States* suggests a uniformity of region, race, class, gender, and viewpoint that does not exist among such diverse places and peoples. Moreover, the uniformity suggested by these terms often assumes White, middle-class men to be the center of the story – or at least the most representative of the whole. While a nation of imagined homogeneity helps forge communal ideas and goals, it also forges communal blind spots. In a society seemingly without "antagonistic differences," the centrality of violent acts – particularly those committed by the state – is obscured. Similarly, the lexicon of the nation can strip humanity from individuals – specifically those who reside within national borders but are largely unrecognized by authorities, like members of Native groups and homeless communities. While nation-based words like "America" and "American" are used in this book, please remember the challenges they raise.[8]

Nations themselves are likewise social and political constructs – a fact that is important to engage in a history of violence. To many elite European theorists, the New World was a crude, organic place. Here, the White settler uncovered a regressive expanse – one devoid of a more advanced ethical and political practice. The preferred term these theorists used for it was a "state of nature." And in this state of nature, Thomas Hobbes explained, "the life of man" was "solitary, poore, nasty, brutish, and short." Such conditions rendered "men apt to invade, and destroy one another." According to classic theory, the liberal state of the eighteenth century arose in response to this supposed chaos.[9]

Violence was, indeed, part of the North American human experience before the European invasion. Indigenous individuals and societies used violence to meet a variety of political and cultural undertakings. Yet life was not a perpetual, aimless fight. So, when Hobbes's description of the so-called state of nature depicted Native violence as frenzied and constant, it served an ideological end: to justify Indigenous dispossession and replacement. Hobbes and other Anglo thinkers helped develop the idea of "confident ascendency," the notion that Europe and Europeans stood superior to Native America and Natives (and Indigenous peoples around the world). This ascendant mindset was not innate to White Europeans, however, and took centuries to construct. Its emergence over time is critical for understanding modern state formation and violence within modern states.[10]

To live in a society where property and persons were protected, European theorists proposed that the violence inherent in the "state of nature" be transferred to liberal government. Thus, the idea of the pre-European state of nature was an important part of what earlier scholars called "colonization" – the process of seizing land and labor from Native communities. Today, we have an updated lexicon that better describes this phenomenon: "settler colonialism" or "settler colonization." Settler societies developed in several British colonial sites: Australia, Canada, New Zealand, South Africa, and the United States. In these places, the aggressive movement of (mostly) White settlers displaced, enslaved, and killed Indigenous populations. In North America, where Spanish, French, and English colonists enslaved Indigenous and African persons, settler colonialism also closely aligned with slavery, another form of exploitation and labor extraction. Through these violent processes, Anglo settlers – and the institutions they created – laid their claim as the land's rightful occupants, with the framework of liberalism responding to and acting on their demands.[11]

Although some scholars designate colonization and slavery as the foundation of American violence, they often fail to do more than briefly identify the existence of these two horribly violent processes. Since Indigenous displacement and human enslavement are found throughout history, simply highlighting their existence in North America does not explain much of anything. The question to understand is how colonization and slavery functioned within the greater political economy of the eighteenth century – the context in which the United States was founded – and how their function transformed in the nineteenth century. Changes and challenges to this broadly defined system from the American Revolution to the Civil War changed, challenged, and reformulated American violence.[12]

A common mistake when confronted with the terms "colonization" and "slavery" is for the reader to map these words on to rather limited spaces and times. "Colonization" is often assigned to the American West and "slavery" to the American South – both are frequently imagined as nineteenth-century phenomena (albeit with seventeenth- and eighteenth-century roots). However, these processes worked together. And counter to such common assumptions about their regional scope and timeframe, colonization and slavery stood as part of a global economic system.

This interconnection can clearly be seen in a case from eighteenth-century Rhode Island. In 1707, Thomas Mumford (eventually the grandfather of Samuel Seabury, the first Episcopal bishop in the United States) lived on a Rhode Island plantation in Kingston. This land had once been occupied by the Wampanoag and Narragansett. On a May day when

Thomas was travelling to Newport, his wife, Abigail, "had some words" with one of the three or four Black persons the family owned as property. While it is unclear whether the enslaved man was whipped by Abigail or by a proxy on Abigail's command, a family record notes that during or soon after the whipping, "he [the enslaved man] struck her down and brutally murdered her." The man quickly ran from the scene and apparently drowned in his attempted escape. When the recovered body of the enslaved person was brought to Newport, the General Assembly ordered "that his head, legs, and arms be cut from his body, and hung up in some public place, near the town, to public view, and his body be burnt to ashes, that it may, if [it] please God, be something of a terror to others from perpetrating of the like barbarity for the future."[13]

Exemplary violence – the performance of a public, violent act in belief that bearing witness to and stories of the act would inhibit future violent activity, in this case slave resistance – was a central means of violence prevention within settler populations in New England in the early eighteenth century. However, current research demonstrates that de-escalating violent settings is key to disrupting cycles of violence. In choosing to dismember and display the enslaved man's corpse, the slaveholding settlers of Rhode Island therefore escalated the stakes. Instead of opting for tolerance and restraint – personal qualities that theorists deem necessary for the success of liberal government – the settlers chose the opposite course of action. And by furthering the violence, they perpetuated a violent system of racialized human slavery.

In early New England, exemplary violence bridged colonization and slavery. Some thirty years before the dismemberment of the unnamed Rhode Island man, settlers in the Narragansett region captured and killed Metacom (whom many Whites called King Philip) near the end of Metacom's Rebellion (King Philip's War). The settlers quartered and beheaded Metacom's corpse and displayed the Wampanoag sachem's head on a pike in the center of New Plymouth. They kept it there for years. In such gruesome displays, the British settler slaveholders made their priorities clear. They supported, developed, and sustained two of history's most violent enterprises, colonization and slavery – systems that packaged together land, race, labor, and violence. The profits of one – slavery and the Atlantic slave economy – helped fund the other: Indigenous dispossession and removal.[14]

These enterprises were global and local, as lethal in other regions of the world as they were in North America. In the eighteenth century and beyond, they worked as part of a specific economic arrangement. Historian Sven Beckert calls this arrangement "war capitalism." In the sixteenth, seventeenth, and eighteenth centuries, global and local hierarchies of land, labor, race, and empire shaped the European perspective. Traditionally known as "mercantilism" or "merchant capitalism," the term "war capitalism," Beckert argues, best shows the "rawness and violence" of a system intimately connected to European imperial expansion. It was a form of capitalism "characterized just as much by massive expropriations as by secure ownership." In other words, we should understand this moment of globalizing economic development less in terms of "contracts and markets" (which were central to industrial capitalism) and more in terms of "violence and bodily coercion."[15]

In 1707 in Rhode Island, the Mumford family profited from the land of killed and displaced Natives. They forced Black persons to clear the fields and labor over stone walls, wheat, peas, corn, and cows, as well as to clean their homes. Slave labor and colonized lands thus provided two essential elements for the Mumfords' participation in market exchange: time (which allowed Thomas to engage in business activities) and surplus goods (crops, cheeses, and livestock to sell). Furthermore, the Mumfords' use of the local and regional markets made available through Newport, especially those in the West Indies, linked the family to a thriving network of trade built on settler agricultural produce and human enslavement.[16]

While the violence of war capitalism often took place on an interpersonal or private level, such as between Abigail Mumford (or her delegate) and the enslaved man, it was also performed and supported by the governments that the settler slaveholders built. The government-ordered corpse desecration and display in 1707 exemplified a trend, with the private–public synergy of violent activity empowering colonizers and enslavers in the colonies. This power led many White colonists to believe that they were central actors in the British empire.[17]

Their perspective was not shared, however, by their counterparts across the Atlantic. A burgeoning industrial sector in Great Britain assigned the producers of raw materials a secondary status. After the Seven Years' War, British leaders signaled this status to North American colonists in a variety of ways, including restrictions on settler movement, the levying of taxes, and the deployment of troops. Faced with an imperial government they could not control, an increasing number of American settlers expressed concern. They demanded that modern political and economic rights extend to settlers in British colonial possessions. Notably, many colonists had celebrated the Redcoats when they countered French and Spanish settlers, Native peoples, slaves, debtors, and the poor. But these Anglo celebrants – by virtue of their alignment with the British empire, Whiteness, wealth, or some combination of factors – considered themselves superior to these groups and wanted the imperial government to respect and reflect what they viewed as their unique role as settler colonial subjects.[18]

By the mid-eighteenth century, questions of legitimacy and violent acts thus lay at the core of the Boston colonists' disputes with imperial governance. British settlers in general – and especially those in North America – had ample reason to view Britain's forces with suspicion. In the 1750s, British troops had forcibly removed seven thousand French Acadians from Nova Scotia, New Brunswick, and Prince Edward Island, and, in the decade starting in 1765, army regulars had acted against protesters in civil disputes throughout Great Britain. In May 1768, a soldier shooting a young boy dead in London's St. George's Fields left a particularly strong impression: Benjamin Franklin referenced it in a piece published two years later in January 1770. Then, in February 1770, just one month following Franklin's publication, a Boston customs official killed a twelve-year-old named Christopher Seider. Following the Boston Massacre in March of that same year, Bostonians' suspicion turned to outrage. In their view, the violence of the imperial state had developed a logic of its own: the government that was supposed to safeguard citizens was instead killing them.[19]

———————◆———————

Who bears the responsibility for murderous government policy? In 1770, many colonists believed that the soldiers in the Boston Massacre bore legal guilt for shooting people dead. To John Adams, this was dangerous thinking. Then thirty-five years old, the lawyer and future American president was no supporter of British rule. He was, however, confident in the mechanisms and justice of the liberal state. He knew that government depended on the law, he knew that the law authorized certain individuals to act with homicidal violence, and he knew how social and cultural difference marked select persons as dangerous – and thus worthy targets of violent acts.

As defense attorney for the British military men involved in the Boston Massacre, Adams believed that a fundamental duty of government was to quell raucous demonstrations. In his view, such uprisings were inevitable. "No form of government, and perhaps no wisdom or virtue in the administration," he said, "can at all times avoid riots and disorders among the people." Citing legal precedent in his trial notes, Adams marked the words of famed legalist William Hawkins: "in some Cases wherein the Law authorizes Force, it is not only lawful, but also commendable to make use of it." On the night of March 5, Adams argued, nine British soldiers followed the law. And the law, he said, indicated a charge of murder if the soldiers attacked without provocation, manslaughter if the protesters had in some way provoked the attack, and acquittal if the shootings were warranted.[20]

To demonstrate the lawfulness of the soldiers' actions, Adams opened his defense with a candid review of state violence. "If an officer, a sheriff, execute a man on the gallows, draws and quarters him, as in case of high treason, and cuts off his head, this is justifiable homicide, it is his duty." And Adams understood that duty – the obligation of the individual to act in accord with command, regulation, and tradition – is the lifeblood of state violence. To Adams, it did not matter that the British government jeopardized the lives of both civilian and soldier by stationing ever more troops in the city. "Soldiers quartered in a populous town," he said, "will always occasion two mobs, where they prevent one." He likewise believed it unimportant to the soldiers' job that the protesters "thoroughly detested" the "statutes, instructions, mandates and edicts" of the British. Implementers not analysts, soldiers were not in Boston to assess the quality of the policy they enforced. Adams thus argued that the violence of empire did not necessarily impart guilt on the empire's agents for the violence they committed.[21]

Adams then asked the courtroom audience to put themselves in the soldiers' place on the night of March 5. By doing so, he suggested, they would see that the military men operated in self-defense. In addition to duty, the individual right to act with violence in defense of person or property offered the possibility that the military members had justly killed five men. "A man is authorised, therefore, by common sense, and the laws of England, as well as those of nature to love himself better than his fellow subject." Self-preservation, said Adams, "is the first and strongest principle in our nature" and the basis of liberal government. "We talk of liberty and property," he told the court, "but, if we cut up the law of self-defence, we cut up the foundation of both, and if we give up this, the rest is of very little value." He then settled his self-defense argument with an example from philosopher Francis Bacon: "If two persons are cast away at sea, and get on a plank . . . and the plank is insufficient to hold them both, the one hath a right to push the other off to save himself."[22]

However, here is the promise and illusion of liberalism. In an equal setting, two persons grappling over the right to survive aboard a plank highlights the sanctity of self-preservation. But theoretical liberalism differs from the liberalism of real life. Widespread equality in liberal societies is pledged but rarely achieved. What happens if one of the plank persons is armed by the government and the other is an unarmed civilian? If one is rich and the other poor? If one is Black and the other White? Who then gets to survive?[23]

9

The answers to these questions reveal an age-old debate over the character of liberal society and the role of violence within it. For a traditionalist such as political scientist Francis Fukuyama, the liberal state, with its tenets of tolerance, is not responsible for the creation of race and racism. It is "simply a pragmatic tool for resolving conflicts in a diverse society." The liberal state, in this view, establishes and maintains a public sphere where diverse opinions can thrive. Here, diversity is not generated by factors such as religion or race (though they can play a role). Rather, this model upholds that diversity is generated by widespread individual expression. According to John Stuart Mill, a "diversity of tastes and talents, and variety of intellectual points of view" develops as individuals learn from each other in a collision of ideas and respectful debate.[24]

Following this conventional view of liberal society, liberal government must protect individual freedoms (such as the freedom of speech, religion, and press) to establish the public sphere and ensure that conflicts generated as a product of diverse perspectives and beliefs are resolved through conversation. The public sphere is thus a neutral meeting ground for individuals. And in the public sphere, liberal individuals are responsible for practicing self-restraint and toleration to ensure the peaceful exchange of opinion. In turn, these nonviolent exchanges secure a foundational liberal belief: that people have a "right to be convinced rather than coerced." Within this standard understanding of liberalism, therefore, violence should not be part of public life. Indeed, the liberal state is responsible for creating and protecting an impartial space where citizens can peaceably interact. In this space, the public sphere, differences of race, class, gender, and sexuality (to name a few) may exist, but they are not created or fostered by the liberal state. Rather, the seeds of division and conflict around such differences are created and fostered by bigoted individuals. Thus, for traditionalists observing the workings of liberal society, differences of class or race or religion *may* influence the result of the two people battling on Bacon's plank, but the liberal state bears no responsibility for the unequal terms of the plank battle.[25]

By contrast, liberalism's critics often look beyond the individual and push for a more systemic view of the role of tolerance and the fact of difference in a liberal society. They find that tolerance of others (and the self-restraint required for it) is not the same as equality, and they note that the many differences cultivated within society are central to liberal life. "In our era, it is not enough to be tolerant," explains Pulitzer Prize-winning journalist Isabel Wilkerson. "You tolerate mosquitoes in the summer, a rattle in the engine, the gray slush that collects at the crosswalk in winter.

You tolerate what you would rather not have to deal with and wish would go away." When paired with the "salvation fantasy of liberalism," the role of toleration is further challenged. This "salvation fantasy" is historian Deborah T. Levenson's expression for how peoples excluded from full social and political participation are forever promised a "more just future" that never comes. In this view, toleration is one more means by which privileged persons delay social and political justice.[26]

Black scholars have led the way in the critical study of liberalism. Often building on ideas from the likes of W. E. B. Du Bois, mid-twentieth-century thinkers like Oliver C. Cox and Cedric J. Robinson rejected the notion that social, political, and cultural difference is solved by shared toleration. They focused instead on how "antagonistic racial beliefs" or "antagonistic differences" maintain the hierarchies of authority and power essential to the liberal capitalist state (arguing along the way that we cannot understand liberalism divorced from its collaboration with capitalism). From this perspective, the state is expected to be neutral for White citizens and non-neutral for non-Whites. For liberalism's critics, therefore, differences of class, race, gender, and access to government power are structured into the liberal state and will directly influence the outcome of the two persons battling to remain on Bacon's plank.[27]

In 1770, while defending the soldiers in the Boston Massacre, John Adams demonstrated the significance of hostile differences to violence and liberal life. He again concentrated on self-defense, noting, "The law does not oblige us to bear insults to the danger of our lives, to stand still with such a number of people round us, throwing such things at us, and threatening our lives, until we are disabled to defend our-selves." But Adams soon made it clear that the dangers in this particular instance did not derive so much from the things being thrown – the snowballs, oyster shells, and white birch sticks – as it did from the people who threw them. He continued, "We have been entertained with a great variety of phrases, to avoid calling this sort of people a mob. Some call them shavers, some call them geniuses." ("Shavers" are young tricksters and "geniuses" are persons channeling the spirit of the age.) "The plain English is, gentlemen, most probably a motley rabble of saucy boys, negroes and mulattoes, Irish teagues and outlandish jack tars. – And why we should scruple to call such a set of people a mob, I can't conceive, unless the name is too respectable for them."[28]

Adams deployed such differences with aplomb, highlighting a rather full range of differences that structured colonial society: age (*saucy boys*), race (*negroes and mulattoes*), ethnicity and religion (*Irish teagues*, a slur for Irish Catholics), and class (*outlandish jack tars*, denigrating seamen in the merchant marine).[29] Then, to counter accusations that soldier Matthew Killroy was inclined to violent acts against Boston's colonists, Adams again trafficked in ethnic caricature. He told the jury that the witness was asking them to believe that Killroy was predisposed to reckless violence – "that he had the spirit not only of a *Turk* or *Arab*, but of the devil."[30]

As Adams's remarks illustrate, individuals and communities unwelcome or excluded from full membership in liberal societies are often marked as especially violent or cruel. Such classification, in turn, justifies a violent discipline of them. Adams presented the views that many White Christian Europeans held of darker-skinned and Muslim individuals. In his reference to Turks and Arabs, he bade his listeners to find it absurd that the actions of a British soldier could equate with the heedless, violent abandon ascribed to outgroups in the White European imagination.

But Adams was not finished. Next, he explained to the jury how Blackness connected with a violent and criminal fate. Building on a report that had Crispus Attucks arriving at the scene at the head of twenty to thirty sailors, Adams said: "Now to have this reinforcement coming down under the command of a stout mulatto fellow, whose very looks was [*sic*] enough to terrify any person, what had not the soldiers to fear?" In other words, Adams suggested that the soldiers had to be afraid because Attucks was an able-bodied Black working man walking the streets with authority. It was, he proposed, the aggressive, "mad behavior" of Attucks – an overly belligerent behavior that Adams attributed to Turks, Arabs, and now Black men – that had "in all probability" caused "the dreadful carnage" of the Boston Massacre. Adams laid the blame on political and social outsiders: working-class, ethnic, racial, and regional outsiders. "A Carr from Ireland, and an Attucks from Framingham, happening to be here, shall sally out upon their thoughtless enterprizes, at the head of such a rabble of negroes, & c.," he cried in disbelief.[31]

John Adams saw hostile differences among peoples because hostile differences organized the liberal world in which he lived. He labeled the marginalized men in the Boston crowd as violent to help obscure the violent acts of the British state and White individuals. To him, the large body of soldiers that crossed the Atlantic to be stationed in Boston were insiders. These insiders were not guilty of murder because they met the expectations of White society. The military demanded rules to be followed, and the soldiers followed the rules. So too did they observe social etiquette. To White elites such as Adams, a large, diverse group of working-class protesters presented strife. By firing into the crowd, the soldiers performed hostile difference within the British empire. The propertied men who sat on the jury in late 1770 agreed. Captain Preston and six of his men went free. Two others had their sentences for manslaughter reduced to the branding of thumbs.[32]

The violence that bolsters antagonistic differences in liberal society (as well as the violence used to resist the structures of liberal life) is not unique or, to borrow terminology from an earlier generation of scholars, "exceptional" in the American experience. It is a global phenomenon often linked to economic structures that fall into two categories: "global White supremacy" and "racial capitalism." *Born in Blood* draws on these complementary theories. The first, global White supremacy, centers on Whiteness as a "political system," as well as the "differential distribution" of wealth and opportunity it entails. Though entwined with and credited to White people, White supremacy is "an equal opportunity employer." As George Lipsitz writes, "Not all white people have to remain complicit with white supremacy ... even non-white people can become active agents of white supremacy as well as passive participants in its hierarchies and rewards." The second theory, racial capitalism, argues that the development of liberal capitalist society is inextricable from the development of hostile differences. Hostile differences are cultivated in many ways, but none as consequential as the marginalization, removal, and enslavement of, and trade in, Indigenous and Black bodies.[33]

Where liberal capitalism thus links the United States to transnational flows of violence, there are other aspects of American violence that are more unique. Some researchers point to social and cultural phenomena for the origins of a violent tradition: an engagement with the so-called frontier, toxic masculinity, rampant individualism, gun culture, and a national mythology of "regeneration through violence." Many of these analyses are not so much wrong as they are symptoms or products of a larger condition.[34]

In this book, the term *American violence* refers to a political formation of violent activity. Crafted in union with colonization and slavery, it is an artifact of the American Revolution, a pathbreaking moment in the history of violent self-determination. Here, the hostile differences of liberal society meet the aggressive, anti-state acts advanced by colonials. What we learn is that "self-determination" and "self-defense," two of the most widely shared justifications for violence against the British, disguised the racial content embedded in their usage. Such phrases often indicated White self-determination and White self-defense. It is unsurprising, then, that the government systems that evolved from this revolutionary moment privileged White men as violent agents of the federal state (the 1792 Militia Act, for example, required soldiers to be White) and as violent actors in their communities.[35]

In many liberal democratic states, a distinct boundary is fixed between the violence of the people and the violence of the state. In the United States, the boundaries between the two were left ambiguous, and tensions unresolved. These tensions are, in fact, encoded in the US Constitution. *Born in Blood* does not argue that the federal government and individuals are in constant war, however. True, there are moments when this could be seen as the case: the span of American slavery, the 1781 mutiny of Continental Army soldiers, and the Great Strikes of 1877, for example, all present significant conflicts between individuals and the national state. There is a temptation, therefore, to frame these moments through the lens of civilians versus government. But American violence almost always incorporates layers of partisan interests – groups of individuals and multiple government agencies prepared for violent action. In the Great Strikes, for instance, private (often wealthy) individuals, local police, state militia, corporate armies, and federal forces merged to suppress the demands and bodies of American workers. At the same time, railroad workers – and soon those who worked in many industries – joined with local sympathizers, including concerned members of the police and state militia, to promote workers' interests through violent deeds. Such deeds often took the form of property damage but, on occasion, labor resistance resulted in serious physical harm or death.

The different layers of partisan interests need not all be actively engaged in violence to nonetheless work in concert toward violent ends. During the "Bleeding Kansas" battles in the 1850s over whether slavery would be allowed in, the federal military largely stood by as slavery's supporters engaged in combat to secure the territory as a proslavery space. At the time, slavery in Kansas was a goal of the president and many Congressional Democrats, so they were content to allow armed individuals to advance this domestic agenda without much interference. Of course, gun-bearing antislavery activists disagreed. And as the territory descended into a guerilla war, progressive Whigs and soon the newly established Republicans demanded that the federal military intervene to protect and ensure legal processes and elections in Kansas. The national government ignored the demands for military action, however, and soon individuals flooded into the territory to fight. In 1861, as Democratic members from seceded southern states exited Congress, Kansas was admitted to the Union as an antislavery state.

As the history of Kansas shows, American violence often has political motivations, but it is not the sole province of any political branch or party. Nor does the appearance of violence in the United States automatically signal social improvement or retrenchment. Throughout American history,

national forces bolstered human bondage and slaughtered Native populations. So too did they help rout the institution of slavery and provide
a foundation of civil rights. Likewise, individuals and communities have
killed and destroyed for both conservative and progressive ends.[36]

Still, a misconception persists. "I need scarcely say," the physician
Thomas Mayo wrote in *Elements for the Pathology of the Human Mind,* "that
violence [is] always wrong." Mayo's sentiment is as pervasive today as when
he said it in 1838. Yet the histories of the battles against human enslavement,
lynching, and genocide suggest something more complex. Violence is
a social and political tool deployed by individuals and nations. Its immorality
is better determined by the context of its use than by fiat. Deployed to
uphold the status quo just as often as to overturn it, violence is a dynamic
instrument.[37]

This book captures the American dynamism in ten chapters organized in
three parts. The chapters in Part I: Early Manifestations explore the groundwork of American state violence and the legal and military cultures that
sustained it. As shown in the first chapter, "A Revolution Restrained," British
military institutions embraced a hierarchy backed by cruel physical punishment. The defiant soldier could face gauntlets, brandings, wooden horses,
floggings, hangings, and firing squads. In certain places in British North
America, though, White male colonists in militias and provincial armies
enacted a more egalitarian design – one that tilted authority toward the
common soldier and curbed the most egregious aspects of military
discipline. Such egalitarianism structured the Massachusetts Army in the
American Revolution. However, the supposedly democratic rebellion would
not feature a more democratic fighting force overall. When George
Washington assumed command of the Massachusetts troops (soon known
as the Continental Army), he made sure that hostile differences and bodily
reprimand shaped the inaugural institutionalization of American state
violence. "Every one is made to know his place and keep in it," said the
Reverend William Emerson of Washington's army, "or be tied up and
receive thirty or forty lashes according to his crime."[38]

Chapter 2, "Life in the Army of the Continent," unveils the gender, race,
and class composition of state violence during the American Revolution
and explores the key interdependence of state finance, state violence, and
military discipline. In 1781, recent military deprivations in clothing, food,
and arms brought a crisis to the American state. Soldier mutiny shook
the Continental Army throughout the year; at times, nearly 30 percent of

Washington's men stood in protest of military authority. When his leaders faced a standoff with a New Jersey unit, Washington wrote to Continental Army General Robert Howe: "If you succeed in compelling the revolted troops to a surrender, you will instantly execute a few of the most active and most incendiary leaders." With five hundred men, Howe was ultimately able to overawe the rebellious soldiers, killing two of them "on the spot." Washington and his generals understood that, to paraphrase the writings of scholar and essayist Elaine Scarry, the problem of violence is bound up with the problem of power. If American nationalism was forged in violent acts against loyalists, as much recent work highlights, so too was it forged in military discipline through the violent acts committed against Continental Army soldiers.[39]

The opening chapters of *Born in Blood* center on the military. This focus is crucial to understanding how the book aligns with contemporary studies – studies that demonstrate how violence is a learned behavior. In the eighteenth and nineteenth centuries, Presidents Washington, Jefferson, Madison, Monroe, Jackson, William Henry Harrison, Tyler, Polk, Taylor, Fillmore, Pierce, Buchanan, Lincoln, Johnson, Grant, Hayes, Garfield, Arthur, Benjamin Harrison, and McKinley had all served in the military or militia. (John Adams tried and failed to earn an appointment as commander-in-chief of the Continental Army.) Their service, when combined with the mechanisms of a settler slave society, reified the hierarchies of liberalism and taught physical punishment as a means to uphold those hierarchies. It also served to develop violence as an important – if not primary – means of communication, especially for the national state and national policy. The military disposition of presidents (and congressmen and governors and judges) helps explain governmental and popular male support for a century of violent Indigenous dispossession, slavery, civil war, and industrial strategy.[40]

The law bolstered what these men learned. "The Code of American Violence" (Chapter 3) reveals how violent individuals and a violent state are structured into the US Constitution. In the Constitution, violent White self-determination (the right of White individuals to overthrow government) and liberal capitalism (the systemic differences central to a liberal state and war capitalism) mix with republicanism (a decentralization of authority that privileges violent acts of citizens – a group most often defined as propertied White men). Focusing on Article IV, Section 4, the Second Amendment, and the Fifth Amendment, this chapter reveals the key formulations and tensions of American violence in this founding document.

16

The chapters in Part II: Evolutions consider the nature of democracy, race and the merit of violent acts, human enslavement, and resistance to human enslavement. Together these chapters track the slow, contested, and ultimately incomplete transformation of state violence away from the interests and demands of slaveholders toward those of the enslaved. Chapter 4, "The 1850s: A People's Government and the Politics of Belligerence," focuses on democracy – specifically, the creation of a violent American political process. By the 1840s, the right to vote expanded to include nearly all White men in the United States. The establishment of this racialized and gendered electoral process put the nation at the global forefront of White male political participation. These voters elected militant candidates, used violence to set boundaries around the electorate, and physically intimidated political opponents. They demonstrated the importance of Whiteness and violence to democratic development.

"The United States Greets John Brown" (Chapter 5) studies the "problem of evil." Violence is a learned behavior, and peaceful interventions and de-escalation disrupt the learning cycles of violence. Black and White abolitionists had been attempting to bring about peaceful interventions to end slavery since the nation's founding. But southern slaveholders were not willing to give up their slave property. Indeed, during the Civil War, enslavers refused President Lincoln's offer of compensated emancipation (being paid market price per slave in exchange for setting slaves free) time and again. This is the problem of evil. How does one disrupt a violent institution when, in this case, slaveholders refused peaceful means of abolishing it? In 1859, John Brown well understood this dynamic when he challenged the greatest enabler of slavery in the United States: the federal government. Brown believed – and the course of the Civil War suggests he was right – that violence was the surest path to slave freedom. This chapter explores understandings of Black violence and Black authority – both threats to the hostile differences of liberal society. It also examines the legal mechanisms used to deploy troops against slave uprisings and interprets Brown's interracial attack on Harper's Ferry in Virginia as a failed attempt to fashion a government that would back the enslaved over the slaveholder.[41]

Chapter 6, "1860: The Undisputed Election that Sparked Dispute," again engages violent White male partisans. Despite the Republican Party's self-promotion as a coalition committed to peaceful law and order (in contrast to the bullying leadership of slaveholders and Democrats), it was an organization built to resist and fight. In the 1860 election cycle, the Wide Awakes – Abraham Lincoln's Republican backer – engaged their

Democratic counterparts in physical battles across the northern, urban landscape. Shootings, stabbings, chasings, and beatings marked these clashes. This chapter explores how partisan fights – both physical and electoral – shaped questions of violence and the national state during the challenging period between Lincoln's election and his assumption of office.

The centrality of slavery in the North and South, Black resistance, and the greatest shift in the domestic use and formation of federal force form the foundation of Chapter 7, "Emancipation's Fury." In the crucible of emancipation, the likes of Robert Smalls, an enslaved boat pilot in South Carolina, the hundreds of thousands of Civil War slave fugitives, Union and Confederate military leaders, President Lincoln, President Jefferson Davis, and others all addressed the consequences of one question: should the United States deploy its forces and its violence in support of slaveholders or freed slaves?

The final section of the book, Part III: Modern Traditions, addresses government and individual violence within the transition to American industrial capitalism. War capitalism, built on taking land and labor, differed from the laws, contracts, property protections, wage labor, and greatly empowered state of industrial capital. New understandings of race, labor, and labor discipline developed. Thus, the final chapters of the book map out the continuities and changes in American violence in the post-Civil War age.

While the war between capital and labor mimicked that of master and slave, the wage labor and contracts of industrial capital introduced new forms of coercion backed by a strong national state. Chapter 8, "To 1877: American Capitalism and the Geography of Violence," investigates how the political and social hierarchies set by industrial capitalism replaced and worked within the hierarchies set by war capitalism and liberal government. It tracks the discipline of Black Union Army soldiers, the sale of guns and weapons of war in the United States and around the world, and the influence of the railroad – an important physical and economic instrument of violence in the United States.[42]

Although the railroad is credited with modernizing the US economy, this modernization was linked to the limits of economic and racial justice in a liberal state. Efforts to rework the system are often costly, just an economic collapse away from being rendered incomplete. And in the postwar United States, financial theorists (otherwise known as the "panic prognosticators") had come to accept two things: "that monetary panics move in cycles," and that the next fiscal crisis always seemed "imminent." "The cycle of boom and panic," printed the *Omaha Daily Bee*, "prosperity and failure roll on." But the rolling on was not without consequences. Chapter 9, "Layering Law and Resistance in the Great Strikes," traces the multiple levels of enforcement (from the personal and local to the state and federal) used in and around the 1877 worker protests that shut down the nation's economy.[43]

Chapter 10, "Words and Ropes: The Postwar Battles over Racial Order," engages the global and historical practice of lynching and situates it within a North American environment of anti-Black terror. Surveying how violence and the construction of race created and upheld relationships of power and economy in the 1870s, 1880s, and 1890s, this chapter links national lawmakers who advocated for White supremacy to the increase and severity of violence against Black individuals (and others). Specifically, it centers on Congressional discussions in the Reconstruction era and the brutal death of Lee Walker, a Black man, at the hands of a White mob in 1893. The creation of a new racial order – one that harkened to earlier forms of racial intimidation – was intricately connected to work, and violence ensured that the linkages between low-status labor, poverty, and skin color remained unbroken.

A fundamental question underlying the formation of modern liberal states is whether their unprecedented concentrations of government and individual force lead to just ends. Far too many people mistake the importance of violence to liberal life to mean that such violence is sensible and fair. This is especially true for state-backed violence and – in the United States – (supposedly) self-defensive violent acts (often) committed by White men.

Liberal life is situated within the hierarchies demarcated by hostile difference. Understanding violence in America can therefore be complex. Violence is an essential means of upholding the relations of power on which these hierarchies rest. Violence is also an essential means through which marginalized peoples challenge entrenched hierarchies. James Baldwin, the Black writer and activist, well understood this dynamic. Pressed by a White interviewer in 1963 on whether Black freedom struggles would be nonviolent (or "legitimate" in the eyes of the questioner) or violent ("illegitimate"), Baldwin spurned the question. "The history of the civilization that you want me to imitate is a history of violence, of bloodshed," he said. "Whether it becomes violent or nonviolent, I repeat, depends on you."

With the word "you," Baldwin indicted empowered White people. He understood that, by and large, empowered Whites had authored a "history of violence" – a history of a deeply stratified United States whose stratification fostered (and continues to foster) political, cultural, and social systems that disseminate and promote violent behavior. And because these systems often frame vicious acts as natural, expected, and (for the victims) deserved, they self-reinforce cycles of violence.[44]

Born in Blood presents readers a starting point for a broader exploration of this "history of violence" in the United States.

PART I

EARLY MANIFESTATIONS

Withhold not correction from the child: for if thou beateth him with the rod, he shall not die.

Proverbs 23:13, Holy Bible, Authorized King James Version, 1611

If you wish to be feard abroad and lovd and respected at Home – establish your Army in its full force. Nothing can give you so much Authority weight and dignity, as an Army at your command superior to all your foreign and domestick Enemies.

Continental Army Major-General Nathanael Greene, 1777

Those who are accustomed to see and inflict horrible suffering . . . lose the power of feeling for their victims, and fancy the infliction not to be sufficiently severe because it has ceased to excite their own sensibility.

British general and anti-flogging advocate Charles Napier, 1837

1

A REVOLUTION RESTRAINED

Established through violent revolution, the United States was born in blood. More than twenty-five thousand Americans died in the War for Independence – the result of battlefield kills and wounds, disease, and death from imprisonment. Based on relative population, this figure translates to 2.8 million deaths today. When we include the British lives lost, as well as the brutal persecutions and dislocations of tens of thousands of loyalists, Indians, and slaves, the outcome is clear: the violence of the American Revolution was an event in its own right.[1]

How should such violence be understood? For a long time, scholars linked the history of violent acts committed by colonial Americans in the Revolution to an ideological change. Raucous parades, mobs, and jail breaks marked just a few ways that colonials subverted legal processes in British North America. In the 1760s and 1770s, participants in these violent actions, according to the renowned scholar Bernard Bailyn, were "newly empowered by widely shared principles and beliefs." Bailyn's notion – that an attachment to democratic ideals pushed Americans to bloodshed – obscures an uncomfortable truth, however. Violent acts by the colonists were not committed in defense of deeply held political ideology. Rather, violence, in both practice and theory, was integral to the formation of the political and social values that underpinned the Revolution.[2]

American rebels used violent measures as a foundational tool in their effort to undermine British authority in the North American colonies. They were not alone. In the eighteenth century, a global conversation was taking place on the societal boundaries of physical force: who is sanctioned for violent acts – individuals, communities, or governments? How are people and institutions so sanctioned? What are the limits and boundaries of their violent activities? The debate over such questions helped launch the American Revolution as well as the subsequent revolutions in Haiti and France. Each nation, responding to varied events and histories, arrived at assorted solutions.

The displeasure expressed by many White British-American colonists on their treatment as soldiers in the Seven Years' War is an excellent place to begin this story. Carrying their displeasure into the Revolution, many everyday colonials tried to implement a new vision in opposition to their experiences within British military institutions. Their intent, formed in the shadows of colonization and slavery, looked to foster through state violence the kind of White democratic participation that later generations strove toward through politics. In places like Pennsylvania and Massachusetts, the Revolution offered the chance for commoners and leaders alike to employ a military organization aligned with a more egalitarian political principle. For New Englanders, whose earlier experiences encouraged them to empower the common soldier in the Massachusetts Army (the Continental Army's precursor), the use of violent acts to curtail protest within army ranks revealed an abandonment of such egalitarianism. It demonstrated to them but one way in which the era's radicalism would unwind.[3]

---◆---

The Seven Years' War reshaped the global order in the eighteenth century. It took place on five continents, but to British colonists in North America, the battles were intimate and direct. In the winter of 1756/1757, French troops threatened important military and economic pathways in northern New York, leaving the New England colonies vulnerable. Its settlers sounded the alarm.

Unfortunately for the British colonists, the French were not alone. They had recruited members of Indian nations, and, in 1757, more than two thousand warriors from around thirty-three communities stood by them at Fort Carillon (Ticonderoga). It was in this place, between Lake Champlain and Lake George, that the war's bloodiest North American battle transpired. Some three thousand French, Indian, and British bodies would litter the surrounding forests by the time it was through – so many that, nineteen years later, in the midst of the Revolution, undersupplied American troops in the area used the dead men's shin and thigh bones to stake tents and drank from skeletal heads. Continental Army General Anthony Wayne would christen the spot "the Ancient Golgotha or place of skulls."[4]

Between 1754 and 1763, New England men registered their strength within the British military. More than a third of military-qualified Massachusetts men served in provincial armies and thousands filled positions to support the war. Yet, reflecting the sort of hostile difference that structured the empire, the British regulars looked down on the provincial military men, from whom they extracted menial labor and who, by a 1754 proclamation, were officially marked as lower in rank. According to the proclamation, for instance, a provincial general stood below an ensign in the British Army.[5]

For provincial soldiers, the increased military discipline they faced during these years was a shock. At first, the colonial men only met the strict disciplinary code of the British Army when their units served alongside those of regulars. But after 1756, leaders subjected all provincial soldiers to regular army rules. New England colonial Rufus Putnam, who joined the Massachusetts Provincial Army in 1757, took note of soldier punishment. Ten days after officers read the Articles of War to Putnam's group, he saw two men receive twenty lashes. "They were the first that were whipped in our Regt.," he reported. They were not the last. In a single day on September 5, Putnam observed two colonists shot and killed for desertion and "a Connecticut man whipped 500 Lashes for Enlisting into York forces." That evening, three men took six hundred of the thousand lashes due as punishment for desertion.[6]

A fellow soldier in the same regiment, Seth Metcalf, witnessed the horror too. He watched a man's back "whipt till the Blood Came Out at the knee of his Breeches" (Fig. 1.1). Luke Ridley, a Connecticut provincial soldier, noticed additional modes of reprimand. He saw a man run the gauntlet "thrugh 30 men," reflecting, "god have mercy on me the Blood flying every stroke this was a sorrowful sight." He saw another man sentenced to "Ride the wooden horse" – a punishment that entailed straddling the sharp edge of a narrow log or board that was supported by four legs with the man's hands bound behind his back (Fig. 1.2). The soldier often had weights (like muskets) added on to heighten the pain while tormentors moved and bucked the horse. In this instance, Ridley reported that the soldier had "4 muskits tieed to his feet." Permanent injury, including emasculation and even death, could result from a ride on the timber beast.[7]

Soldier discipline and the separation of ranks distinguished the order found in units of British regulars. Reflecting the structures of hostile difference in British societies, it forged an unequal system of military justice where the enlisted, more so than their officers, stood exposed to corporal punishment and the death penalty. A later general called this strict code "the *despotic government of the army in the field.*" When it was applied to provincial soldiers, though, it practically upended the White American colonials' world.[8]

Fig. 1.1 A military flogging. © 1977 University of Oklahoma Press. Reprinted by permission of the publisher.

White colonists entered provincial armies from provincial militias. These militias often operated on ideals far different than those of the British military. Rufus Putnam, for example, had served in the militia in Brookfield, Massachusetts. Here, many of the region's able men between sixteen and sixty participated in military drills. Notably, in a mix of racism and elitism, the colony exempted from militia service slaves, Indians, ministers, civil magistrates, and Harvard students and faculty. The shared sense of local camaraderie and security found in the militia forged the bonds that led Putnam to "a Provincial Regiment of Foot" in the "Company of Capt. Ebenezer Learned."[9]

Putnam's experience was common. Provincial recruiters relied on the militia's relationships of community and kin to fill army ranks. Recruiters for the British Army, by contrast, often used a variety of coercive and deceptive methods to sign on lower-class men. The logic, as once expressed

Fig 1.2 Riding the wooden horse. © 1977 University of Oklahoma Press. Reprinted by permission of the publisher.

in Parliament, that "the worst men make the best soldiers" was based in the belief that such individuals responded satisfactorily to physical punishment. Soldiers and officers in provincial service were thus bound more by association than by authority. To British leaders, the provincial army men appeared untrained, disorganized, and disobedient. And as imperial leaders increasingly implemented new forms of discipline for provincial soldiers, the colonial men pushed back. To those in the American colonies, who had grown accustomed to electing the militia officers who served over them, life in the provincial army developed into something strange and harsh.[10]

Yet the choice to enlist in "His Majesty's Service" for a man like Putnam was probably an easy one. Putnam's father, a farmer who was a civil, militia, and religious leader in the town of Sutton, Massachusetts, had died in 1745. This left the young Putnam in a precarious position. For two years, he lived with his grandfather; then with his stepfather, Captain Sadler, an illiterate man who forbade Putnam from attending school; and, after Sadler's death in 1753, Putnam was bound as an apprentice to a local millwright. Farming, trade work, and laboring were the three central professions in

Massachusetts colony. As the youngest of eleven children, Putnam had failed to access one familiar path to farm ownership: the inheritance of land. And the possibilities available to him in mill construction and repair, it seems, were less attractive than the avenue opened by war. A provincial soldier enlisted for an annual term, and while a private in provincial service earned just as much per month as a common laborer, soldiering was steady work and the army awarded attractive bonuses. By the end of his year of service, Putnam could have saved enough to purchase more than one hundred acres of land near Brookfield.[11]

Indeed, the violent capability of the imperial state in North America was linked to economic opportunity. Provincial men, whose interpersonal relationships had crafted a less repressive military experience in the militias, connected to the British polity in contractual terms. In 1757, Rufus Putnam passed muster in "New Braintry" (current-day New Braintree) and, two weeks later, received "arms and clothing at Worster" (Worcester) – the central site for Massachusetts troops headed to northern New York. As shocked as he might have been by the deliberate disciplining of fellow soldiers during this time, however, he saw too the near-inevitable result of untrained men and guns. In July, he wrote: "There was a man shot off his gun accidentally, & shot a man in the next Tent through the body; who never spoke any more words than these: I am a dead man; the Lord have mercy on me."[12]

Putnam reported on wartime's direct brutalities too. He saw "a great No. of Invalids" (wounded veterans) who marched past his camp on their way home and detailed the sufferings of fallen provincial and British soldiers. The corpse of one provincial man was described to Putnam as having been "found barbecued ... with his nails all pulled out, his lips cut off down to his chin and up to his nose, and his jaws lay bare; his scalp was taken off, his breast cut open, his heart pulled out and his bullet pouch put in the room of it ... a Tomahawk left in his bowels." (Significantly, British colonists and other Europeans often highlighted physical mutilation when Natives committed the act; they failed to note when they themselves disfigured enemy and Indigenous bodies.) A few weeks after hearing this grisly tale, Putnam learned of Lieutenant Dormit, "found with his head and arms cut off and his body cut to pieces."[13]

Yet the accidents and designs of war appeared to bother Putnam less than its broken promises. As a provincial soldier, he expected to see – and perhaps fall prey to – torture and death. But he and the colonial men with whom he served wielded a clear sense of what such risks were worth. On July 27, 1757, for example, Putnam and fellow soldiers (then stationed at

Fort Edward) refused "to go a scouting without some consideration for it." To scout – to locate and detail enemy locations – was dangerous duty. The Fort Edward men also served as rangers, patrolling the area to provide early warnings of attack. In a sign that provincial soldiers did indeed resist the rigid command structure of the British, Putnam and friends brokered a deal. The commanding officer of the fort, Major Fletcher, offered "three dollars per month" for ranger duty and "half a pint of Rum when" the soldiers scouted. Putnam was quick to note, however: "The Rum we got sometimes; but the money we never see."[14]

The broken deal that July proved the least of Putnam's woes. When most of the 1,800 men with whom he had entered provincial service were discharged in November, Putnam was among the 360 "drafted to stay." Winter weather put a stop to the war's open fighting, and the young soldier's ability as a millwright proved invaluable to the military. He worked as a carpenter. But then, just when his year of military service was officially set to end on February 2, 1758, Putnam learned that he might be forced to keep on. A message from Major-General Abercrombie to leaders at the fort intimated that since Abercrombie did not yet "know what the government intends to do with" the men, the soldiers had to wait for their discharge. British superiors further explained that anyone who left without proper orders would "Suffer Death." Unsurprisingly, the provincials immediately dissented. Neither their commanders "nor the Province could hold us any longer," they argued, and "by going off" they asserted that they were not breaking any law.[15]

The next morning at 3 a.m., seventy provincial soldiers acted on this belief. The men left the fort as they had joined – bound now by shared experience as well as community and kin. The close ties between common soldier and officer were apparent. Captain Learned himself led the rebellious group. Clad with snowshoes, the men carried three days' provisions. It was not enough. After a terrible winter storm their first night, the group followed the wrong river and soon became lost. But, to the men's approval, Learned announced, "I will die in the woods before I go back." By the third day, the men had all but consumed their rations. The occasional turkey, killed and roasted, was not enough for such a large contingent. With snow five feet deep and low temperatures, many suffered from frostbite as well. On February 8, the starved soldiers killed "a large dog" who had travelled with them. "None can tell what a sweet morsel this dog's guts and feet were but those that eat them as I did the feet and the riddings of the guts," Putnam reported. Canine butchery made what was taboo for the soldiers more routine. "With respect to the meate of a Dog," Putnam later said, "I have ever Sence . . . believed it to be very good eating, and that I could at any time eat it without disgust." Finally, after eight days of marching, the group found Hawk's Fort in Charlemont, Massachusetts, on February 10.[16]

The British blamed Captain Learned for the incident and would not offer him another commission in the war. But Putnam and the men who walked away knew that Learned had not imposed his beliefs on them. When Learned shouted that he would rather die than turn back, the men "all cried out that they would die with him." This bond, forged in respect, relationship, and righteousness, highlighted an early American conception of how government force might work. It was a participatory system with power more equally divided than it was in the oversight of the British regular forces. Yet, even when the British system failed – as was seen in the regimental rebellion and what Putnam referred to as "Sufferings in my return home" – provincial service and its economic lure remained attractive. Only two months after his 1758 Massachusetts homecoming, Putnam enlisted for another year.[17]

The spaces of equity forged within provincial military work, though, were not open to everyone. Distinguished by race, class, gender, education, and empire, the Massachusetts military men were as varied as the population of the colony they represented. White male colonials of British background, regardless of their economic situation, tended to enjoy most of the privileges afforded by kin and community in provincial militaries. Free Blacks, Indians, and deserters from the enemy (Putnam noted men of French and Dutch descent) inhabited a different place in the organization. In summer 1757, for example, Captain Learned contracted smallpox, was "carried into the Hospital," and, a month later, was provided furlough in New England. But when a free Black scout fell sick during a twelve-day campaign near Ticonderoga, his captain left him "in the woods with two Indians to look after him." The trio remained there for several days, scouted on by the French and French-allied Indians, before forty men, including Putnam, rescued them.[18]

Here, amid more equality and opportunity for some, provincial service in the Seven Years' War prefigured modern political and social forms. While men like Putnam enjoyed a relatively progressive military life, the impoverished, unfree, and disenfranchised often experienced what would also be an American tradition: uneven access to and deployment of physical force by governments and individuals.

The war helped colonists imagine a military that transcended local borders, and the effect lay a foundation for the tumult that led to revolution in the 1770s. At first, New Englanders and others in the colonies – especially those who had served in the conflict – felt great imperial pride and promise, the result of being on the winning side. But the war was followed by severe economic depression in North America, the product of wartime demobilization and plans that accentuated the region's cash shortages. These troubles began to seed doubts. In Philadelphia and New York, the courts compelled property sales to cover debt at a rate two to three times that of recent years. The poor packed almshouses beyond capacity. And rural migrants in search of opportunity collected in the Carolina backcountry, where loosely structured legal systems gave way to vigilantism and mob law. Indeed, the postwar period was not a good time for policy changes that expected more from British North Americans. And yet, that is just what the politics of empire in London demanded.[19]

A basic economic question started the trouble. Between 1689 and 1763, British military expenditures had more than tripled. In the Seven Years' War alone, the British deficit increased from £74 million to £133 million. At times in the eighteenth century, more than 40 percent of annual British revenue was used to service national debt. In 1764, the ever-frugal Chief Minister George Grenville shifted the financial burden for North American security to the colonists who lived there. Some ten thousand British soldiers stood ready to stave off Indigenous and French attacks on the North American frontier. They stood ready too to try and stop westward settler expansion over the Appalachians to enforce the Proclamation Line of 1763. To underwrite these armed forces, British leaders levied well-known taxes such as the Sugar Act, Stamp Act, and Townsend Revenue Act of the 1760s. In other words, state violence and the ability to pay for such violence stand as central causes of the British–American conflict.[20]

Financial considerations often drove military decisions in the British empire. In the late seventeenth century, for example, regular troops based in Jamaica and Virginia were removed after the colonies failed to locate enough funds to cover the cost of the men stationed there. Yet Grenville's decision in the 1760s marked a decided shift. Since the 1690s, the empire had funded its militarism through economic growth. By and large, the approach had worked. Where other European governments' military costs exceeded 80 percent of their annual public expenditures in times of war, the British spent less: between 61 and 74 percent. Armed with the world's greatest navy and a formidable army, Parliament funded measures to bolster social and economic life in its colonies. This changed in 1764. Rather than promote the expansion of producers and consumers, British leaders targeted production. In the North American colonies, tax, trade limit, and migration restraint established extraction and cost reduction as the new means to pay down British debt. Akin to the modifications Grenville helped introduce to the British navy (an amplified form of authoritarianism), the British government now embraced enforcement. "He that accepts protection, stipulates obedience," said London author Samuel Johnson to the American colonists.[21]

As the British–American controversy heightened in the 1760s and 1770s, the use of physical force by individuals and governments was not the issue. Many colonials, especially men, accepted violence as a means to regulate family, work, and society. Animals, children, criminals, slaves, and the poor represented some of the groups viewed as receptive to or in need of physical discipline. As they advanced on to Native lands, as well as those occupied by Spain and France, White American colonials also asked for British soldiers to shield them against Indigenous communities. Meanwhile, in principle and practice, Redcoats guarded colonial American slaveholders who, along with masters of indentured servants, sustained a brutal system of labor control.

But just as slaves and indentures resisted such authority, White colonials turned on British forces that acted as colonial police. Tension and hatred had arisen between British soldiers and settlers in Virginia during Bacon's Rebellion in 1676 and in New York during the Leisler Rebellion in 1691. A similar pattern held in 1763, when the British government cracked down on White migration, and in 1766, after British troops looted and destroyed property during a Hudson River manor tenant protest. As these later deployments represented a change in British colonial strategy, American rebels identified the problem: it was not government soldiers, but a lack of influence over how soldiers were used.[22]

In the cry "no taxation without representation," White colonial Americans packaged together several complaints. They understood that financial resources are the foundation of the violent capability of a state and that the state's ability to act with violence ensures its monopoly on taxation. The famous words also summoned deep-rooted precedent. The relationship between taxes and political influence had been established in the Middle Ages in France and England. Liberty, as developed as a White, Western ideal, exchanged economic and physical extraction (in taxation, mercantilist plans, and troop placement) for a voice in government (in a representative form). American rebels rejected the British claim that they had virtual representation – an assertion that each member of Parliament stood by himself an agent of empire and every citizen therein. The White colonists, buoyed by the recent war victory over France, imagined

themselves full British citizens. Their treatment as colonial subjects, however, failed to sustain such imaginings. It mattered little to the colonials that
British citizens in Sheffield, Birmingham, and Leeds were likewise unrepre-
sented and yet still taxed. Representation was local, they said, and only
representatives who originated from a particular locale could operate with
the consent of the governed.[23]

Often recognized as a lynchpin of American rebel political ideology,
such thinking directly affected notions of state violence in the colonies.
"Keeping a standing army in the province in time of peace without
consent of the representatives is against law," said the Massachusetts
Provincial Congress in October 1774. This well-known argument – that
without representation, without consent, the British treated American
colonials not as citizens, but, in the parlance of the Revolution, as slaves –
framed the perception of White colonial victimhood. And this status,
many in the colonies came to believe, sanctioned violent acts against
British aggression.[24]

However, like many of the ideas that authorize war, notions of White
American victimhood often stood divorced of reality. First, the deployment
of British regulars in Massachusetts was not extraordinary. The colonists
lived and had lived in a system that consistently privileged the soldier over
the citizen. While military authority in the American colonies was centralized and controlled by a commander who reported to London, political
authority was dispersed among colony governors. As historian John Shy
notes, "No American commander ever lost a battle with a royal governor."
The deployment of several thousand troops in the North American interior
after the Seven Years' War highlighted this imbalance. The military readily
put the men in place, but the colony leaders could not raise funds from
colonial Americans to pay for them. The great irony of the 1770s is that
within a structure that favored military response, colonial protest – and its
consequent collapse of civil authority – only furthered the very dynamic the
American rebels set to destroy: British militarization devoid of White colonist influence. Second, White American colonials knew that their treatment
by the British failed to mimic the accepted, interpersonal violence that
buttressed racialized slavery in the empire. Still, they loudly declared such
treatment unacceptable for White male recipients. And the false analogy of
British politicians ruling White American slaves provided a potent result:
the talk of White suffering prepared the colonists to act with violent,
supposedly self-defensive acts.[25]

Eventually members of both sides, British leaders and American protesters, concluded that the most appropriate way to communicate was

through force. In Parliament, Whig statesman William Pitt was confident that "in a good cause, on a sound bottom" (by which he meant that popular opinion and the law stood in the empire's favor) the British military could "crush America to atoms." By 1770, British commander Thomas Gage appeared ready to test Pitt's theory. "America is a mere bully, from one end to the other, and the Bostonians," he said, "by far the greatest bullies." One such Boston bully was the intellectual Mercy Otis Warren. Warren claimed that once British authority was asserted through physical coercion – in other words, once it became destructive instead of protective – the relationship between the colonies and mother country collapsed. She likened the British state to "an unnatural parent" who "has plung'd her dagger into the Bosom of her affectionate offspring." It was "the law of nature," John Adams said to explain the colonial response, "to repel injuries by force."[26]

The rebels grounded their use of armed resistance in the idea of self-defense – a common practice to support violence exercised by individuals and government. When colonists seized Fort Ticonderoga, for example, they portrayed the event in a defensive light. The capture, marked as the "taking of Ticonderoga," was an early American pre-emptive strike. "Defence and preservation," along with the "overruling law of self-preservation," explained the Continental Congress, mandated the attack. This need for American violence in self-defense soon defied even religious contradiction. Benjamin Franklin looked to recruit known adherents of nonviolent confrontation, Quakers, to the cause, as they would "arm in a defensive war." "The principles of self-preservation," explained minister Zabdiel Adams, sanction "the *humble* and *quiet*, the *meek* and *inoffensive* to turn their attention to the art of war ... And while they breathe the pacific spirit of the gospel, furnish themselves with the instruments of slaughter."[27]

But how such violent instruments should be created and wielded proved a muddied task. When the Massachusetts Provincial Congress eyed Fort Ticonderoga, for instance, its lawmakers appointed Connecticut businessman Benedict Arnold to direct an attack. The provincials authorized Arnold to gather an army of no more than four hundred men, which could act beyond the bounds of their authority in "neighboring colonies." Rather than raise his own troops, however, Arnold rushed to meet a group of Vermonters. Ethan Allen, a backwoods renegade, also sought Ticonderoga. And Allen's men, a militia in the loose sense of the term, cheered as Arnold brought the official support of Massachusetts to their mission. Tension soon arose, though, over who was to lead the attack and why. Arnold, who flaunted his commission from the Provincial Congress, believed the expedition was his by right. Allen's men, in contrast, "were shockingly surprised when Col Arnold presumed to contend for the command" and refused to "be commanded by any others but those they engaged with." Unable to decide whether the people themselves – the Vermont soldiers – or the people's representative governed the American forces, both leaders proceeded into the battle.[28]

As British activity in Massachusetts increased and imperial soldiers marched in Boston's streets, the province's leaders promptly rejected the rigid social and military hierarchy associated with the empire. Massachusetts lawmakers mused that a violent American state, one that coupled popular violence and elite prerogative, had to be different. The New Englanders borrowed on experience from the Seven Years' War and on a host of thinkers – from sixteenth-century classicists to seventeenth-century English radicals. In the end, they sided with Italian Niccolò Machiavelli, who identified the republic – where power channels from the consent of the governed – as a reasonable means to control state violence. Other forms of political organization lauded the violence of the state over its people. Republican violence, by contrast, derived from within – from armed citizens in a militia. Citizens (most often White, wealthy individuals) had a stake in the success of the republic; thus, less violence was needed to sustain a republican society. When state violence allied an armed citizenry with national achievement, Machiavelli believed, (White) liberty was the result.[29]

Republican thoughts were no doubt on Massachusetts Committee of Safety member Joseph Warren's mind when he spoke of a nation in which "every member feels it to be his interest, and knows it to be his duty, to preserve inviolate the constitution on which the public safety depends." Warren's committee was ready "to alarm, muster, and cause to be assembled with the utmost expedition and completely armed, accoutered, and supplied with provisions . . . so many of the militia" as it deemed necessary. The resolves of October 26, 1774, recognized the role of the people in this militarized condition. The Provincial Congress valued the "knowledge and skill in the art military" of the men of Massachusetts, who it deemed should be properly "armed and equipped." If the men were unable to arm themselves, the towns and, ultimately, the province would supply them. Further, the legislature "recommended to the several militia in this province who have not already chosen and appointed officers, that they meet forthwith and elect officers to command respective companies." These armed citizens would defend Massachusetts, but only for as long "as the safety of the province" required it.[30]

Armed by private and public means, democratic in its election of officers, impermanent, and manned by militiamen, the Massachusetts Army created a military form familiar to New Englanders. But much like its earlier manifestations in colonial militias, the democratic impulses in the Massachusetts Army tended more toward a flawed than an efficient fighting machine. The selection of officers by vote bound those supposedly in authority to their men rather than the other way around. In reaction to an irksome order or reprimand, therefore, many militiamen opted to elect a new officer or simply decamp. These soldiers were "armed tourists," who "did as they pleased and went where they pleased." Still, the Massachusetts leaders applauded themselves for the creation of an armed force "without any such severe articles and rules ... as are usually practiced in standing armies." A popular militia manual went so far as to condemn the use of violence as a pedagogical tool. Soldiers in training, it suggested, would "be quite confounded" by physical discipline "and rendered incapable of learning any thing at all, and even forget what they already know." In short, the Provincial Congress created an army of consent.[31]

By early spring 1775, though, the Massachusetts Army had suffered setbacks. The men gathered in Cambridge and Roxbury required food, shelter, and arms – expenditures which the province struggled to disburse. Chaos ruled: 3,700 men set out from Connecticut for Boston; within ten days, about 2,500 of them returned. Among the comings and goings, the American generals found it difficult to assess their numbers. For those who did stay, sanitation was an issue. Pit latrines – "sinks" as they were called – were routine for an eighteenth-century army; here, they were substituted by nature. As historian Paul Lockhart writes, "Men urinated and defecated whenever the mood struck them, sometimes right outside their tents, sometimes in close proximity to supplies of fresh water." This assemblage witnessed other unfortunate but easily foreseen events, as well. On April 28, for example, while on parade with his regiment, eighteen-year-old Abiel Petty of Walpole fired his musket by accident. The mistake cost twenty-two-year-old Asa Cheney his life. Eager and spirited, these soldiers were untrained and dangerous.[32]

Headed by General Artemas Ward, a Shrewsbury shopkeeper whose first general order required a record of soldiers by race, the coagulation of men on the Boston town commons was clearly a failure. Massachusetts leaders instituted a new oath of service, but the army of consent suffered from direction not allegiance. The local representatives soon turned to the Continental Congress, which had just convened its second meeting in Philadelphia. "The prospect of deciding the question between our mother country and us, by the sword, gave us the greatest pain and anxiety," they wrote, "but, we have made all the preparation for our necessary defence." They worried, however, that while Massachusetts had created an army, it had yet to assume the "reins of civil government." With an army but no government, the members of the Provincial Congress acknowledged that they were in violation of a key republican principle: that "the sword should in all free states be subservient to civil powers." To correct this problem, the provincial men offered two solutions. The first option placed the Massachusetts Army under the yet-to-be established civil authority of the Provincial Congress. The second, which members of the Provincial Congress preferred, placed the Massachusetts Army under the control of the Continental Congress. The local lawmakers even suggested that the Continental Congress meet closer to Boston, where advice "may be more expeditiously afforded upon any emergency." But no matter which corrective course was chosen, the existing records from the Provincial Congress reveal that the formation of the Massachusetts troops predated the formation of a civil authority to oversee them. This suggests that the establishment of state violence drove American political development.[33]

Though the Massachusetts legislators expressed concern over the army that they created, many of them enthusiastically endorsed the use of physical force to counter British authority. Take, for instance, Joseph Warren who helped to author several letters sent from the Provincial Congress to the Continental Congress in 1775. Like most of the more than 230 Provincial Congress members, Warren, a Harvard graduate and physician, had been active in the colonial turmoil since the 1760s. British troop buildup and colonial disarmament frightened the Massachusetts slaveholder. "Even if a private gentleman carries one [gun] out of town with him for diversion," Warren explained, "he is not permitted to bring it back again." There was hope in the prospect of a colonies-wide militarism, though, and he trusted the Continentals would agree. "The exactness and beauty" of the British troops will "inspire our youth with ardor in the pursuit of military knowledge." This circulation of violence, Warren assured, would work toward American ends. "The mistress we court is LIBERTY; and it is better to die than not to obtain her." White American rebels, rich and poor, bonded in this belief: physical sacrifice validates social and political faith.[34]

Warren and his Provincial Congress colleagues picked a near-perfect time to proposition the Continental Congress. In spring 1775, militant tones resounded in the large rebel assembly. The delegate and enslaver from North Carolina, Richard Caswell, wrote home from his Philadelphia seat, "Here a Greater Martial Spirit prevails, if possible, than I have been describing in Virginia & Maryland. They have ... near 2000 men who March out to the Common & go thro their Exercises twice a day regularly. Scarce any thing But Warlike Musick is to be heard in the streets." Caswell advised his son to become a soldier "to defend our Country & Support our Liberties." Fellow delegate Joseph Hewes, who enslaved at least ten Black people at the time, confirmed that, in Philadelphia, "nothing heard but the sound of Drums & Fifes, all Ranks and Degrees of men are in Arms." Along with others, Hewes was especially impressed that "all the Quakers except a few of the old Rigid ones have taken up arms ... one or two of the Companies are composed entirely of Quakers."[35]

Meanwhile, Connecticut's Continental Silas Deane, who also enslaved Black persons, observed the uniforms of Philadelphia militiamen. "Their Coat is made Short, falling but a little below the Waistband of the Breeches, which," he said to his wife, "shews the Size of a Man to a very great advantage." The sexual overtones were unmistakable. Hardly unique to the United States, a link between male physicality, particularly sexual virility, and violent prowess would persist in America. Deane, who displayed a keen eye, made another connection transparent: "Their Cartouch Boxes are large, with the Word Liberty." Again, size marked a heightened power, but, more importantly, coupled violence – the cartouche box carried ammunition – and liberty.[36]

This environment, where White colonials embraced such forceful displays of dress and action, sounded clear notes in the ears of those in the Continental Congress who would soon agree to the Massachusetts military request. On June 2, 1775, the delegates acted quickly after receipt of the Provincial Congress application and moved to take command of the "Army now collecting from different colonies." The next day, Saturday, June 3, they charged a committee to borrow six thousand pounds to purchase gunpowder to be used by what they now referred to as "the Continental Army." And by the end of the following week, the congress orchestrated a unified defense. It ordered the removal of provisions and armaments from places like New Hampshire, Rhode Island, and western New Jersey to the most likely sites of conflict: Boston, New York, and Philadelphia.[37]

Alone among the thirteen colonies, only Georgia did not participate in the Continental Congress's Philadelphia assembly. Therefore, only Georgia did not agree at this time to the creation of the Continental Army. Its leaders feared their "dreaded" and "vast number of negroes [slaves]," as well as the "bad effects of an Indian War." The Georgians believed that "none but Great

Britain" could provide "such powerful aid and assistance" necessary to overawe the enslaved and Indians. Of course, the representatives from the twelve other colonies disagreed and established an American military.[38]

Founded on notions of White consent, justified by the laws of nature and nations, and integral to the formation of colonial unity, the violent American state would thus be built on a robust foundation. Yet the men who met in Philadelphia for the Continental Congress still harbored doubts on assuming control of the Massachusetts Army, which was on the verge of dissolution and lacked discipline, arms, and latrines. They discussed the possibility of raising a whole other army. However, "the difficulty of collecting another and the probability that the British Army would take Advantage" of their disorganization subdued the discussion. What was apparent to the likes of Ethan Allen weeks before in Vermont was now a more widespread opinion: "a war has already commenced between Great Britain and the colonies ... To fight the king's troops has become inevitable."[39]

Insofar as the transfer of violence from the "state of nature" to a political body marks the creation of liberal government, the Continental Congress founded America on Thursday, June 15, 1775. It was on this day, after weeks spent in preparation for the formation of the Continental Army, that the Continental Congress "Resolved, That a General be appointed to command all the continental forces, raised, or to be raised, for the defence of American liberty." The Virginia slaveholder and delegate Edmund Pendleton's words speak plainly to the significance of what the group decided that day: "Colonel Washington is appointed General and Commander in chief of all the American Force."[40]

The selection of George Washington was no accident. By 1775, the forty-three-year-old had a long history of military service. Back in 1754, an openly ambitious Washington persuaded Virginia Governor Dinwiddie to appoint him lieutenant-colonel for an assault in the Ohio country. He won a quick victory over French and Native forces, but his success was soon overshadowed. During the battle, a French delegate bearing a diplomatic note was killed. Then, in a surprising turn of events, the French opposition overran Washington and his men at a makeshift defense dubbed Fort Necessity. In the rain and dark, Washington, who forever claimed there had been a deception, capitulated – with terms that admitted his responsibility for a diplomatic assassination.[41]

The supposed slaughter of an ambassador placed Washington at the center of an international brouhaha. To make matters worse, the French stole his diary and printed its contents. French leaders fully blamed the

British for the killing, to the extent that the incident stands as one of the immediate triggers for the Seven Years' War. The occasion was so notable in its time that Washington's name appeared in John Barrow's *A New and Impartial History of England, From the Invasion of Julius Cæsar, to the Signing of the Preliminaries of Peace, in the Year 1762.*[42]

Despite this initial disaster, Washington established himself as a no-nonsense military man. A doomed campaign in the western theater at Fort Duquesne in 1755 highlighted his steely nerve. British Major-General Edward Braddock, who led the attack, was killed. His aide, Washington, lived to brag of the "4 bullets through [his] coat and two horses shot under." With pride, Washington kept his battle-scarred hat. "I heard Bulletts whistle," he wrote to his brother, John Augustine, "and believe me there was something charming in the sound." (One memoir has it that King George II, upon hearing the anecdote, responded, "He would not say so, if he had been used to hear many.") The next year, the *Boston Gazette* welcomed Washington as "the Hon. Colonel Washington, a gentleman who has deservedly a high reputation of military skill, integrity, and valor, though success has not always attended his under-takings." The *Royal Magazine* described him as "a young gentleman of great bravery and distinguished merit."[43]

A willingness to play the disciplinarian bolstered Washington's military worth. In opposition to the underlying ideals of the Massachusetts Army, he believed that men, particularly of the non-elite class, responded best to violence. He held this belief from the very start of his career. Washington especially saw the need for this disciplinary standard when it came to the Virginia militiamen, whom he found "obstinate, self-willed, perverse; of little or no service to the people, and very burthensome to the Country." To combat the disorder, especially the high desertion rates that plagued his Virginia Regiment, he regularly meted out whippings and hangings. In his orders for early July 1756, Washington sustained the sentences of John Leigh and Andrew Simmons at 250 lashes; Andrew Lockhart at 400 lashes; John Jenkins at 500 lashes; and William Pritchard, William Davis, and Robert Yates at 1,000 lashes apiece – all penalties for desertion, repeated desertion, and influencing others to desert. Washington appeared only slightly more charitable in practice, demanding "the above prisoners to receive as much of their punishment as the Surgeon (who must attend upon this occasion) shall judge they are able to bear."[44]

The British military, of course, was organized under such practices, and Washington chose to follow custom. A noted military manual of the era states: "The Drum-major counts every lash with a loud voice; the Adjutant stands by to see the punishment properly inflicted; and the Surgeon, or his Mate attends, that no punishment may extend to life or limb." However, that flogging was not intended to kill or maim did not prevent the killing or maiming of the victim. Nor did such boundaries shelter recipients of the lash from horrific torture. British Major-General Charles Napier, who began his army career in the 1790s, offered this:

> I have seen hundreds of men flogged, and have always observed that when the skin is thoroughly cut up, or flayed off, the great pain subsides. Men are frequently convulsed and screaming, during the time they receive from one lash to three hundred lashes, and then they bear the remainder, even to eight hundred, or a thousand lashes, without a groan; they will often lie as if without life, and the drummers appear to be flogging a lump of dead, raw flesh.

Massachusetts provincial soldier David Perry agreed. He upheld whipping as "the most cruel punishment I ever saw" and noted that after 300 lashes on two soldiers, "The flesh appeared to be entirely whipped from their shoulders, and they hung mute and motionless as though they had been long deprived of life." Perry remarked, too, that the surgeon on hand then signaled that the men could "bear it yet" – meaning that they could receive more lashes.[45]

According to one estimate, George Washington ordered (in a military setting) on average 613 lashes based on data from May and July 1757. This average placed him a touch under the 713 annual average for the British Army. Despite the small sample size, some scholars point to this study as evidence of Washington's humanity (while ignoring the whippings and other punishments received by Washington's slaves). Such sentiment, it is important to note, stands in contrast to actions and requests over the course of his career as a colonial and American military leader. In the service of the British and, later, the Continental Congress, Washington made repeated requests to make the punishments available to him more severe.[46]

Severe punishment never seemed to stem the outflow of Washington's units in the 1750s. Yet he continued to order lashings, place men in shackles, and throw them in "dark rooms" (for example, solitary confinement) for desertion. It was not enough. Along with Governor Dinwiddie, he petitioned the legislature to allow executions for desertion and other disobediences. The young colonel believed, in the vein of an early New England Puritan, that violent public example served a civic good. "Henry Campbell, for Desertion, is to be shot on sunday morning at seven of the clock," Washington ordered in June 1756. To bring home the lesson, he further ordered "all the Soldiers and Draughts to attend the execution." To Dinwiddie he wrote: "These Examples, and proper encouragement for good Behaviour, will I hope, bring the Soldiers under proper Discipline."[47]

Washington's practice of exemplary violence fit well within White societal norms in the British empire. It reflected an arrogant belief that the lower classes, including Black slaves, were uncontrollable without physical chastisement. The famed slave trader and sea captain, John Newton, active between 1748 and 1754, demonstrated this mindset on the high seas. "Without a strict discipline," he said, "the common sailors would be unmanageable." Anthony Whitting, who managed George Washington's estate in Virginia, echoed this conviction when he whipped Charlotte, a Black enslaved woman at Mount Vernon. He wrote, "She will behave herself for I am determined to lower her Spirit or Skin her Back." Washington agreed with the method, responding, "Your treatment of Charlotte was very proper."[48]

Though White enslavers like Washington sustained exemplary violence across a variety of British and soon American institutions, such as the military and human slavery, this does not suggest that the victims of those institutions, the common soldiers and the enslaved, suffered similar fates. For example, flogging (or whipping) was a form of physical torture used in a variety of settings. The whipping of a Black person in enslavement, however, sustained a system described by the sociologist Orlando Patterson as the "permanent, violent, and personal domination of natally alienated and generally dishonored persons." In other words, the violence of slavery created and defined a racialized group of "disposable" people. Meanwhile, harsh military discipline – the internal violence of the military – created and continued a regimented military workforce. To conclude, the broader implication is that Washington and other leaders readily deployed violence in many different settings, even though the meaning and function of violence in each setting was different. And regardless of the setting, although on occasion Washington opted for peaceful means to manage confrontation, his default mode was for further violence.[49]

By the 1770s, Washington had settled more into the life of a Virginia planter than that of a military leader. The British Army had shunned him from its regular ranks, as it did most colonials. But when the Revolutionary crisis arose, Washington quickly turned back the clock. As a delegate for the Continental Congress, he arrived in Philadelphia with his outfit and colors from the Fairfax militia. Most likely it was the same clothing he wore for a 1772 portrait by Charles Wilson Peale. Washington had never abandoned his martial leanings and, more than two weeks before the

Continental Congress appointed him general, John Adams noted, "Coll. Washington appears at Congress in his Uniform and, by his great Experience and Abilities in military Matters, is of much service to Us."[50]

Six feet in height, with wide, muscular hips that made him a great horseman and dancer, Washington stood tall above his peers. On horseback, he dominated the scene. Such physical presence only reinforced the perception of his military prowess. The well-known physician Benjamin Rush was hardly alone in observing that Washington "has so much martial dignity in his deportment that you would distinguish him to be a general and a soldier from among ten thousand people." John Adams gushed like a schoolboy after seeing the Virginia colonel in uniform. "Oh that I was a Soldier!" he declared. So inspired, he continued, "I will be. – I am reading military Books. – Every Body must and will, and shall be a soldier."[51]

And men were not the only ones drawn to Washington. Married to a soldier, Martha Daingerfield Bland had much to say of the Virginian. Observing his attributes, she said, "Now let me speak of our Noble and Agreable Commander (for he commands both Sexes) one by his Excellent Skill in Military Matters the other by his ability, politeness, and attention." Indeed, Washington's virility was bolstered by his wealth and rank, and extended to many flirtations with women. "He can be down right impudent sometimes," Bland explained to a friend, "such impudence, Fanny, as you and I like."[52]

Under Washington's command, the Continental Army stands as the first instance of American institutionalized violence. That the individual in charge of it sported a manly vigor linked to authoritarian ways and a dominant physical presence cannot be overstated. In 1775, Abigail Adams remarked upon it when she wrote to her husband, John, "I was struck with General Washington ... Dignity with ease, and complacency, the Gentleman and Soldier look agreeably blended in him." Notably, Washington was among the wealthiest men in America, a Virginia planter whose manner and dress often mimicked that of the British aristocracy. At the same time, he was unschooled – a somewhat self-made man, to borrow the phrasing of later generations – and had a clear record of ferocity. As portraitist Gilbert Stuart said of Washington, "had he been born in the forest, it was his opinion that [Washington] would have been the fiercest among the savage tribes." Stuart's statement reflects the image found in the proverbial "colonial mirror," as it is described by anthropologist Michael Taussig. This view "reflects back onto the colonists the barbarity of their own social relations, but as imputed to the savage or evil figure they wish to colonize." It is therefore significant, from this perspective, that Stuart failed to acknowledge that Washington often deployed his ruthlessness in pursuit of Native lands and, as a military leader, in destruction of Native communities.[53]

In the Continental Congress, Washington was one of several candidates who jockeyed for position before the final decision announced him as the chief of the Continental Army. Artemas Ward, for example, who served as general of the troops under the aegis of the Massachusetts Provincial Congress, was in the mix. His candidacy rested on the belief that the New England soldiers already "had a General of their own" and "appeared to be satisfied with him." At the time, Continental Congress President John Hancock, an enslaver of two or three Black persons in Massachusetts, also had open designs on the military post. But even though John Adams marked him a thorough patriot, "the Delicacy of his health, and his entire Want of Experience in actual Service ... were decisive Objections." Hancock's "Ambition to be appointed Commander in Chief" worked against his campaign as well. Political men in the late eighteenth century often held grand notions of civic service – they frowned on individual aspiration or financial profit as motives for public duty. Delegates were duly impressed, then, that whenever Washington's name was mentioned, the colonel "from his Usual Modesty darted into the Library Room" away from the debate. Washington was, in fact, a genius at playing the politics of virtue. He convinced many in the Continental Congress that, even though he arrived in Philadelphia in military garb, he did not crave the position.[54]

Southerners were keen to support the selection of George Washington. Talk of liberty exposed a growing rift over race and labor in the colonies. Significantly, White leaders in the North were not unyielding advocates of Black slave emancipation – there were tens of thousands of northern slaves. Indeed, many northern politicians proved wedded to White supremacy during the processes of slave abolition that would eventually start in several northern states. But, as seen in Georgia's initial refusal to join the Continental Congress, the maintenance of robust state violence was necessary for plantation life and a significant southern concern. In New Hanover County, North Carolina, representatives understood the importance of the Battles of Lexington and Concord, but said that only when combined with "the dread of instigated [slave] insurrections in the colonies" did it justify "the use of [American] arms." White men in Wilmington, North Carolina, watched in disbelief as the British commander of Fort Johnston "basely encouraged slaves from their masters, paid and employed them, and declared openly, that he would excite them to an insurrection." The Committee of Safety in Pitt County denounced the commander's "atrocious and horrid declaration" and placed a "Poll Tax on all the Taxable Negroes." The monies would pay for slaves "Killed or disabled" by White American "Patrolers" – men authorized to shoot "Negroes" in groups larger than four found off their plantations and who "will not submit." Southern delegates needed George Washington – an enslaver of hundreds of Black individuals – because they needed a general who shared their view on slavery. They thus opted for a man who at times wore dentures formed of teeth torn from the mouths of slaves.[55]

The debate over Washington's selection did expose some of the earliest divisions between the northern and southern colonies, however. Southern delegates flummoxed John Adams, who strained to understand why they were so adamant for one of their own to lead. He questioned whether their stance was sincere or "mere pride and a haughty Ambition." But Washington's personal character, military reputation, and the ideological unity brought by a southerner at the head of what was then a New England army persuaded him. "There is something charming to me in the conduct of Washington," Adams said. "A gentleman of one of the first fortunes upon the continent, leaving his delicious retirement, his family and friends, sacrificing his ease, and hazarding all in the cause of his country!"[56]

In no small part, Washington earned the trust of leaders in the North and South with his record of coercion. Yet he demonstrated a deft ability to downplay the link between physical, economic, and social domination and his acceptance of the leadership position. When offered the generalship, Washington received the command with the expected propriety. Speaking to the Continental Congress, he moderated his military skill – "I do not think myself equal to the command I am honored with." He even refused to earn a salary, opting only for reimbursement of expenses incurred, stating, "I do not wish to make any proffit from it." In private, he continued in this vein. To Martha, his wife, he wrote, "so far from seeking this appointment I have used every endeavor in my power to avoid it." To Burwell Bassett, his brother-in-law, he laid blame for the move on the Continental Congress: "I have been called upon by the unanimous Voice of the Colonies to the Command of the Continental Army – It is an honour I by no means aspired to."[57]

On June 19, 1775, the "Commission from the Continental Congress" authorized Washington as "GENERAL AND COMMANDER IN CHIEF for the defence of American Liberty and for repelling every hostile invasion thereof." It specifically conferred on him "full power and authority to act ... for the good and Welfare of the service." In this wording, the delegates made clear their expectation that Washington would put an end to the disorder that plagued the army. Not only did they tell Washington to "require all officers and soldiers under your command to be obedient to your orders," they demanded the general bring about "strict discipline and order." On June 22, the Continentals elaborated on these instructions: "You shall take every method in your power, consistent with prudence, to destroy or make prisoners of all persons, who now are, or who hereafter shall appear in arms against the good people of the United Colonies." In the Continental Congress's orders, the self-defensive logic of the Revolution was thus reversed: the Americans had become the state, and they justified the use of violence since they upheld order.[58]

Now the most powerful American, Washington faced a difficult task. He had to bring stability to the army in Massachusetts and "destroy" the British empire in North America. And a letter dated June 24, 1775, alerted the general to yet another problem. Five of his slaves had run away from his Virginia plantation. Instability in the slave system, the very scenario feared most by many White southerners, was coming to pass. A few months later, Lord Dunmore added fuel to the fire, offering freedom to all American slaves and indentured servants who would fight for the British. It was an effective gambit. "There is not a man of them, but woud leave us, if they believe'd they coud make there Escape," Lund Washington, the manager of Washington's Mount Vernon estate, reported of the workforce in December. "Liberty is sweet."[59]

General Washington recognized that orderly slaves and White American liberty depended on his wise deployment of violence on behalf of the would-be American state. Toward that end, he removed himself to Boston to organize his army and survey the British (Fig. 1.3). Though the term "Continental Army" was already in use, Washington called his men the "Troops of the United Provinces of North America." On July 4, 1775, he released orders stating, "it is required and expected that exact discipline be observed, and due Subordination prevail thro' the whole Army." This, he claimed, would help the Americans avoid "shameful disappointment and disgrace." He reminded the soldiers that army regulations forbade "profane cursing, swearing & drunkenness," and insisted on "punctual attendance on divine service." Washington had further instructions for his officers, whom he commanded to keep the "Men neat and clean – to visit them often at their quarters, and inculcate upon them the necessity of cleanliness, as essential to their health and service."[60]

Only three days after his arrival in Boston, Washington proved that he meant business, ordering a "General Court martial" for July 6, 1775, at 10 a.m. One man was charged with insulting a sentry, one with leaving his

Fig. 1.3 *Washington Assumes Command.* Ralph Ludwig Boyer, American, 1879–1952, Printed by Henry E. Carling, London, Published by the George Washington Memorial Association, New York, Wadsworth Atheneum Museum of Art, Hartford, CT. Anonymous gift in honor of Dr. George C. F. Williams, 1933.172.

post, another with theft, and two with sleeping at their posts. In the upcoming days, the general arranged trials for desertion, "rescuing a Prisoner when in lawful custody," and cowardice. On the last, he reflected, "the Cowardice of a single Officer may prove the Distruction of the whole army."[61]

Through punishment, Washington looked to instill in his inexperienced soldiers the regimented European military ethos that he had learned over the course of his career. As he was well aware, drilling and discipline have served to transform ordinary citizens into killers across time and cultures. The power and coercion needed to enact such change, Washington believed, was most effective when issued from a central authority. And it was for this reason that he continued to doubt the militia. These temporary units of citizen-soldiers were often regulated under provincial control rather than that of Washington. As a result, they seemed insufficiently disciplined to the general. Writing to John Hancock, Washington reflected that "No Dependence can be put on the Militia for a Continuance in Camp, or Regularity and Discipline during the short Time they may stay."[62]

Once Washington took command, the men in Cambridge and Roxbury were subjugated to a general who sought to create a rigid, British-styled military force. Now, with its earlier restraints loosened, the violence of the United American Colonies was freed to discipline and punish – the very situation that the architects of the Massachusetts Army had tried to prevent. And the clash of the two structures of state violence, the Continental Army and the Massachusetts Army – one more authoritarian, the other more egalitarian, both tied to the hierarchies of liberal life – forged a lasting American legacy.

Indeed, as Washington instituted a new command structure, which placed many southerners in charge, Andover's Samuel Osgood reported on the resistance of the common soldier. "Is the faithful obedient Soldier to be contemned because he says I know my own Colony Men, I choose to be commanded by them? . . . Can anything, Sir, fire upon us a more infamous Name, than that we are able to raise Men, but cannot officer them!" Osgood explained that many soldiers of the Massachusetts Army would refuse to re-enlist thanks to Washington's military reorganization. He already had anecdotal evidence. The "Connecticutt Soldiers . . . at present appear to be determined to Leave the Camp" and the Massachusetts "Men will dance to the same Tune when their Time is ended."[63]

Washington supporter John Adams also voiced concern over the changes the general and his southern supporters demanded. The new military leaders had found the pay scale of the Massachusetts Army "too high for privates, and too low for the officers." They immediately altered it. Adams now feared "our people," New Englanders, would find the increase in officer salaries "extravagant, and be uneasy." Adams, like Osgood, believed that freeholders deserved more power and pay in the military. To them, it was an essential right of property-owning and, as was often the case, Whiteness. Each held fast to a belief in the sanctity of all men with property (as opposed to just that of men with significant holdings). This ideal, they argued, created "a Kind of Equality" in New England.[64]

But Washington and his southern commanders were not persuaded. As army chaplain Reverend William Emerson observed of the changes in Boston:

> There is great overturning in the camp, as to order and regularity. New lords new laws. The Generals Washington and Lee are upon the lines every day. New orders from his Excellency are read to the respective regiments every morning after prayers. The strictest government is taking place, and great distinction is made between officers and soldiers. Every

one is made to know his place and keep in it, or be tied up and receive thirty or forty lashes according to his crime.[65]

Clearly, American leaders such as Washington and Adams disagreed on the contours and boundaries of White, male authority in the American provinces. Significantly, though, they did not question the racial, religious, and gendered assumptions at its core. Adams held notions of a more democratic environment for property-owning Whites, but he found it "dangerous" to "confound and destroy all Distinctions, and prostrate all Ranks, to one common Levell." He also dismissed the broader political and social aspirations of Indians, Catholics, slaves, and women inspired by the Revolution's egalitarian rhetoric. These movements, Adams said, were nothing more than a divisive campaign hatched by the British.[66]

Indeed, that the future American president, like its general, remained firm in such beliefs is a testament to the commitment to hierarchy and institutionalized inequity at the center of the nation's founding. When his wife, Abigail, asked for change in married women's dependent legal status, for example, John refused to answer in a rational tone. "General Washington, and all our brave Heroes would fight" such "Despotism of the Petticoat," he replied. "We know better than to repeal our Masculine systems." And yet, while Adams was right to highlight the masculine structures in place at the time of the Revolution, violent acts on behalf of a colony or province had never been an exclusively White, male domain. And during the Revolution and beyond, women, like other groups traditionally framed out of full rights and privileges, contested the military roles that men such as Washington found suitable for them.[67]

2

LIFE IN THE ARMY OF THE CONTINENT

The formation of the Continental Army offers insight into how White male leaders understood inclusion and exclusion in their political and military worlds.

General Washington tried with varying success to exclude women, Blacks, and Indians from his troops. The question was not only about who could serve, but about the nature of that service. Meanwhile, American military elites grappled with the link between public funding, military budgets, and military discipline, which was the internal control of state violence. Political leaders often underfunded and undersupplied the Continental Army. Washington's soldiers (specifically, the White men who formed the bulk of the troops) fought at times without pay and frequently without adequate clothing, food, and arms – a condition that would repeatedly prove disastrous within the repressive military culture the general had created.

Throughout the war, the American soldiers protested and, even when Washington acknowledged the legitimacy of their complaints, he subjected them – or at least those whom officers identified as protest leaders – to physical punishment. Severe bodily abuse of the army protesters, Washington believed, would prevent future demonstrations of discontent. During the American Revolution, however, that future was never realized. Instead, many common soldiers continued to rebel while Washington stood firm in his belief that, for the class of men beneath him, following command was more important than individual or communal claims to justice.

Within the Continental Army, hostile differences situated in class, race, and gender informed and sustained an early American nationalism that would come to permeate the social fabric of the United States well beyond the battlefield.

———————◆———————

In 1775, George Washington was confident that the security of the American provinces demanded a manly force. "We," he said, speaking for provincial men, "have taken up Arms in Defence of our Liberty, our Property, our Wives, and our Children." Thus linking political rights, personal assets, female spouses, and minors, Washington announced the masculine duty of a physical defense: "We are determined to preserve them, or die."[1]

Yet, over the course of the American Revolution, fighting women and women who worked in support of army troops continually exposed Washington's male military ideal for what it was – an idea that was often out of sync with the realities of war. Margaret Corbin, for example, was a nurse who followed her husband into battle in 1776. John died in the conflict at Fort Washington and Margaret immediately assumed his post loading cannon. Hit by grapeshot and crippled for life, she would receive a veteran's pension. Corbin was not alone in female military service. Ann Bailey enlisted as Samuel Gay, Ann Smith as Samuel Smith, and Deborah Sampson served as Private Robert Shurtleff. Discharge, fine, and jail met Bailey and Smith. Sampson, who soldiered for several years, received honorable discharge and a Massachusetts pension.[2]

Years later, Sampson drew on the widely accepted gendered dynamic of violence to explain her former military role. Throwing off the "soft habiliments of *my sex*," she said, she assumed "those of the *warrior*." However, Sampson knew full well that her time in the army was groundbreaking and that one of the barriers she had broken was set by gender expectations. Her soldiering, she explained, presented an "opportunity which custom and the world seemed to deny [to women], as a natural privilege."[3]

During the American Revolution, army men rejected such fluid performances of gender and viewed female soldiers as offensive. To them, the definition of womanhood – especially the revered elite, White womanhood – indicated an incapacity for violent acts. As a result, military and political leaders typically disparaged the character of fighting females. These male leaders, who regularly praised the selfless sacrifice of White male soldiers upon receipt of signing bonuses and salary, charged that women who joined the army were selfish, motivated solely by economics – namely, signing bonuses and military salary.

Only female soldiers who proved able to fight and endure battlefield harm successfully challenged male sexism. The battle-scarred Corbin and Sampson, for instance, earned mild reprimands and veteran benefits for their military sacrifice. Female recruits and soldiers unmasked before they faced combat and combat injury, however, were met with legal punishment in the form of imprisonment, economic punishment in the form of fines, and social punishment. In New Jersey, for example, when recruiters suspected the biological sex of a potential enlistee, they commenced a physical examination and then marched her in male clothes through the streets.[4]

Where fighting women appear as exceptions in the Continental Army, women who served in military support roles were common. Often from society's lower classes, these women cooked, washed, sewed, and nursed for the soldiers. They also socialized and copulated with the men, and then raised their children. Perhaps unsurprisingly, Washington tried to hide his military men's physical and emotional reliance on these women. When Continental troops arrived in Philadelphia, he ordered, "Not a woman belonging to the army is to be seen with the troops on their march thro' the city." Over the course of the war, he also tried to limit female access to army transport. "The women are expressly forbid any longer, under any licence at all, to ride in the wagons," he said in 1777. The thousands of women who supported the army, though, remained steadfast. They fell in line behind the troops and, when the opportunity arose, hopped a ride in the military caravan. Washington, irritated by his inability to make the women disappear, even directed officers "to inflict instant punishment" on those who followed his men against his orders.[5]

A Christian understanding of female danger drove the general. Washington coupled it to a theory of feral male heterosexual desire. "Once the Woman has tempted us, & we have tasted the forbidden fruit," he said to poet Annis Boudinot Stockton, "there is no such thing as checking our appetites, whatever the consequences may be." Washington adhered to this vision of male sexuality to an impressive degree. After the army executed Thomas Hickey for mutiny and sedition, for example, the general identified Hickey's downfall as being due to women. It was not dishonesty or duplicity, though the soldier had been arrested for circulating counterfeit currency and corresponding with "enemies of the said Colonies." Rather, Washington noted that Hickey's contact with "lewd Women" had triggered the trouble.[6]

Lewd women, in the general's mind, were those who were not genteel. The wives of officers, for instance, often visited the troops in their winter encampments without issue. Upper-class women served as shining objects of admiration, living examples of the wealthy, refined life the soldiers engaged to defend. The presumed chastity of elite women also established a gendered-class model of superiority. Lower-class women, by contrast, expressed a wild sexuality. And unlike earlier Italian and current Spanish militaries, which recognized sexual labor as part of operations, the American one did not. Following British example, Washington objected to his common soldiers having sex, whether engaged on a contractual or consensual basis. The general thus tried without success to restrict male–female interaction in the troops, saying, "I conceive it to be a right inherent with Command to limit ... the proportion of Women to the Men of an Army." But, as much as women vexed Washington, he found it equally difficult to govern his men.[7]

Who a state allows to fight, as well as the nature of their military participation, is key to the study of the violence among individuals and nations. In histories of the American Revolution, however, a nuanced understanding of army demographics, enlistment conditions, and the economy of war is often supplanted by romanticized visions of the militia. After all, if the Americans defeated the British with decentralized groups of citizen-soldiers, then they reflect the perfect response to the centralized, regular army of the British. But few who served in the Continental Army would lay claim to this romanticized depiction. George Washington, as general and later president, upheld the fundamental role of a professional, permanent force to the American victory and national security.

Significantly, Washington's centralized army operated in wartime. Many American rebels considered themselves adherents of Jonathan Trenchard, who, in *A Short History of Standing Armies* (1698), equated peacetime military deployments with undue coercion. (Of course, the Americans conveniently ignored Trenchard when he endorsed the use of British troops to counter what he called "rebellion" in Ireland.) Wartime deployment allowed Continental Army leaders the ideological leeway to embrace the use of government force.[8]

They also disavowed the presumed alignment between republican virtue and militia service, a correlation that had fostered the chaos of the Massachusetts Army. Instead, as the Revolutionary conflict progressed, political and military leaders coupled individual gain, especially financial profit, with military commitment. By the end of the war, the Continental delegates had paid army recruits in allotments of clothing, land, and cash. When many in the officer class began to resign, the Congress guaranteed them a seven-year pension. For a while, it appeared Washington was right when he observed, "A small knowledge of human nature will convince us, that, with far the greatest part of mankind, interest is the governing principle."[9]

"Interest" in the success of the American cause arrived with expectations. American soldiers who fought believed that the possible sacrifice of life earned them entry into cherished realms of citizenship. For those commissioned as officers, this expectation often meant a land portion large enough for economic self-sufficiency. For the common soldier, it was land, enfranchisement, or, in the case of slaves, emancipation. In late 1775, for example, Philadelphia artisans and journeymen made such hopes explicit when they demanded the right to vote for all militiamen with no regard to age or fiscal condition. During a failed attempt to persuade southern leaders to recruit slaves into military service, Continental Congress delegates similarly understood the relationship between soldiers' willingness to fight and expectations for their service. They attempted to stipulate "that every negro who shall well and faithfully serve as a soldier to the end of the present war, and shall then return his arms, be emancipated and receive the sum of fifty dollars." Although their efforts did not succeed in this instance, it was clear that the violence of the American colonies yoked the American cause to a pathway for political authority, freedom, and financial gain.[10]

By September 1776, Washington had secured permission to create a more permanent fighting force. Against a volunteer citizen model that detailed a clear preference for well-to-do, landed men as soldiers (an ideal that was never met), state officials now filled the regular ranks with whomever they could find. And in a society captivated by a link between soldiering and citizenship, debates over the decision to refashion the army anticipated the limits and boundaries of belonging in the emergent nation.[11]

The new American fighters often represented the poorest men of society, where the bottom third held less than one percent of all wealth. Signed to long-term contracts, these Continental Army soldiers were paid, bought, or compelled to serve. In the mid-Atlantic region, the soldiers most often derived from landless, unskilled workers who were often recent immigrants (Scots, Irish, English, and German). The southern soldiers were likewise poor, young, landless, and, in half the cases, immigrants. Maryland went so far as to permit local courts to remand men charged as vagrants to at least nine-months' service in the army. Virginia, meanwhile, quelled draft protest by declaring "each and every person or persons so misbehaving" to be "soldiers for the war, in this states quota of continental troops." New Englanders who served shared the common threads of youth, poverty, and lack of social connection. A debtor named Ezekiel Brown, for instance, who was recruited from Lexington, Massachusetts, claimed to have heard the fateful "shots heard round the world" on April 19, 1775, from his nearby jail cell.[12]

Despite the demand for able male bodies, not all were openly received. The initial forces collected in New England included a significant number of free Blacks and Indians. George Washington tried to change this. He stood against Black enlistments of any kind. In fall 1775, military and civilian committees agreed with him that "Negroes" should be "excluded from the new Inlistment especially such as are Slaves." Washington repeated these resolutions in orders given at the end of October. To Washington the army leader, free Black soldiers in northern units were of no more use than unfit old men and "boys unable to bear arms." To Washington the enslaver, Blacks should not be furnished weapons. As the ongoing dialogue over who could wield the violence of the American state percolated throughout the Revolution, George Washington held it to be the domain of White men.[13]

When Lord Dunmore issued his proclamation on November 7, 1775, that slaves would be freed in exchange for British military service, the American general was thus especially outraged. Dunmore's proclamation successfully raised a so-called "Ethiopian Regiment" of about three hundred soldiers made up from among the eight hundred slaves who fled to Dunmore and his protection. The former bondsmen wore military regalia adorned with the words "Liberty to Slaves." While Dunmore failed to realize victory over the Americans, his policy opened the way for some twenty thousand Black slaves to join British forces. This included about twenty-four individuals enslaved by Thomas Jefferson who escaped to General Cornwallis late in the war.[14]

As Washington struggled to hold together the American Army, Dunmore's move and a need for recruits eventually pushed him to relent on his White soldier ideal. On December 31, 1775, Washington wrote to Continental Congress President John Hancock that he now feared the "free negroes" who already served the American cause might switch sides because of his earlier anti-Black declaration. "I have presumed to depart from the Resolution respecting them," he said, "& have given Licence for their being enlisted." The Continental Congress certified his decision more than two weeks later, specifying, "That the free negroes who have served faithfully in the army at Cambridge, may be re-inlisted therein, but no others."[15]

In the American provinces, however, Black participation in the Revolution extended beyond those who served in the "Cambridge army." Over the years, 6–12 percent of Washington's forces were African American, a level of military racial integration not seen again in US history until the second half of the twentieth century. Black soldiers largely represented New England, where the White to Black population ratio was much higher than in regions farther south. Six states in total accepted the work of slaves in military life in exchange for emancipation. The list includes Rhode Island, Massachusetts, New Hampshire, New York, Maryland, and Virginia, where five hundred slaves were freed for their service.[16]

Still, the use of armed Blacks in a racially stratified society that viewed military labor as a civic duty and an opportunity for personal advancement created much dissent. One southern Council of Safety demanded that all Blacks yield their guns and ammunition for use by White militiamen and troops. In Massachusetts, where roughly twenty-one free Blacks fought at Lexington or Concord and more than eighty-eight at Bunker Hill, representatives objected to the use of enslaved recruits. Because enslaved soldiers highlighted the connection between White liberty and Black slavery, the Committee of Safety declared "that no slaves be admitted into this army upon any consideration whatever."[17]

Rhode Island leaders, however, worked around such concerns. They accepted slaves into military service, compensated slave-owners at market price, and "voted and resolved, that every slave, so enlisting, shall, upon his passing muster before Col. Christopher Greene, be immediately discharged from the service of his master or mistress, and be absolutely FREE, as though he had never been encumbered with any kind of servitude or slavery." Nevertheless, Rhode Island leaders feared that "neighboring states" would see their Black soldiers "in a contemptible point of view, and not equal to their [White] troops; and they would therefore be unwilling that we should have credit for them." Needless to say, Georgia and South Carolina politicians never allowed such a situation to occur. In March 1779, when the Continental Congress suggested they recruit three thousand slaves for wartime service, those states' leaders nearly abandoned the war effort altogether. Racism in the North and South, the centrality of enslaved labor in the South, and the lack of a universal plan to trade military service for emancipation meant that, despite the push against slavery from the enslaved, the American cause was fought for White liberty, not Black freedom.[18]

But, as quick as American leaders were to make promises to the men who bore arms, Black and White alike, they were slow to follow through on them. So slow, in fact, that they frequently imperiled the American military effort. Hardship, no pay, little food, and inadequate clothes, as well as a shortage of arms and ammunition, typified the plight of American forces two years into the war. Military leaders complained non-stop about the lack of necessities. "I beg you will exert yourself in procuring Shoes," wrote George Washington to James Mease, the clothier general whom Washington would soon accuse of incompetence. Later, informing Continental President Henry Laurens of the soldiers' deprivations, Washington wrote, "We have now a great many men entirely destitute of Shirts and Breeches and I suppose not less than a fourth or fifth of the whole here, who are without Shoes." In 1778, he reported that "the distress of this army for want of arms is very great; we have a number of men intirely destitute, and many recruits are dayly coming in from whom we can derive no service on the same account." When pressed to supply troops in Wilmington, Delaware, the general bristled: "The distress of this army for want of provisions is perhaps beyond any thing you can conceive."[19]

Years later, the soldiers' memories tended to corroborate Washington's complaints. More than anything else, scarcity marked army life. Richard Vining recalled "the sickness and hardship" of a campaign in late 1775, when "his company was obliged to kill a dog and eat it for our breakfast." Richard Durfee, a Rhode Island soldier, went home to Tiverton "almost without shoes, money, or clothing." In the winter of 1779–1780, Joseph Plumb Martin saw "men roast their old shoes and eat them." Others remembered marching on "bare feet" after their "shoes gave way" and going for weeks on scant food.[20]

Military leaders blamed the shortages on corruption and legislative inaction. Some believed the scarcities to be a figment of the soldiers' imaginations. By 1778, though, when dire economic conditions enveloped all Americans, civilians and soldiers, a power beyond graft, indecision, and individual fortitude was clearly in play. Caught in a ghastly fiscal situation of its own make, the Continental Congress needed to establish taxes to fund the violent industry it had created. But, amid a war over the colonial revenue system, the Continental delegates, powerful enough to muster thousands of men and move them like pawns through thirteen states, were too weak to aid the economy. "The true point of light then, in which to place, & consider this matter," said Washington in October, "is . . . whose Finances (theirs or ours) is most likely to fail."[21]

Faith in overwhelming force (a mindset traceable in American military endeavors from the Revolution to more recent times) elicited short-term plans, both military and economic. John Adams said to Moses Gill, the chairman of supplies for the American Army at Cambridge, "In my opinion Powder and Artillery are the most efficacious, Sure, and infallibly conciliatory Measures We can adopt." To match the quick efficiency of government force, rebel lawmakers turned to currency expansion as their fiscal fix. In the spring of 1775, Continental Congress delegates issued two million dollars for the war effort. This figure ballooned to six million by the year's end and, one year later, the Continentals had printed twenty-five million dollars.[22]

These measures, however, soon proved a makeshift solution. In December 1778, about seven paper Continental dollars equaled one "specie dollar," or money coined from a precious metal. One year later, the rate soared to forty-two paper dollars and, by the end of 1780, nearly one hundred paper dollars per specie dollar. To battle the currency devaluation, the Continental Congress issued loan certificates – essentially government bonds that accrued 4 and soon 6 percent interest until three years after the war's end. As the certificates largely failed to generate enthusiasm from the public, Congress pushed for the states to bring in five million dollars through taxation. State leaders demurred, however, recognizing that the issuance of a tax was politically untenable. With the viability of government arms at stake, the Continental Congress remained committed to printing dollars, sought international assistance, and continued to try to obtain funds from the states to pay for the war effort.[23]

When currency depreciation combined with price inflation (which was the result of the vast wartime expenditures), a true crisis peaked. The British paid in pounds sterling, a far more stable tender, and American farmers began to skirt regulations and sell to the red-coated troops. They sent loaded wagons operated by women and children, hoping that American sentries on the lookout for illegal exchanges would ignore them. Washington abhorred the "avarice" of these farmers, telling Brigadier-General John Lacey, Jr., to arrest just one who, "if found guilty," he would execute. The example, Washington said, would make all American farmers "sensible of a like Fate." Notably, however, there is no record of a farmer being executed in this fashion by the Continental Army.[24]

As prices soared by 50–100 percent from 1776 to 1783, spending in the military's commissary and quartermaster departments likewise exploded. In the opening year of the conflict, the combined cost of the two units equaled 3.3 million dollars. In 1779, it was 109.4 million. Army salaries during the same period did not even double, moving from 9.4 to 15.8 million dollars. Though the issue at hand was macroeconomic in nature, the Continental Congress saw fit to combat military costs through administrative reform. Popular lore blamed corruption in the divisions responsible for army supply. The changes instituted in 1777, and again in 1779 and 1780, helped rationalize a bureaucratic structure by demanding strict documentation and personal accountability. Largely useless as a solution for currency depreciation and price inflation, the governmental oversight put in place for military supply nonetheless represented the kind of capable infrastructure more often assigned to the Civil War era or later.[25]

It took a lot to feed an army. Even during one of the worst shortages of the Revolution, the winter from December 1777 to February 1778, the soldiers consumed 2.25 million pounds of beef, 2.3 million pounds of flour, and 500,000 gills of rum and whiskey. Yet, despite the large volume of goods provided to the forces, inflation ensured that there was never enough. "I can neither Send on any more stores or procure any thing from my department," one supply official said; "the money depreciates so fast no body will trust the Continent one day." Indeed, the phrase "not worth a Continental" came into widespread use during this time to label the valueless Continental dollars. Meanwhile, Washington increasingly turned to the military impressment of goods to prevent the disbandment of the army. "It is of the utmost Consequence that the Horses Cattle Sheep and Provender within Fifteen or Twenty miles west of the River Delaware between the Schuylkil and the Brandywine be immediately removed," he ordered Nathanael Greene in February 1778. His purpose was two-fold. Washington wished "to prevent the Enemy" from securing such bounty, but he knew full well it would help "to supply the present Emergencies of the American Army."[26]

Expropriation, even when committed with full intent of repayment, was risky. The American Revolution was one of the first modern wars in that it was less a battle of military prowess and more a fight over the loyalty of the people. Washington learned this lesson early on and thus feared the "bad tendency of pushing Military Impresses too far." Too far was when the impressment of supplies elicited local opposition. Nevertheless, Washington noted the dilemma of a severely undersupplied military. There was an "impracticability of keeping the Army supplied without it [military impressment], or *money*." Indeed, Washington's "Military Impressess" became so common that Pennsylvania leaders soon demanded the Continental Army receive their approval for any impressment activity.[27]

As much as the general fretted over "oppressing the people," "souring their tempers – and alienating their affections," the need was clear. Washington harbored more concern over the condition of his troops than the feelings of the public. "And what Officer can bear the weight of prices, that every necessary article is now got to?" he wondered. "A Rat, in the shape of a Horse, is not to be bought at this time for less than £200 – A Saddle under Thirty or forty – Boots twenty – and Shoes and other articles in like proportion!" Washington predicted that "unless some measures can be devised, and speedily executed, to restore the credit of our Currency," the American Army was doomed.[28]

Meanwhile, disobedience and desertion plagued American forces from the start. The soldiers were, after all, an eager, untrained lot – and the situation only worsened when the economy collapsed. "The constant firing in the Camp, notwithstanding repeated Orders to the contrary, is very scandalous," Washington said in August 1776, "and seldom a day passes but some persons are shot by their friends." In 1777, 40 percent of the forces from New Jersey deserted along with about 33 percent of the privates who enlisted from New York. Captain Henry Lee identified southern Delaware, which had little in the way of patriotic governance, as an "asylum to deserters from the continental army." Later, Washington said the same of Vermont.[29]

The signs of unrest could not be ignored. In spring 1779, the officers of the North Carolina Line, who suffered a northern winter underdressed and underpaid, held a meeting at West Point, New York. They informed authorities that they were prepared to resign en masse unless changes were made. North Carolina's delegates in the Continental Congress appealed to Governor Caswell for help: "The grievances of which they complain, we are convinced, press them with difficulties much more severe than they have expressed, and the prices of necessaries, which they have stated, are far from being exaggerated." Bankrupt and determined to stop printing money, they explained, the Continental Congress had to rely on the states. In the end, the North Carolina General Assembly granted the officers, who by virtue of their position were White, improved provisions of rum, sugar, soap, and tobacco. Far more significantly, it promised them half-pay for life and a tax exemption on lands received upon their commission. The officers accepted the terms even though the government proved unable to satisfy their prior, less generous arrangement.[30]

Dissent spread through the ranks in 1779–1780 after the coldest winter of the war. Arguments flared over the expiration of enlistments throughout the Continental Army. Some wanted out only to re-enlist under better terms, while others felt a need to attend to their families and homes. All were frustrated by delayed or missing pay and the privations of daily army life. "Lack of food constitutes the single biggest assault upon morale," noted a twentieth-century military leader. "Apart from its purely chemical effects upon the body, it has a woeful effect upon the mind." In the American Revolution, General Anthony Wayne was more succinct: "Discontent ever produces Desertion." The Continental Army's shortages of food, clothing, and shelter are well documented. When combined with the stresses of killing and the possibility of being killed, Continental soldiers bore a heavy burden.[31]

In addition, Washington's belief in linking personal interest to government defense soon collapsed.

———————◆———————

On January 1, 1780, about one hundred soldiers in the Massachusetts Line struck out from their quarters believing that their three-year commitments had expired. Forcibly returned, the men were mostly pardoned. By March, however, scores of officers from the same disgruntled unit resigned. Then, on May 25, a warm and dry day in Morristown, New Jersey, where Washington had headquarters, officers discovered an unsigned letter of complaint. The soldiers of the Connecticut Line hinted that if provisions were not provided immediately, they would "march in the Country."

And that's exactly what they did.

At night, after roll call, beating drums broke the calm, summoning malcontented soldiers to action. Two armed Connecticut regiments began to march – that is, until officers and a contingent of Pennsylvanian troops were able to pacify them. With the uprising's leaders under arrest, the Connecticut commander Jonathan Meigs wrote to George Washington. Since the "Brigade is now ten days deficient in Meat," he said, it was not "a case where mutiny can be admitted the event." Washington agreed. "There are certain bounds, beyond which it is impossible for Human nature to go," he said to Connecticut Governor Jonathan Trumbull. "We are arrived at these. The want of provision last night produced a mutiny in the army of a very alarming kind."[32]

The incident exposed Washington's dilemma. Experts calculate that between 2 and 3 percent of human beings are enthusiastic killers – the rest of the human population requires conditioning and social pressure to take the life of another. In the Continental Army, drilling and a severe code of conduct helped turn the American recruits into a fighting force. But what happens when a lack of provisions, which saps military determination, and broken promises, which undermines the chain of command, are the sources of soldiers' objections?

"Their complaints are, that they have too long served the public without any present, or prospect of future recompense," wrote army surgeon James Thatcher of the Connecticut men. "These circumstances are known to be substantially true, and in justice they ought, and undoubtedly will, be admitted in extenuation of the crime which they have committed." However, Thatcher also recognized a problem with leniency. "It is never-theless indispensably important that every symptom of insubordination should be crushed as soon as discovered lest the example become conta-gious and involve the whole army in ruin."[33]

In Morristown on May 26, the day after the mutiny, a scheduled execu-tion of eleven soldiers was held. It was an event that bore no relation to the previous night's proceedings. When ten of the men received reprieve from the commander-in-chief, the ceremony followed custom. Intended to present Washington as merciful and magnanimous, the reprieve likewise enhanced the profile of his godliness. The only unusual circumstance took place when James Coleman, who had forged discharges for more than one hundred soldiers, strode to the gallows as the lone soldier to be executed. A large man, Coleman broke the rope and was but bruised on the first attempt. However, Thatcher reported, after requesting a stronger cord, Coleman "was launched into eternity."[34]

In June 1780, army unrest continued as thirty-one men of the 1st New York Regiment abandoned Fort Schuyler in northern New York. Upset over a "want of pay and the necessary clothing, particularly shirts," the armed band announced its intent to reach the British at Oswegatchie on the St. Lawrence River. Infuriated, Lieutenant Hardenberg equipped himself with a party of Oneida Indians, who, unlike the White men still under his command, lacked close ties to the protesters. He then set off in pursuit. The deserters were located just after fifteen of them had crossed the Grand River. "A fire was immediately commenced," reported George Washington, and "thirteen of the sixteen" who remained in sight were killed. The rest of the men escaped.[35]

Hardenberg's actions demonstrate why state violence, here embodied by Native American troops under Continental command, often appeared impersonal. Familiarity with targeted individuals, army leaders believed, raised soldiers' resistance to killing. This explains why leaders repeatedly requested outside help when in pursuit of military personnel.

When news of the incidents at West Point, Morristown, and Fort Schuyler reached the enemy, the British commanders saw an opportunity. They launched a campaign to win the minds of American soldiers. "You are neither clothed, fed, nor paid," read a widely distributed British hand-bill. "In order to procure your liberty you must quit your leaders and join your real friends." American politicians and military officers, who by then expected additional French support in soldiers and credit, were chastened by the boldness of their enemy. They well understood that no foreign power would support what appeared to be a failing cause – and nothing signaled defeat more than disobedient forces. In winter 1780–1781, significant portions of Washington's soldiery had been unpaid for up to twelve months, and a full third of the eight thousand soldiers in the Continental Army were unfit for duty due to being sick, unclothed, or unarmed. A comprehensive mutiny appeared more likely than comprehensive victory. "I can only say that we are bankrupt with a mutinous army," wrote James Lovell, the Continental Congress delegate from Massachusetts.[36]

The lack of provisions, soldier discontent, and British guile all fed the powder keg that was now the American military. In late 1780, General

Anthony Wayne, who commanded the Pennsylvania Line, sensed that the mindset of his troops was "much soured by neglect & every extreme of wretchedness for want of almost every comfort & necessary of life." A promise of "solid landed property" as reward for their "past services & their more than Roman Virtue," Anthony proposed, would "Insure fidelity."[37]

But no action was taken. And on January 1, 1781, between 9 and 10 p.m., more than a thousand Pennsylvanian soldiers refused to obey General Wayne. Camped at Mount Kemble near Morristown, New Jersey, they "paraded with their Arms" and "seized the Artillery of the division." At 11 p.m., the group "scoured the grand parade with round and grape shot from four field pieces," and, "advancing in solid column with fixed bayonets," delivered "a diffusive fire of musketry in front, flank & rear."[38]

During the fracas, the mutineers killed Captain Biting. They also shot Lieutenant Francis White in the thigh and Captain Samuel Tolbert in the stomach. While early reports list the men as having fatal wounds, White and Tolbert survived. "They continued huzzaing and fireing in riotous manner," said Lieutenant Enos Reeves, "so that it soon became dangerous for an officer to oppose them by force." Wayne asserted that the "rioters" suffered casualties too (Fig. 2.1). "Many of their bodies lay under our horses' feet," he reported, "and others will retain with existence the traces of our swords and espontoons."[39]

When the troops appeared ready to march off, Wayne and his officers blocked the road to Elizabethtown, a route that could lead the discontented men to the British. Instead, the rebellious faction moved south, toward Princeton. George Washington soon described the event as his worst nightmare. To fellow enslavers George Clinton and John Hancock, he wrote that the event was something he had "long apprehended." To Philip John Schuyler, who also owned Black individuals, he said, "The event, which I have long dreaded would be the consequence of keeping the Army without Pay, Clothing, and (frequently without) Provisions, has at length come to pass."[40]

On January 2 at 4:30 a.m., Wayne reported to George Washington that "every possible exertion was used by the officers to suppress [the mutiny] in its rise." However, "the torrent was too potent to be stemmed." The use of swords and short pikes (espontoons) was no match for the many men armed with muskets and artillery. The situation no doubt drove General Wayne mad. An adherent of discipline, he was accustomed to deference and having the violent upper hand. During a mutiny of a rifle company in 1777, for instance, he demanded the leader to step out. When the man followed the command, Wayne "presented a Pistol to his Breast" and made him beg for

Fig. 2.1 *Mutiny of the Pennsylvania Line*, by James E. Taylor (engraved by Edmund A. Winham). From the Wallach Division Picture Collection, New York Public Library.

his life. Wayne noted with pride how such measures wrought compliance. But when he cocked his pistol in 1781, the soldiers, according to a diarist, "instantly presented their bayonets to his breast, saying, 'We respect and love you; often have you led us into the field of battle, but we are no longer under your command; we warn you to be on your guard; if you fire your pistols, or attempt to enforce your commands, we shall put you instantly to death.'" When the Pennsylvanian mutineers inundated the "grand parade" – the Mount Kemble grounds reserved for marching and drilling – with gunshot and munitions, their muskets and artillery voiced opposition to Wayne's exacting ways.[41]

The commander's autocratic style, though, was more a trigger than a cause of the rebellion. This was made clear by the soldiers' six articles, which they provided to Wayne after creating a more democratic chain of command (the men elected their own officers). The first four articles distinguished between when soldiers had enlisted (1776 or 1777), the length of enlistment (three years or for the war's duration), and the bounty paid (between $20 and $120). No matter the case, the soldiers demanded the discharge of those who had fulfilled their arrangement and an immediate compensation for "all arrearages of Pay . . . and all arrears of Clothing." In the last two articles, they declared a unanimous consent over the grievances.[42]

The soldiers clearly marked the economic and contractual nature of their dispute. These were matters that George Washington also understood on a personal and professional level. On January 3, 1781, for instance, he complained, "I have not been able to obtain any Money for my own expences, or table for More than three Months." Before he had seen the demands from the leaders of the mutiny, Washington had already written to John Hancock that they wanted pay, provisions, and clothing. The general predicted "that unless some immediate and spirited measures are adopted" – by which he meant the protesting men had to be overpowered in a sudden, harsh attack – "the worst that can befall us, may be expected."[43]

At the opening of the mutiny, Washington and Wayne appeared to discount the stated concerns of the Pennsylvania troops. They worried more over other possibilities: that the Pennsylvanians were headed to the British or that the spirit of mutiny might spread. In a letter the day after the event, Wayne, relieved that he found no indication of betrayal, wrote that "their general cry is, to be discharged, and that they will again enlist and fight for America, a few excepted." By taking this stance, the men demonstrated that the alignment of state violence with promises of soldier prosperity was more effective than mercenary contracts. When the French stopped paying Swiss mercenaries in 1602, for example, the Swiss simply abandoned the French cause. In 1781, when the governments failed to pay and provide for the Continental Army, the soldiers sought a guarantee of their terms and, if possible, looked to secure even better ones. Money was one way, albeit an imperfect one, to bring a soldier in line with the American effort.[44]

Violent reprisal was, of course, another. Advisers John Laurens, who implored Washington that "nothing but a superior investing Force will reduce them to reason," and Arthur St. Clair, who stated that "nothing but Force" would get the job done, both demanded an overwhelming response. But Washington, whose first impulse was to rush to New Jersey, found himself detained by "the temper of the troops" at his New Windsor camp. They lacked "Flour – Cloathing and in short every thing," he said; it was unwise for him to leave. Violent reprisal would have to wait.[45]

Nevertheless, the general understood the seriousness of the protest in the Pennsylvania Line. Numbering as many as 2,500 men, the soldiers in rebellion represented more than 30 percent of the entire American Army. Anthony Wayne, with some several hundred officers in New Jersey, was outmatched. Of the mutinous troops Washington said: "Should they finally go to the Enemy, they will be a considerable augmentation of strength against us, or should they be dispersed, their loss to the service will be severely felt." Henry Knox's recommendation appeared the most prudent: "There being but few regular continental troops in Jersey except the Pennsylvania line," he suggested, "force cannot be opposed to them with success. Lenitive measures only will answer." Washington, for now, agreed. The protesters' appeal would be heard.[46]

Unhinged by the widespread fiscal crisis of the American experiment, the regimented order of the Continental Army – the pillar of state-backed violence – was ineffective against such a large protest. Anthony Wayne was lost without an ability to use force. He promised the soldiers in rebellion "on the *Honor* of a gentleman and a *Soldier*" that he would "exert every nerve to obtain a redress." Yet his assurance offered little comfort and his contempt did not help: "the General hopes Soon to return to Camp with all his brother Soldiers who took a little tour last evening." The mutineers soon announced an intent to march to the Continental Congress in Philadelphia.[47]

The impact of the mutiny was felt far and wide. From Madrid, the diplomat William Carmichael reported that "the mutiny of the Pennsylvania line has had a bad effect in Europe, and our enemies have been indefatigable to represent it in the worst colors." British newspapers joyously blamed the uprising on "the Bankrupt Condition of the Congress's Finances" and British leaders sent two agents to offer generous terms to the soldiers to change sides. On the ground in the American states, military and civilian leaders scrambled to respond. The Marquis de Lafayette, commissioned as a major-general by the Continental Congress, wrote home to France that "no European army would endure the tenth part of such sufferings" and praised American soldiers, "who are more hardy and more patient, I believe, than any others in existence." Meanwhile, Washington started to assemble "as large a Detachment to march ... as could be spared."[48]

In New Jersey, Anthony Wayne continued to negotiate to no avail. On January 7, Joseph Reed, Pennsylvania governor and former Continental Congress delegate, left Philadelphia for a summit with the protesting troops. Acting without fear of discipline, the Pennsylvania soldiers had settled in Princeton, which, George Washington noted, was "(to them) a favourable intermediate point between Congress and the enemy." Here, Wayne all but ceded control of the situation to Reed. The troops were anxious for Wayne and his officers to exit the town. The general, however, in his ever-haughty tone, replied that while he wanted to leave and allow the men "to follow their wild & ungovernable inclinations," Reed and Washington had directed him to stay.[49]

It was a combustible situation. British General Henry Clinton offered the protesting American soldiers, with no expectation of military service, a pardon for their treason to the Crown along with "immediate Payment of all Arrears of Pay, Clothing Provisions," and "Depreceation" due to them by the Continental Congress. Armed with the offer, the leaders of the mutiny enjoyed a powerful position. In just one day, Governor Reed, after the soldiers had turned over the two foreign emissaries, agreed to terms similar to those offered by the British. A three-person committee would adjudicate enlistments, back pay was awarded with acknowledgement of currency devaluation, and every soldier, even those whose enlistments were determined complete, was to receive "A Pair of Shoes, Overalls & Shirt." The one dispute was over appointments to the committee. Reed refused the soldiers a voice in its selection. "This implies such a Distrust of the Authority of the State," he said, it could not be granted.[50]

From the moment he first heard the demands of the protesters, George Washington opposed them. "They are so extravagant," he said, "it will end in the dissolution of the line." The main thrust of the general's concern, no doubt, focused on enlistments. To lose even a quarter of the Pennsylvania Line could prove crippling. Still, in his use of the words "extravagant" and, in another letter, "exorbitant," one hears tones of Washington from two years before. "All that the common Soldiery of any Country can expect is food and clothing," he declared from the position of a man sheltered by riches. "The idea of maintaining the families of our Soldiers at Public expence is peculiar to us, & is incompatible with the finances of any Government." The general was particularly peeved, then, that the leaders of the mutiny intended to use the British overture "only by way of threat" to broker a deal. He noted the terms were "very favourable to the revolted Troops" and that "witht any intention I am persuaded of fulfilling them." While he had previously advised Wayne against the measure, Washington now searched for a force large enough to overawe the Pennsylvanians. Uncertainty about the men at his New Windsor camp slowed him. On January 9, 1781, he stated that "whether they would act agt the mutiniers is a matter of some doubt." So Washington continued to plot against the rebellious troops, waiting for the moment when "the reduction of them by force ... would not be difficult."[51]

It was while he was delayed that Governor Joseph Reed stepped in – and Reed already had an agreement with the leaders of the mutiny by January 13, when Washington, not yet up to date on events in Princeton, brought a thousand men to a state of readiness. The general believed that "the support of Military authority, was so essential, as to be attempted at almost every hazard." One can imagine Washington's disappointment, then, upon receiving the news of Reed's settlement. In written correspondence, Washington remained largely silent. A letter dated January 21 states: "I shall therefore content myself with adding, that the Civil Authority having undertaken to settle the dispute, there would have been an impropriety in my interfering in their conciliatory Measures, which would not have suited the principles of Military discipline."[52]

Indeed, as the arbiter of government arms, the general believed that the proper way to arrive in Princeton was backed by a prodigious force. His thoughts thus reveal a tension in the typical historical interpretation of Washington's character and beliefs. "It has ever been a point of delicacy with me, while acting only in a Military character," he explained, "not to interfere in the civil concerns of the Continent or the Legislatures, except where they are intimately connected with Military matters." This is the George Washington whom scholars uphold as the standard bearer for civilian oversight of state-sponsored violence. And, while it's true that Revolutionary military culture gave voice to the notion that, as one soldier wrote, "the Military must be subservient to the Civil," it was an idea – much like the original form of the Massachusetts Army – that aligned well with the greater political culture of White consent.[53]

However, Washington wielded the violence of the state in a far more dynamic manner. In July 1775, for example, he requested "a more immediate & frequent Communication with the Congress" expressing a need for "Assistance & Direction from them." Yet, in practice, he just as often subverted legislative supervision. Few examples are more glaring than the management of his spy network, which he often funded through private donations. He rode with a saddlebag filled with hard currency to insure the secrecy of his campaigns. Nor was Washington always clandestine. As mutiny raged within the Pennsylvania Line, he boldly petitioned the states for provisions. He understood this step, which he had taken time and again during the war, as a clear abuse of power. "It is not within the sphere of my duty to make requisitions without the Authority of Congress, from individual States," Washington said to Massachusetts Governor John Hancock, "but at such a Crisis as this, and circumstanced as we are, my own heart will acquit me."[54]

The strain between honoring legislative decisions and Washington's own belief in the importance of exemplary violence soon came to a head. On January 20, 1781, about one hundred and sixty soldiers in the New Jersey Line followed the recent example set by the protesting soldiers from Pennsylvania. They struck out against their officers, marched all night, and paraded around the town of Chatham. The commanding officer, a slave-owner named Frederick Frelinghuysen, chased the troops for two days. When he caught them, he read aloud a recent resolution of the New Jersey legislature that promised to improve their conditions. "The greater part of them expressed the greatest Satisfaction," Frelinghuysen wrote to Washington, "and agreed to return to their duty." The rest "however declared they would persist, untill similar Terms were offered them to those granted the Pensylvanians." When he accounted for the "Lenity exercised towards the more criminal" mutineers from Mount Kemble, Frelinghuysen opted to pardon all the men who agreed to come back into service. He assured General Washington "that no very evil Consequences will follow from this partial Revolt."[55]

Washington was in no mood to listen. Though he did, at first, accept the recent deal struck by Pennsylvanian politicians to end their soldiers' uprising – "Every thing wore a favorable aspect for an accommodation," he wrote to Continental Army General Robert Howe on January 15 – he was quick to blame that arrangement for his new problem. The "affair of the Pennsylvania Line" was mishandled "by the intervention of the State," he said in one letter. In another, he added that the "interposition of the Civil Authority of the State" produced the current "disturbances in the Jersey Brigade." He dashed off correspondence to New Jersey Governor William Livingston "in order to prevent any compromise being made with the mutineers." "The most dangerous consequences may ensue unless an immediate stop shall be put to such horrid proceedings," Washington declared. A protest for food, clothing, and earned pay was indeed so "horrid," he believed, and the need to stop it so pressing, that he declared, "I am now taking the most vigorous coercive measures for that purpose."[56]

Washington did not waver. He sent forces under the command of Major-General Howe, with orders to "compel the mutineers to unconditional submission." "If you succeed in compelling the revolted troops to a surrender," he further directed Howe, "you will instantly execute a few of the most active and most incendiary leaders." When Howe arrived on January 25, he learned that the British "sent out a spy with a proclamation offering the Same terms to the Jersey revolters that they offered to the Pensylvanians." Though the soldiers had already been pardoned by

Frelinghuysen, Howe questioned their conduct. "I understand enough to think that it is but little better than the second part of the pensylvania tune which I, by no means, am inclined to dance to," he said. Howe, another significant enslaver of Black persons, reported to his commander that the New Jersey soldiers acted more as if they were "following advice than obeying command."[57]

Soon, in response to the increased rigor Howe put in place, the troops reached another breaking point. One soldier presented a bayonet to an officer's breast and, when he was knocked down, a full-blown resistance re-emerged. Again, the men paraded fully armed. Howe, however, believed that "no medium lay either for Civil or Military bodies between dignity and Servility but Coertion." That night, he marched about five hundred men to the scene, blocked the five exits of escape, and sent orders for the protesters to lay down their weapons. The rebels had five minutes to comply. As the unarmed men came out, Howe asked the officers of the New Jersey troops to single out the greatest troublemakers. "A Field Court Martial was presently held," Howe reported, "and they received Sentence of death by the unanimous decree of the Court. Two of them were excuted [sic] on the Spot, the third I have reprieved." He added, "I thought it would have a good effect to appoint the executioners from among those most active in the mutiny."[58]

With no sense of irony, Washington characterized the response to the New Jersey incident as a bloodless success. "This business was happily effected without bloodshed," he wrote. "Two of the principal actors were immediately executed on the spot and due subordination restored." One day later, Washington revealed to George Clinton the military mindset wherein response to the executions helped authorities gauge the need for more killing. Howe "had two of the most active Instigators immediately tried and executed. It was judged unnecessary to extend the example further, as there was every appearance of genuine contrition."[59]

In General Orders for January 30, 1781, Washington laid the recent uprisings to rest. "We expected to encounter many wants and distresses and We should neither shrink from them when they happen nor fly in the face of Law and Government to procure redress," he said.

> The General is happy in the lenity shewn in the execution of only two of the most guilty after compelling the whole to an unconditional surrender – and he flatters himself no similar instance will hereafter disgrace our military History – It can only bring ruin in those who are mad enough to make the attempt; for lenity on any future occasion would be criminal and inadmissible.

In a series of letters Washington trumpeted the success of his repressive methods: "Nothing can revive the spirit of discontent among any of the Troops, which, where ever it has appeared, seems now to be extinguished."[60]

Washington's sense that the spirit of mutiny had ended proved wishful, however, as small protests and desertion continued to plague his units for the war's duration. But the quick, violent response showcased by Howe against the New Jersey soldiers – as opposed to legislative negotiation – became a hallmark of the American Army. As the official report of the Continental Congress on the Pennsylvania mutiny cautioned, "soldiers never to separate severity from justice and to temper severity with mercy." The Congress expected the men to accept the army's lethal response to protest as reasonable and be grateful when merciful leaders opted not to kill or maim them for protesting.[61]

---◆---

Earlier in the eighteenth century, a Huron man named Kandiaronk explained to Westerners that they could opt for less brutal ways. In an exchange with Baron Lahontan, a Frenchman, Kandiaronk asked, "What sort of Men must the *Europeans* be?" He answered the question for himself: "The *Europeans*, who must be forc'd to do Good . . . have no other Prompter for the avoiding of Evil than the fear of Punishment." Kandiaronk questioned a society structured around reprisal. What would happen if persons were stimulated by reward instead? The Native leader pointed to the horror of the many innocent persons trapped and disciplined in the Western legal system. Overall, he blamed a culture of bodily repression on European greed. "I affirm that what you call Silver is the Devil of Devils . . . and the Slaughter-House of living Persons," he said.[62]

Baron Lahontan presented a central tenet of Western liberal societies in his response. "To avoid the lash of those Laws," he replied, "which are severe only upon the wicked and criminal Persons, one needs only to live honestly, and offer Injuries to no man." But this logic, focused on individual behavior and accountability, ignores how factors such as race and class influence understandings of criminality and sidesteps the terror and fear central to the system.[63]

A system of terror and fear appeared in full in the last years of the American Revolution. In April 1781, when Anthony Wayne faced a new mutiny in the reconstituted Pennsylvania Line, he instructed his officers to "put to death instantly any man who stirred from his rank." Wayne then commenced an immediate court martial for about twenty of the protest's leaders. Seven were found guilty and, as the rest of the soldiers marched by, executed by a firing squad. "This was an awful exhibition," said Major Ebenezer Denny. "The seven objects were seen by the troops just as they had sunk or fell under the fire. The sight must have made an impression on the men; it was designed with that view."[64]

Washington's increased embrace of force to maintain compliance as the war went on further spoiled his estimation of the militia units, the groups of citizen-soldiers that continued to represent the common soldier in the minds of many Americans. "A moderate compact force, on a permanent establishment, capable of acquiring the discipline essential to Military operations," he said, was far superior to "the throngs of Militia." He felt stymied "that coercion . . . cannot be exercised upon" militiamen and thus found it "impracticable to detain the greatest part of them in service."

To Washington and the commanders of the Continental Army, then, violence trumped consent. And the general was certain of one other detail: "The want of Pay, Cloathing, & Provisions is productive of evils, from which we scarcely know how we shall be able to extricate ourselves." In these years, American leaders learned that state violence subsists on economic support; the men, that it spirals inward to face defiance – and both discovered deep defects in the arrangement.[65]

3

THE CODE OF AMERICAN VIOLENCE

Most American military leaders, like George Washington, believed that Continental Army soldier activism demonstrated a need for more order, that more physical punishment was needed to enforce it, and that centralized authority was the best means to achieve it. After the mutiny of the Pennsylvania Line, the military officers were not alone. For two years, Maryland legislators had refused to approve of the Articles of Confederation, a new political framework proposed to organize the American states. The near disintegration of the Continental Army in January 1781 changed their minds. "The advantages and necessity of one general established power, to draw into action the force of the United States, is obvious," said the state's House of Delegates in newfound support. In the Maryland senate, officials observed that confederation was "a means of negotiating loans in Europe." They declared that "without such resources, or a foreign subsidy ... the states cannot prosecute the war with vigour." Clearly, a concentration of force and an increased ability to secure funds to pay for such force justified the formation of a new nation.[1]

The Articles of Confederation bound thirteen disparate states into a confederacy, "a firm league of friendship with each other, for their common defence, the security of their liberties." So called "The United States of America," the confederation forged "a perpetual union" and empowered a federal congress to arbitrate disputes. However, the Articles were conceived in the 1770s, years before the crisis of 1781. And as the war drew on, the Articles would soon come to disappoint proponents of American centralism.[2]

Along with Maryland's leaders, many hoped that the new arrangement would create clear lines of authority. George Washington wrote, "The confederation being now closed will, I trust, enable [the national] Congress to speak decisively in their requisitions of the respective States." As decisive as the Congressional delegates' speech may have been, however, their mandate under the Articles was unenforceable. Congress, authorized to borrow money, often failed to pay interest on its loans because it could

73

not impose taxes or compel the states to pay their share. Permitted to fashion international treaties, the Congress lacked the power to implement them. Even the primary function of the Confederation – to ensure a "common defence ... against all force offered to, or attacks made upon" the states – remained decentralized. The states provisioned and trained armed forces in times of peace that, like the fortification of the Continental Army, would turn over to Congress for control in time of war. In other words, the Articles rationalized, not revolutionized, American governance.[3]

Suspicions over the centralized violence of the confederated states triumphed in the drafting of the first general charter. Three-quarters of the states had to vote in support for the national Congress to "engage in war" or even to budget or plan for (let alone raise) an army or navy. The militia model of the citizen-soldier dominated. "Every State shall always keep up a well-regulated and disciplined militia, sufficiently armed and accoutered," declares Article VI, while Article VII makes clear that decision power over the militia remains within individual states. However, militias were still viewed as a potential threat. According to the charter, states could assemble their forces only in wartime (a condition declared by Congress), or in peacetime with direct approval of Congress. Such provisions mimic several found in Revolutionary-era state constitutions. Massachusetts and Virginia, for instance, banned permanent armies in times of peace without explicit legislative approval.[4]

Some American states at the time went further when it came to codifying their fears of an oppressive centralized force. Maryland forbade men from holding military and civil posts at the same time, banned gatherings of soldiers at voting places, and prohibited ten or more militiamen from the same company from visiting a single poll in succession. The state also outlawed all armed persons from election sites "to prevent any violence or force being used."[5]

Many in the former colonies understood that prevention of this sort was a fundamental object of White government. Under the Articles of Confederation, the Congressional templates for treaties and alliances stood "against all Violence, Insults, Attacks or Depredations" and "To prevent entirely disorder and violence." But, as Continental Army mutiny and the possibility of losing the war rendered centralized state violence in a new light, Maryland's House of Delegates saw the need for national forces as a balance struck between individual liberty and protection from foreign and domestic enemies. On the Articles of Confederation's creation of federal violence, the state legislature wondered whether the national Congress possessed "too little for our defence, or too much for our liberty?"[6]

The answer to this question was quickly made apparent, insofar as the Articles sanctioned the faulty system of supply and payment already in place for the Continental Army. Unable to raise funds from the states, the new national government did not and would not rectify the military situation on the ground with dwindling supplies and mutinous soldiers. Indeed, respect for the Confederation Congress reached such lows because of this situation that, by 1784, the Virginia House of Delegates considered a motion to allow Congress to make states pay "their respective quotas, by means of an armed force." This proposal did not pass, but its aim had been to federalize the design set by Continental Army leaders to stymie soldier protest in the Revolution. The message was: if you fail to comply, we will force you to do it.[7]

A few years into the national experiment of confederation, an increasing number of American leaders saw an insolvent nation besieged by political stalemate. An effort to reform the Articles was already underway when a 1786 campaign of farmers in western Massachusetts, led by Continental Army veteran and local official Daniel Shays, put the ineffectiveness of the national Congress on full display. Living amid a horrific economic slump, the men demanded relief from measures that foreclosed on their lands, sent debtors to jail, and, in some cases, sold debtors to work to meet obligations. That October, when the distressed farmers moved to attack the Confederation armory (with its 450 tons of military goods, including 7,000 small arms) at Springfield, Massachusetts, Congress tried to raise a half million dollars for army expansion. This effort, which looked for private backers, failed when the states refused to guarantee tax support for loan repayment – but this was cold comfort for the Massachusetts farmers now engaged in what would come to be known as Shays's Rebellion.[8]

That the Congress was not even authorized to requisition troops to suppress a domestic rebellion added to its woes. Officially, the legislators asked for soldiers to fight Indians. But with no help expected from the national government, state leaders sought a resolution. Militia members in Springfield sympathized with Shays's rebels and refused to reinforce the armory's defenses. And, like his counterparts in Congress, the Massachusetts state treasurer failed to secure loans to support a volunteer army. In the end, General Benjamin Lincoln, the slaveholder from Hingham, Massachusetts, personally raised monies to fund forces to combat Shays's rebels. The rout was effective. Lincoln and his men readily captured and dispersed the protesters in January and February of 1787. Notably, on February 21, Congress then sanctioned a convention in Philadelphia for widespread reform of the Articles of Confederation.[9]

That summer at the Philadelphia Convention (now remembered as the Constitutional Convention), many delegates arrived with an appreciation for the idea of a centralized, perhaps permanent, federal military. The mutiny of 1781 and the recent protest led by Shays had left them shaken. Some believed the Articles of Confederation had provided the Congress with "too little" of the powers of physical force – and one of their main objects was to correct the deficiency.

Hailing from diverse geographic regions, the fifty-five Constitutional delegates were all White men whose ideas on state violence and the personal uses of force were shaped by several key institutions. Thirty of them were veterans of the Revolutionary War and twenty-five enslaved Black persons. Many more profited from human enslavement and the slave trade. But the military and slavery were not the only institutions known for circulating lessons on Whiteness, physical power, and hostile difference. Colonization and the exploitation, command, and killing of Indigenous peoples – a process forged by White settlers and their governments – were central to the lives of all the delegates. Whatever legal changes might be made in Philadelphia (formerly the land of the Lenni-Lenape), the White men in charge of making them were steeped in at least one of several cultures of American violence.[10]

At the convention, delegate Charles Pinckney, a veteran and enslaver from South Carolina, analyzed political life under the Articles of Confederation: "No Government has more severely felt the want of coercive Power than the United States." Virginia's Edmund Randolph, another veteran and enslaver, gave a gloomy assessment too. He found "the prospect of anarchy from laxity of government everywhere" – and fellow Virginian enslaver George Mason agreed. The present Confederation, he said, is deficient in "providing for coercion and punishment against delinquent states." Even though these men were eventual opponents of the Constitution (Randolph refused to sign the document and Mason fought ratification), they acquiesced on this point.[11]

Connecticut's Oliver Ellsworth also assessed the American dilemma. "How far the federal Govt. can or ought to exert coercion," he observed, is "a question of great importance." Convention attendees sought a measured response to Ellsworth's query. Alexander Hamilton, delegate from New York, listed "Force" as one of the five principles of "good government" – "by force," he said, "I mean the coercion of law and the coercion of arms." Pennsylvanian slaveholder James Wilson felt "the government ought to possess not only, first, the force, but, second, the mind or sense of the people at large." While delegates agreed that they must rework and strengthen the violent capacity of the American state, however, they failed to offer a unified approach.[12]

The debate over what was then called the sixteenth resolution, an argument over when the federal government could unleash violence on citizens or member states, highlights the problem. In June, George Mason was adamant: "Rebellion is the only case in which the military force of the state can be properly exerted against its citizens." Yet when text of the proposal surfaced in July, it provided for a more expansive idea. The national administration was to guaranty "a republican form of government" to each state and to protect each state "against foreign and domestic violence." Luther Martin objected. The Maryland slave-owner thought it best for "States to suppress rebellions themselves." Mason countered that the federal government must have the "right to suppress rebellion" lest it "remain a passive Spectator of its own subversion."[13]

In the first major draft of a new constitution, dated August 6, 1787, what was now Article XVIII read, "The United States shall guaranty to each state a republican form of government; and shall protect each state against foreign invasions, and, on application of its legislature, against domestic violence." At the end of the month, the group considered revision: "It was moved and seconded to strike out the words 'domestic violence,' and insert the word 'insurrection.'"

To modern readers, such a change may appear insignificant. But within the greater dialogue of state aggression in the eighteenth century, it is clear that proponents sought to limit the use of violence by the federal government. "Tumult," "convulsions," "violence," and "riot" were used to represent the most general forms of social and political resistance. Each could escalate into an insurrection, a localized disruption of civil society. Here most users specified the actors involved – insurrection of the Negroes, Indians, or peasantry, for example. More virulent than an insurrection was rebellion, a widespread collapse of law and order. In the 1780s, the term "revolution" – understood by White Americans as a legitimate challenge to authority – often went unused except, in the aftermath of independence, to evoke the "late revolution."[14]

The motion to replace "domestic violence" with "insurrection" was rejected six to five. "There may be resistance to the laws which cannot be termed an insurrection," James Madison later explained. "A riot did not come within the legal definition of an insurrection." But just as they refused to narrow the violence of the new federal state, the delegates would not expand it beyond what was already on the page. Pennsylvanian war veteran John Dickinson, who had recently freed the people he had enslaved, sought to delete the words "on the application of its Legislature" from the resolution. He feared cases when "domestic violence . . . may proceed from the State Legislature itself." Gouverneur Morris just found the clause illogical. "We first form a strong man to protect us, and at the same time wish to tie his hands behind him." Another war veteran, New Jersey's Jonathan Dayton, "mentioned the Conduct of Rho. Island" to support "giving latitude to the power of the US on this subject." (The lone state to boycott the convention, Rhode Island was often derided as "Rogue's Island" because its debtor-controlled legislature had forgiven an array of financial obligations.)[15]

But these words, in effect a state-level check on national violence, satisfied the demands of the likes of George Mason, who believed state consent was necessary for the centralized use of violence. And, in the end, Dickinson's motion lost in a vote of eight to three. The delegates did approve the removal of "foreign" from "foreign invasion," however, as a phrase they found redundant. Article IV, Section 4, of the American Constitution now states: "The United States shall guarantee to every State in this Union a Republican Form of Government, and shall protect each of them against Invasion; and on Application of the Legislature, or of the Executive (when the Legislature cannot be convened), against domestic Violence."[16]

Notably, upon first reading Article IV, Section 4, many citizens of the time objected. "This clause meddles too much with the independence of the several States," reflected William Symmes in Massachusetts. Indeed, the new national government had violent capabilities.[17]

With the question of when the federal government could deploy violence largely settled, the delegates turned to how. "This could be done only in two ways," said James Madison at a state convention in Virginia for the new Constitution, "either by regular forces or by the people." A widespread belief in the purity of the citizen-soldier as embodied by the militia – "the people" (or, more appropriately, the White people) – should have made the decision easy. Yet even this choice for the federal government to deploy violence through militias elicited debate. New York's Gouverneur Morris had already grumbled that northern states "are to bind themselves to march their militia for the defense of southern states for their defense against those very slaves of whom they complain." On the other side of this issue was Madison, himself an enslaver of many Black people. He noted, "the Southern States are, from their situation and circumstances, most interested in giving the national government the power of protecting its members." Madison thus argued in favor of national authority over state-raised militiamen.[18]

George Mason disagreed with Madison and acted the part of the conspiracy theorist. He feared "the extreme danger" of national leaders grasping for control. They would establish "cruel martial regulations," he forecasted, in order to render "the militia odious to the people themselves." Mason conjectured that citizens, loath to serve in a heavy-handed militia, would thus beg for the formation of a standing army. While Mason predicted tyrannical doom, others in the Virginia convention deliberated. "The militia is to introduce a uniform system of discipline," said Edmund Pendleton, "to pervade the United States of America." Here, White southerners, in need of extensive and overwhelming force to maintain human enslavement, would win. Article I, Section 8 transferred ultimate control over state-organized militia to the federal Congress. Under the Articles of Confederation, control had remained within individual states.[19]

The delegates at the Constitutional Convention, however, had gone even further in bolstering the military capabilities of the national government. Article 1, Section 8 of the Constitution empowers Congress to raise an army and navy – a so-called "standing army" – with no stipulation against permanent national forces in times of peace. This measure roused the critics in the debates over the Constitution's ratification. "A standing army!" said Major Samuel Nason in disbelief in Massachusetts. "Time would fail me, were I to attempt to recapitulate the havoc made in the world by standing armies." He continued, asking "the gentlemen of Boston ... [to] bring to their minds the fatal evening of the 5th of March, 1770, when by standing troops they lost five of their fellow-townsmen."[20]

Nevertheless, Nason's attempt to sway his state's delegates against ratification fell short. The Massachusetts men approved of the Constitution by a count of 187 to 168. Similar scenes of criticism against permanent, national forces played out across the ratification debate in several states. For example, in a ratification meeting in Maryland, a group proposed the following amendment: "That no standing army shall be kept in time of peace, unless with the consent of two thirds of the members present of each branch of Congress." It was a proposal that failed to gain the majority's support.[21]

On the other side of the table, the war veteran and enslaver Richard Henry Lee offered the supportive view of state violence as written into the Constitution. At the Virginia ratification meeting, he spoke of the valiant, honorable, and, at times, unreliable militiamen that he had commanded in the Revolution. He then explained that the new Constitution correctly offered the federal government two forms of physical force. "This plan provides for the public defence as it ought to do," Lee said. "Regulars are to be employed when necessary, and the service of the militia will always be made use of." Not only did the new national government have violent capabilities, but it would have at its disposal a standing army and the control of state militias.[22]

The US Constitution's opening verbs dictate the powers of the central state to "form, establish, insure, provide, promote, and secure." Violence is thus located in the federal government, a body granted the authority "to declare War," create an army and navy, organize the militia, return escaped individuals to enslavement, "suppress Insurrections and repel Invasions," protect states from "domestic Violence," and "declare the Punishment of Treason." The Bill of Rights, enacted as the first ten amendments to the Constitution in 1791, is often conceived as a shield for citizens against this robust authority. Thomas Jefferson expressed this perspective in a 1788 letter, saying, "I hope therefore a bill of rights will be formed to guard the people against the federal government."[23]

While the Constitution and the initial amendments shape the use of physical force by national (and state) institutions and individuals, however, it is incorrect to claim that one establishes federal authority while the other the authority of citizens. A careful look at the Second and Fifth Amendments challenges Jefferson's ideal and confirms the intricacies of how violence is structured in the United States. Individual violence sits at the foundation of the Second Amendment: "A well regulated Militia, being necessary to the security of a free State, the right of the people to keep and bear Arms, shall not be infringed." But this right has a direct correlation to the violence of the federal state: "A well regulated Militia," "the security of a free State," and "the right of the people to keep and bear Arms" signal a relationship in which armed individuals come together in a militaristic setting to act as the defense for a nation-state. It is an individual right (to keep arms) that stipulates a civic expectation (to protect a community).[24]

Niccolò Machiavelli supported such an arrangement for republican forms of government. So too did Englishman Algernon Sidney. "The body of the people is the public defence, and every man is armed and disciplined," he said. "This makes men generous and industrious; and fills their hearts with love to their country." Benjamin Franklin, a slave-owner and now antislavery supporter from Pennsylvania, voiced a similar notion within an American context, observing, "A Body of Freemen, animated by a Love of Liberty, and trained to the Use of Arms, afford the most certain and effectual Defence."[25]

The Revolution, however, muddied this association between individual armament, patriotism, and national defense. "The people shall be judge," said John Locke, who, in 1690, unwittingly fostered the logic for the American rebellion. It was the people's right to "provide for their own safety and security" once political leaders, due to "ambition, fear, folly or corruption," breach the trust (or consent) of the governed. "It is the Right of the People to alter or to abolish" government, wrote Jefferson in the Declaration of Independence, "whenever any Form of Government becomes destructive." In the minds of many early Americans, then, armed White citizens secured the right of popular revolution. And the example of 1768, when the British banned imports of tools of violence such as gunpowder and ordered Bostonians to hand over guns, informed their view. (Note the ideologically conflicted politics of early American gun rights, however: in 1776, states such as Massachusetts passed laws to disarm British loyalists and those who refused to proclaim allegiance to the "United American Colonies.")[26]

How far personal armament ought to extend as an individual, self-protective right was a topic of much debate in North America and the world in the late eighteenth century. "The people have a right to bear arms for the defence of themselves and their own State, or the United States, or for the purpose of killing game," stated Pennsylvanian representatives. In Massachusetts, the Revolutionary Constitution specified that "The People have a right to keep and bear arms for the common defence." But critics in the town of Northampton suggested that "the people have a right to keep and bear arms as well for their own as the common defence." And Williamsburgh citizens said that "to keep Arms in our houses for Our Own Defense" is an "essential privilege," one that could be curbed by a legislature which "may Confine all the fire arms to some publick Magazine." (Owing to a prevalence of firearm deterioration and the volatility of gunpowder, public storage was common and at times mandated.)[27]

A first draft of the federal amendments by Thomas Jefferson therefore included a staunch defense of individuals with guns. "No freeman shall ever be debarred the use of arms," it said. Jefferson, who believed that guns give "boldness, enterprize and independence to the mind," drew from the philosophy of Italian thinker Cesare Beccaria. Beccaria felt that the logic of removing arms from upstanding citizens was equivalent to banning "men of the use of fire, for fear of their being burnt, and of water, for fear of their being drown'd." "The laws of this nature," he said, "are those which forbid to wear arms, disarming only those who are not disposed to commit the crime which these laws mean to prevent." In other words, Beccaria argued, don't disarm the law-abiding people, for then only the criminals have guns.[28]

White American leaders quarreled over the right of individuals to commit violent acts, but they focused on the function of violence, not its need or existence. The legacy of the Revolution and British anti-gun mandates ensured that most leaders believed that people – regular, everyday White people – should have access to guns. The nature and limits of gun use, however, would remain poorly defined in the United States. This was unique in a greater Atlantic world that produced other new national charters in places such as France, Haiti, and throughout the Americas.

The 1791 French Constitution, for example, declared men to be citizens, with a component of citizenship mandating service in the National Guard (the French militia). Clear proscriptions were placed against people, as individuals and as part of the militia, using violence to challenge central authority. "Liberty to citizens to assemble peaceably" was granted only when they assembled "without arms in accordance with police regulations." The document banned armed citizens from voting in the assembly and banned, in general, "armed force" from electoral assemblies. Citizens could not gather as the National Guard without "legal authorization" and, in words that echoed throughout the French constitutions of the era, "The public force is essentially obedient; no armed body may deliberate." King Louis XVI, in a September 1791 proclamation that sanctioned this Constitution, emphasized that citizens were armed only "for the maintenance of the law." "The revolution is over," he said.[29]

It was not. Louis was killed by guillotine in 1792. And the more radical Constitution of 1793, which codified as "most sacred" that "insurrection is for the people," demonstrates the difficulty of limiting popular violence. It justified the defensive use of force against extralegal, violent acts – but also attempted to restrain individuals through a particular definition of liberty: "to do whatever is not injurious to the rights of others." The Constitution declared, "all Frenchmen shall be soldiers; all shall be trained in the handling of arms," and it upheld ranks of distinction only within military service. When another collapse of French society led to the Constitution of the Year III in 1795, however, a more conservative approach was taken. Like the 1791 charter, the Constitution of the Year III attempted to constrain the violence of the people, introducing a warning that "every armed gathering is an attack upon the Constitution; it shall be dispersed immediately by force."[30]

Absent in the United States Constitution, such declarations against armed action are found in a range of early nineteenth-century constitutional documents. The 1825 Guatemalan charter, for example, echoes language once used by the French: "The public force is essentially obedient: no armed group may deliberate." In Argentina, the wording was more specific. "No Soldier of the Army of the Line, or Militia, national or civic, to whom arms have been entrusted, shall use them factiously against any Inhabitant of the State." Several constitutions feature voting clauses like that of Panama in 1841: "The elections will be public, and no one will participate in them with arms." Notably, limitations on armed individuals, especially government-armed individuals, are paired in these charters with protections for individual gun rights, but such rights often arrived with additional constraints. An Argentinian citizen could enjoy firearm owner-ship for the protection of person and property – but only "in those urgent cases in which he cannot avail himself of the protection of the Magistrate." "All the inhabitants may have their own arms for their defense and that of the State," decreed Guatemalan leaders in 1839, but they paired gun rights and gun control: individuals "may not be deprived of their use, except in cases established by law."[31]

Given the national and global conversations of the age, American leaders in the 1780s and 1790s had a range of prescriptive language avail-able to them for addressing the intersections of individual, state, and gun violence. The amended Constitution that they produced, however, raised more questions on a relative scale than it answered. Does the First Amendment's right to peaceable assembly include those carrying weapons? How secure is an individual's gun rights outside a "well-regulated militia?" Toward what end can a gunowner discharge a weapon? In their ambiguity, the Founders bequeathed to generations of Americans battles over the boundaries of individual violence, especially as it relates to guns and the formation of force for states and the national government.

Military discipline as seen in the Continental Army's example was another means of controlling violent acts by individuals – as well as control-ling the individuals themselves. The 1795 French Constitution offered this definition: "The army on land and sea shall be subject to special laws for discipline, the form of trials, and the nature of penalties." The specialness or exceptional nature of military discipline created some stark contrasts. In 1801, in Saint-Domingue, where the Haitian Revolution was currently raging, certain claims from within the former French slave colony's first national constitution appear to conflict. "That the law is the same for everyone with regard to both protection and punishment" was denied in a separate measure stating that "crimes committed by soldiers are dealt with by special courts." Meanwhile, the United States Constitution handles the matter implicitly in Article I, Section 8, which authorizes Congress to prescribe discipline for state militias, and in the Fifth Amendment, with the exclusion of individuals "in the land or naval forces, or in the Militia, when in actual service in time of War or public danger" from the right to grand jury indictment in criminal cases.[32]

Indeed, military justice and military discipline have been standard practice for thousands of years. Evidence reveals special tribunals for war crimes in the Peloponnesian War in 405 BC and throughout the wars of the Middle Ages. As a British general explained: "The object of Social Law is to punish crime . . . The object of military law is to produce prompt and entire obedience." Within society, military justice creates a class of approved killers whose killing necessarily stands independent of civil law. Within the armed forces, it creates a brutal system of internal management. In the age of democratic revolutions at the end of the eighteenth century, the constitutional incorporations of military justice made clear that, while ideas of human equality (often White human equality) drove much political reform, violence – as a tool of the state – would serve as the greatest authority.[33]

Concern over military justice in the early United States therefore targeted its control and severity. In the Revolution, Washington and other military leaders had chafed at limitations set by the Continental Congress on the total number of lashings a soldier could receive. "The Number allowed to be inflicted, are too few," wrote John Laurance, the Judge Advocate General, in 1778. "Soldiers, who have transgressed . . . must be made to feel in order to prevent their committing the like Acts in future." Laurance said that the men considered one hundred lashes "a trivial punishment" and pushed General Washington to seek Congressional modification of the Articles of War. Though Washington argued for them, the changes did not take place.[34]

Now, in the Constitutional era, several leaders looked to retain military justice as a source of violent authority for the states. George Mason's concern that severe militia discipline would push citizen-soldiers to favor the formation of a standing army (and thus transfer military control from individuals and states to the federal government) was joined by other anxieties. The federal Congress, some suggested, might refuse its Article I, Section 16 duty to organize and arm a militia. In effect, the national government could disarm the states. A North Carolina resolution for the Bill of Rights looked to prevent this scenario. "Each state respectively shall have the power to provide for organizing, arming, and disciplining, its own militia, whensoever Congress shall omit or neglect to provide for the same." In a further attempt to secure local control, Carolinian senators proposed that the militia, "when not in the actual service of the United States, shall be subject only to such fines, penalties, and punishments, as shall be directed or inflicted by the laws of its own state."[35]

The final wording of the Fifth Amendment failed to explicate such measures of local autonomy, but the importance of the debates remained. Even without constitutional support, many Americans believed individuals and states (and the force they may wield) acted as safeguards on federal authority.

In its drive to exact obedience, military justice is directed at the bodies of soldiers. In the army, the early American legal system often featured an alarming lack of procedure. When a critic questioned the 1799 conviction of Joseph Perkins, a soldier sentenced to death for desertion, Secretary of War Alexander Hamilton issued a tart response. "It is enough that the Military Code does authorise such a punishment for such a crime," he said. "The Court need not lay its finger upon particular clauses. To require a nice detail of this sort would be to fetter and clog the operation of Military Justice by the subtil forms of special pleading." Perkins was hanged at Fort Jay on New York's Governors Island in July.[36]

Even without Hamilton's extreme view, the creation of military justice in the United States fostered disparity – just as it did elsewhere. Protection from double jeopardy (being tried twice for the same crime) is, along with the right to a trial by grand jury and protection from self-incrimination, a centerpiece of the Fifth Amendment. Double jeopardy safeguards stood at odds, however, with the two distinct legal codes – civil and military – sanctioned by the Constitution and its initial amendments. George Washington foresaw this conflict in 1779. He suggested that the mistreatment of civilians by soldiers was "as much a breach of military, as civil law and as punishable by the one as the other." A 1962 military handbook was thus more straightforward. A member of the armed forces, it read, "may in certain cases be subject to both a court-martial and a civilian court for the same offense."[37]

The Fifth Amendment exhibits the social consequence of the lessons learned by Washington's mutinous troops – that violence, not adequate pay or provisions and certainly not the claims of protesting soldiers, generates compliance. The creation of a separate, stricter legal code for those in the armed forces and active militia shatters the reading of the Bill of Rights as protecting individuals. A society formed to empower Whiteness that can imagine different standards of justice among its White citizens and servicemen would have little trouble maintaining different standards for more vulnerable populations such as the poor, Indigenous communities, and communities of color.[38]

The first two Militia Acts present a final coda in the codification of American violence. In summer 1789, President George Washington suggested to Congress that a "uniform and effective system for the Militia of the United States" was of "national importance." Henry Knox, the secretary of war, formulated a plan. "All men of the legal military age, should be armed, enrolled, and held responsible for the defence of the state." Notably, as Congress debated the legislation to create and discipline the militia, it rejected any form of religious exemption. At the time, New Jersey Senator John Rutherford, who thought militiamen were of a better class than military regulars, also proposed to limit the severity of militia military justice. He suggested a ban on loss of life or limb or "any corporal punishment" from militia court martial sentences, except in cases of desertion, abandonment of post, or treason. But his proposal failed to gain support.[39]

In 1792, Congress passed two legislative pieces to govern the formation of the American militia. The first softened the system of military justice insofar as only militia officers would serve in courts martial of militiamen. The second, signed into law on May 8, required healthy men between eighteen and forty-five years old to serve. A militiaman had to "provide himself with a good musket or firelock, a sufficient bayonet and belt, two spare flints, and a knapsack," along with "a pouch with a box therein to contain not less than twenty-four cartridges." In addition to the governmental mandate for armed males, one requirement stands out: the federal government demanded that "each and every free able-bodied white male citizen" perform in the militia. Within an early American society that increasingly cordoned off access to suffrage and other rights for women, Blacks, and Native Americans, state-sanctioned violence would thus become structured by ableism, race, and gender.[40]

As the Constitution (relative to the Articles of Confederation) shifted authority from the states to the federal government, the Washington administration further established federal force over states and individuals. In 1790, Kentuckians explained to the president that their state militia, with its "officers and privates having their all at stake," was "preferable to the best regular troops" of the United States for "offensive or defensive" strikes against Indigenous communities. They wanted local control, and grounded their argument in tactics. Local men, they argued, knew how to deploy an "indian mode of warfare" – what historian John Grenier calls America's "first way of war," the brutal targeting of enemy civilians, including elders, women, and children. Washington, however, knew full well that national troops were versed in the "first way of war." During the American Revolution, for example, he had directed Continental Army troops against communities in the Haudenosaunee League: Washington explained in 1779, "The immediate objects are the total destruction and devastation of their settlements and the capture of as many prisoners of every age and sex as possible." In 1790, he thus dismissed the request from Kentucky with a promise to "keep the protection of the frontiers steadily in his view, and use the means in his power according to his best judgement."[41]

In 1794, Washington's "best judgement" helped him institute the federal military by sending General Anthony Wayne to the West. It was at the American victory in the Battle of Fallen Timbers in Ohio that the United States asserted its sovereignty over Native peoples. But not all White Americans celebrated the occasion. Henry Knox, Washington's long-time military confidante, resigned his cabinet post in protest. He claimed that Wayne's war against Indians was worse – more morally corrupt – than anything perpetrated on them by the European empires in North America.[42]

Washington's military sense wrought further consequences in 1794. Months after the US Army conquered western Indian lands that summer, Washington became the first (and still the only) active US President ever to lead troops in the field. In western Pennsylvania, where settlers clashed with federal officials over a tax on whiskey, he commanded some twelve thousand White militiamen in the military response. By the time the soldiers arrived, though, most of the so-called whiskey rebels had disbanded. Washington's message was nevertheless clear: political liberty meant obedience to the federal state – taxes would be paid and domestic protest cured through national force. Where Knox critiqued the president's use of federal violence against Indians, however, Thomas Jefferson viewed the Washington-led militia as an "inexcusable aggression." When Jefferson's Republican Party gained control in 1801, it repealed the whiskey tax and with it the need to showcase federal authority.

The 1794 lessons in constitutional structure endure. Federal soldiers – as regulars – are deployed against those framed as external threats, including against the nineteenth-century North American Natives. Militiamen today are federalized and deployed against internal threats. The lines separating the two forms of national strength, however, have never been quite as rigid as the Constitution suggests. Army regulars, for instance, often helped combat domestic disturbance in slave rebellions and labor strikes. Moreover, political partisanship in the United States performs a central role in the use of government force.[43]

In early America, there seemed no way to reconcile these tensions. At the time, they were most aptly represented by George Mason, who declared, "Once a standing army is established in any country, the people lose their liberty"; James Madison, who said, "There never was a government without force"; and Elihu Marvin, who declared, "In every Nation a Military force is absolutely Necessary (Under Heaven) for the Purpose of Guarding the lives & property of the Citizens." Instead, the Constitution and its early amendments created hybrids. The armed citizens of the Second Amendment were positioned to be a revolutionary force capable of over-throwing government yet essential to serve as its national defense. The American military, specifically a standing army and navy, had its funding limited to two-year stints – a gesture indicating that regular forces were somehow less than permanent. And the state militias, the citizen-soldiers meant to protect against national despotism, could be called into service by the federal government "to execute the Laws of the Union, suppress Insurrections and repel Invasions."[44]

The United States had been fashioned in revolution, and that event left an indelible mark. Violence is now secured in its Constitution in multiple ways and multiple sites. The document explicitly protects the right of the federal government, the states, and the people to commit violent acts. And, in its original form, it overtly sanctioned racialized violence in the practice of American slavery. Here lies the fateful com-promise of the American Revolution. A product of a society born in blood, the United States represents a White people willing to draw on the coer-cive, violent capacities of individuals and institutions. The violence so central to understanding the American experience is not inexplicable but is precisely what one expects.

PART II

EVOLUTIONS

Slaves rather weaken than strengthen the State, and there is therefore some difference between them and sheep; sheep will never make any insurrections.

Esteemed Continental Congress Delegate Benjamin Franklin, 1776

Is there one law of submission and non-resistance for the black man, and another law of rebellion and conflict for the white man?

Antislavery activist William Lloyd Garrison, 1852

The democratic method of resolving social conflict, which some romanticists hail as a triumph of the ethical over the coercive factor, is really much more coercive than at first seems apparent.

Christian theologian Reinhold Niebuhr, 1932

4

THE 1850S: A PEOPLE'S GOVERNMENT AND THE POLITICS OF BELLIGERENCE

In 1831, the French government charged two noblemen, Alexis de Tocqueville and Gustave de Beaumont, to study the United States prison system. Over nine months, the men traveled from Rhode Island and New York to Michigan and Louisiana and many points in between. They collected documents, interviewed inmates, and, soon after their return, deposited a report titled *On the Penitentiary System in the United States and its Application in France*. Each was captivated by their American experience, however, and continued to write. In 1835, Beaumont published *Marie, or Slavery in the United States*. Tocqueville published *Democracy in America*.

In all three works, the French elites demonstrated their acceptance of liberal society and theories of hostile difference. Together in *On the Penitentiary System*, the two expressed a belief that "alms, however well distributed, tend to produce poverty: and assistance afforded to a forsaken child causes others to be abandoned." Here is the conservative faith that public assistance makes poor people lazy (producing more poverty) and delinquent (generating more abandoned children). "The abuse of philanthropic institutions is as fatal to society as the evil itself which they are intended to cure," they observed. For this reason, Beaumont and Tocqueville argued that social institutions in America such as houses of refuge must bend toward a prison model, and away from that of a school. Punishment, the Frenchmen believed, not education, development, or uplift, is the best response to impoverishment.[1]

In *Marie*, Beaumont, working at the junction of class and race, continued this line of thought. And though he wrote with compassion on the plight of Black slaves in the United States, he also subscribed to notions of greater (White) and lesser (Black) civilizations. In *Democracy in America*, Tocqueville likewise proclaimed the superiority of "Anglo-Americans." "Three races naturally distinct, and I might also say hostile to each other, are discoverable among them [North Americans]," he wrote. "Among these widely differing families of men, the first which attracts attention, the superior in intelligence, in power, and in enjoyment, is the white or

European, the MAN pre-eminent; and in subordinate grades, the negro and the Indian."[2]

Tocqueville's racism led to an unapologetic analysis of American democracy and society. For instance, he understood "the Indians and the negroes" as "two races" best viewed in relation to White Americans. And since White Americans were "the democratic people" of the New World, Tocqueville considered "the Anglo-American Union" (the United States) a result of White superiority. These racial views led Tocqueville to misinterpret American life. For example, he advanced the idea that "the equality of conditions is the fundamental fact" in America that makes for a successful democracy. He failed to note, though, that this cherished "equality" was a figment of his White imagination. In his belief that only White persons had achieved the necessary tools for democratic self-government, Tocqueville felt justified to look only at White society. The French aristocrat found that the White American social classes were more equal – an economic and political valuation – than those found in Europe.[3]

Similar analytical blind spots mark Tocqueville's engagement with violence and democracy. When exploring the Constitution, he said: "The great end of justice is to substitute the notion of right for that of violence; and to place a legal barrier between the power of the government and the use of physical force." Tocqueville did not comment on what happens when the so-called "legal barrier" fosters government force. Enslaved African Americans, marked as a form of property protected by the Constitution, confronted this tension. The fugitive slave clause found in Article IV, Section 2 of the US Constitution implicitly sanctioned human slavery and endorsed the recapture of runaway slaves. This was a system of violence sustained by American government and individuals who were mostly White or who benefited from systems and structures extending them certain privilege within White society supremacy. And, while Tocqueville did note of Black men that "violence made him a slave," he was referring to the kidnappings and cruelties of the Middle Passage rather than the many forms of governmental and individual violence that perpetuated enslavement. Tocqueville was, in fact, a proponent of antislavery, but akin to many White antislavery supporters was nonetheless prejudiced against Black people. Standing in concert with many American slaveholders, he framed Black people as a menace. One part of a chapter in *Democracy in America* is even titled, "Situation of the black population in the United States, and the dangers with which its presence threatens the whites." An early progenitor of the theory that American democracy required the subordination of communities of color, especially Black and

Indigenous people, Tocqueville thus obscured and justified the many layers of force used on them.[4]

Tocqueville's New World discovery, a democracy of White men, may not have missed the racialized and gendered structures of American society, but it did miss the intent behind them. Most states had permitted Black men to vote in the late eighteenth century. However, in the forty or so years before Tocqueville's visit, the right to vote increasingly became the province of White men. As the historian Kate Masur notes, among states formed after 1800, Maine alone allowed Black men to vote and the "older states increasingly restricted Black men's right to vote or disenfranchised them entirely." At the same time, in a process that would be complete by the 1840s, the right to vote was granted to nearly all adult White men. Democracy in America was White, not because, as Tocqueville said, Whites had achieved a more advanced place in society. It was White because White political leaders – men who believed like Tocqueville that Whiteness and maleness were superior in government – sought to make it so. Their success placed the United States among world leaders in reformulating global White supremacy to fit within and uphold a liberal democratic state.[5]

Once bound by property and other wealth-based qualifications, the expanded and Whitened male electorate of the 1830s and 1840s used violence to protect and extend the privileges of their Whiteness. Then, in the 1850s, when popular sovereignty – the theory that White male voters in local spaces were best positioned to decide on the national question of slavery – fused with electoral politics, a nation steeped in violence and hostile difference was fully on display.

Tocqueville and Beaumont thus visited the United States at a key moment in 1831. The 1828 election of General Andrew Jackson as president helped direct the belligerent practice of American democracy toward territorial expansion and fixed the expansion of voters to violence and race. Jackson gathered the support of New York's Bucktail Democrats, who largely disqualified property-owning Blacks from voting, and White men who lived on slavery's frontier in places like Alabama, Kentucky, and Tennessee. These voters adored the military man for his self-righteous volatility and reputation as an individual beholden to no one.[6]

In the 1828 campaign cycle, Jackson's critics detailed his violent ways. They published, for example, a handbill decorated with eighteen coffins (see Fig. 4.1). The so-called Coffin Handbill represented each of twenty-three individuals whom Andrew Jackson had put to death. "Some Account of Some of the Bloody Deeds of General Jackson" reads the political handout. Prominent at the top of the page are six coffins representing soldiers

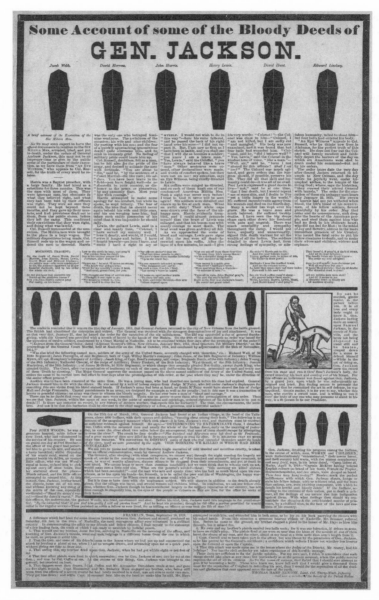

Fig. 4.1 "Some Account of Some of the Bloody Deeds of Gen. Jackson." "Coffin Handbill," Hurja, Sir Emil (1892–1953) Collection 1793–1953 (THS), Box 8, Folder J - 31, 42366, Tennessee Historical Society, Tennessee Virtual Archive.

whose death sentences Jackson had sanctioned in January 1815. These six coffins symbolize those singled out and killed as leaders of a 200-soldier mutiny. The dispute had been over enlistment length (three or six months). One condemned man, John Harris, the text explains, was so overcome by the unjust punishment that he surrendered to a "feminine weakness" and "sunk In unmanly grief" on execution day.[7]

The detractors behind the campaign material hoped the revelations of his past violence would sabotage Jackson's political future – after all, authoritarianism was supposed to be inappropriate for a president in a democracy. But many of the newly empowered voters found the candidate's violence attractive. Jackson embodied an unbowed White masculinity that raged throughout the antebellum United States. To his supporters, Jackson would never succumb to the emotional and physical weaknesses then ascribed to women. When the Coffin Handbill decried Jackson's murder of Indian "men, WOMEN, and CHILDREN," it further enhanced his profile. Jackson, an enslaver of nearly a hundred Black persons in 1828, headed a generation for whom anti-Indian violence had developed into a nationalist, racial fervor and genocide. His supporters knew and approved of the 1814 Battle of Horseshoe Bend, for example, where Jackson planned to eliminate not just a Red Stick village, but the Red Sticks themselves. He led a military force that killed between three hundred and five hundred Red Stick individuals – the deadliest single campaign ever waged by the federal government on a Native community.[8]

Jackson's supporters flaunted their candidate's history of casual willingness when it came to killing in the interest of White Americans. "COOL AND DELIBERATE MURDER," announced one Jacksonian newspaper. "Jackson coolly and deliberately put to death upward of fifteen hundred British troops on the 8th of January 1815, on the plains of New Orleans, for no other offense than that they wished to sup in the city that night." But in 1828, Jacksonians also issued threats of their own. One newspaper in Virginia reported that Jackson enthusiasts said that "if Mr. Adams was not put out by the voice of the people, they would be willing to put him out by force." They voted in droves. Andrew Jackson thrashed John Quincy Adams 178 to 83 in the Electoral College and collected 56 percent of the popular vote. Based on exclusion, American democracy in the nineteenth century represented two things: a cultural identity of White entitlement centered on a violent manliness, and a governmental practice that made White supremacy readily accessible to nearly all White men.[9]

To traditionalists like Tocqueville, who had arrived in America during the first administration of President Jackson, the genius of the Constitution ensured that political citizens in the United States could look at identical information, arrive at opposite conclusions, and continue to partake in the same civic system. In its allowance for the expression of the White, male minority voice, American democracy, he observed, was a system that defended itself against violent conflict. "In America," said Tocqueville, "the citizens who form the minority associate . . . are therefore peaceable in their intentions." But the violence that near-universal White male suffrage brought to the polling place – inexorable revelry that scared away some women, extreme partisanship, and physical intimidation to threaten political opponents – signaled that voting (and by extension democracy) was not inherently peaceful. Elections, said a New Orleans editor, are a "hell's holiday of drunkenness and perjury and bludgeons."[10]

At no single point in the American past was a wager on democracy more highly staked than in the 1850s. A fervent belief in political localism by conservative leaders led to the abandonment of federal oversight and governance in American territories. Southerners such as John C. Calhoun, James Mason, and Jefferson Davis, men who looked to protect, sustain, and expand human enslavement, pursued a course to make radical localism a national standard. The results were stunning. Violence became an ordinary tactic to win elections and retain political control in places like Kansas and Utah. In 1860, such local lessons jumped to the national scene. Despite the rhetoric that voters, in their capacity to elect leaders, retain the ultimate authority in the United States, Americans, voters and non-voters alike, realized violence as the true judge.[11]

A democracy can advance the means for fraudulent elections and violence – as in the Kansas Territory after the Kansas–Nebraska Act of 1854 – as well as for fair elections and violence, as in the succession of Abraham Lincoln to the presidency in 1861. In the face of stark dispute, American politicians and citizens professed that force provides a clear solution. The question that demands an answer is not whether democracy is prone to violence, but how do violence and democracy work together? How do they work together to defend and uphold the hostile differences central to liberal life?

———————◆———————

In the decade before the American Civil War, political compromise tended to draw out the worst in those involved. The passage of the Fugitive Slave Law in 1850 was a prime example.

"I voted for the fugitive slave law because I did not doubt its constitutionality, and I understood and believed it would be satisfactory to the people of the southern states," said Iowa Senator Augustus Caesar Dodge. "Unless we were willing to acknowledge that the Constitution was a failure" – that certain parts of the document could be ignored – Dodge continued, he felt compelled to back the legislation. He called his support "an act of justice."[12]

For more than a decade, northern protesters had flouted the 1793 fugitive slave law. In places like Syracuse and Boston, Black and White abolitionists, unafraid to use physical force, rescued captured slave runaways from jail. The Fugitive Slave Law of 1850 sought to put an end to such brazen, unconstitutional deeds. It subjected to fines and imprisonment "any person who shall knowingly and willingly obstruct, hinder, or prevent" runaway recapture. It also authorized American enslavers to "pursue and reclaim" runaways and greatly expanded the mission and reach of the national government. A newly created federal administrator, the US Commissioner, would decide on fugitive cases and certify a runaway's re-enslavement. No state or federal court could challenge the commissioner's decision. Indeed, no local or state action could interfere with this federal right, a retroactive authority that threatened even those former slaves who had lived in freedom for decades.[13]

Signed into law on September 18, 1850, the new regulation for fugitive recapture immediately impacted Black communities throughout the United States. Before the month was out, a US Commissioner in New York remanded James Hamlet to the custody of Marylander Mary Brown. Brown asserted that Hamlet had fled from enslavement. The first fugitive forced back to slavery by the federal government under the Fugitive Slave Law, Hamlet was among the more fortunate. Activists collected $800 to purchase his freedom, and he soon returned to New York. In October, White residents of New Bedford, Pennsylvania, hunted ten fugitives, killing one and wounding another. The United States Commissioner paid $225 to the man responsible for the capture of the remaining eight. This was thanks to a federal subsidy that now supported armed White men in capturing Black individuals seeking safety and liberty.[14]

Antislavery advocates battled back. In October 1850, members of Detroit's Black community supplied themselves with guns to free a man captured by a federal commissioner. In January 1851, a slave runaway shot and killed his apprehender in Ohio (federal authorities soon arrested and bound the shooter to re-enslavement). And in September, the enslaver Edward Gorsuch pursued four Black individuals to Christiana, Pennsylvania. With the help of free Blacks, the fugitives fought Gorsuch, a federal marshal, and a posse. The Black men killed Gorsuch and the runaways fled to Canada.[15]

The new legislation, an open attempt to sustain racial difference in the United States, helped galvanize northern opinion against human enslavement. Black activists such as Hartford's S. M. Africanus found the Fugitive Slave Act "both unjust and unreasonable." It required only a "general description" of an escaped slave, which made every "colored person" a target. Africanus boldly claimed that the denial of proper legal channels to Blacks deprived "the citizen a Jury Trial, where his liberty, and perhaps his life, is at stake." Many Black and White protesters agreed with Africanus when he insisted that the Fugitive Slave Law had "no binding force."[16]

An elaborate deal, the Compromise of 1850, had brought about the Fugitive Slave Act. The Compromise admitted the territory of California as the thirty-first state. Black slavery was banned in this new state, although traffic in Native slaves remained robust. The Compromise also abolished the slave trade in the District of Columbia. Such measures looked to satisfy a growing antislavery constituency in the North. The deal rewarded southern enslavers with federal funds for debt incurred by the Republic of Texas (now a slave state), a guarantee of Congressional nonintervention in the domestic slave trade, and, of course, a renewed license to pursue and capture slavery's fugitives. Both sides celebrated a final point: the territories of Utah and New Mexico would be organized "with or without slavery." Officially, "every free white male inhabitant, above the age of twenty-one years" who was a territorial resident was to decide by ballot on the legality of Black human property. A belief that the Utah and New Mexico soils could not sustain crops amenable to enslaved labor marked this passage as an antislavery measure. At the same time, though, the Compromise of 1850 upended an important, earlier Congressional deal. The Missouri Compromise in 1820 had set a line marked by the southern border of Missouri to govern American expansion and slavery. Territories claimed by the United States above this line would enter the nation without human slavery and those below the line with slavery. Now, in 1850, however, slaveholders registered a clear win. Two American territories north of the line, Utah and parts of New Mexico, were thus opened up to the possibility of slavery despite their location.[17]

Many White men believed the Compromise of 1850 to be the foundation of liberal democracy. But, as White men oversaw and celebrated such dealmaking, it is not surprising that members of Black communities voiced harsh criticism. Samuel Ward, a Black abolitionist in New York, declared that compromise "is always the term which makes right yield to wrong; it has always been accursed since Eve made the first *compromise* with the Devil." Disappointed Americans wound satanic imagery into many complaints. In October, one month after Millard Fillmore signed the new law, William P. Newman, a Baptist clergyman, fugitive slave, and now advocate of violent, Black resistance to federal authority, wrote to Frederick Douglass, "It may be properly asked, would not the Devil do well to *rent out hell* and move to the United States, and rival, if possible, President Fillmore."[18]

The Compromise placed the fate of enslaved Black individuals and the political processes to manage the legality of slavery safely in White hands. The new Fugitive Slave Law undeniably involved the federal government as a guarantor of the cruelties and Black dispossession required to maintain the slave system; popular sovereignty undeniably empowered White male voters in the territories to make decisions that would affect Black individuals and families. From this viewpoint, the Compromise of 1850 is among the most blatant acts in support of hostile racial difference in United States history.

Among the most vocal supporters of White superiority in Congress, Senator Dodge could not imagine that the growing regional dispute over human enslavement would "embroil the States in a war in which American blood is shed by American hands." (Notably, Dodge used the term "American" to signal "White.") But in December 1853, he helped to create exactly such a scenario. Dodge introduced a bill "to organize the territory of Nebraska; which was read the first and second times, by unanimous consent, and referred to the Committee on Territories." By January 1854, the bill further asserted that both the 1793 and 1850 fugitive slave laws would be "in full force within the limits of said Territory" and made clear other expectations. "In order to avoid misconstruction," it read, "the true intent and meaning of this act, so far as the question of slavery is concerned," is that "the people residing" in any states created from the territory will make decisions regarding slavery. In its final wording, this clause upheld the premise of "non-intervention by Congress with slavery" and declared "the people thereof perfectly free to form and regulate their domestic institutions" – the southern euphemism for slavery – "in their own way."[19]

The recent Fugitive Slave Law had increased federal force in support of human enslavement. This bill sought the near opposite. It favored individuals and locales over the authority of the United States. In short, political supporters of slavery secured the violence of the United States *and* the violence of individuals to protect and expand human bondage in the nation.

The Kansas–Nebraska Act, as it would be known, encompassed a swath of 485,000 square miles, which today includes the states of Kansas, Nebraska, North Dakota, South Dakota, Montana, and parts of Wyoming and Colorado. The territory was nearly 7 percent larger in size than all the free states east of the Rocky Mountains and contained about a thousand White settlers. Unconcerned that Indigenous communities contested the status of the land, the legislation focused only on how Whites would extract value from it. As prescribed by the act, the White citizens in a territory would vote on the lawfulness of human enslavement.[20]

For American enslavers, who had been moving to the West and South throughout the nineteenth century, national expansion was intimately linked to material success. Counter to the legends of enduring, magnificent plantations that dominated popular culture after the Civil War, the story of most slave-owning families was that of regular geographic mobility. Slaveholders moved to buy cheaper and larger parcels of land, land that was often more fertile, and, importantly, land that was farther away from free states. Here, in places like Texas, White Americans built cotton and sugar kingdoms from the enslaved labor of Black Americans.[21]

There was more to slaveholder mobility than the desire to sustain and expand human enslavement, however. At the time, the federal government's sale of public lands annually filled about 40 percent of the national treasury. The dispute over the legality of human bondage in American territories was a dispute over the foundation of federal economic authority. And federal economic authority was intertwined with the capability of the federal government to act with violence. Often the question of whether the American territories would support enslaved or wage labor is posed as an abstract fight, a battle of ideals. These ideals, however, had significant consequences. A federal government essentially funded by slave labor was a federal government bound to protect and uphold systems of human bondage. If funded by free labor, the mission of the federal government and national forces would be different.[22]

When made public, the Kansas–Nebraska Act captured national attention. "The report of the Committee on Territories in the US Senate, which we publish today," announced the *NY Journal of Commerce*, "is an important document, and will be much spoken of hereafter." The *New York Times* defined the northern antislavery position on the legislation. It framed the statute as a "Renewal of the Slavery Agitation" for two reasons. First, the act formally repealed the 1820 Missouri Compromise. Second, in a related complaint, the *Times* understood how popular sovereignty (giving territorial citizens the power to decide on the slavery question) ushered in a new era.

Human enslavement was now possible in all the land to which White Americans aspired, the newspaper said. The Kansas–Nebraska Act would be "fatal to the public peace."[23]

In the South, many publications were more coy. They willfully ignored the legislation's slavery-expanding potential. The *Mississippi Free Trader* thought the question of slavery in Nebraska insignificant, since nothing, not cotton, sugar, nor "anything upon which slave labor could be profitably employed," was harvested there. One Florida newspaper was more direct when it threw support to Congressmen who stood behind the bill: "Let the South stand fast by the men who are true to its interests." No matter which side a newsroom supported, the sheer volume of coverage overwhelmed. "We have little room for editorial or general matter to-day," said the *Daily National Era* in late January, "in consequence of the large space occupied by the debate on Nebraska."[24]

The fight over the status of the American territories was taken up in Congress by Democrat Stephen A. Douglas of Illinois. Douglas, whose name would soon be tied to the idea of popular sovereignty, stewarded the Kansas legislation through the Committee on Territories. "Popular sovereignty" and its counterpart "states' rights" were theories of political economy that proposed to shield slave labor from federal administration. Under the guise of individual social and entrepreneurial freedom, Stephen Douglas argued for a right to choose. "You must provide for continuous lines of settlement from the Mississippi valley to the Pacific ocean," he said; "you must decide upon what principles the Territories shall be organized; in other words, whether the people shall be allowed to regulate their domestic institutions in their own way." Here, of course, "the people" specified White male settlers prepared to "regulate" American slavery. Douglas feared the alternative to popular sovereignty: "congressional interference."[25]

President Franklin Pierce signed the legislation on May 30, 1854. The Kansas–Nebraska Act, which some people called the "Dodge and Douglas law," removed the uncertainty of slavery's extension from Congressional jurisdiction. To solve questions on human slavery, the people of a territory – an ill-defined group of White citizens – were to vote in an equally ill-defined election. The Congress had diminished the authority of the federal government and arranged for a questionable, issue-based ballot. Extreme localism, where White men would supposedly vote, was to settle a national debate.[26]

In theory, popular sovereignty was a centrist plan that expressed the burgeoning democratic spirit of the nineteenth century. "If man is capable of self-government," said Governor Willis Gorman of the Minnesota Territory, "leave the question of Slavery to the people, to whom it properly belongs." President Pierce touted the "great principles of popular sovereignty which, under the Constitution, are fundamental in the whole structure of our institutions." What could be more (White) American than to vote to settle a dispute? In practice, popular sovereignty aligned with the rough-and-tumble world of the White male electorate. "When the laws thus enacted are not executed," said leaders of San Francisco's Committee of Vigilance, a group of violent vigilantes, "the power returns to the people, and is theirs whenever they may choose to exercise it." Such self-interested rhetoric – the group asserted to speak for all the city's inhabitants – demonstrates how popular sovereignty sanctioned a fierce mode of personal liberty and let loose an individual righteousness that appeared to know no bounds. The Kansas–Nebraska Act was an accelerant poured on to the fire of American expansion and slavery. It taught Americans that elections and government are weak.[27]

In 1854 and 1855, men and women from across the United States risked their lives to claim Kansas as a slave or slave-free state. Thanks to the Kansas–Nebraska Act, the decision hinged on votes – and votes rely on the number of voters. With American elections framed as winner-takes-all events, a nationwide push ensued to stack the Kansas ballots. Residents from nearby Missouri (a slave state) were the first to rush in. Their presence, according to a special investigation by the United States House of Representatives, manifested an "unlawful interference" in the initial elections. "*Every election*," declared the House statement, "has been controlled, not by actual settlers, but by citizens of Missouri." Those who moved to Kansas, such as Dr. John H. Stringfellow who relocated just after passage of the federal law, believed that "the conviction was general that it would be a slave state." Amos Rees, another White Missouri transplant, agreed. "It was generally understood that Kansas would become a slave state."[28]

The situation quickly worsened. Groups such as the proslavery Sons of the South and the antislavery Emigrant Aid Company collected dues and coordinated the passage of individuals, families, and munitions into the territory. It was, to borrow words from the federal report, "an organized invasion." One meeting of Missourians on June 18, 1854, declared, "That we recognize the institution of slavery as already existing in the Territory, and recommend to slaveholders to introduce their property as fast as possible." Another of its resolutions read: "That we afford protection to no abolitionists as settlers in Kansas Territory." The secretary of the Emigrant Aid Company, Thomas H. Webb, explained his organization's low-cost travel packages: "No pledges are required from those who go; but as our [antislavery] principles are known, we trust those who differ from us will be honest enough to take some other route." In Kansas, one antislavery committee proposed, "every reliable free-State man in the Territory be furnished with a rifle, a brace of pistols, and a sabre, gratis." So-called "emigrant aid guns" stood stockpiled in a Lawrence warehouse.[29]

In October, the lawyer Abraham Lincoln appraised popular sovereignty. "The people are to decide the question of slavery for themselves; but WHEN they are to decide," he said, "or HOW they are to decide" was unsettled. "Is it to be decided by the first dozen settlers who arrive there? or is it to await the arrival of a hundred?" Born into a frontier family, Lincoln bore witness to the coarser side of the White American dream. He did not need to be in Kansas Territory to understand the outcome. "Bowie knives and six-shooters are seen plainly enough; but never a glimpse of the ballot-box." "If this fight should begin," Lincoln asked, "is it likely to take a very peaceful, Union-saving turn?"[30]

Events proved his skepticism right. Partisan settlers attempted to sway the Kansas ballot through loyalty oaths, falsified votes, and, increasingly, physical intimidation. "For the benefit of those who intend to emigrate to Kansas," read one New England advertisement, "we now have in store a large supply of COLT'S REVOLVERS; fine single and double barrel GUNS ... which we offer at the *lowest prices*." The proliferation of inexpensive firearms, which Samuel Colt's technological advances made faster and more accurate, fed into a growing consensus. The situation in Kansas wasn't an electoral fight, it was democracy as war. "Last week," noted antislavery activist and Massachusetts transplant Hannah Ropes, "a man living about six miles from here upon a claim, while walking towards a blacksmith's shop, was shot down by a party of Missourians, without any provocation." To her mother, Ropes explained, "I have loaded pistols and a bowie-knife upon my table at night, three of Sharp's rifles, loaded, standing in the room."[31]

After their probe of the Kansas elections held between November 29, 1854, and October 1, 1855, the House committee was "unable to find that any political power whatever ... has been exercised by the people." "The elections," the report read, "were preceded and followed by acts of violence on the part of those who opposed them." It concluded "that in the present condition of the Territory a fair election cannot be held without a new census, a stringent and well-guarded election law, the selection of impartial judges, and the presence of United States troops at every place of election."[32]

Though Kansas required stronger federal oversight to ensure fairness, the object of the Kansas–Nebraska Act was to remove the national government from the process. President Franklin Pierce thus acted against the recommendation of the House investigation. He refused to supply troops "to preserve the purity of elections either in a State or Territory." "To do so," Pierce explained, "would be subversive of public freedom." Apparently, the president believed that the "public" – White men acting outside their homes – was free to interrupt democratic processes.[33]

Notably, Pierce blamed the outbreak of violence in Kansas on White settler migration – a stance that was as odd as it was true. The purpose of territorial status was to announce a federal land claim in hopes that White settlers would migrate. White settlers had historically used violence – against one another, Indigenous persons, and free and enslaved Black people. That the settlers acted out in violence was a matter of course, therefore. Nevertheless, Pierce called the White migration an "aggressive intrusion" and said such movement would be met by "any available forces of the United States." Luckily, the president's other statements clarified his intent. Popular sovereignty, the right of White men to vote, he declared, is "fundamental in the whole structure of our institutions." Such principles cannot be met with disregard. "The dire calamity of an arbitrament of arms in that Territory," Pierce said of Kansas, "shall be between lawless violence on the one side and conservative force," which is "wielded by legal authority of the General Government." The Kansas battle had two participants, in other words, one progressive or radical ("lawless violence") and the other conservative (the federal government).[34]

Pierce, a Democrat, was clear about which group of White migrants were the troublemakers. He said that the "primary causes" of the Kansas chaos originated in "that pernicious agitation on the subject of the condition of the colored persons." This, he said, has "excited individuals . . . to toil with misdirected zeal in the attempt to propagate their social theories." Wedded to hostile racial difference, Pierce identified antislavery activists as fomenters of rebellion and enemies of the United States. He said that they were revolutionaries, stating, "our system affords no justification of revolutionary acts." Thus, the president directed federal troops in Kansas to target the abolitionists, and Secretary of War Jefferson Davis complied. In his annual report, Davis observed that the army "arrested violators of the peace," "expelled lawless bands from the Territory," and "met and disarmed bodies of men organized, armed, equipped, and advancing for aggressive invasion." Davis did not mention that such "violators," according to the Pierce administration, were always antislavery advocates.[35]

The president was right that some abolitionists in Kansas looked to upend the very structures and inequities essential to liberal life. None would become as famous (or well remembered) as John Brown. Though

Brown did not begin the violence in the Kansas Territory, he started to embrace violence as a means to combat the evils of the slave system. In late June 1855, he attended the inaugural convention of the Radical Abolition Party in Syracuse, New York. A founding member, he adhered to the party's sweeping call for immediate and comprehensive emancipation, universal suffrage, and land reallocation (to offset economic inequality). The Radical Abolitionists believed that slavery was a state of war. The proper response to slavery, then, was not compromise or ballot boxes, but force. Brown and his cohorts believed that God directed such action. And in August, when Brown set out for Kansas, he was on the lookout for religious signs.[36]

Whether or not God crafted the omens Brown would find, national events and the near-war underway in Kansas fostered his righteousness. In spring 1855, a newly elected Kansas legislature provided legal sanction to slavery by making speech against human enslavement a criminal offense. John Brown arrived in the territory a few months later, on October 7. About two weeks after his arrival, a proslavery settler killed yet another free-state supporter. The scope and scale of the troubles worsened in 1856. On May 21, more than seven hundred proslavery men – "a military force consisting in part of US soldiers, and in part of an infuriated mob," said the *Hartford Courant* – attacked the antislavery town of Lawrence. Led by the proslavery sheriff, Samuel J. Jones, they destroyed newspaper presses, set homes on fire, and exploded the so-called Free State Hotel.[37]

Some justified the endeavor with banners that read "Southern Rights!" and "The Superiority of the White Race!" The *New York Tribune* called it "A Reign of Terror in the Territory." Of President Pierce, the *National Era* asked, "Is he anxious to stain his soul with blood, to go down to posterity, branded as the butcher of American citizens?" "Assassinations, robberies, outrages and violence of every description are freely practiced," said the *Albany Evening Journal,* "while the United States troops are forbidden by orders they have received from the President to do anything to protect the Free State settlers from slaughter ... Such is the result of Popular Sovereignty."[38]

When word circulated that the Kansas governor intended to demand antislavery and free-state supporters hand over their guns and munitions, the liberal activists quickly turned to the Second Amendment. "The Constitution of the United States prominently recognizes the right of holding arms," they said. And this legal defense of the people's right to violence sat perfectly well with John Brown. He was exasperated by the destruction at Lawrence. "We must show by actual work that there are two sides to this thing," he said, "and that they [proponents of slavery] cannot go on with impunity."[39]

As Brown prepared his revenge, the war over Kansas flared in Congress. It was nearly as violent. On May 22, South Carolina Representative Preston Brooks, who was armed with a cane, beat Massachusetts Senator Charles Sumner senseless. In a speech on the Kansas Territory, Sumner had spoken against South Carolina's Andrew Butler, accusing him of keeping a curious mistress: "the harlot, Slavery." "For her," he said, Butler's "tongue is always profuse in words." Brooks took offense on his colleague's behalf.[40]

Thanks to injuries suffered in the attack, Sumner would not resume his senatorial duties until 1859. Meanwhile, reflecting on the antislavery community's response to the Lawrence and Sumner incidents, New York's Democratic *Weekly Herald* observed: "The nigger worshippers are boiling over with rage." Notably, the use of the "n-word" as an anti-Black slur surged around the 1820s in the United States, the same time that northern states disenfranchised many free Blacks. As the historian Elizabeth Stordeur Pryor states, the meaning of the word is complex, often summoning histories of racial violence and diminishment when spoken by Whites; indeed, the use of the word in this context can be marked as an act of violence in itself.[41]

Though some scholars draw a clear link between the May 22 assault on Sumner and John Brown's subsequent killing spree, the evidence is anecdotal at best. As a Radical Abolitionist, Brown fully embraced violence, which for him, unlike the many antislavery supporters who carried a popular reputation for pacifism, had moved beyond a theoretical realm. He perceived proslavery men as despots, a status borne out by the numbers in Kansas. Fifty-two bodies marked the territory's battle over slavery between 1855 and 1858 – and thirty-six of them, nearly 70 percent, were antislavery or free-state adherents. Of the sixteen proslavery deaths, two died in accidents, one was shot after he disrupted an antislavery meeting, and eight were murdered. On the night of May 24, 1856, John Brown slaughtered five of those eight.[42]

Eyewitnesses to Brown's murders near Pottawatomie Creek in eastern Kansas spoke to the House investigation committee. Near eleven at night on May 24, James P. Doyle and his sons, William and Drury, were kidnapped by John Brown and members of the self-styled "Army of the North." Mrs. Doyle reported that James "was shot in the forehead and stabbed in the breast;" William's "fingers were cut off, his head was cut open." There is no record of what they did to Drury. Mrs. Doyle, undoubtedly too pained to look on her other son's body, refused to view it until the funeral. Then, at midnight, Brown and his men grabbed Louisa Jane Wilkinson's husband, Allen – a member of the Kansas legislature – "in the name of the Northern Army." He was found the next morning 150 yards from his house "with a gash in his head" and "cut in the throat twice." At about two in the morning, Brown and his "Northern Army" cohorts took William Sherman. Sherman's skull was "split open in two places and some of his brains were washed out . . . his left hand was cut off." Representative Mordecai Oliver of the House investigation committee noted that "those who were killed, it is testified, were proslavery people."[43]

The women who recalled these stories stood as survivors and victims of horrific acts. Execution by gunfire is one thing, but Brown and his gang had killed through torture. They stabbed, shot, crushed, and dismembered these men. Yet this bloody truth about John Brown failed to register in the North, where coverage of the massacre blamed Indians and the proslavery victims themselves. Some articles claimed Brown acted in self-defense: Doyle, Wilkinson, and Sherman were set to hang a free-state supporter, claimed the *New York Times*, and Brown and his men killed to save their friend.[44]

With the extent of Brown's cruelty thus largely concealed, it was easier to promote the antislavery cause in Kansas. "Brown is just the man we need in Kansas," said one appeal in the *Hartford Daily Courant*, "and if every man who loves Freedom and can spare a dollar or two, would put it in Brown's purse, we will warrant they get their money's worth out of Brown, hereafter. Let us back up the men who are fighting our battles."[45]

The violent righteousness of John Brown, though admittedly an extreme example, highlights the troubled aspect of mid-nineteenth-century America. In the 1850s, men and women, often influenced by Christian ideology, cultivated clear moral visions. Estimates suggest that 40 percent of the population at the time, more than ten million individuals, associated with evangelical Christianity – by percentage one of the largest minority cultures in American history. "I tried to lay down in my own mind certain great rules of right and wrong, truth and falsehood, vice and virtue," said future president Andrew Johnson. Such moral rectitude hardened both sides in the slavery debate. "We hold it here that African Slavery is an ordinance of God, and that it is a political blessing in the *US*," said Daniel P. Braden, a well-to-do Tennessee farmer. John A. Copeland, Jr., one of the five free Black men who accompanied John Brown in the failed attempt to overthrow slavery at Harper's Ferry, Virginia, wrote from the jail where he was kept before his execution: "remember the *cause* in which I was engaged; *remember it was a holy cause.*"[46]

Into this mix, the Democratic Party, in control of the White House and the Senate (they gained full control of the House in 1857), enacted a violent competition for control of Kansas to help determine the future of America.

Fig. 4.2 Killing free state supporters in 1858. In Albert D. Richardson, *Beyond the Mississippi* (Hartford: American Publishing Company, 1867). Courtesy of the Watkinson Library, Trinity College, Hartford, CT.

Based on a radical localism, they took a national issue, slavery, and tossed it into Kansas. Here, violence, not votes, formed the basis for a new social and cultural order – it allowed for quick access to and control of economic and political resources. But whether the violence would support freedom or slavery was up for debate. The federal government leaned to one side (proslavery) while citizens on both ends fought to determine a winner. (See Fig. 4.2.) President Pierce and the likes of Stephen Douglas and Augustus Dodge created an environment for terror – a backhanded effort of state violence that cost fifty-two White American lives. John Brown and his proslavery adversaries all went unpunished.[47]

The results of popular sovereignty had registered. In 1857, Kansas remained embroiled in lawlessness and partisan panic. And for James Buchanan and Abraham Lincoln, the fiasco in the territories was fundamental to the next round of political violence.

In 1856, the Democratic Party nominated Pennsylvanian James Buchanan for president in large part because he was untainted by Pierce's management of Kansas. Buchanan was the American minister in London during the controversy, and the Democrats correctly calculated that his distance from the territorial fray would entice enough northern voters to defeat the fledgling Republican Party. He arrived in office in 1857 with a strong belief in anti-abolitionism, local government, law and order, and the American union. Buchanan now endeavored to continue what the Democrats had started with the Kansas–Nebraska Act: the protection of slavery through a sanction of local and regional authority. It was a political logic that prevented him from the direct deployment of federal force.

In a line of thought repeated throughout his career, Buchanan accused antislavery activists of inadvertently provoking slave rebellion. "The natural tendency of their publications is to produce dissatisfaction and revolt among the slaves," he had said in 1836. "The history of the human race presents numerous examples of ignorant enthusiasts, the purity of whose intentions cannot be doubted, who have spread devastation and bloodshed over the face of the earth." In 1850, he had restated the principle. "Agitation in the North on the subject of Southern slavery must be rebuked and put down by a strong, energetic, and enlightened public opinion." When the subject of *Uncle Tom's Cabin* – the best-selling novel anecdotally responsible for inspiring broad-based White support for emancipation – arose in London, Buchanan blamed the British, chiding the British Anti-Slavery Society and "its interference in our domestic concerns." Though examples of White abolitionist-inspired slave rebellion were nonexistent in the United States when he made these remarks, Buchanan's sympathies with southern enslavers helped him imagine them as real.[48]

The future president was more forgiving of "angry political discussions" divorced from slavery. He paraphrased Thomas Jefferson to say, "It would seem that such storms are necessary to purify the political atmosphere of the Republic, (though they are sometimes much more violent than agreeable.)" He believed in the "peaceable aid of the [White] people, in their sovereign capacity, to remedy" evils. "They are the source of all power," he said in 1837; "they are the rightful authors of all constitutions." Though his initial impulse led him to support the extension of the Missouri Compromise line as "the best mode of finally settling the question," Buchanan, ever the Democratic stalwart, soon backed popular sovereignty instead. When nominated as presidential candidate in 1856, he felt convinced that "the recent legislation of the Congress respecting domestic slavery" – the Kansas–Nebraska Act – "promises ere long to allay the dangerous excitement" through "the will of the majority."

Buchanan was no fool, however, and saw a clear contradiction in the political environment. Unlike former President Pierce, he supported the right of White people to rebel against American government. It is "sanctified by the declaration of independence," he said. It was a right that he held supreme. The central government had no authority, Buchanan claimed, to categorize White rebellion as "domestic violence." And the president could not put a White rebellion "down by force of arms." To do so would be "an attempt to suppress an insurrection of the people against themselves." If the people (here meaning White southerners) are the foundation of the American republic, surely they cannot be the republic's object of war. Of course, while Buchanan exempted White male proslavery partisans from instances of "domestic violence," he would not do the same for White abolitionists, free Black individuals, or the enslaved.[49]

The Declaration of Independence attracted Republican Abraham Lincoln too. But where Buchanan linked the document to White popular sovereignty, Lincoln saw it as the wellspring of male freedom. "The theory of our government is Universal Freedom," he said in Springfield, Illinois, in October 1854. "'All men are created free and equal,' says the Declaration of Independence." The phrase was "an abstract truth, applicable to all men and all times." Interpretations of it that limited freedom and equality to Whites, he believed, committed "violence to the plain unmistakable language of the Declaration." A few days after giving this speech, Lincoln emphasized another phrase from Jefferson's famed document: "DERIVING THEIR JUST POWERS FROM THE CONSENT OF THE GOVERNED." Anchored in notions of equality and consent, Lincoln unlocked his antislavery stance and his opposition to the Kansas–Nebraska Act.[50]

Lincoln followed the Republican Party line when he questioned the validity of slavery, which depended on the right to property in man. The "just application" of popular sovereignty in Kansas, he said, "depends upon whether a negro is *not* or *is* a man." And while Lincoln was ever careful to avoid an assertion of full equality among Whites and Blacks (for a long time he supported "returning" freed Blacks to Africa to amend the international slave trade's "ruthless hand of fraud and violence"), he was certain that Black men were, simply, men. Black men were due the same eternal truth granted to White men: they must provide consent to be governed. "The master not only governs the slave without his consent," Lincoln said, "but he governs him by a set of rules altogether different from those which he prescribes for himself. Allow ALL the governed an equal voice in the government, and that, and that only is self government." In other words, popular sovereignty, a government of Whites, failed to engage the equality espoused in the Declaration. And by default, popular sovereignty failed to sustain its own most profound claim – that decisions made on a local scale best reflect the will, or consent, of the people.[51]

In Lincoln's mind, popular sovereignty was an unmitigated evil. He wrote on the Kansas–Nebraska Act to Joshua Speed, his closest friend who, in 1850, owned nineteen Black persons in Kentucky: "I look upon that enactment not as a law, but as violence from the beginning. It was conceived in violence, passed in violence, is maintained in violence, and is being executed in violence." The legislation destroyed the Missouri Compromise, ignored the will of all people (all men), and promoted aggressive sectionalism. Lincoln scolded his friend Speed for chasing Stephen Douglas's political fiction:

> You say if you were President, you would send an army and hang the leaders of the Missouri outrages upon the Kansas elections; still, if Kansas fairly votes herself a slave state, she must be admitted, or the Union must be dissolved. But how if she votes herself a slave state unfairly … would you hang men? Must she still be admitted, or the Union dissolved?[52]

As the Democrats clamored for ways to develop and maintain human enslavement in the United States, they crafted an ideal federal state that catered to White economic and social interests. They sought – and in the Dred Scott decision realized – constitutional guarantees for the forthright movement of slaves throughout the country. It required a certain moral obtuseness, but southern leaders supported a rigid social and economic inequality. The violence of the American state was appropriate to guard the perpetual enslavement of individuals. This included the return of slavery's fugitives and the defeat of slave revolt. Violent and constitutional structures needed to be set up, but beyond such security and legality, the federal state should not intervene. Only American enslavers understood the importance of slavery to local places.[53]

The southern desire for a White American empire of slavery was never constrained to those localities. It extended beyond California, Kansas, and Nebraska to Cuba, Mexico, and South America. Such vision required a central state that was both severe in police capacities and flexible in transferability to distant lands. Popular sovereignty met these criteria because enslavers believed they could influence elections or intimidate voters on a local scale. At the same time, popular sovereignty tapped into a long history of mob aggression, election-day riots, and the right of White men to revolt against governance with which they disagreed. The American body politic in the 1850s showed how discord and state abrogation foster violent unrest.[54]

Where Buchanan located fairness within the mechanism of popular sovereignty, Lincoln found bias. However, the two men, who fundamentally

111

disagreed on national policy, did coalesce around the need for a powerful response to Mormon resistance in the Utah Territory. In 1856 and 1857, Governor Brigham Young armed his followers and sought to exclude White Protestant settlers and US soldiers from Utah. Buchanan, who was so adamant about the right of the people to rebel and the prohibition on the federal government to counter, clearly excluded White religious outsiders like Mormons from his assessment. "We ought to go there with such an imposing force," he said in his first annual message to Congress, "as to convince these deluded people that resistance would be vain." Buchanan's overconfidence in violence, an American tradition in itself, shone through. "We can in this manner best convince them that we are their friends, not their enemies." Lincoln too supported the deployment of national troops in Utah. "If they are in rebellion, they ought to be somehow coerced to obedience."[55]

This, then, was the American inheritance in a decade marked by profound disjuncture: beyond an apparent consensus that White Americans should settle on Indigenous lands, there was an entrenched debate over how, when, and against whom violence could legitimately be deployed. And as the American frontier expanded, so, too, did division over the character and governability of local and regional space in relation to national concerns.

5

THE UNITED STATES GREETS JOHN BROWN

In the early United States, denying Black people a right to rebel against an unjust authority, the direct use of federal force to maintain human enslavement, and, in the words of philosopher Charles W. Mills, a "white misunderstanding, misrepresentation, evasion, and self-deception on matters related to race" worked together to forge an American conundrum. Violence is a learned behavior and, in a slave society such as that in America, violence was a core principle. So, how does one disrupt the cycles of violence perpetuated by a violent institution? This was the problem of the slaveholders' evil.[1]

American slave-owners positioned themselves within longstanding traditions in Western civilization. At the dawn of the African slave trade, White theorists had decided that the violence of slave masters was justifiable and that the violence of slaves (slave rebellion) was not. They often said this was so without openly acknowledging the racial dynamics of modern slavery. In the 1600s, for example, the Dutchman Hugo Grotius reasoned that the rightfulness of violent resistance to enslavement depended on timing. "Submission [slavery] is a hard lot, and it is honourable to fight in order to avoid it," he said. "But when a person has once been overcome in such a struggle, if he shake off the yoke, he is no longer a lover of liberty, but an insurgent slave." John Locke, the British political philosopher, followed this line of thought, declaring that "by resisting the will of his master" a slave draws "on himself the death he desires." The implication for slave rebellion was evident: enslavement was legal, for a slave to fight enslavement was not. And Grotius added one more point: "Life, which is the foundation of all temporal and the occasion of eternal good, is of more value than liberty." In other words, being alive was more important than being free – a very self-gratifying statement for White thinkers in societies that enslaved Black and Indigenous peoples.[2]

A century or so later, the relationship between slavery, violence, and freedom was turned on its head, but the result was much the same. Slavery may be legal, said White liberal scholars, but it is not natural or divine.

The practice required manmade law – positive law – for sanctification. Human enslavement, argued Swiss legalist Emmerich Vattel, represented a perpetual state of war. A favorite example originated in ancient history. "The Scythians said to Alexander the Great, 'There is never any friendship between the master and slave: in the midst of peace the rights of war still subsist.'" Slavery as war meant that slavery was a form of death. In his influential *Le Droit des gens* (*The Law of Nations*), Vattel wrote: "Is it lawful to condemn prisoners of war to slavery? Yes, in cases which give a right to kill them ... In every circumstance, when I cannot innocently take away my prisoner's life, I have no right to make him a slave." If slavery was death, then violence to escape slavery was the essence of freedom. "Men of spirit, to whom life is nothing, less than nothing, unless sweetened with liberty," said Vattel, "will always conceive themselves at war with that oppressor." In other words, being free – or attempting to be free – was more important than being alive. In this formulation, freedom seemed to necessitate a readiness to use violence. Such ideas helped promote the American, French, and Haitian revolutions.[3]

But the link between freedom and violence was intended for Whites alone. In the American Revolution, John Adams used this idea to shame the White leaders in Barbados and Jamaica who refused to support the American colonists' cause. Reflecting that news of slave rebellion in the Caribbean was not uncommon, Adams said of his West Indian counterparts, "Their Negroes, seem to have more of the Spirit of Liberty, than they." George Washington directed a similar thought at White male colonists in North America. "The Crisis is arrivd when we must assert our Rights," he explained in 1774, or the British "will make us tame, & abject Slaves, as the Blacks we Rule over with such arbitrary Sway." From this perspective, White freedom won through violence was purposeful – its purpose was freedom. Black violence was different – a threat and an aberration where Black docility was expected.[4]

White leaders in the United States believed the purpose of slave violence was uniquely hateful and aimless or, when it had an aim, it was to exterminate Whites. To incite "insurrections of our slaves," Thomas Jefferson noted, is among the "most barbarous principles." In the Revolution, the fact that no White individual had been killed in a slave rebellion in the history of Virginia – by far the largest slaveholding region in mainland North America at the time – did nothing to change the views of colonial leaders. The empowered Whites who formulated the United States thus leveled the violence of the federal state against slave rebellion – and there were those who felt that the United States must do even more. Connecticut Governor

Oliver Wolcott, an enslaver of six African Americans, wrote of his concerns to President Washington in 1797. The nation needs "the enrollment of a Land force," he said, "principally with a view of preventing insurrections of Slaves in the Southern States." Ten years later, merchant Michael Walton advised President Jefferson to garrison the South with "small Forts or Block houses." Should Black men and women "endeavor to seize the Arms, Ammunition &c of their Masters," Walton said, "the Fort wou'd be a terror to them."[5]

Even certain White Americans with antislavery leanings worked against Black-led violence to overthrow enslavement. Pennsylvanian Quakers were religious pacifists and among the first White antislavery voices in North America. Yet in a Revolution-era petition for conscientious objector status to avoid military service, some of them professed a willingness "To suppress Insurrections of Slaves or disaffected Persons during an Attack." Most White Americans in the early national period would agree with John Adams when he reassured Virginian John Randolph: "Perish the New England Wish, if any One Should ever be uttered or conceived, for any Insurrection among your Domesticks."[6]

Late eighteenth-century White American leaders situated themselves within a tradition that defended the use of force over persons whom they deemed manageable only by such force. Disorderly, uncontrolled, and destructive of civilians and property, slave rebellion was an unjust revolution, they said. Only the violence of disgruntled White men was warranted. Empowered Whites thus criminalized slave rebellion (and other forms of Black violence) in a political society that emerged only through the process of violent insurrection. Such thinking helped vindicate the force that the United States deployed to uphold Whiteness, human enslavement, and the widespread exclusion of Blacks from politics and society. For, if Black violence was forbidden, and violence was a primary means to obtain freedom, then Black freedom could be limited too.

The US Constitution structured the deterrence of Black freedom and slave rebellion into Article IV, Section 2 (the fugitive slave clause) and Section 4 ("domestic insurrections"). But, as much as the document captured a racist mindset, the response of many White leaders to international and domestic events shows how their thinking operated. For this, the slave rebellion in Haiti, which became the Haitian Revolution, is an important example.

The Haitian Revolution (1791–1804) was born in the philosophy of natural rights ("the cry of 'les droits de l'homme' is echoed thro their Camp," wrote one American observer of the Black rebels). Men and women with dark-complected skin expanded on White American and French ideals

115

to apply a more universal standard to natural rights doctrine. "All men are created equal," announced the American Declaration of Independence; "Men are born and remain free and equal in rights," said the French Declaration of the Rights of Man. For the enslaved in colonial Saint-Domingue, this rhetoric included themselves.[7]

Yet the first United States president to confront the crisis in what would become the nation of Haiti saw things differently. The event was not an expression of rights inherent in humanity, nor an instance of colonial resistance (though Saint-Domingue/Haiti was a French colony). George Washington described the start of rebellion in Haiti as a "daring and alarming" slave uprising. Thus, when French authorities contacted Washington for assistance, he was "happy" to report that the United States was prepared to quell the "alarming insurrection of the Negros in Hispaniola [Haiti]." To help battle the rebellious slaves, Secretary of War Henry Knox sent Captain Constant Freeman to the West Point public stores for 10 barrels of powder, 1,000 muskets and bayonets, 5,000 gun screws, 110,000 cartridges, and "every other article to render the equipment perfect."[8]

When John Adams assumed the presidency after Washington, he continued the hard stance against slave violence, including by refusing to conduct open trade with the new nation. "The hopes of our merchants, of great profit from the trade," Adams said, "will be found too sanguine & the evils in store seem not to be foreseen." Adams never shook the suspicion that Haitian independence was the "worst & most dangerous condition." An advocate for gradual emancipation measures under White leadership, the second president had little tolerance for immediate, Black-led approaches to slave emancipation. "Violent means and measures," he said – here meaning the violence of Black people – "produce greater violations of Justice and Humanity, than the continuance of the practice [of slavery]."[9]

The early American injunctions against Black violence were just as strong when such events took place in the United States. When the insurrectionary plot of an enslaved man named Gabriel was uncovered in 1800, for instance, even John Quincy Adams – who, in the 1850s, was touted as the theorist of American military emancipation – supported Gabriel's demise. The younger Adams, much like many White Americans (including his father, John), tied the American slave's plan to the Haitian precedent. "I hope however that the dreadful catastrophe which befell the french islands of the West-Indies will yet be avoided in every part of our country," he said, "and above all that any insurrection of the blacks will, far from meeting any encouragement in the eastern States, have every exertion of their energy employ'd for its suppression."[10]

The focus of such "suppressive energy" was physical force backed by Whiteness and hostile racial difference. In 1822, after an attempted slave insurrection led by free-Black artisan Denmark Vesey, Supreme Court Justice William Johnson wrote to Thomas Jefferson on the topic of rebellious slaves: "You know the best way in the World to make them tractable is to frighten them to Death." A White leader in Charleston, South Carolina, where the Vesey rebellion transpired, was equally direct. Speaking of enslaved Black Americans, he said, "There is nothing they are bad enough to do that we are not powerful enough to punish."[11]

The notoriously violent Virginia enslaver William Byrd once observed that "superiority has from the beginning ungenerously imposed slavery on those who are not able to resist it." In the twentieth century, scholars refuted the racist intimation that there was an inherent flaw in Black Americans, whom Byrd framed as too docile, too weak, and too dim to fight enslavement. Yet the same scholars failed to better explain the first part of Byrd's equation, the factors behind the imposition of slavery in the nation. Human enslavement demands an active consolidation of authority and violence. In the United States, no organization was better suited for the role than the national government.[12]

However much it pales in comparison with its later strength, the violence of the nineteenth-century federal state was a daunting presence capable of stopping slave rebellion in fact and imagination. John Brown learned this lesson well. By 1859, he had developed a more nuanced critique of violence in American life. Where in Kansas he had raged against proslavery individuals, he arrived at the federal arsenal in Harper's Ferry, Virginia, an abolitionist prophet aware of slavery's dependence on government force. Here, Brown confronted the laws of the Constitution and American systems of hostile difference. Directing White and Black men to instigate a slave rebellion, he sought to upend centuries of racism and Black dispossession. He believed that an antislavery and antiracist show of force – a call that an increasing number of Black abolitionists had been making – was the only means to engage with enslavers and disrupt their violent institution.

In the end, the national government defeated Brown's strategy in a demonstration that showed strength, but also the growing limitations of federal force regarding slavery. As the popular 1860s song "John Brown's Body" declares of its namesake, "his soul goes marching on." A little more than three years later, in the midst of the Civil War, Abraham Lincoln, military leaders, and members of Congress authorized the mobilization of Black men in the Union Army and started to hand over guns to former slaves.

◆

On October 17, 1859, Lieutenant J. E. B. Stuart rode to Arlington plantation. As Jim Parks, an enslaved man forced to work on the property watched on, Stuart delivered an urgent message to Robert E. Lee: Lee was being summoned to the War Department. Lee went to Washington, where he met with the president and other members of the Buchanan administration. The early reports were sketchy, but their import was clear: a slave insurrection was taking place at Harper's Ferry, Virginia, and it had to be stopped. "Negroes are led by about two fifty (250) white men," alerted a telegram from railroad workers. Henry Wise, the Virginia governor and owner of more than twenty Black individuals, had already summoned the state militia. Area residents started melting pewter dinnerware for bullets. Secretary of War John B. Floyd sent eleven officers and 142 men from Fort Monroe to Baltimore and another group was dispatched from New York Harbor. The troops at Fort McHenry were put on alert. Now, Special Orders No. 194 directed Lee, with a detachment of ninety-one United States marines, to take charge of the scene.[13]

At 10 p.m. that evening, Lee arrived in Harper's Ferry aboard a special train sent by the Baltimore and Ohio Railroad. Initial counts placed the number of insurgents anywhere between a hundred and three thousand. The situation, Lee learned, was more constrained but still unruly. Local citizens and the militia had chased a band of fourteen White and five Black men from several strategic locations. The rebels now held ten hostages inside the federal arsenal; earlier, more than thirty additional hostages had made an escape. As the federal soldiers disembarked from the train, disorder reigned. "Every man had a gun, and four-fifths of them were under no command," noted Maryland militia captain John Sinn of the forces aligned against the rebellion. "Men who were intoxicated were firing their guns in the air." Lee swiftly replaced the militiamen and locals with the marines, who, given the more limited engagement than anticipated, left their Howitzer field artillery on the train. Lee wanted to order "the attack at once," he said, but he feared for the safety of the captives. Instead, he waited, showing a patience that, by and large, he abandoned in the Civil War.[14]

At daylight on October 18, Lee sent Stuart to deliver a message to the rebels under a flag of truce. By now, Lee knew that John Brown, "of some notoriety in Kansas," was his adversary. "Colonel Lee, United States army, commanding the troops sent by the President of the United States to suppress insurrection at this place, demands the surrender of the persons in the armory buildings." The note continued that, upon peaceable surrender, the rebels "shall be kept in safety to await the orders of the President." Lee also issued a warning: if he had "to take them by force he cannot answer for their safety." But he did adopt precautions. In preparation for a fight, the military commander ordered his men "not to injure the blacks detained unless they resisted" and "to attack with the bayonet" to avoid accidental shooting of the hostages. He also established guidelines on "how to distinguish our citizens from the insurgents." In other words, how the soldiers could distinguish the White captives inside the building from the White insurgents.[15]

The moment Brown refused to yield, a "storming party" of twelve marines – backed by another party of twelve held in reserve – broke through the doors of the armory (Fig. 5.1). They rushed "in like tigers" and, despite Lee's orders, started to fire. Armed with a sword, the marine leader, Israel Green, struck Brown, who still managed a quick shot from his revolver. Brown's shot killed one marine, but, knocked unconscious himself, he

Fig. 5.1 "Storming of the Engine-House by United States Marines," by David Hunter Strother in *Harper's Weekly*. From the Wallach Division Picture Collection, the New York Public Library.

119

suffered a "deep saber cut in the back of the neck." The soldiers also mortally bayoneted two of Brown's men. One, Jeremiah Anderson, was skewered to the rear wall of the building. Then Green demanded that the killing stop. In less than three minutes, national forces had crushed John Brown's slave rebellion.[16]

But the aftermath of the violence had only just begun. On the first day of the resistance, Dangerfield Newby, a slave who had hoped to free his family in the rebellion, had been shot dead through the neck. Left on the armory's streets, Newby's body attracted pigs that foraged in its wounds; locals poked it with sticks and sliced off the ears. William Leeman, who at twenty was the youngest rebel fighter, abandoned Brown's cause when the arsenal position turned hopeless. Unarmed and with hands raised in surrender, Leeman was shot in the face during a failed escape through the Potomac River. Sentries on a nearby bridge riddled his corpse with gunfire until it floated downstream.

The federal presence in the town dampened the rowdy treatment the rebel men had received the day before, but the crowd remained riled up after Brown's capture. A lynch mob formed and crowded the government's captives, but Brown was escorted safely to a nearby paymaster's office. When Lee's marines moved the wounded and dead outside the armory buildings, the crowd could not get enough. Taken down from the wall, Jeremiah Anderson, in the last stages of life, started "vomiting gore." "Gentlemen, can't you stand back and let the ladies see the corpses?" asked an onlooker navigating the push of people amid the morbid curiosity and excitement. Another spat in Anderson's face. When he died, his cadaver was sent to a medical school for dissection.[17]

Thanks to the US marines, John Brown was alive and in custody. But the incident concluded so fast that the legitimacy of the federal force in Virginia was never clearly established. The Constitution (Article IV, Section 4) and Militia Acts of 1795 and 1807 required an application for federal assistance from the state legislature or state executive ("when the legislature cannot be convened"). But Brown and his men had first targeted the telegraph and railroad to isolate the town. Officials of the Baltimore and Ohio Railroad were thus among the first alerted to the attack. A business leader, not a state official, thus made the request for United States troops – a scenario that would become common in post-Civil War America. "Telegraph advises present a serious affair at Harpers Ferry, where United States armory and our bridges are in full possession of large bands of armed men said to be abolitionists," cabled railroad president John W. Garrett to Secretary of War and enslaver John B. Floyd. "Can you authorize the

Government officers and military from Washington to go on our train at three twenty this afternoon to the scene?"[18]

The answer was "yes." In the absence of a request from the state legislature or executive, the Militia Act allows for the domestic use of federal force when an insurrection or invasion obstructs the laws, or the execution of the laws, of the United States. President Buchanan prepared Lee for such a condition. As stipulated by Congress, to deploy the violence of the national state in a domestic context, the president must "forthwith, by proclamation, command such insurgents to disperse, and retire peaceably to their respective abodes, within a limited time." Buchanan, a government report noted, "issued the usual proclamation, which was intrusted in manuscript to Colonel Lee, to be published at Harpers Ferry on his arrival." However, Lee never distributed the proclamation – he returned it to the secretary of war after Brown's capture.[19]

American presidents have fulfilled, ignored, and questioned the proclamation requirement. Millard Fillmore, wanting federal force to operate in more secrecy, suggested eliminating the prerequisite. "Such a proclamation," he said in 1851, defeats "the whole object, by giving notice to persons intended to be arrested." Buchanan, though, was less wily, more often content with the limitations in place. Prone to convoluted legal justification, he no doubt authorized Lee to act within two distinct scenarios. The first drew authority from the Constitution and the Congressional Militia Acts. A failure of Virginia's leaders to make a request of the federal government and the engagement's limited scope rendered it difficult to justify national troop deployment on such grounds. The second positioned Lee and his men as a posse comitatus, an armed body charged to enforce civil law under the jurisdiction of a federal marshal. The marines who broke through the arsenal door functioned not under a military commission, but under civil authority. This explains why Lee turned over the captives to the "hands of the marshal of the western district of Virginia and the sheriff of Jefferson county."[20]

The use of national troops as a posse comitatus had gained in popularity in the 1850s. The status was granted to army and naval forces in Massachusetts (1851 and 1854), California (1856), Kansas (1856–1861), Utah (1859), and Virginia (1859). Unrest in the pre-Civil War years, which neither overturned civil authority nor threatened the general security of a state or territory, demanded the use of federal violence that was at once more dynamic and less beholden to Congressional oversight than that issued by the Militia Act. The fugitive slave crises highlight this fact. A revised fugitive slave law in 1850 transferred the responsibility for runaway recapture from the states to the federal government. Opposition to the Fugitive Slave Act was a clear obstruction of the United States legal processes that sanctioned Black enslavement. Such opposition readily fit the requirements for the more robust deployment of national force in a domestic setting. Yet the posse comitatus became the preferred means to guard enslaver interests in northern states. It drew on the capacity and strength of the federal government, preserved lines of authority largely within presidential purview, and, all the while, recognized civil authority and civil law.[21]

In February 1851, for example, Shadrach, a Black Bostonian waiter, was arrested and placed in the custody of a deputy US marshal. An interracial group of activists broke Shadrach free from detention and shuttled him to Canada. In response, President Fillmore issued a proclamation, which, similar to the events at Harper's Ferry in 1859, signaled the possibility of martial law. "Lawless persons, principally persons of color," Fillmore announced, "combined and confederated together, for the purpose of opposing by force the execution of the laws of the United States." To arrest those involved, Secretary of War Charles Magill Conrad opted for a display of national force that was bound to civil authority. He ordered the commander of US troops in Boston Harbor to act "as a part of a posse comitatus ... under the control of the marshal ... as may be deemed adequate to the purpose."[22]

Three years later, after a failed attempt to free a recaptured and imprisoned fugitive slave named Anthony Burns on May 26, 1854, national leaders deemed the Shadrach case instructions to be still in effect. A federal judge directed the US marshal to call a posse comitatus to enforce "the laws of the United States in the case of Anthony Burns." The marshal, in turn, charged "all the military force" at Fort Independence to appear under his command. "Two batteries of the Fourth Artillery, 2 officers and 42 men, with two field pieces" from the fort and a group of sailors and marines from the Charlestown naval yard joined with the local militia to secure Boston. When a judge sentenced Burns to return to his one-time master, the marshal demanded more federal troops to guarantee the enslavement. General Winfield Scott responded by readying men in New York City, but the federal forces on hand were up to the task. Protesters who lined the route to resist the Burns procession were arrested. Some were beaten and stabbed. Ushered to a US revenue cutter by as many as 1,600 armed men (a combination of infantry, marines, militia, and police), Burns arrived at Boston Harbor unfree but physically unharmed. From there, his ship sailed to Virginia "under the escort of several naval vessels." Activist minister Theodore Parker cried out, "United States soldiers loaded their pieces in

Court square, to be discharged into the crowd of Boston citizens . . . The Law of Massachusetts was cloven down by the sword of the Marshal."[23]

In the end, the federal government had spent more than $40,000 to fortify the city and secure American slavery. It was a military exploit that had a lasting effect. "Since the disgraceful capture of poor Burns," wrote free Black intellectual Charlotte Forten, soldiers "are more hateful to me than ever." At the time, Boston had a robust African American community, and many Bostonians believed, like Forten, that the United States government had in effect executed Anthony Burns. "He has been sent back to a bondage worse," she said, echoing the reflections of Emmerich Vattel, "a thousand times worse than death."[24]

When Colonel Lee and his men acted the part of a posse comitatus at Harper's Ferry in 1859, they joined a recent pattern of federal troops acting as civilian authority in defense of human enslavement. The only exception may have taken place on the afternoon of October 18. After Lee subdued Brown and his men, families from nearby Maryland started to arrive. They had fled, they claimed, from slaves who were killing Whites. In response, Lee marched twenty-five marines four and half miles to the site where he found "the inhabitants of Pleasant Valley were quiet and unharmed." While it is conceivable that Lee acted on orders from the federal marshal, his official report suggests that he did not. "I thought it possible that some atrocity might have been committed," he said, "and I started . . . for the scene of the alleged outrage." To complete this maneuver, the marines – national soldiers – exited the property of the United States government (the arsenal) and marched on the soil of two different states. Clearly, the mandate of White supremacy superseded the mandate of the Constitution. It allowed Robert E. Lee to ignore the law.[25]

Southern Democrats and enslavers assailed the federal government in the wake of the failed rebellion. National leaders had left the armory unprotected, which facilitated John Brown's design, they argued, and then mounted a far too limited response. Virginia Governor Henry Wise led the criticism with an unmatched bravado. He said that if he had arrived in Harper's Ferry before Colonel Lee, he would have immediately "proclaimed martial law," recaptured the arsenal showing "no quarter," and, "by court martial" shot survivors "on the spot." Wise wanted a swift, severe military justice to rule the occasion. He scoffed at the federal troops "playing *posse comitatus* to a United States marshal." Indeed, before Brown's execution, the governor impersonated a military dictator. On November 19, he called 500 men into service – notably, after Buchanan had ignored a call for help with a supposed plot to free Brown. In the days to follow, he summoned

563 more men, and 560 again after that. In less than two weeks, Wise issued two years' worth of armaments to citizens of the state. He also closed railroad travel for civilians such that only militia members could board a Virginia train. It was an exorbitant response. "Wise is making a fool of himself & the State," complained W. C. Bruce in Norfolk.[26]

Amid the displays of Virginian violence, John Brown well understood his plight. In Virginia, one could be jailed simply for asserting "that owners have not right of property in their slaves." The penalty for inducing "a slave to rebel or make insurrection ... whether such rebellion or insurrection be made or not" was death. Not only charged with "advising and conspiring with slaves and others to rebel," Brown faced two other capital accounts: treason (for "levying war against the state") and "murder in the first degree." The abolitionist warrior did not complain, however. When asked if he had anything to say in defense of himself, the court records show "he said he had nothing but what he had before said."[27]

In fact, John Brown agreed with violent, liberal governance. But he preferred to be in control of it, and for it to bend toward gender equality and racial justice. His "Provisional Constitution," which Lee and the marines discovered on members of his antislavery army, called slavery in the United States "an unjustifiable war of one portion of its citizens upon another portion." Notably, it addressed both "the Citizens of the United States" (White individuals) and "the Oppressed People" (Black individuals). The Provisional Constitution laid out new rules for state violence (military appointments and courts martial) as well as displays of individual force. Article XLIII stated that "all persons known to be of good character and of sound mind and suitable age ... whether male or female, shall be encouraged to carry arms openly." Those who bore concealed weapons, by contrast, were deemed "suspicious" and subject to search and investigation without formal complaint or warrant. According to the document, everyone was to adopt Brown's revised legal code "to protect our Persons, Property, Lives, and Liberties; and to govern our actions."[28]

When the state of Virginia sentenced Brown to "be hanged by the neck until he be dead" on December 2, 1859, it sought to kill a man who had tried to overturn in word and deed the American racial hierarchy and the national government used to maintain it. His was a revolutionary effort to improve the American liberal experiment.[29]

However, while there were many southern critics of the US government's reaction to John Brown's attack, Henry Wise offered a unique assessment. He was adamant that the act be classified not as a slave rebellion (unrest that originated in the state of Virginia involving enslaved African

Americans) but as an invasion – a military exploit of a foreign nation. Brown's deep ties to free Black communities in Canada and the copies of his Provisional Constitution found among his men bolstered this interpretation. "Here there was no 'insurrection:' no case of force from within," Wise said in December 1859. "Invasion was threatened from without, by citizens of one state against another state." Such criticism focused on a perceived failure of the federal government to protect the state of Virginia. Since national leaders refused their duty to defend the states, Wise claimed, "*We must rely on ourselves, and fight for peace! . . . Organize and arm!*"[30]

Wise's theory of state vulnerability ignored the overall outcome of John Brown's rebellion: the national military had entered Virginia and secured the practice of American slavery. Still, the governor may have had a point. Earlier instances of national violence deployed in support of slavery demonstrate a lack of restraint compared with 1859. In 1831, for instance, the United States government was far less concerned with jurisdiction and more focused on prodigious displays of national strength. Merely on the suspicion of slave rebellion in Louisiana, the War Department moved two infantry companies to New Orleans and held nearby posts in a state of readiness. Later that summer, as slave unrest and the rumor of slave unrest spread through Delaware, Maryland, Virginia, and the Carolinas, national leaders deployed five companies from northern sites to Fort Monroe on the Virginia Peninsula. When the Nat Turner slave insurrection broke out in Southampton County, Virginia, in late August, government officials also ignored constitutional and Militia Act procedure. Mayor Holt of Norfolk called on the commander at Monroe to request "150 to 200 men," stressing "the imminent and pressing necessity of the occasion." Without instruction from the War Department or the president, the commander, Colonel House, sent the 115th Virginia Regiment to check the "insurrectionary movements of the blacks in the neighboring counties." Again, the mandates of White supremacy supplanted those of the Constitution.[31]

The troops did not, however, see action during Turner's 1831 attack on slavery. Adjutant-General Jones approved House's orders two days after the fact – reporting that President Andrew Jackson and Secretary of War Lewis Cass expressed their "entire satisfaction" with the developments.[32]

But barely ten days had passed from the outbreak of Turner's rebellion before slave insurrection fears pushed the secretary of war to further action. He delivered arms to the White civilians in Hampton, Virginia, and deployed a company of artillery from Fort Monroe to Newbern, North Carolina. Notably, the Carolinians responded to the federal show of force in a manner opposite to that of Virginians three decades later in 1859.

Newbern's leading Whites were upset that the government offered, not too little protection, but, as the federal force remained for weeks, too much. The townsfolk feared the national soldiers would make them "less vigilant" in their enslavement and oversight of Black Americans. Captain Whiting reported that local sentiment indicated "the presence of United States troops is no longer necessary as a protection against their slaves."[33]

In 1859, Governor Wise and other southern leaders could look to the summer of 1831 as a highpoint in the domestic use of national force to bolster American slavery. Add in its foreign corollary – the international use of troops to secure slavery's expansion in the 1840s during the Mexican–American War – and, clearly, federal troop deployment as a posse comitatus looked weak.

But, for all the complaints in his time (and in ours) over a lack of consistency and backbone in Buchanan's policies, the president was remarkably consistent in his use of federal force. He followed the general guidelines established by his predecessor, Franklin Pierce, to govern the situation in the Kansas Territory. Pierce had set a federal response according to exigency. The first level was a commitment of troops to enforce civil authority – that is, the deployment of national arms as part of a posse comitatus. If that did not restore order, Pierce claimed, the president "may call forth the militia of one or more States for that object, or employ for the same object any part of the land or naval force of the United States." Violence, in Pierce's thinking, intensified and defused in a somewhat linear fashion. The violence of the national state should likewise proceed from a local and civil or national and civil to a national and military concern (and back again) based on the severity of a situation. In the greater Atlantic world, a central government's exercise of force was often calibrated to such prospects. An American correspondent noted of the 1858 rebellion of Black workers in Antigua, for example, that "the French troops had arrived, but would not be landed as they were not required." There is no reason to suspect that Buchanan sought to deviate from conventional policy in October 1859.[34]

Federal leaders and Governor Wise did stand in close agreement on an entirely different front, however. They believed that Black participation in the John Brown affair was compelled, not volunteered. Robert E. Lee was among the first to foster this analysis. The military commander and enslaver understood full well the significance of Brown's actions. In a slave society – the United States in 1859 ranks among the largest slave societies in human history – slave rebellion represented the ultimate breakdown of political and social life. Many American Whites understood Black violence as the very definition of chaos – a time when indiscriminate killing gave way to a racial anomaly: Blacks lording over Whites. Charleston lawyer Edwin C. Holland explained: "Let it never be forgotten, that 'our NEGROES are truly the *Jacobins* of the country; that they are the *anarchists* and the *domestic enemy*; the *common enemy of civilized society,* and the barbarians who would, if they could, become the destroyers *of our* [White] *race.*"[35]

To diminish the fear of Black violence at Harper's Ferry, Lee underscored an absence of Black American collaboration with Brown. He cast the White abolitionist as the lone person of importance in the event. Brown was a kind of enchanter, "a fanatic or madman," Lee explained in his initial report, whose "object was the liberation of the slaves of Virginia, and of the whole South." Brown, in Lee's eyes, was deeply "disappointed in his expectations of aid from the black as well as white population." "As far as I could learn," Lee stressed, "the blacks whom he forced from their homes . . . gave him no voluntary assistance."[36]

Governor Wise joined Lee in laying the responsibility entirely on Brown and thus highlighting the submissive disposition of Virginian slaves. Brown was exceptional, Wise claimed, trained in Kansas with "the skill of the Indian in savage warfare." His civility removed, Brown thus waged an "unnatural war upon negro slavery." Brown's mistake? The abolitionist deluded himself over the "disposition of the slaves." "The slaves taken refused to take arms," Wise declared, and they had no incentive to enlist. In an inadvertent claim for the disarmament of civilian Americans, Wise focused on the first fatality in Brown's raid: Heyward Shepherd, a free African American railroad worker who turned and fled from the antislavery soldiers in the dark of night early on October 17. Brown's men shot Shepherd in the back, a casualty of the insecurity and adrenaline endemic to armed attacks. Wise said that there was "no danger from our slaves or colored people" because "the first man killed was a respectable free negro who was . . . shot running from the philanthropists who came to liberate the black race!"[37]

In Wise's understanding, the antislavery soldiers had undermined their cause. Any slaves who participated in Brown's exploits had had to be "forced to fight to liberate themselves." The dominant theme of American enslaver and Democratic Party rhetoric – that abolitionists were the central problem – ruled the day. In 1859, White Virginians were scared not of their slaves, said a farmer, but "from the uncertainty as to how far the negroes had been tampered with."[38]

The 1860 senate report on John Brown, authored by Democrats James Murray Mason, Jefferson Davis, and Graham N. Fitch upheld this view. "It was owing alone to the loyalty and well-affected disposition of the slaves that he [Brown] did not succeed in inciting a servile war." The report documented Brown's weapons cache – "200 Sharp's rifled carbines," "200 revolver pistols," "900 or 1,000 pikes" – and munitions – "many thousand percussion caps in boxes," "a large supply of powder in kegs," and "ample stores of fixed ammunition." "Not one of the captured slaves, although arms were placed in their hands," the senators said, "attempted to use them." In addition, they noted that the slaves "hastened" back to bondage once released from Brown's custody.[39]

There is ample reason to disregard this depiction of enslaved people's participation in Brown's assault, however. Brown and his army captured Lewis Washington along with three of his slaves at 1:30 a.m. on October 17. When they returned to the federal arsenal, the rebels placed enslavers and slaves in different rooms. One group, the White individuals, stayed as hostages; the other, the Black individuals, was armed and, in Brown's eyes, freed. After the event, Washington noted the upending of the status quo of White mastery. When his slaves entered the captives' room to warm themselves by the stove, "each negro" had "a pike in his hand." Washington's friend and neighbor, John Allstadt, whose family was captured along with seven of their slaves, reported a similar situation. "They had armed the negroes with spears, and they would occasionally walk in to the stove." Other slaves, Washington said, were put to work drilling gun holes to help mount a defense.[40]

Shields Green, a fugitive from South Carolinian enslavement, also helped defend the arsenal. He was the only former slave to join Brown's gang before the attack; he did so at a meeting in August 1859. (Frederick Douglass, who attended the same meeting, saw fit to steer clear of the White abolitionist's plot.) Lewis Washington recalled that Green was armed "like the rest" of the antislavery soldiers: "with a rifle and revolver, and a butcher knife in his sheath." The Congressional committee asked directly whether Green fired his guns: "yes, sir, very rapidly and diligently," said Washington. The slave-owner found Shields' expressions of authority "very impudent." "I saw him order some gentlemen to shut a window," he said, "with a rifle raised at them."[41]

Other slaves took part in activities outside the armory buildings. Some shuttled arms from Brown's cache outside the town. One slave, Jim, who was hired out from a Dr. Fuller to work as Lewis Washington's driver, was absent when Brown's army arrived at the plantation. Jim joined the abolitionist forces later and helped guard an arsenal building, but drowned while trying to escape from local residents who mounted the first counterattack. The *New York Herald* described him as a slave who "had joined the rebels with a good will."[42]

Still, Jefferson Davis wanted to know more. He inquired of John Allstadt, "What was the conduct of those negroes at the time they were walking about with pikes in their hands? Did they appear hostile to you?" Allstadt responded, "Not at all; they did not appear hostile to any one." Likewise, most White southerners opted to overlook the Black violence perpetrated by John Copeland and Lewis Leary, two free Black Ohioans who participated in the raid. Copeland took up as a slave liberator thanks in part to his misreading of the American Revolution. "[George] Washington entered the field to fight for the freedom of the American people – not for the White man alone," he wrote to his brother on December 10, 1859. Yet, when Senator Mason wanted to know whether the event excited "any spirit of insubordination amongst" the "negroes," Lewis Washington responded, "Not the slightest."[43]

Significantly, the senators only enquired about Black violence from verified enslavers, asking first, "Are you a landholder and slaveholder?" And in their responses, the White enslavers who answered questions about Black violence ignored a crucial dynamic. The balance of power among slave, master, armed abolitionist, and federal soldiers shuttled back and forth over the course of the Harper's Ferry slave rebellion. On the morning of October 16, enslavers wielded the most authority in the town. It was based on labor, the extraction of work from male and female bodies, racism, a belief in White superiority, and violence. White Virginians had been enslavers for more than two centuries, and their violent authority was a means of upholding labor discipline, racial hierarchy, and tradition. The armed band of White and Black men (both freed and free Black men) thus shook the slaveholders from their perch.[44]

For more than twenty-four hours, the rebel liberators created a different reality: one-time slaves walked around with pikes while their former enslavers huddled on the armory floor. At this moment, the abolitionist forces, in full expectation of support from the thousands of slaves in nearby counties, brandished the most authority – and hope. Brown started to dictate terms. He followed Article XXXIII and Article XXXVI of his Provisional Constitution: Whites who "voluntarily deliver up their slaves," Brown announced, are "entitled to the fullest protection of person and property." They "shall be treated as friends." Forty-two-year-old Terence Byrne, a Maryland landowner and enslaver, testified to the senate committee that Brown's men followed their leader to this effect. They promised "to protect my person and property" if I gave up "my slaves voluntarily."

Byrne refused. "I looked to the State government," he said, "or, if that failed, to the federal government to protect me." Full of confidence, Brown's men "remarked they would have them [Byrne's slaves] any how."[45]

Nevertheless, when only a few of the town's two hundred slaves – who represented but a fraction of the state's half a million enslaved – joined with John Brown and his men, the slave insurrection collapsed beneath its weighty ambition and expectations. Byrne was right to place his faith in the federal government. So too were the slaves who, in their inaction, sensed the scope of the violence that upheld American slavery.[46]

As the federal troops raided the arsenal, the quick-thinking Shields Green tried "to represent himself as one of the slaves." He threw down his hat and weapons, which distinguished him as Brown's crusader, and used his dark complexion to camouflage himself as a local. Green's attempt reveals the political reality for Blacks inside the federal arsenal. A quick look outside the building in the moments just before federal forces entered clearly showed that Brown's emancipatory scheme had turned suicidal – if it hadn't been so from the beginning. Once the marines knocked down the door – the violence of the federal state clearly siding with human enslavement – the enslaved, whether they were captured by Brown or willing recruits, had everything to lose by standing against the government and their enslavers. As they lay down their weapons, perhaps it is no wonder that White southerners so readily perceived them as unwilling participants in the bloody event.[47]

However, the slaveholder interpretation of the lack of Black autonomy at Harper's Ferry was unique to that occasion – an instance when a White man, John Brown, had planned for and led a violent antislavery effort. By 1859, there was a much more robust history in the United States that suggested something different: White enslavers knew full well the power and strength found in enslaved communities. And in response to this strength, slave-owners had targeted Black individuals and their families with threats, punishments, and violence. For example, in November 1774, James Madison, the Virginian political theorist and enslaver, expressed a concern to William Bradford that local slaves had been planning to take advantage of the growing hostilities between the White Americans and British. "When the English troops should arrive," Madison explained, the slaves "foolishly thought ... that by revolting to them they should be rewarded with their freedom." He assured Bradford that the "proper pre-cautions" were "taken to prevent the Infection." Indeed, insurrection was often imagined as a site of contamination. It had to be isolated and cut off to prevent its spread. The preventatives alluded to by Madison involved separation of family and friends through slave sales, physical beatings, and capital punishment. "It is prudent such attempts," Madison said of the planned insurrection, "should be concealed as well as suppressed."[48]

The dominance of slave-owner views is no coincidence, and their efforts to conceal Black violence in the American slave past had concrete effects. Slave testimony in official records is often silenced, ignored, or, when it does appear, coerced. At times, for example, enslavers beat confessions from Black individuals. Here, at the intersection of federal violence and White enslaver authority, is where the fuller picture of American slavery is buried. After the discovery of the slave insurrection planned by Gabriel in 1800, James Monroe explained to Thomas Jefferson that officials did all they could "While it was posible to keep it secret." Secrecy also shrouded the largest slave revolt in United States history, which took place outside New Orleans in 1811. It involved as many as five hundred slaves but remains one of the least documented instances of American slave rebellion. It was "very soon quelled by the prompt and decisive Movements of the armed Force of the United States, and the Body of the Militia," but Louisianan enslavers quelled knowledge of the uprising too – so much so that the event continues to remain hidden in the historical record and historical memory.[49]

Slaveholders believed the "problem" of slave resistance was best quickly overpowered and kept concealed. John Brown had met White southerners on their terms and on their soil. He tried to consolidate antislavery and antiracist violence – largely in the form of violent Black individuals – within a central body. But the protections of his "Provisional Constitution" proved no match for the federal state and United States Constitution, and, in the end, the official pattern of concealing Black violence undermined the legacy of his grand vision. Violence proved an effective means to achieve political and social ends in nineteenth-century America, but only White violence backed by the United States government seemed to reign supreme.[50]

6

1860: THE UNDISPUTED ELECTION
THAT SPARKED DISPUTE

Established in opposition to the Kansas–Nebraska Act in 1854, the Republican Party served as the main political conduit for northern resistance to slavery. By 1860, the party's progressive supporters understood the "question of human rights" to be "paramount." But many more Republicans sought a moderate agenda. They maintained that natural rights were for all men (but that voting was not necessarily a natural right), that slavery could not expand in the United States (though immediate emancipation was not necessarily wise), and that the violent acts of the past decade were the fault of Democrats and enslavers – or, as one Republican poet described them, "those fierce southern bullies, *so hostile to brains.*"[1]

Abraham Lincoln, "an earnest antislavery man" who would uphold the rule of law over his own views, embodied this centrist Republican vision. Through him, the party forged an identity balanced on northern White men, wage labor, slavery's non-extension, and White superiority to Native peoples. Indeed, he seemed to embody such a balance. An 1860 campaign biography noted that western places like Illinois, where Lincoln had moved "when the foot of a white man had barely begun to tread its magnificent prairies," embraced free, wage labor. The "dark and bloody ground" of Kentucky, Lincoln's birthplace, supported slavery.[2]

The 1860 Republican platform elaborated on the freedom and slavery divide. It noted in horror the recent events in the Kansas Territory and condemned "the lawless invasion by armed force of any State or Territory . . . as among the gravest of crimes." "The normal condition of all the territory of the United States," said the Republican Party, "is that of freedom [not containing slavery]." The platform denounced President Buchanan's ploy to impose a proslavery Kansas constitution in 1857 as an "unvarying abuse" of power. Because Kansas voters had recently submitted an antislavery constitution for Congressional approval, the Republicans demanded the admittance of Kansas as a slave-free state.[3]

The 1860 Republicans also took issue with recent talk of disunion (soon to be known as secession) among Democratic supporters. A threat of disunion, they said, was the contemplation of treason. The Democrats had issued threats of disunion in reaction to the Republican Party's stance on slavery and, to a lesser degree, race. Such issues did, indeed, appear in the platform's later resolutions. The Republican platform's seventh resolution called the Dred Scott decision, which provided a national sanction of slave property and declared that Blacks could not be citizens, "a dangerous political heresy ... subversive of the peace and harmony of the country." The ninth resolution stated that the "re-opening of the African slave-trade" – a proposal supported by slaveholders in South Carolina and the Mississippi Valley – was "a crime against humanity." Presented as a necessary countermeasure, the Republican Party's principles, said its supporters, offered the means for a "peaceful and constitutional triumph."[4]

In accepting the processes of American democracy, these Republican men nonetheless embraced the limitations of their political world. The United States Constitution, for example, offered no clear means for the federal government to oversee slavery in the states. Republicans thus looked to stop the spread of slavery into US territories. Yet, on the whole, party members were not keen on the idea of a significant population of free Black people in the United States either. Nothing better illustrates the Republican dilemma than its members' support for colonization. The racist agenda of colonizationists proposed to "repatriate" Black American individuals to Africa and to Christianize Black persons already in Africa. For Whites, the historian William B. Hart explains, removing African Americans from the United States addressed the "pernicious problem of slavery" and solved what was to them another truth: that Blacks and Whites cannot peaceably live together. Antislavery advocates, not antiracists, Republicans often upheld hostile racial differences – the very differences that forged and sustained Black enslavement in the United States.[5]

Positioned against both slavery and full human equality, the Republican Party fostered a complex dynamic. Many of the more radical abolitionists, such as Frederick Douglass, believed that the institution of slavery was the root cause of racism. The party's stance against slavery thus signaled to them, despite the abiding bigotry of most Republican candidates, the possibility of a race-free world. At the same time, many recent White immigrants supported the Republican Party in hope that White wage labor would prevail in American spaces where slavery was banned. Mostly, however, Republican supporters focused more on slavery as a corrupt institution than on the plight of the enslaved. Notably, this focus would find the Lincoln administration and national military unprepared to address the demands of Black families and communities suddenly freed amid the Civil War.

Yet, while a majority in each major political party agreed on racist, not antiracist principles, the parties did not coalesce in their racism. Democrats advocated for human enslavement and Republicans for free labor. This did not mean, however, that Republicans as a whole endorsed free *Black* labor, a fact confirmed by the support in the party for Black removal via colonization. Where the parties did align, however, was on a fundamental relationship to violence.

Despite its self-promotion as a party of lawful peace and its condemnation of John Brown's use of antislavery violence, the Republican organization was built to resist and enforce. The party, born in an environment of violent, White male partisanship, was soon supported by violent, White male partisans. While the most extreme, like John Brown, looked to overturn the hierarchies of American life, many others believed the structures for change were already in place. They argued that slavery was an anomaly in the Constitution and that antislavery principles were the foundation of the nation. As a result, most offered an unwavering faith in the liberal society they lived in.

In the progression of the 1860 national election, the violence of Republican backers in word and deed centered on the issues that had resonated in the White political sphere throughout the 1850s. In Lincoln's campaign materials and activities, Kansas took center stage. Where Kansas antislavery activism had previously focused on victimhood ("In Kansas bled our noble dead"), it was now transformed into a space of Republican power: "We'll guard our country's ballot box, Till *Stuffers* learn our path to shun ... If rogues their daring schemes advance ... We'll show them how by Vigilance, Can make them from the country run!" With such statements, party patrons appeared to accept the terms of popular sovereignty: White American democracy required violence and the "vigilance" of Republican individuals. Notably, this theme had first appeared in the party's 1856 platform, which, in light of the Democrats' attempts to disarm Kansas antislavery proponents, had focused on denouncing Second Amendment infringements threatening the "right of the people to keep and bear arms."[6]

Republican vigilance was fused to Republican righteousness – an unwillingness to compromise, particularly on the non-extension of slavery. Abraham Lincoln's "MIGHTY BACKBONE" featured prominently in the 1860 election. Righteousness, though, pervaded the whole organization. When Virginia Governor Wise planned to obstruct Republican actions, Republican Congressman Thaddeus Stevens laughed. Only "the knees of a few old women in pantaloons" are shaking, he said. The party's supporters stood by their leaders. One Philadelphian Republican society, organized in military fashion, went by the name The Invincibles. To move "Forward," admonished J. J. Clarke, Republican men must "unsheathe the freeman's sword . . . Till SLAVERY knows a freeman's power! Obeys a freeman's will!"[7]

Righteousness requires violence or an inclination to violent acts for effectiveness. The fullest expression of Republican force thus developed in northern spaces with the greatest Democratic support. In 1860, the state of Connecticut was one such place. Here, Republican William Buckingham would win the governorship by fewer than six hundred votes. On February 25, after a speech by Republican Party founder Cassius M. Clay, Hartford dry goods clerks grouped together to guard Clay's return to his hotel. The men, dressed in black capes and glazed caps (a hat partially waterproofed by lacquer, often worn by firemen) and carrying oil-based lanterns, were part of a new movement. Calling on a tradition of citizen militias in the United States, this was a grassroots political movement of young male Republicans. In a name that captured their political awareness, the blaze of their torches, and the spirit of their nighttime parades, these Republican organizations were called the Wide Awakes.[8]

During the 1860 campaign, Wide Awake chapters organized in towns and cities throughout the North. Black capes, glazed caps, and torches, which took on several forms including that of a rifle, became the association's hallmark. The Wide Awakes coordinated political displays through military regulation. One Wide Awake drill in Hartford combined men from Massachusetts, New York, New Jersey, and Connecticut in an elaborate parade. A *New York Times* reporter noted that colored lanterns differentiated among the Wide Awake officers. "The Captain carries a red lantern; his lieutenants, according to their rank, blue, green and so on," he said of the July 1860 event. "They were drilled in the Wide Awake manual and exhibited a degree of proficiency that is rarely attained in military companies of the same magnitude." In October, a *Harper's Weekly* artist captured a large New York demonstration for his newspaper (Fig. 6.1). It shows an army of torch-wielding men passing by the offices of the *New-York Tribune* at 154 Nassau Street and the *New York Times* at 41 Park Row near City Hall. Wide Awake signs and insignias are joined in the image by an enormous transparency of the Lincoln–Hamlin candidacy attached to a light box and a Free Speech display shooting fireworks. Thousands of torches throw off light and smoke amid tens of thousands of spectators.[9]

The Wide Awakes in the image appear intriguingly stoic. One parade observer noted the sounds of fireworks and of spectators against a widespread "silence like the quiet flow of a vast river." These were grave

Fig. 6.1 "Grand Procession of Wide Awakes at New York on the Evening of October 3, 1860." From the Irma and Paul Milstein Division of United States History, the New York Public Library.

young men who took up the Republican mission. The hiss of burning torchlights (which ran on coal oil or low-grade kerosene to emit a vile smell) and bonfires, along with the sounds of bands, rockets, and cannon-ade, marked the celebrations. But, for all the sights, sounds, and silences of Wide Awake festivities, historians have too often failed to grasp their impact. It was much more than an "emotional appeal." The group is "the most numerous, the best disciplined and the most effective political organization this country has ever seen," said the *New York Times*. By contrast, the *Clinton Democrat*, a publication in support of the Democratic Party, considered the Wide Awakes Republican agitators and noted their "debauchery, drunken-ness, profaneness, violence and riot." Regardless of how one read their gatherings, it is clear that in an age focused on violent political activity, Wide Awake men harnessed violence for the Republican mission.[10]

On September 25, 1860, New York Wide Awakes erected a pole decor-ated in support of the Lincoln and Hamlin candidacy in front of the Republican headquarters on Broadway. When Democratic supporters passed by and shouted their critique, Wide Awake General J. H. Hobart

Ward ordered his men to attack. The Democrats took cover in a nearby hotel and then rallied, chasing the Wide Awakes through the streets. Police arrested several men during the altercation, and the Republicans lost "a number of their torches." The partisan battles over political rights to urban space captured headlines: "Political Riot at Troy," "The Fight between the Wide Awakes and Firemen," "Republican Mass Meeting – Democratic Assault," "Assault Upon a Republican Meeting." Male bodies most often suffered in the beatings. An Indiana Democrat shot a Wide Awake in the shoulder, and an Illinois Wide Awake stabbed an opposition leader. Poised on a precipice between violent symbolism and violent deed, the Wide Awakes often provided a lesson in how one leads to the other.[11]

Wide Awake men appeared to Democrats and southerners as a new manifestation of the Kansas antislavery soldiers. In Pennsylvania, the *Columbia Democrat* connected the name "Wide Awake" to John Brown's Ossawatomie soldiers and remarked that "under this disguise the Abolitionists of the North are at this moment completely organized as *a military body of men.*" The *New York Herald* called the Wide Awakes Lincoln's abolitionist "posse comitatus." However, while Wide Awake members did organize to protect Republican interests before the November 1860 election, they did not – despite Democratic and southern intimations – plan to invade the South.[12]

As the Wide Awakes created a defiant and forceful Republican Party – one willing to fight in the streets for Republicanism – the Democrats, who represented the sole national political party, began to fall apart. In the summer of 1860, leading Democrat Stephen Douglas refused to endorse an explicitly proslavery platform. He chose instead to sustain the same principles on which James Buchanan had won. The so-called Cincinnati Platform of 1856 upheld the "popular will," limited the powers of the federal government, and refused Congressional authority over slavery. Senator Jefferson Davis of Mississippi believed it was "a cordial approval of all who believe these United States to be, what their very name imports, a union of States, equal, sovereign, and endowed in all respects with equal rights." The platform did not satisfy the many southerners who sought a more strident position on the "cardinal principles on the subject of slavery in the Territories." These men soon designed a Democratic platform of their own.[13]

On paper, the two Democratic codes appear nothing more than a game of semantics. Following on the Dred Scott decision to which each side was pledged, slavery was protected. But politics is just as much about personality and appearance as actual creed. Fifty delegates stormed out of

137

the Democratic convention in a dramatic, staged event. In the end, two distinct Democratic caucuses selected two sets of candidates: the southern Democratic ticket was headed by John Breckinridge, Buchanan's vice-president; the Democratic or northern Democratic ticket was led by Stephen Douglas.[14]

"No person can fairly contend that either assemblage ... at the time the nominations were made was a Democratic National Convention," declared President Buchanan on his party's woes. Tennessean James B. Lamb said, "I am entirely at a loss – clear out to Sea – in politics – I don't even know what *democrat* means now!" Despite the convulsions, many remained confident. Initially a Breckinridge advocate, Buchanan was critical of Douglas's popular sovereignty. It "alienated the South," he asserted. But soon the president started to support Douglas from behind the scenes. "I heartily desire his election," he wrote in a private and confidential letter in September 1860, "because it may be the means of defeating Lincoln."[15]

As confusing as the intra-party battles appeared, the reason for the divisive presidential contest was clear. "The issue before the country is the extinction of slavery," said the *Charleston Mercury*. The matter of slavery was a comprehensive one. It framed understandings of the past and linked to the future, a place where imperial visions of the North American continent buoyed a diverse set of individual and national dreams.

The 1860 election, at its core, was a referendum on the meaning of America (and the violence that sustained the nation). Was it, as candidate John Bell and the Constitutional Unionist Party suggested, a strict veneration for "THE CONSTITUTION OF THE COUNTRY, THE UNION OF THE STATES AND THE ENFORCEMENT OF THE LAWS?" The Constitutional Unionists, one newspaper noted, attempted "to ignore the existence of slavery." Or was the new America aligned with Stephen Douglas and the northern Democrats, who adhered to the Constitution, acknowledged the variety of opinions on slavery, but ultimately deferred to the Dred Scott case – "the decision of the Supreme Court of the United States upon these questions of Constitutional law."

Bell and Douglas presented the most obliging positions. The platform of the southern Democratic Party led by John Breckinridge, however, was more direct. It highlighted the "acquisition of the Island of Cuba" (where slaveholders looked to expand their economy), insisted that the rights "of person or property" cannot be "destroyed or impaired by Congressional or Territorial legislation," and denounced opposition to the Fugitive Slave Law as "hostile in character, subversive of the Constitution, and revolutionary in their effect." Breckinridge courted southern supporters with an "ultra principle on slavery," an idea for a nation in which White personal liberty and property, protected by state and national force, extended full sanction to human bondage (but not to freedom of speech or assembly, which they granted only to supporters of slavery).[16]

Abraham Lincoln and the Republicans suggested something altogether different. They quoted from the Declaration of Independence to state "That all men are created equal," maintained the "rights of the states ... to order and control [their] own domestic institutions," and, at the same time, upheld "that the normal condition of all the territory of the United States is that of freedom." On one issue Lincoln was sure: "For, whether we will or not, the question of Slavery is *the* question, the all absorbing topic of the day." Bombarded with the four positions during the campaigns, White male voters found their exasperation voiced by one New England newspaper on election day: "We are all sick of the slavery topic."[17]

The victory of Abraham Lincoln in November 1860 remains one of the great pivot points in White American national politics. A Democrat had filled thirteen of the previous fifteen presidential terms – a Republican would hold fourteen of the next twenty. Even more importantly, Lincoln, a northerner who represented northern interests, had captured the White House. "For sixty out of seventy-two years last past, the South has controlled our Government," announced a publication in the North. Why were southerners "entitled to this preponderance?" On November 7, 1860, the *Hartford Daily Courant* celebrated with the headline: "The Day of Jubilee Has Come! The Battle Fought and Victory Won! LINCOLN OUR NEXT PRESIDENT! Bring Out the Big Gun, Boys!" The article opened in a militant mode of salvation: "The Army of Free Men have pledged their standard upon the hilltop, and with their glorious leaders, LINCOLN and HAMLIN, at their head, say ... 'the day of your deliverance has come!'"[18]

The results confirmed what Lincoln suspected. "If the rotten democracy shall be beaten in 1860," he said about the Democratic Party, "it has to be done by the North." Lincoln gained nearly 40 percent of the popular and almost 60 percent of the electoral vote (he received 180 votes and needed 153 to win). The South, where Lincoln went unlisted on most ballots, provided the next president with no electoral support whatsoever. John Breckinridge captured the second most electoral votes with 72, while Stephen Douglas ended in an unusual situation. He collected about 30 percent of the popular vote, which placed him second to Lincoln, but stood fourth, last, in the electoral tally with only 12 votes. Lincoln's strength in states with the largest electoral share, New York (35 votes), Pennsylvania

139

(27), Ohio (23), Indiana (13), Massachusetts (13), and Illinois (11), proved insurmountable.[19]

The November election reverberated throughout the world, and many understood the Republican Party as far more committed to slave emancipation than its stated position. In France, the *Constitutionnel* declared that Americans had rejected slavery's legality throughout their country, while another journal celebrated "the abolition of slavery is a noble cause to defend and bring to a triumphant conclusion." *Le Progres,* the Haitian newspaper, called the American president-elect "the great Abolitionist." "The biggest things that are happening in the world today," Karl Marx wrote, "are on the one hand the movement of slaves in America ... and on the other the movement of the serfs in Russia." French politician Count Agenor de Gasparin agreed. "What an immense step America has just taken!" he said. "Between the presidency of Mr. Buchanan and that of Mr. Lincoln, there is the distance of social revolution."[20]

The Russian Baron de Stoeckl, who held that "religion and humanity condemn slavery," was more measured. He believed that American emancipation would take time. "To accomplish this end it is necessary to combine with intelligence adequate legal measures, proper timing, and a willingness to give up some property rights," he said. And not everyone who understood the American election as an abolitionist accomplishment viewed it in a positive light. "All over the world people believe that the abolitionists' only aim is to achieve the emancipation of the Negro," said the French geographer and anarchist Elisée Reclus. He believed White American antislavery, founded on a fear of Black labor, was driven by "hatred ... and not love of the black race."[21]

In the North, free Blacks were divided on the Republican Party. It is a party, said a letter in *Douglass' Monthly,* "who would wield the whole power of the Government to shoot down John Brown, and return the bondman to the hands of his oppressor." The violence of the federal state was the cornerstone of American racial injustice. Black activists doubted that this was something Lincoln could change. "The Republicans are for *white* reasons," said one skeptic. Thomas Hamilton, in the *Weekly Anglo-African,* chastised the party's conservative racial policies: "Their opposition to slavery means opposition to the black man – nothing else."[22]

H. Ford Douglas, however, who saw no "essential difference" between Stephen Douglas and Abraham Lincoln, nonetheless threw his support to the Republican. He said that Lincoln and his party displayed an element of antislavery principles, "and though the party will do nothing for freedom now, that element will increase." For his part, Frederick Douglass had applauded Lincoln's nomination. "He is a radical Republican," said the famed abolitionist and former slave. Yet the Republican Party platform disappointed him. Douglass wished for it to declare "'Death to Slavery,' instead of 'No more Slave States.'" Notably, however, Douglass changed course after the presidential victory. He subsequently challenged the description of Lincoln as an "Abolition President" and was certain that, after four years, the Republican would be known more for his "pro-slavery truckling, than for doing any anti-slavery work."[23]

Southern bondsmen, in recollections of 1860 colored by a post-emancipation glow, were more optimistic. "The slaves prayed to God for his success," recalled Thomas L. Johnson, who was born into Virginian slavery in 1836, "and they prayed very especially the night before the election. We knew he was in sympathy with the abolition of Slavery."[24]

Indeed, White southern alarm at the Republican presidential victory was instant. "The Northern people, in electing Mr. Lincoln," declared the New Orleans *Crescent*, "have perpetrated a deliberate, cold-blooded insult and outrage on the people of the slaveholding states." Such crisis rhetoric pervaded the South. "Reports of the election leave little doubt that the event you anticipated has occurred," Jefferson Davis wrote on November 10. "I doubt not that the Gov'r of Missi. has convoked the Legislature ... to decide upon the course which the State should adopt in the present emergency." Four days later, Baltimore's *Sun* reported that "the vital question now presented to American Patriots is how and in what manner can a constitutional Union be preserved?"[25]

Such actions and questions were not the normal response to an election – especially when most agreed that the election had proceeded "not by trick, or fraud, or violence; but by the fair, open, deliberate, constitutional suffrages of the People." Texas Governor Sam Houston offered a rare, moderating voice in the Deep South. "The election of a President in the mode pointed out by the Constitution is no just cause for revolution and a dissolution of the Union," he said. Many of Houston's compatriots, however, were unmoved by the lawfulness of the Republican win. "Shouts and cheering for a Southern Confederacy" rang throughout Charleston, while, in Kentucky, the cry was for "Secession or Abolition."[26]

Much like John Brown and the Radical Abolitionists who viewed slavery as a state of war, a group of southerners – the staunch secessionists – experienced Lincoln's election as a forthright attack. Branding Republicans as supporters of Black men and women, they quickly developed the epithet "Black Republican" to characterize their foes. In 1859, well before Lincoln's nomination, the Mississippi legislature, as well as the

Mississippi Democratic Party, declared that "the election of a Black Republican, on the avowed purposes of that organization," would be regarded "as a declaration of hostility." Democrats in Raleigh, North Carolina, agreed. They were "bitterly opposed" to "federal-ism," the strength and authority of the national government that imperiled the politics of localism, and "black republican-ism." "Let the South Arm!" declared an Alabama newspaper in anticipation of Lincoln's success. "*Every one who can point a shotgun or revolver should have one.*" In Georgia, Governor Joseph E. Brown requested from his legislature an immediate state convention, a one-million-dollar war chest, and "an official call to war." "A convention of the seceding States ... should immediately be assembled," said a South Carolinian pamphlet. By March 4, when "Mr. Lincoln takes his seat in the Presidential chair," it declared, the South must have a fully functional government prepared "for our defence."[27]

The illegality of their arrangements did not sway southern leaders from embracing this path. Article I, Section 10, of the US Constitution reads, "No State shall, without the Consent of Congress ... keep troops, or Ships of War in time of Peace, enter into any Agreement or Compact with another State ... or engage in War unless actually invaded, or in such imminent Danger as will not admit of delay." Soon-to-be attorney-general, the Republican Edward Bates, explained the ramifications: "Armed resistance to a lawful President is but the beginning of civil war." Yet the South continued to race along the road to armed rebellion.[28]

A private Atlanta group was an early proponent of southern force. The so-called "Minute Men" in 1860 exploited the right to violent, White male self-determination as a legacy of the American Revolution. They resolved to "unite our [White] people as a band of brothers – in resistance to Northern aggression – and in defence of ourselves, our property [slaves], and our firesides against federal power wielded by a black republican administration." "The Republican party is a standing menace," said Jabez Curry, an Alabama Representative and owner of sixty-nine Black people. "Its success is a declaration of war against our property and the white race." Curry sanctioned pre-emptive acts. "The law justifies the taking of a life in advance of injury ... The like rule of self-preservation applies to a people endangered." To the most indignant of the southern states, there were two choices: a revolution through White male southern violence ("armed resistance by the South") or southern enslavement ("the more dreadful revolution incident to Southern submission").[29]

Indeed, Jabez Curry mourned Lincoln's success. "The recent election has consolidated and made permanent a political revolution, which has for several years been in process of establishment," he said, adding, "Did it never occur to such persons, that ... the Constitution is what the President and majority in Congress determine it to be?" Louisianan Senator Judah P. Benjamin likewise observed that "the difficulty seems to arise chiefly from a difference in our construction of the Constitution."[30]

The Constitution, of course, had not yet changed. With the power they had wielded for so long now curbed, southerners announced an unwilling-ness to play by the rules of White American government. They imagined a monolithic North bound to Republicanism, antislavery, and racial equal-ity. In so doing, they turned from potential allies – northern Democrats, whose own abiding racism led to a fear of emancipation, and Republican supporters who called for "Free Territories for free white men." Had the eleven southern states that formed the Confederacy remained in the Union, the Democrats would have retained control in the Senate and southerners would have continued to dominate the Supreme Court. Instead, southern enslavers staked their authority on the domestic and global influence of cotton (a product of slavery) and a belief in their inherent right to violence. They retaliated against a perceived northern attack because, within the culture of human property, slaveholders defined their liberty vis-à-vis the enslaved. And enslaved individuals in law (though less often in practice) could not strike back. Not only did southern enslavers believe themselves untouchable, they understood northern Yankees – and the slaves they were perceived as supporting – as mentally and physically weak.[31]

John B. Jones, a southern sympathizer who fled Philadelphia to Richmond at the outbreak of war, knew better. "It will be found that they will learn how to fight," he said of northerners in his diary, "and will not be afraid to fight." His assessment was correct. Wide Awake organizations were among the best prepared to feed a forceful, northern response. "We must foil the design of traitors," explained one Wide Awake advocate after Lincoln's election. "Your brother Wide-Awakes of Alleghany have already formed themselves into a military body – Will you imitate their example?"[32]

———————◆———————

President Buchanan guided the nation in the four months between Lincoln's election and inauguration. His presumption that disunion talk would subside was quickly proven wrong. On December 3, 1860, the presi-dent offered his first public response to the growing crisis. First, he con-demned the "long continued and intemperate interference of the northern people with the question of slavery." How, he wondered, could a White southern calm prevail when fears of "servile insurrections" abounded?

He then turned to the secessionists. "The election of any one of our fellow-citizens to the office of President does not of itself afford just cause for dissolving the Union."[33]

Buchanan explained that the United States of America "was intended to be perpetual" and that the national government "has at command a physical force for executing the powers committed to it." But he was torn. Natural laws, he said, which exist "independently of all constitutions," are vital to the American experiment. "The right of resistance on the part of the governed against the oppression of their government cannot be denied." He followed his reasoning to argue that secession was a "revolution," not "an inherent constitutional right." Buchanan, who denounced Black resistance as "servile insurrections," believed that White people had a natural right to overthrow an unjust government. He did acknowledge, though, that even White revolutionary action violates the law in force. "It may or may not be a justifiable revolution," the president said, "but still it is revolution."[34]

A man caught between his constitutional duties and the uproar from his southern constituents, Buchanan produced an awkward stance against secession. "Some overt and dangerous act on the part of the President elect," he said, must occur "before resorting to such a remedy." He assured southerners that the president was tasked with no more than to "execute the laws" and that, apart from the Missouri Compromise, no antislavery legisla-tion had ever been enacted. Buchanan scrutinized the Militia Acts of 1795 and 1807, which gave authority to the president to federalize and deploy the militia. They were enforceable "whenever the laws of the United States shall be opposed or the execution thereof obstructed, in any state, by combinations too powerful to be suppressed by the ordinary course of judicial proceedings." On the advice of Attorney-General Jeremiah Black, Buchanan argued for the use of force to defend federal property, such as forts or post offices.[35]

But then he undermined the use of national power in the case of secession. He said the absence of "judicial authority" in a seceded state prevented the government from implementing federal law with troops. Without functioning federal courts, the proper legal channels were not in place to sanction acts of federal agents. When the whole White population of a state supports lawlessness, Buchanan explained, there is no mechanism to return them to a lawful direction. Does the general government have the power to make war upon a state? he asked. "After much serious reflection, I have arrived at the conclusion that no such power has been delegated to Congress or to any other department of the federal government." "If we possessed this power," Buchanan said as he eviscerated the federal state of its recourse to physical force, "would it be wise to exercise it under existing circumstances?" He answered with a definitive "no." The foundation of the American union was "public opinion," which "can never be cemented by the blood of its citizens shed in civil war."[36]

Buchanan's judgement thus confirmed the fears of those who supported Article IV, Section 4 of the US Constitution at the Constitutional Convention. George Mason's 1787 alarm that the federal government would be "compelled to remain an inactive witness of its own destruction" had come to pass.[37]

As a solution, Buchanan offered a Constitutional amendment "defining the rights of the South in exact accordance with the decision of the Supreme Court." He believed in an America that would forever uphold slavery, sanctify popular sovereignty in its territories, and strictly enforce the fugitive slave law. So, in his first public response to the growing crisis, he affirmed the violence of the American state was not to be used against White, southern citizens. It was more appropriate to buttress the South's system of racialized slavery. Buchanan's dream of a White republic, which enslavers would enact in the Confederate States of America, was the fulfillment of the Dred Scott case: Black people could not be citizens of the United States and the national pledge to uphold slavery was eternal.[38]

According to the *Constitution*, published in Washington, DC, "The Message yesterday transmitted to Congress by Mr. Buchanan" was "the most important document emanating from the President of the United States since the formation of the Government." Other newspapers were less celebratory. "While the President presents an unanswerable argument against the right of a State to secede," said the *Sacramento Daily Union*, he claims that "the General Government possesses no constitutional right to use force to compel a State to remain." In Indiana, the *Vincennes Gazette* was more critical still. "The message we think is too much against secession to please traitors, and too little on the side of the Union to please patriots." Newspaper coverage throughout the nation tended to sustain this analysis. The *Portland Journal*, an antislavery paper, said "the North will never submit to being made slave-hunters" and was confident Buchanan's proposed amendment would "only increase and intensify the contest." The Kentucky antislavery editor and immediate emancipationist William S. Bailey agreed in a published letter, adding that the "slaveholding lords" were "aching for chastisement, and the President should not delay."[39]

The *Daily True Delta* in Louisiana presented the southern view. It accused the president of accepting influence from an "unprincipled herd of renegade abolitionists." His tactic to allow state secession and to control federal property in a seceded state, declared the *Macon Telegraph*, signified war: "The General Government will wait to be assailed." As this accusation of warmongering demonstrates, even the slightest assertion of federal authority from a pro-southern president was enough to affront southern leaders.[40]

The response to Buchanan's address was not just a matter of public debate, however. The Senate, too, debated the meaning of Buchanan's speech. Despite the president's refusal to act against seceding states, many southern senators found cause for complaint. North Carolinian Thomas Lanier Clingman compared the condition of the South under a Republican government to that of Ireland, "represented nominally, but really as powerless as if the semblance of representation was not given to it at all." "It is not, for example, merely that a dangerous man has been elected to the Presidency of the United States," he said, but that Lincoln was elected "*because he was known to be a dangerous man.*" Kentucky Senator John J. Crittenden, however, fought back, insisting that members of neither party in his home state would support Clingman's claim. He then homed in on Buchanan's speech. "There is no right to secede on the part of any State, (and I agree with him in that)," he said, but to claim "that the Union has no right to interpose any obstacles to its secession, seems to me to be altogether contradictory." Indeed, a Reuters telegram that arrived in London gave an inaccurate account of the reception of Buchanan's speech when it stated that "The Message is condemned by those of extreme opinions from both North and South." The president had managed to disappoint men in the North and South, but those like Crittenden were by no means extremists.[41]

Abraham Lincoln himself remained silent on Buchanan's December address. After his November victory, he devoted his time to the formation of a cabinet and selecting political appointments. In place of public remarks, speculation and rumor satisfied a widespread call for Lincoln's opinion. "Mr. Lincoln is a discreet gentleman, and keeps his own counsel," said British correspondent John J. Pettus. Pettus confidently predicted, however, that the next American president would wield with daring the violence of the American state. "He is more likely to re-enact the part of General Jackson than that of Mr. Buchanan." A Maryland paper, the *Easton Gazette*, reported on an enslaver's supposed conversation with the president-elect. Would Lincoln permit South Carolina to secede? "He replied that he would let her go if Congress did not pass a 'force bill.'" Would he abolish slavery? "He concluded by advising the Mississippian to purchase as many negroes as he needed; and expressed the opinion that, in twelve months, slave property would be worth more than it ever has been." Another popular anecdote had Lincoln declare, "any concession in the face of menace" is "the destruction of the government itself." Rumor had it, too, that he abhorred the idea of American democracy beginning to look like the "disorganized state of affairs in Mexico."[42]

From a historical perspective, the offer of a cabinet position to William Henry Seward on December 8, 1860, fills the void left by Lincoln's own silence on the matter. The position of secretary of state, which Seward held from 1861 to 1869, carried a stature in the nineteenth century that is largely lost today. Seward's placement was a clear sign of the new president's backbone: Lincoln had little intention to yield to slaveholder threats. In the spring of 1860, Seward had been the party's presumptive presidential nominee. But one reason Republicans had opted for Lincoln instead was Seward's radical, well-known stance against slavery. As New York governor in the 1840s, he had rejected Virginia's fugitive-slave extradition requests; as a senator in the 1850s, he formulated multiple attacks on slavery. Seward had even coined two of the era's most repeated antislavery catchphrases: "higher law," to indicate the natural and moral laws above the Constitution to which Americans were beholden, and "irrepressible conflict," to characterize the battle between freedom and slavery as inevitable.[43]

Seward represented, in the words of the *New York Times*, the very "incarnation of that hatred" of the South that elicited enslavers' "worst fears." In September 1860, Seward was in Madison, Wisconsin, where he spoke about the effects of the 1787 exclusion of slavery from the Northwest Territory. Looking at the growth and prosperity in the region, he wondered, how was such abundance possible? "The reason is a simple one," he said to listeners in the badger state. "Your soil had been never polluted by the footprints of a slave."[44]

Lincoln was on the record with a personal abhorrence of slavery. But he was aware that, as a peacetime president, he was powerless to directly affect slavery in the states. His was a problem faced by political abolitionists for decades. Slavery, a national concern, was governed as a domestic or local issue. To combat this problem, Republican Party adherents developed two scenarios. The first offered a gradual end to slavery. In the 1850s, the likes of Charles Sumner, William Henry Seward, and Salmon P. Chase advanced the idea that slavery would end in the South just as it had in the North: through gradual, state-led emancipation. The Republicans adopted measures so that slave-state leaders would recognize the economic, political, and moral backwardness of their ways. A "cordon of freedom" – the code for surrounding slave states with free states and territories – would isolate slavery, expose it as unfeasible, and spur a southern antislavery awakening.[45]

Republicans' second scenario threatened a more direct method of ending slavery. Its basis was that, in times of war, the federal government assumes exceptional powers, among them the ability to emancipate slaves. John Quincy Adams is credited as the author of this approach. Adams had served as secretary of state during the aftermath of the War of 1812. At the time, American planters sought to retain some 3,600 slaves who had fled to British forces – 300 of whom had served in the Royal Colonial Marines in the Chesapeake. The dispute dragged on until 1818, when the Russian czar stepped in to arbitrate. He decided the Americans were due fair compensation from the British for slaves who were "carried away." Whether the term applied to slaves who sought British protection remained unclear.[46]

Adams's experience with this sort of military emancipation no doubt shaped his speeches in the House of Representatives in the 1830s. Infuriated by the gag rule passed in 1836 to quell Congressional discussion of slavery, Adams looked for opportunities to speak out on the topic. One chance arose on May 26, 1836, when the House discussed the distribution of rations to refugees of the recent Seminole Indian war. He began with an outline of how the British emancipated American slaves in the 1810s. "The war power of Congress over the institution of slavery in the States is far more extensive," he explained. Imagine, for example, a situation in which the national government needed "*to suppress a servile insurrection.*" There might be the need for the "master of the slave to recognize emancipation" in a treaty that brings about national peace. "From the instant your slaveholding States become the theatre of a war, *civil, servile, or foreign war*," he warned White southerners, "from that instant the war powers of Congress extend to interference with the institution of slavery."[47]

In 1859, Democrat Andrew Johnson pointed to Adams's ideas on immediate, military emancipation as legitimating southern fear of the Republican Party. "What are we to infer from teachings like these?" he asked. What will happen when the "Federal Government is called upon to interfere" and would "emancipate all your slaves?" Adams had constructed an end run around slavery, localism, and constitutional qualms. Slavery may have been a state institution, but send in federal troops and human enslavement is suddenly a national concern. His claim was brilliant, and almost certain to ensure that any serious opponent of slavery would find the logic of federal military action irresistible. Yet it did provide proslavery supporters with even more reason to resist Republican federal authority.[48]

Secessionists attacked early and often to appropriate weapons and key federal military sites. United States secretary of war, the Virginian John B. Floyd, sold ten thousand smoothbore muskets to South Carolina in a secret exchange. These proceedings started on November 5, 1860, which was just before the presidential election. Then, on December 20, White politicians in South Carolina seceded from the United States. "Prescribing to none, she will be dictated to by none willing for peace," explained the *Charleston Mercury*; "she is ready for war." In January 1861, the *New York Times* printed a list of federal sea vessels confiscated by determined southerners. Off the Florida coast at St. Augustine, for instance, the schooner *Dana* "was reported *seized*." Governors in Alabama, Georgia, and Florida ordered the takeover of federal arsenals and forts in their states during the first week of the New Year. Some of this appropriation transpired even before a state's official declaration of secession.[49]

The antagonistic climate in the South pushed President Buchanan past his southern sympathies. He authorized the resupply of Fort Sumter in Charleston and agreed that Major Robert Anderson, the fort's commander, was entitled to return hostile fire. "The right and the duty to use military force defensively against those who resist," said Buchanan in a special message to Congress on January 8, 1861, "is clear and undeniable." But the letter that explained the president's decision failed to reach Anderson in time. Shots rang out across Charleston Bay early on January 9, 1861. The federal resupply ship, *The Star of the West*, fled while the guns at Fort Sumter stayed silent.[50]

The secessionist moment transformed the dialogue of American violence. In the election cycle, debate had focused on slavery, popular sovereignty, and US territories. By early 1861, the discussion tended toward constitutional concerns: the validity and structure of American government. Moderate voices were soon drowned out. Sectionalism, some southerners argued, revoked the promise of White representation – the promise of consent affixed to the national democratic process. The Republican Party "has no foothold or resting place south of a geographical line," said the South Carolinian enslaver William Dennison Porter. Void of a governmental voice, southern leaders felt they had a duty to secede. Once again, the right of White self-determination ruled the day. But to arrive at this point, politicians in the South flaunted an inverted reasoning. They had banned the Republican Party from most southern states, such that they could now argue that it was not a true, national party. The Republican Party and its Republican president thus could not represent the South. Makers of their own crisis, White southern leaders found their solution in secession. By the end of February, six additional states of the lower South abandoned the federal union.[51]

The most widespread explanation for secession rested on the protection of slavery through the principle of states' rights, a position that had percolated throughout the country for years. Where British North America had been a collection of independent and distinct colonies, they were brought together in part to consolidate and concentrate the violence of the central state. Now, more than six decades later, the states were being torn apart to disperse that strength once again.[52]

Article VI of the 1783 Treaty of Paris was among the first national documents to expose the state-centric tensions bubbling beneath the surface of the United States. It required that no state take legal action against British loyalists – a statute that most states ignored in a belief that it unduly impaired their authority. The confiscation of loyalist property in New York, for example, only intensified after the treaty went into effect. Then, in 1798, the Kentucky legislature passed resolutions on the primacy of the state in respect to the nation. "The several States composing the United States of America," read one resolve penned by Thomas Jefferson, "are not united on the principle of unlimited submission to their general government." Each state "has an equal right to judge for itself" the extent of any infraction as well as the "mode and measure of redress." Here was born the states' rights theory, which placed ultimate American sovereignty in the states. By 1822, slavery apologist Edwin C. Holland had cause to characterize the United States as "an immense empire, composed of different sovereignties."[53]

States' rights thinking is what led to the Nullification Crisis in 1832. South Carolina leaders disagreed with federal protective tariffs placed on manufactured goods. In their Ordinance of Nullification, passed on November 24, the state's representatives "nullified" not only the tariff, but any "application of force by the federal government." In the greatest internal (White) challenge to the violence of the national state since the whiskey rebels in 1794, President Andrew Jackson responded with the Force Bill. Approved by Congress on March 2, 1833, the bill authorized using military force to induce compliance with federal law. But Senator Henry Clay made moot the legislation by working on a compromise tariff to avoid a military showdown.[54]

Years later, Union General Winfield Scott called the peaceful end to nullification a mistake. South Carolina's states' rights position in 1832 was treason, he declared, and Americans had failed to learn "a most needful lesson – that *playing treason is a dangerous game!*" He recognized that federal force was constructive only to the extent that it was feared; and fear was cultivated through the demonstration of federal force.[55]

Yet southerners were not the only White leaders to employ the states' rights doctrine. Supreme Court Justice Joseph Story took the crisis of nullification to heart. His 1834 *Commentaries on the Conflict of Laws* stated that "no [White] people are found to enforce, or hold valid in their courts of justice any contract, which is injurious to their public rights, or offends their morals, or contravenes their policy, or violates a public law." In 1836, a Massachusetts court, influenced by Story's work, freed an enslaved young woman named Med, whose enslaver had brought her into the state. Since Massachusetts did not recognize a right to property in individuals, the court decided Med was free.[56]

States' rights would remain a potent form of local resistance to national authority throughout the antebellum period. In the 1840s, southern theorists such as slaveholder Abel P. Upshur, President Tyler's secretary of state, maintained the doctrine of states' rights. In the wake of British emancipation in 1834, Upshur had panicked that the Crown wished to set free slaves worldwide. In subsequent years, he maintained that the preamble of the Constitution ("We, the people of the United States") actually meant "we, the people of the states united." He (correctly) imagined that "the most direct conflict between the state and federal governments" would arise over slavery. "The question whether the act of congress forbidding slavery, or the laws and constitution of the state allowing it, should prevail," he suggested, would sit at the crux of the dispute. As a supporter of states' sovereignty, the answer was clear: the two sides "could not be convened before the supreme court"; states wielded definitive authority.[57]

In the 1850s, southern Democrats and their northern advocates transformed states' rights – and its equivalent for American territories, popular sovereignty – into a central principle of American political and economic thought. As they argued for an omnipotent localism within the United States, one that included a state supremacy to deploy violence, these Democrats marked a clear aversion to political compromise. They proposed that personal and financial well-being was tied not to the federal promotion and protection of wage labor, but to the promotion and protection of a White republic. A nation that recognized White, southern supremacy, that protected property in human slaves, and that promoted free markets, was a federal state that could satisfy southern demands. Where Republicans placed a limit on market relations in a burgeoning industrial society (as Lincoln noted, Republicans put "the man before the dollar"), Democrats embraced the market over the man and the federal government. It was in enslavers' interest to obliterate political restraint upon their economic activity. States' rights and popular sovereignty weakened the power of the federal state and made it more flexible to their needs.[58]

Jefferson Davis was among the strongest proponents of states' rights in the secession crisis. "All that is not granted in the Constitution belongs to the States; and nothing but what is granted in the Constitution belongs to the Federal Government." Davis's logic was correct. The Tenth Amendment cedes "to the States respectively, or to the people" powers that are not specified, and secession went unmentioned in the Constitution. But the Constitution also grants the federal government the power to "suppress insurrections and repel invasions," an authority that Congress in 1795 extended to times when the laws of the United States were opposed or obstructed. Secession was not mentioned by name in the Constitution, but by deed it was illegal. Yet this truth did not stop some, like Louis T. Wigfall, from making bold declarations. "The right of secession," said the Texan, is "a legal, peaceable, constitutional right, *as if it had been contained in the body of the Constitution itself.*" Davis, Wigfall, and other secessionists discounted the authority granted to the national government – and southern actions often violated federal law.[59]

St. George Tucker, a Virginia law professor, gradual emancipationist, and enslaver, wrote in his 1803 classic that southern states benefited most from federal protection. The South was prone to slave insurrections, he said, addressing the divide over racial violence in the United States. He therefore argued that southern Whites "ought to be particularly tenacious of a constitution from which they may derive such assistance in the most critical periods." To Tucker, the Constitution was grounded in proslavery protections. And several planters in 1860 still believed this to be true. South Carolinian James Chesnut, Sr., for example, credited American slavery's success to "the aid and countenance of the whole United States." But generations of southern White Americans had also learned something different. Robert E. Lee pointed to the work of William Rawle, *A View of the Constitution of the United States* (1829). It was required (and, for a national military academy, subversive) reading at West Point. In a chapter on the "permanence" of the United States, Rawle acknowledged that "the paternal power of the Union" could "*repress domestic violence.*" Such power was offset, he argued, by state authorities who forever had the option to "continue" or "wholly withdraw from the Union." The White right to violent self-determination, a foundation of liberal life in America, was repackaged by White state politicians into states' rights and secession.[60]

Article IV, Section 4 of the US Constitution and Article 1, Section 8 (which led to the Militia Acts) are the passages that provide for national assistance in the face of domestic unrest. In 1861, these fell prey to a changed political current. Where Buchanan had said that the Constitution was useless when the White leadership of an entire state rebelled, Lincoln said the opposite. In July, the new president pointed to the constitutional clauses as justification to deploy national troops against the slaveholder uprising. These contrary readings of the Constitution measure the scope of the political divide. It mattered whether the president was a Democrat or a Republican. It mattered whether the government supported or opposed slavery. And it mattered because the slavery question now triggered the means to deploy violence that had been written into the Constitution.[61]

That said, the Republican administration was also developing a means to downplay the centrality of slavery in their deployment of national troops. On April 1, 1861, William Henry Seward issued a memorandum to the president suggesting that Lincoln demand "satisfactory explanations" from Spain and France. Their interference in Mexico, a country on the verge of its own civil upheaval, Seward said, was worthy of an international war declared by America. This proposition has earned Seward's piece the title of the April Fool's Day Memorandum. But he was serious. A foreign war, Seward undoubtedly believed, would unite White Americans on the home front. Indeed, there was nothing insincere about the memo. Seward was simply just as prone to fantastic outbursts as he was to brilliant insight. On the domestic disaster faced by Lincoln, he advised more steadily: "*Change the question before the Public from one upon Slavery, or about Slavery, for a question upon Union or Disunion.*" The result, he claimed, would shift talk from a partisan concern – the Republican Party's stance against slavery – to the more agreeable ideas of "*Patriotism or Union.*" Toward this end, Seward recommended the abandonment of Fort Sumter, which stood in the rabid proslavery state of South Carolina. The reinforcement of other southern federal sites under national control better suited his play for the patriotic position.[62]

Lincoln's written response, the substance of which was likely delivered in conversation, displayed that the two had an ongoing dispute. "Again," Lincoln wrote, "I do not perceive how the reinforcement of Fort Sumpter [*sic*] would be done on a slavery, or party issue." Clearly, the men agreed that the federal government was endowed with a right to act with force; they appear, at first glance, to joust simply over how to justify its use. Lincoln took a legalistic tone and recalled his recent inaugural address:

"The power confided to me will be used to hold, occupy and possess the property and places belonging to the government." But, ultimately, the two men pushed for the same thing. Lincoln's argument, based on power and constitutionalism, was one aimed at patriotism and unity. Seward merely reformulated Lincoln's stilted tone and translated it for widespread public use: the federal government had the right to deploy state violence in defensive situations.[63]

The success of the Lincoln administration in turning the dialogue of state violence away from slavery was apparent in spring 1861. In the wake of the April 12 fall of Fort Sumter, Ulysses S. Grant wrote to the slaveholder and Democrat Frederick Dent, his father-in-law. "I know it is hard for men to apparently work with the Republican party but now all party distinctions should be lost sight of and evry true patriot be for maintaining the integrity of the glorious old *Stars & Stripes*, the Constitution, and the Union." On July 4, President Lincoln affirmed this idea in a message to Congress, echoing a central concern of the men at the Constitutional Convention: "Must a government, of necessity, be too strong for the liberties of its own people, or too weak to maintain its own existence?" Lincoln was confident that the question at hand was "whether a constitutional republic, or a democracy – a government of the people, by the same people – can, or cannot, maintain its territorial integrity, against its own domestic foes." The battle, to borrow from Seward's memorandum, was "a question upon *Union or Disunion*." He then requested an army of 400,000 men and a war chest of $400 million.[64]

Lincoln and the Republicans had good legal and political reason to distance their war resolve from slavery. The authority for federal force was intimately linked to domestic disturbance and public safety – which included slave insurrection, not slave emancipation. Beyond legality, though, stood a need to secure volunteers for the Union Army, as well as the support of the slave states of Delaware, Kentucky, Maryland, and Missouri. In shifting focus, the federal government dictated a story of violence aimed to attract the most support. White northern racism paired better with patriotic Unionism than antislavery. Indeed, the slave states that had not joined the Confederacy continually looked for the constitutional protection of slavery as a condition of their loyalty to the Union.

Because of their attack on the Union – and because secession was the extreme result of popular sovereignty and states' rights – Lincoln maintained that White southerners required an education through violence. "Such will be a great lesson of peace," he explained. "Teaching men that what they cannot take by an election, neither can they take by a war – teaching all the folly of being the beginners of a war." In the North, many took the Lincoln administration's call for violence and Unionism to heart. One US colonel explained to a southern foe, "we have come down here to teach you the Republic is a success!" In New England, James Russell Lowell echoed the emphasis on education. "It is the very life of the nation that is at stake," he said. "The lesson we have to teach them now is, that we are thoroughly and terribly in earnest." Federal force was instructive, and many northerners stood as willing educationalists. With only 35 percent of the school-aged, free population of the South enrolled in school – and with the average number of southern school days in a year at eighty – the rhetoric of learning had a particular resonance. The comparable figures for the North were 72 percent and 135.[65]

While its domestic announcements centered on retaining the Union, the Lincoln administration was more transparent about the Civil War in foreign lands. In 1862, the US ambassador Henry S. Sanford met with Belgian Prime Minister Charles Rogier. "The war, I went on to say," Sanford reported of his conversation, "had its origin in the ambition of a few politicians who had sought to build up a slave empire for the benefit of themselves and a small oligarchy of slaveholders, and for the overthrow of liberal institutions and universal suffrage." Sanford ignored the fact that American liberal institutions upheld racial difference and human enslavement, as well as the fact that a so-called "universal suffrage" allowed only White men to vote. Instead, he begged for patience and support from European leaders. While Europe witnessed economic hardship due in part to the sudden end of cotton exports from the American South, the Europeans had also "reproached" Americans "with the crime of slavery, and urged upon us its abolition." Sanford thus proceeded with prudence. "Our present care," he said, "was to restore the authority of the laws [the Union]; if slavery, the cause of it, was destroyed in the process, it would be for us to provide as we could for that event."[66]

Rogier, however, was suspicious about the administration's ability to follow through on this promise. "The condition of the Negro, if free," he said, "did not seem to be much ameliorated in the northern States, where he was not tolerated as an equal." He asked, "what would be done with the slaves if emancipated?" Sanford's reply illuminates the grip of hostile racial difference on White American political society. He acknowledged that there "certainly was a prejudice in the United States against the African race," and, as if to prove that statement, he added, "certainly the negroes, a tropical race, had not thriven nor could thrive in the temperate regions of the north." Reflecting a popular climate theory of race, Sanford argued that Whites could not work the crops of the South and "that the negro, or some

155

other tropical race, would always be needed there to cultivate the free cotton and rice." In his comments on climate and work, the American ambassador revealed a racial capitalist mindset committed to making Black and Brown bodies work in hot and humid fields. From this viewpoint, the violence of the federal state in the Civil War, often referred to as a force for "freedom," was committed to a project of racial hierarchy and degradation.[67]

Meanwhile, Congress began to put things in order, debating over the enduring issues of standing armies, soldiers' pay, and lengths of enlistment. On August 5, 1861, the punishment of flogging, which summoned visions of planters lording over slaves, was abolished in the Union Army. On the next day, the government took its first step toward acknowledging that the war was over slavery. "An Act to Confiscate Property Used for Insurrectionary Purposes" stated that enslavers who used their slaves in work to support the Confederate military would forever forfeit their "claim to such labor." Leaders in the United States government decided that the violence of the central state was more legitimate than that of its constituent parts. This represented a thorough rejection of popular sovereignty and states' rights.[68]

Of course, discussions about the origins and legality of violent action often meant little to the soldiers in a war that cost upwards of 740,000 lives. The ideological battles over democracy, wage labor, and slavery wrought consequences that were horrific and clear. A Confederate surgeon reported on a battle in which the "Seventh Iowa was almost annihilated." "In the woods and in the field," he wrote, "the dead were so thick that it required careful riding to keep from tramping their bodies." He said that "the wounded men groaned and moaned, yelled and shrieked with pain." One young soldier whom he knew, James Walker, appeared "shot through the rectum." In other battles, soldiers remembered comrades "all torn to pieces leaving nothing but their heads or their boots." "*Strings of flesh*" hung from trees. When a six-pound ball tore through a pack of five rebels, a Union corporal reported, "one had been cut in two at the bowels and nothing held the carcass together but the spine."[69]

Violence, however conceived on a theoretical level, was a great equalizer. Lundsford P. Yandell, the Kentucky slave-owner, noted in November 1861: "There is a terrible sameness in the appearance of all the dead men I have ever seen."[70]

7

EMANCIPATION'S FURY

In the Civil War, the federal government eventually looked to excise human enslavement – a central political, economic, and social structure – from the nation. The result brought the most significant change in state violence in the history of the United States. Forged by hundreds of thousands of fugitive slaves, the path to freedom sought to resolve the tensions of a society built on enslaved and free labor as well as the racial hostilities embedded in these types of labor. The transition to a state that supported the formerly enslaved, though, was a slow, tortuous, and ultimately incomplete journey.

The Civil War was a revolution that addressed the problem of evil (how to respond to those who refuse to peaceably dismantle an unjust system) and disentangled a nation entrenched in war and industrial capitalism. This project nearly tore apart the American liberal democratic state. Even powerful individuals confident that people should never be categorized as property, such as Abraham Lincoln, struggled to find the legal mechanisms to achieve slave emancipation. Federal troops proved to be both part of the problem and central to the solution. But, as much as an expanded federal state – one that ended slavery and sought to protect African American rights – forged a new way forward, it strained against the systems of White supremacy layered into American politics and society.

The promises of the Emancipation Proclamation – slave freedom, Black male soldiering, a right to African American self-defense, and a federal state capable and willing to use physical force to uphold these pledges – were only realized in part. This chapter documents individual and collective resistance, a Union Army struggling to uphold the laws of slavery and freedom, and political leadership steering a government teetering toward justice.

◆

"We pass fort Sumter ½ past 4 o'clock," noted Robert Smalls. In the early hours of May 13, 1862, one year into the American Civil War, the twenty-three-year-old Smalls was sailing the steamship *Planter* toward Union blockaders outside Charleston harbor in South Carolina. As the one-time cotton transport passed the Confederate defense, sentinels saw no reason to sound an alarm. With Smalls at the wheel, the ship was steady – he had been navigating these waters for more than a decade. The *Planter*, employed by the Confederacy to run arms and munitions, was also known as a "guard-boat." "It is by no means unusual for the guard-boat to run out at that hour," said Confederate Major Alfred Rhett. But this trip was different.[1]

The *Planter*'s white officers, Captain C. J. Relyea, Mate Samuel H. Smith, and Engineer Zerich Pitcher, were not on the vessel. They had been negligent and left the ship unattended, defying the Confederate command that "officers and crews at the wharf" must remain "on board day and night." In their stead, Smalls cruised with an assortment of eight men, five women, and three children. Four of the men were from the *Planter*'s regular crew. Another was a crewman from a different ship. Hannah Jones Smalls, Robert's wife, and Elizabeth Lydia Smalls, his three-year-old daughter, were there too.[2]

"We arrive at blockade squadron at Charleston Bar at ¼ to 6," he reported. As they neared the USS *Onward*, the *Planter* men hurried to take down the Confederate flag and replace it with a white one. "We give three cheers for the Union," Smalls wrote in his log. The commander of the *Onward*, Lieutenant J. F. Nickels, steered toward the rebel ship. He brought his "port guns to bear" on Smalls's boat and prepared to fire. Then he saw the "white flag set at the fore." "I immediately boarded her," Nickels said, "hauled down the flag of truce, and hoisted the American ensign." "It was the steamer *Planter*," Nickels wrote to his superiors. "She was wholly manned by negroes, representing themselves to be slaves."[3]

For weeks, northern newspapers continued to reprint the *Planter* incident report from the commander of the South Atlantic Blockading Squadron, Samuel Francis Du Pont. "This man, Robert Smalls, is superior to any who has yet come into the lines, intelligent as many of them have been," he said. Readers, imbued with the American racial hierarchy, understood what Du Pont meant. "Many of them" were the Black slave fugitives who sought security and hoped for freedom within Union military lines. The first such individuals appeared in northern military records in March 1861. On March 11, seven days after Lincoln's inauguration, "a negro boy" canoed across the harbor from Charleston to Fort Sumter. "He was at once sent back," said Captain J. G. Foster. The next day, "four negroes (runaways)" arrived at Fort Pickens in Florida. They entertained "the idea," wrote First Lieutenant A. J. Slemmer, "that we were placed here to protect them and grant them freedom." More than a month before a full-blown conflict developed between the Union and Confederacy, Slemmer announced with pride that he "delivered them to the city marshal to be returned to their owners." At that point, the violence of the federal state was aligned with the proslavery Constitution and the Fugitive Slave Act.[4]

By the time of Du Pont's report in May 1862, however, the tens of thousands of escaped enslaved men and women had changed the tenor and tone of the war and the slavery debate. Union leaders would not return Smalls and his cohorts to their Confederate enslavers. "The bringing out of this steamer, under all the circumstances, would have done credit to anyone," said Du Pont. "I shall continue to employ Robert as my pilot on board the *Planter*." The most renowned naval man in the North, Flag-Officer Du Pont had captured Port Royal, South Carolina, in a major victory in November 1861. Now, he asked that the *Planter* be marked a prize of war with "this man Robert and his associates" as the claimants.[5]

"Gallant Act of a Negro Pilot" announced the *Chicago Tribune*, which, along with other newspapers, erased the possibility that the women on board had anything to do with the "daring" act. The *New York Herald* credited the capture of the *Planter* to the "heroism of nine colored men." Glory for the deed fell mainly on Robert Smalls, who was praised as the mastermind – although his name was often misspelled. "Robert Small, a Sable Hero," read Pennsylvania's *Union County Star*. In Washington, DC, the *Evening Star* linked Smalls to Lincoln and Republican antislavery violence: "A Wide-Awake Contraband Accomplishes a Coup d'Etat."[6]

"Contraband" was Union General Benjamin Butler's term for the scores of escaped slaves who sought refuge at Fort Monroe in Virginia. In spring 1861, Butler argued that if these Black individuals were property, as the Confederacy maintained, such property can be taken as contraband of war. The name "contraband" stuck to the slave fugitives, and the legal claim provided the logic for subsequent military guidelines. Yet Butler's policy failed to acknowledge a greater process underway. Emancipation wasn't an "appropriation" (a White-led process that removed enslaved property and labor from the Confederacy) but a *conversion* – a Black-led demand to transfer the violence of the federal state away from enslavers to the formerly enslaved. A complex progression, conversion demanded the recalibration of national and state regulation, legal procedure, and the custom and practice of American individuals, Black and White.[7]

With his bold stroke, Smalls explained to northerners and southerners what an antislavery renovation of the United States might look like. He had taken the *Planter*, a 300 ton, 147 foot long ship built of cedar and red oak, armed with a 32 pound gun "on pivot," "a fine 24 pounder

(a)   (b)

Fig. 7.1 "Robert Smalls, Captain of the Gun-Boat 'Planter'"; "The Gun-Boat 'Planter,' Run out of Charleston, SC by Robert Smalls, May, 1862." From the Wallach Division of Prints, the New York Public Library.

howitzer," and four other guns on deck as well as a "7-inch rifle." It had been anchored on the docks in front of the residence of Confederate Brigadier-General Roswell S. Ripley when Smalls started his perilous adventure. He sailed the ship to a different wharf to gather the others, including his family members, and then on to the Union blockade. The removal of the *Planter* and enslaved labor from Confederate control directly impeded the violence of a slaveholding society and bolstered that of its northern counterpart – a society in the midst of extricating itself from slavery (Fig. 7.1).[8]

In the history of human bondage in North America, countless enslaved men and women completed acts of what was often called self-emancipation. Examples include the likes of Ona Judge, Martha Washington's enslaved personal maid, who fled the presidential mansion in May 1796. In a more publicized event, George Latimer and his expectant wife escaped Virginia for Massachusetts in 1841. Newspapers called Latimer "the man who stole himself." Such "stealing" demonstrated the grip of slavery throughout the United States. If there was no such thing as a right to property in humankind – which is the basis for a society set on freedom – then the slave fugitive had nothing to steal.[9]

Robert Smalls explained his emancipation as a self-awarded, masculine deed in an open letter in 1862. "A party consisting of nine men, myself included," he said, "conferred freedom on ourselves, five women and three children." At the same time, Smalls understood freedom as a gift, part of an exchange. "To the government of the United States we gave the Planter."[10]

Congress acted quickly to make Smalls's trade complete. Though legislation that freed slaves at work in the Confederate military had been long since enacted, Representative Owen Lovejoy introduced a special bill to emancipate "Robert Small and his fellow passengers." On May 19, 1862, six days after the *Planter* left Charleston, Senator James Wilson Grimes, who sat on the Committee on Naval Affairs, followed Du Pont's suggestion to award prize compensation to the Smalls group. The Grimes bill passed "by unanimous consent" in the Senate and, a week later, by an overwhelming majority, 121–9, in the House. It provided one-half of the total value of the *Planter* to Smalls and his crew with one qualification: the secretary of the navy could invest the money on behalf of the Black recipients in "United States securities" until "such time" that he "may deem it expedient to pay . . . the principal sum."[11]

The government assessed the *Planter*'s total worth at $9,168. Of the half-sum awarded to the crew, the men involved received the greatest share. Robert Smalls, for example, earned $1,500, an impressive amount, while the two unmarried women in the group each secured $100. In its 1862 handling of the Smalls event, the federal administration thus simultaneously sanctioned the seizure of Confederate arms, legitimated personal freedom as secured by enslaved individuals, and enshrined gender inequity in the settlement. The federal government also capped Black empowerment from violent acts, a dominant American theme, in this case by consigning the economic bounty of the Smalls troupe to the hands of a White investment steward.[12]

Robert Smalls did not complain, however. Rather, in a move that anticipated the end of slaveholder authority, he used the monies to purchase his former enslaver's home in Beaufort. He also served the Union military as an informant and pilot, a rank denied to Blacks in the South, and welcomed his status as a northern hero. A week after the appropriation of the *Planter*, Du Pont, using "information derived chiefly from the contraband pilot, Robert Smalls," ordered Commander J. B. Marchand to reconnoiter the Stono River, which the Union navy soon secured. Then, in June 1862, Smalls piloted the *Planter* in raids up the North Edisto and Wadmalaw rivers. He visited New York City that fall. There, Smalls attended to the fundraising mission of Rev. Mansfield French, a man with government support to feed, house, and educate the thousands of Black individuals "reclaimed from Slavery, by the arms of the United States."[13]

At the Shiloh Church on Prince Street in New York, free Blacks celebrated Smalls for embodying two interrelated concepts: the loyalty of "the four millions of black Unionists" (the southern slaves), and the value and wisdom of "the doctrine of immediate emancipation." The congregants presented Smalls, who was in attendance with wife and child, a gold medal. On its face, the medal wore an image of "Charleston harbor, with the steamer *Planter* and Fort Sumter in the foreground, and the Union squadron in the distance." Indeed, view the case of Robert Smalls from almost any angle and, here, deep within the relationship between federal violence and the actions and desires of enslaved individuals, lies the answer to two important, interrelated questions posed by historians James McPherson and Steven Hahn: "Who freed the slaves?" and "Did we miss the greatest slave rebellion in modern history?"[14]

Notably, Charleston harbor had been an active site for self-emancipation from the start of the war. There was, of course, the young man who canoed to what he thought was freedom just days after Lincoln assumed office. But as the war developed, many more enslaved individuals in the area fled from bondage. In December 1861, nine Black men – six of whom were sailors – found refuge and work aboard the USS *Susquehanna*. And two weeks before Smalls ran off with the *Planter*, Gabriel, an experienced boat pilot and enslaved man, stole a small barge from General Ripley and led fourteen fugitives to the USS *Bienville*.[15]

If many White northerners were hesitant to acknowledge such events as rightful flights to freedom, southerners were swift and clear in stating their disapprobation. "This gives Robert and every traitor, black and white, the right to confiscate vessels and slaves," complained a Georgia newspaper. "We soon expect to hear of Negro Congressmen in Washington." And indeed, between 1874 and 1886, Robert Smalls served five terms in the House of Representatives.[16]

When Smalls escaped with a warship – a direct blow to his Confederate masters – he laid to rest questions on the worth of self-emancipation. In Congress and the media, Smalls's feat was compared to that of William Tillman, a free Black man who had been celebrated in the summer of 1861. Tillman served as the cook for the northern merchant ship *S.J. Waring*, which was captured by a Confederate privateer on July 9. As the ship sailed under a Confederate prize crew toward Charleston, Tillman killed three of the five sleeping prize crew with an axe. He forced the remaining two to sail the ship to New York. One year later, Smalls was seen as the enslaved version of Tillman. "The two most desperate and gallant achievements of the war," announced the *Cass County Republican* in Michigan, "are those of the negro who recaptured a vessel taken by a Confederate cruiser, killing the prize crew; and the running of the steamboat planter out of Charleston harbor." Despite the history of self-emancipation in South Carolina during the opening years of the war, escaping from bondage was not enough. For Whites in the North, it took audacity and force to make Black freedom legitimate. Of this, the *Daily Nashville Union* was sure: "The first sign of slaves helping themselves is the running away of Robert Small with the steamer Planter from Charleston."[17]

Slaves had been helping themselves and the cause of freedom since the start of the conflict. But a White, northern dialogue centered on the loyalty, trustworthiness, and intellectual capabilities of Black men and women constantly raised barriers. Emancipation on this front was more about White national values – how freed Black Americans would enhance or diminish the White experience in the United States – and less about the needs of enslaved individuals or a shared humanity. Union records are replete with examples, particularly those that equated slave fidelity with exchanges of knowledge and labor. This dynamic played out, for example, on August 6, 1861, when the commander of the USS *Penguin* saw four fugitive men in a small boat off the North Carolina coast. "I took them on board; found them intelligent; they gave me useful information." Similarly, in November of that year, Commander Drayton reported that the slaves "assisted us voluntarily wherever we wanted their aid." "I overheard one of them say that it was but fair that they should do so for us, as we were working for them." A naval secretary for the North Carolina expedition, Henry Van Brunt, noted in early 1862 that he had obtained "much local information . . . from negro Ben and his brother, escaped slaves from Roanoke Island." And in a deposition, Northern General James Blair Steedman stated that "most of the information we received while the army was in Mississippi, Alabama, and Tennessee came from negroes." He added, "I think nineteen out of twenty of the slaves of the disloyal states are friendly to the Union cause."[18]

As northern Whites looked for signs of merit among slave fugitives, Black individuals shed the burden of proof to claim for something far more radical: that the violence of the United States stand by their side. As a result, whenever slaves discovered the Union military, they expected security and safety. It was a claim made by the vast number of slave fugitives who crossed over to Union lines in addition to being made by word. For example, on August 12, 1861, John Smith, Prophet Washington, Silas Smith, and Iris and Catherine Grevins came alongside the USS *Minnesota* in a "small, open boat." They demanded "food and protection." Men in the Union squadron that passed Beaufort, South Carolina, saw "great numbers" of slaves who "came down to the shore with bundles in their hands, as expecting to be taken off." Captain Rufus Saxton relayed from Port Royal that "contraband negroes are coming in great numbers." "Near 400 slaves came down to the steamers and were taken aboard," said the commander of the USS *Albatross*. Indeed, General Grant reported in 1862 that "Negroes [were] coming in by wagon loads."[19]

In New Orleans, General Butler found the flow of slaves overwhelming. "They are now coming in by hundreds, say thousands, almost daily." And when the Union took control of the St. John's River and Jacksonville in Florida, S. W. Preston noted that "the most tangible result of this movement is that upward of 2,000 negroes from the territory adjacent to the river have sought the protections of our arms." Enslaved individuals analyzed the role of federal violence, and if it stood against southern enslavers, many believed it must be on the side of the enslaved.[20]

The key role of the military in emancipation is seen in the interaction between slave fugitives and Union authorities – a dynamic featured in a racist lampoon of Robert Smalls. "What, steal a steamer and four cannon, and a full complement of rebel flags, and a valuable $2,000 nigger, (that's Robert himself,) and a whole black crew, fireman, cook and cabin-boy, with five wenches and three children, altogether a good $10,000 worth of nigger property?" No "federal officers can countenance such acts." But, of course, federal officers did. For if the Union military had failed to support slave fugitives, as the article continued, "Dupont sends the black rascal and his stolen property straight back to Gen. Ripley."[21]

Though the half a million Blacks who fled enslavement during the war could not end the system of slavery by themselves, they were essential to its abolition. If slaves were content in their circumstance, as their enslavers maintained, then the moral foundation of the antislavery position was false. The men, women, and children who risked their lives to escape taught White leaders two lessons: first, the inhumanity of enslavement; second, that the federal state was the only possible guarantor of universal emancipation during the war. This was true no matter how many enslaved men and women prayed "constantly for the 'day of their deliverance'" (in the words of Robert Smalls) or ran away.[22]

When asked about emancipation and freedom in an interview, nine Georgia freedmen liberated in the war sustained the argument that slave emancipation needed the Union military. For example, fifty-two-year-old James Hill was a Savannah slave "up to the time the Union army come in." His answer, that the slaves had been "freed by the Union Army," articulates an understanding of the structure and flow of government power and violence in American life. It marks the evolution of federal force as pivotal to American emancipation. The simple scholarly question "who freed the slaves?" demands a simple answer – one that may ignore the centrality of enslaved persons to their own freedom. And here the answer seems to be: the men of the Union Army. Indeed, January 1, 1863 – when Abraham Lincoln issued the Emancipation Proclamation – marks the first time in US history when the United States military backed the interests of the enslaved over those of enslavers. To this day, it represents the greatest shift in the domestic use and formation of federal force. A more complex answer, however, acknowledges that this shift in federal force would not have arrived without the demands of freedom being made by the enslaved. But, ultimately, before addressing the full scope of factors involved in slave freedom, more attention needs to be paid to how it came about that the US military transformed into a liberating force.[23]

At the start of the Civil War, Union leaders were far from being the defenders of freedom mythologized by later generations. True, slavery in the North had been abolished. But the measured emancipation processes of the northern states, which stretched the end of slavery in the region over several decades, exposed the power of human bondage in national life. Gradual emancipation valued White enslaver economics and tradition over human dignity. It accepted the idea of human property even when holding such property was seen as cruel and inhumane. Connecticut's 1784 Gradual Emancipation Act, for instance, freed the state's slaves born after March 1, 1784, but only when said individuals reached the age of twenty-five. From the view of northern slaves unaffected by these statutes (those born before March 1, 1784, in Connecticut), such acts brought "gradual abolition" rather than emancipation.[24]

And gradualist legislation did nothing to break the intricate social and economic web that bound the North to the robust slave system in the South. Through the first six decades of the nineteenth century, northern shipbuilders, insurers, manufacturers, banks, universities, and more prospered from the enslavement of Black individuals throughout the Americas. When Republican Party advocates like Charles Sumner argued in the 1850s that freedom was a national disposition, they spoke of the future. The Civil War did not remake the South in a northern image; it remade the whole – transforming a slave society into a society without slaves.[25]

When southerners threatened secession before the war, Republicans proposed the use of military powers to sidestep the federal government's inability to affect slavery in American states. However, the White southern rebellion forged a political landscape hostile to such direct antislavery effort. In 1861 and 1862, the loyalty of the so-called border states was at stake. Delaware, Maryland, Missouri, and Kentucky, all slave states, remained in the Union. Many, including the president, believed the North would lose the war without them. In a war against a brazen slave-holder alliance, the United States government was pledged to uphold slavery so as not to fall apart altogether. Ten days after the southern attack on Fort Sumter, Union General Benjamin Butler thus tendered troops to Maryland enslavers distressed over the possibility of "an insurrection of the negro population." We will "with an iron hand crush any attempt at [slave] insurrection," said General George B. McClellan.[26]

Four weeks later, though, the same General Butler, now in the seceded state of Virginia, welcomed the contrabands who fled to his camp. Such was the push and pull of slavery and freedom in the United States. While military leaders like Butler, General Harney, and General Sherman pacified border state leaders with federal slavery protections, others in the Union worked on antislavery measures. Congressional Republicans approved the emancipation of slaves at work for the Confederate military (August 1861), banned army men from returning fugitive slaves (March 1862), abolished slavery in Washington, DC (April 1862), and abolished slavery in American territories (June 1862). President Lincoln, as the chief executive and commander-in-chief, supported the laws and regulations of both sides.[27]

Divergent policies around slavery impacted the military. One part of army leadership believed that the Civil War was waged in the most literal sense over a restoration of the United States. The slave society that existed in 1860, it supposed, could be brought back to life. Major-General John A. Dix was one such individual. In August 1861, Dix wrote to the secretary of war about three Black men, slave runaways, who arrived at Fort McHenry. The military installation was in the border state of Maryland. "I take it for granted they are fugitives," he said. "But I suppose the matter should be treated precisely as it would be if we were in the occupation of Virginia. We would not meddle with the slaves even of secessionists." A northern Democrat who briefly served as the secretary of the treasury for President Buchanan, Dix took the position of his political party into the field. Slaves had nothing to do with the war, he claimed, only the traitorous Confederate leaders were to blame. As for himself and his soldiers, "we have nothing to do with slaves." In an oft-repeated line, Dix declared that "we are neither negro-stealers nor negro-catchers, and that we should send them [the slaves] away if they came to us." The army was not a band of liberators ("negro-stealers") or fugitive policemen ("negro-catchers"). When two slave runaways navigated to the ship of Captain Henry Nones, Dix thus instructed Nones to "please deliver them up with the canoe and sail" to their owners. As thousands of fugitives flooded to Union positions, Dix believed that contrabands, or "Colored Refugees" as some Whites preferred to call the escaped slaves, did "nothing but consume rations." He called them "a useless burden."[28]

While Democrats such as Dix and McClellan banned fugitives from military lines and remained committed to the rights of enslavers, Republicans such as James Henry Lane, the Kansas senator and military leader, and General John C. Fremont, the 1856 presidential candidate, stood at the other extreme. When General Samuel Davis Sturgis questioned the purpose of Lane's Kansas Brigade in Missouri, Lane gave a two-faced reply. "My brigade is not here for the purpose of interfering in anywise with the institution of slavery," he said. "They shall not become negro thieves nor shall they be prostituted into negro-catchers." Lane then undercut his statement with an antislavery clarification: "The institution of slavery must take care of itself." Here Lane indicated that, when provided a safe space by the military, the slaves would run away. "In my opinion the institution [slavery]," he said, will "perish with the march of the Federal armies."[29]

Lane then argued that the military should take a more active stance to punish enslavers. "Confiscation of slaves and other property which can be made useful to the army should follow treason as the thunder peal follows the lightning flash." As Lane pushed for more comprehensive emancipation measures, he and his Congressional colleagues had already found a constitutional means to direct the violence of war. Article I, Section 8 of the Constitution authorizes Congress "to make rules concerning capture on land and water," and on August 6, 1861, the president approved "An Act to Confiscate Property Used for Insurrectionary Purposes." Known as the First Confiscation Act, the measure declared property deployed in the Confederate rebellion the "lawful subject of prize and capture wherever found." Its last section singled out slaves who worked "in or upon any fort, navy yard, dock, armory, ship, entrenchment, or in any military or naval service whatsoever, against the Government." An owner of such individuals, accordingly, "shall forfeit his claim to such labor." In other words, slave freedom was punishment for White Confederate actions. However, by acknowledging that slaveholders indeed had a "claim" on Black labor, the federal government still recognized slaves as human property.[30]

The fits and starts of the national state's evolution toward freedom can easily be seen in responses to the First Confiscation Act. General Fremont was annoyed by it and, when he proclaimed martial law in the border state of Missouri on August 30, he ignored its provisions. Looking to chasten Confederates, Fremont did so on merciless terms. "All persons who shall be taken with arms in their hands within these lines shall be tried by court-martial and if found guilty will be shot," he said. An equally strong measure followed. The slaves "of those who shall take up arms against the United States . . . are hereby declared free men."[31]

Southern and northern White leaders quickly realized that Fremont's Missouri orders represented emancipation more than confiscation. Confederate Secretary of War Judah P. Benjamin called Fremont's act "an invitation for the slaves to revolt" and named "the Yankee General" and Union leaders not only Confederate enemies, but "enemies of the human race" (by which he meant the White race). President Lincoln took note of Fremont's action, too, and disagreed with it. "Should you shoot a man according to the proclamation," he wrote to his general on September 2, "the Confederates would very certainly shoot our best men in their hands in retaliation, and so man for man indefinitely." Indeed, Fremont's declaration garnered this very response. Jeff Thompson, the Confederate commander for the Missouri State Guards, promised to "*hang, draw,* and *quarter* a minion of said Abraham Lincoln" for each man shot under Fremont's instructions.[32]

Lincoln was clearly upset. Still, he did not direct Fremont to rescind the proclamation in full. Though the Union president maintained that Fremont's proposed executions were abusive and would perpetuate a cycle of violence, he allowed for the courts martial and, on presidential approval, executions of Confederates. The commander-in-chief believed Fremont had acted within the lines of military authority on the issue of Confederate soldiers. But the emancipation of slaves was a different determination. Lincoln worried that Fremont's fiat was illegal and would alienate border state citizens. He ordered the general to alter the proclamation "to conform" to Congress's Confiscation Act. Fremont could not liberate all slaves held by Confederate masters. As dictated by the recent legislation, only slaves directly at work for the Confederate military could be freed.[33]

The president's instructions to Fremont closed with a revealing statement: "This letter is written in the spirit of caution and not of censure." Censure would have indicated antagonism in spirit and legal interpretation toward Fremont's emancipatory impulse. Lincoln chose caution, which he admitted responded to political realities. Freeing slaves "will alarm our Southern Union friends," he worried, "and turn them against us – perhaps ruin our rather fair prospect for Kentucky." On Lincoln's command, federal soldiers could execute Confederate sympathizers, but they could not yet unilaterally free Confederate sympathizers' slaves. This view resonated with certain members of Congress. "Our fathers intended us to hang" a Confederate rebel, said border state Representative John Menzies, "but not to take his property from his wife and minor children, if we take his life." In the United States, where liberal property protection was sacrosanct and Black individuals were property, the government could kill with much more ease than it could confiscate. Indeed, such thoughts would soon foster strong ties between industrialists and the national state.[34]

Fremont and his Confederate counterpart, Commander Thompson, did not engage in the promised rounds of prisoner executions. On September 12, though, when Fremont emancipated Frank Lewis and Hiram Reed, he made no effort to meet Lincoln's demand. Whether the two slaves worked for the Confederate military, as was required for their freedom under the confiscation law, we do not know. On record, however, Fremont freed them because their enslaver, Thomas L. Snead, was an active enemy of the Union government. While Lincoln did not reprimand the general, Fremont nonetheless lost his command – for incompetence, not insubordination or emancipation – in 1862.[35]

During the opening years of the war, the fluctuation of federal and state forces in relation to the enslaved made for confusing, perilous conditions. Black men and women in Missouri pushed back against General McClellan's attempt to evict them from his lines. In response to questions on their legal status, the contrabands "all stoutly asserted that they were free." After Colonel Ross removed Black persons from his camp, he soon noted, "Some have returned." At Fort Pickens in Florida, Colonel Harvey Brown refused to "send the negroes back," but agreed to "hold them subject to orders." When Maryland enslavers arrived at Camp Hall to locate runaways, they shot at a Black individual "with an evident intention of taking his life."[36]

In Washington, DC, Virginian slaves freed under the Confiscation Act witnessed the hopelessness of a system built on slavery and freedom. As the freed men and women gravitated to the nation's capital, the city's police, at work in a district where slavery remained legal, arrested many of them. It was "upon presumption arising from color" that the police believed them to be "fugitives from service or labor," wrote Secretary of State William Henry Seward. For every step in a new direction, it seemed, law and hostile racial difference appeared to pull it back. Right away, Seward directed the arrest of anyone who seized a person freed under the Confiscation Act. On April 16, 1862, the "intent to re-enslave," selling into slavery, or the re-enslavement of any person in Washington, DC, was made a felony.[37]

The Confederate States of America did not suffer from uncertainty about the social and legal status of Black individuals. In London, southern diplomats explained how the American founders "made their famous declaration of freedom [the Declaration of Independence] for the white race alone." An attempt to forge a stark, new slaveholder nation, the Confederacy dedicated its violence abroad and at home in support of it. In August 1861, Commander Raphael Semmes, owner of at least seven Black persons, docked in the Dutch colony of Surinam. In Paramaribo, he found the city's slaves had too much autonomy – "niggerdom will not work *sua sponte* [on its own accord]," he said. But it was when his cabin and wardroom stewards ran away that he became livid. "One of these deserters being my personal servant," he wrote to a Dutch official, "has no doubt been tampered with by some unscrupulous person, possibly some resident or shipmaster of the United States." He demanded searches of the home of the local US diplomat and the American ships in the harbor. Semmes offered a private, financial award to the city's police chief and informed Surinam's procurer-governor, "the negro" slave is "valuable private property."[38]

In the end, the fugitives were not caught, and Semmes went on his own warpath. At other stops in South America, he expounded on how the Confederates "were fighting the first battle in favor of slavery": the "true issue" of the Civil War, he declared, was "an abolition crusade against slave property." Notably, this was about the same time that US Secretary of State Seward started to work with Great Britain on a slave-trade treaty. When ratified in 1862, the British could search and seize American ships suspected of involvement in the Atlantic slave trade. Along with the United States navy in Africa and the West Indies, the treaty helped cut the number of African slaves sold in Cuba from fourteen thousand in 1861 to four thousand in 1863. The trade ceased a few years later. Clearly, Semmes was fighting an uphill battle for international support.[39]

On North American soil, meanwhile, the Confederates were asserting new policies and practices of enslavement and re-enslavement. In August 1861, for example, General John Bankhead Magruder commanded troops "to capture and send up to the works at Williamsburg all the negroes to be found below a certain line." "These duties," he recorded, "were well performed by Colonel Johnston and some 150 negroes were captured and delivered." Johnston said of the Black people he apprehended, they "evinced the strongest dislike of being taken." Also in 1861, a US commander discovered, islands near Charleston were "infested with gangs of rebel cavalry, whose principal, if not sole, object is to drive the negroes into the interior" away from federal troops. On a raid to burn cotton in the Union-controlled district of Port Royal, Confederate Colonel Martin explained to General Lee how he "concealed his men in a dense thicket and allowed no negroes to pass," "guarded every negro house and the country around," and "took every negro who was passing into custody." After Confederate forces seized the steamer *Harriet De Ford* in spring 1865, "the negroes captured in the steamer were taken to Kilmarnock and sold at auction." In Arkansas, a Confederate officer dragged back a slave fugitive to his master's home, confirmed he was a runaway, and, on the spot, shot him dead.[40]

Surveilled, traded, intimidated, and killed, Blacks in the South understood full well what a slaveholder victory meant. And, while enslaved Black men did on occasion fight alongside rebel troops, such as those from Texas and Georgia who battled in Tennessee, it was not the preferred choice of slaves or enslavers. Only in desperation at the war's very end, when they put in motion a widespread measure to arm slaves, did Confederate leaders begin to break from their pure vision of a White republic.[41]

The northern ideal – wedded to White dominance, but not Black subjugation – was less threatened by African American military service. The arming of Black men, especially slave fugitives, started as early as 1861 in the Union military. It would revolutionize the role and foundation of force and government in the United States. In 1862, however, measures for widespread emancipation and Black militarization faced an impediment: slavery's vision of race and property continued to pervade the North.

The US Constitution restricts how personal property can be seized in general and as a punishment for treason. Where the Fifth Amendment demands the "due process of law" and, if property is taken for public use, "just compensation," Section 3 limits "an attainder of treason" – the forfeiture of property for the crime of treason – to "the life of the person attainted." These demands caused fits for White Union politicians. In most parts of the rebellious states of the South, federal courts (the means of providing "due process") could not function. And, while Abraham Lincoln worked hard to foster support for an abolition program linked to the "just compensation" of slave-owners, his efforts failed. The final constitutional hurdle, that the forfeiture of property for treason be limited to the lifespan of the owner, was impossible to reconcile with emancipation – wherein human "property" was to be set "forever free."[42]

With the Constitution deeply bound to slavery, Union leaders sought alternatives. A move to engage the much-talked-about military powers of the federal state coincided with a collapse in bipartisanship. In early 1862, a militant antislavery coalition formed around the Republican majority and a northern public angered over "the uncoffined bones of thousands" of Union soldiers. Lincoln sensed the change and its possibilities. In February, he approved the hanging of Nathaniel Gordon, the sole slave-trader in American history convicted and killed under federal law. Soon, the president warned border state leaders who refused gradual, compensated emancipation that stringent abolition terms would follow.[43]

Congressmen took the lead. "The olive branch has been held out," said Representative Samuel Blair. It is time to engage the "powerful engines of military policy." These are "extraordinary powers," explained Wisconsin Senator J. R. Doolittle, that are "without limitation" and bound only to "the laws of necessity and of humanity." Military powers authorized by the Constitution in desperate times worked around the peacetime regulations on property seizure, and radical Republicans pushed for their widespread use. "If no other means were left to save the Republic from destruction," said Representative Thaddeus Stevens of Pennsylvania, "I believe we have the power; *under the Constitution* ... to declare a dictator." Confederate defeat, he went on, required immediate emancipation and the armament of former slaves. In a crack at Lincoln's gradualist approach, Stevens proposed a six-month resurrection and dictatorship of Andrew Jackson. Jackson would "abolish slavery as the cause" of the rebellion, arm all Black men, and "end the war by a wholesale hanging of the [Confederate] leaders." In this absurdist critique of Lincoln, of course, Stevens conveniently ignored that Jackson had owned a significant number of Black people and was an unlikely abolitionist. And, while Jackson had deployed free and enslaved Black men in the Battle of New Orleans, he also broke his promises of freedom to the slave soldiers and sent them back to their owners.[44]

Stevens was known for his dramatism, but northern constituents and newspapers egged him on. "The people are anxious to have Slavery wiped out, believing it to be the cause of the war," wrote Pennsylvanian Frederick Miles. Citizens of three New England towns petitioned "for the emancipation of slaves, under the war power of the Constitution." Editors in Pennsylvania and New York picked up on the theme. They chided national legislators stuck in debate over a new confiscation bill when Congress granted Robert Smalls and his crew prize compensation. The Smalls award confirmed "the right of 'contrabands' to confiscate vessels and slaves – a power they deny to Congress and the President."[45]

Indeed, Smalls's stature as Black hero served as a conduit for several attacks by the invigorated Republicans. "It would be an act of public justice to send the colored pilot Robert Small to act as Governor of South Carolina," said Congressman Charles B. Sedgewick. "There is not a loyal slaveholder in the country." Owen Lovejoy of Illinois rankled the Kentuckian Charles Wickliffe. Would you "return Robert Small as a fugitive?" "I'll answer no more questions," Wickliffe responded. As Republicans radicalized, they increasingly called for a stronger, sweeping approach to emancipation and the arming of Black men for the Union cause.[46]

Despite the increasing antislavery aggressiveness, many northern politicians remained torn over measures that met the standards of a peacetime Constitution and those aimed at the problems of a war-torn nation. Proof of this tension can be found in the Second Confiscation Act of July 17, 1862. Among the most important pieces of legislation of the Civil War era, the new law created policy that was fixed to old ways while pointing to new. Its first parts laid out the court punishments for treason: the emancipation of one's slaves and death; or emancipation, imprisonment, and a large fine. For those who assisted in rebellion, the sentence was slave emancipation, imprisonment, and fine. These penalties extended Butler's contraband policy as codified in the First Confiscation Act. However, directed at White southerners – the allegiance of Blacks was not in question – the regulations framed freedom as punishment and slaves as property.

The act then moved to uncharted realms. It authorized the president to seize the estates and property of leading White Confederates to support the Union military and, after a "proclamation" and sixty-day "public warning," to seize the estates and property of all others "engaged in armed rebellion against the government of the United States." In this iteration, slaves of disloyal owners were not contrabands but "captives of war." They "shall be forever free of their servitude, and not again held as slaves." Significantly, loyal owners could still make claims on fugitive slaves upon taking an oath to the United States. Section 11 also sanctioned the military use of Black individuals – the employ of "as many persons of African descent" deemed necessary by the president "for the suppression of this rebellion." Here is the genesis of a federal state emboldened to form and protect the rights of the oppressed.[47]

"The confiscation and emancipation act," as one editor called the new measure, mixed peacetime constitutionalism and war powers, human property and freedmen. To the most discerning minds, it was a groundbreaking charter. Secretary of the Treasury Salmon P. Chase called it "the Emancipation Bill" and detractor General McClellan, who still believed slavery outside the scope of military aims, agreed. "I fear the results of the *civil* policy inaugurated by recent Acts of Congress." Karl Marx elaborated: "So far we have witnessed the first act of the Civil War – the *constitutional* waging of war. The second act, the *revolutionary* waging of war, is now at hand."[48]

Marx and the others missed an important point, though. The Second Confiscation Act was innovative more in the path it laid than in the outcomes that resulted. No Confederate was convicted of treason under the law. This explains why modern-day critics regard the act as impotent. But only one man was convicted of treason during the whole Civil War, and federal courts did not take part in that instance. Rather, it was General Butler, in New Orleans, who convened a military court for William Bruce Mumford for having torn down an American flag. Mumford was hanged on June 7, 1862. Moreover, there was no way to gauge the numbers of slaves freed by the legislation. Despite early proposals to issue certificates of freedom or create a national registry, the act made no provision to document the names or numbers of the slaves it freed. Ultimately the key to the legislation is its closing section, which empowered the courts to do all things "necessary to carry" the act into effect. The new confiscation measures, in other words, were bound to courtroom constitutionalism. The Civil War and emancipation were gained on the battlefield.[49]

While the Second Confiscation Act clung to the vestiges of a United States wrenched between slavery and freedom, it asked the president to move the nation beyond. The question was whether federal violence sided with the enslaved or their enslavers. Was the commander-in-chief to employ military powers for a widespread Confederate confiscation? Could he fix emancipation policy to humanity instead of human property? Would he take the most significant step toward both goals and arm Black Americans?

By 1862, Abraham Lincoln understood what his secretary later called the "awful arithmetic" of the Civil War. The two armies were world leaders in military technology and technique – either would have presented a great challenge to the more heralded soldiers of Russia, Prussia, or France. The Union military had more men than its southern counterpart – at times the overall advantage was near two to one. But, aside from landing one grand, finishing blow – an idea that the South forced its adversary to drop – attrition was the most likely means for northern triumph. But a war of attrition takes time and horrific emotional and physical sacrifice. Confederate leaders thought that if they held out for long enough – for a European nation to back them, Lincoln's Democratic opposition to score victory, or northerners to lose their will – then they would win. Lincoln's army needed men, and to have men, the federal government needed money. Once he had money and men, the commander-in-chief needed military leaders willing to suffer the relentless losses of a strategy built on "friction and abrasion" – the slow erosion of Confederate forces.[50]

Money was on the minds of those who looked to avoid the war and those who sought to embrace its violence. "We have heard of plans to buy off slavery by paying some twenty-five million dollars a year for twenty-five years to States voluntarily emancipating their slaves," said the editors of the African American *Christian Recorder*. "Better by far to pay all this, and ten times more." The "Wall street view," meanwhile, adhered to the market-place crafted by American slave-owners. "The government might make a splendid speculation of this war," announced the *New York Herald*. It observed that federal forces should capture slaves and then, in peacetime, sell them back. At three hundred dollars per head, the national government could earn "the neat indemnity of seventy-five millions of dollars." But "Honest Abe Lincoln," the paper assessed, was not up to the task.[51]

One year later, Lincoln was still focused on economics when he pivoted toward the idea of abolition. "Have you noticed the facts that less than one half-day's cost of this war would pay for all the slaves in Delaware, at four hundred dollars per head? – that eighty-seven days cost of this war would pay for all in Delaware, Maryland, District of Columbia, Kentucky, and Missouri at the same price?" The accounting was purely financial, intended to prove what Lincoln had often expressed: human property – a price tag on individuals – was the source of slavery's wicked ways. But enslavers shook him of this belief. Money was not the sole issue.[52]

While the meaning and limits of human equality constituted a topic of much debate, a different national legacy was at stake. The Revolutionary origins of American violence suggests that beliefs are meaningful only to the extent that one is willing to die for them. At the heart of the current conflict was the possibility that violence – mostly armed, White violence – was the ultimate means of creating and enforcing social and political values. When White northern leaders acknowledged that military strength (violence) was more important than the military's racial composition, they upheld the supremacy of federal force in creating and enforcing freedom of enslaved Black men and women.

President Lincoln began to recognize these ramifications in July 1862. "It is a military necessity to have men and money, and we can get neither in sufficient numbers or amounts if we keep from or drive from our lines slaves coming to them." Although money was a great concern, the North already had methods in place to address it. In abandoned and captured southern fields, the Union put former slaves to work. Government bonds aligned personal and business interests with the

United States. And a variety of taxes, including the first national income tax, made the nation in war the most taxed polity in the nineteenth-century world. From 1861 to 1865, the Union spent $1.8 billion, which was more than all government expenditures in the nation's prewar history added together. It was manpower that presented the greater challenge. The initial rush of more than 640,000 recruits by December 1861, which derived mostly from state militias, represented those most willing to serve. As the war continued and the death toll rose, however, the patriotic fervor dimmed. The federal government took note. So, in July 1862, US citizenship was guaranteed to foreign-born men who served honorably in the army – an offer that attracted more than a half-million immigrants to a Union force of a little more than two million men.[53]

Northern deployment of Black soldiers created far more debate. The United States Army started experiments to arm former slaves in late 1861, but it came amid controversy and concern. A foremost racist fear of White leaders centered on whether a Union attack on South Carolina's coastal islands would foster violent slave unrest. When federal troops aboard the USS *Wabash*, "sublime in her destroying energy," gained control of the region in November, observers reported mixed results. Fort Walker, said Union Captain John Rogers, became "a Fortress Monroe in South Carolina. Negroes are pouring in." In Beaufort, though, the Black refugee population chose violent resistance. As southern enslavers shot at slaves who refused to flee the oncoming northerners, Black individuals fired shots back and, a Union officer revealed, "parties of negroes were breaking open houses and plundering at leisure." A New York correspondent described what he saw: "A perfect saturnalia had begun."[54]

Samuel Francis Du Pont ordered Union forces to counter "any excesses on the part of the negroes" and, after panic subsided, Captain Bankhead posted a sign on the most elegant home in town: "Every effort has been made by us to prevent the negroes from plundering their masters' houses. Had their owners remained and taken care of their property and negroes, it would not have occurred." Though the lawlessness surrounding the attack was nothing other than the disruptions that accompany armed conflict, most Union leaders expected and thus witnessed mayhem from African Americans. Unlike the celebrated, Black-directed violence of individuals (in the mode of Robert Smalls or William Tillman), White northerners feared that when committed by contraband groups, most would call it slave insurrection. In the North, no less than in the South, White people accepted the notion that White military troops should regulate Black actions. *Frank Leslie's Illustrated*, a northern middle-class staple, bragged,

"We have shown how our troops punish treacherous and murderous Negroes."[55]

Once in charge of the Atlantic coastal region, Union military leaders faced a different security question: how to protect the coastlines and islands for the Black men and women who worked on them. White labor to build defensive works or stand guard was unavailable. Military leaders had foreseen this problem. One month before the incursion, the War Department authorized Brigadier-General Thomas W. Sherman to "employ" the area's contrabands "either as ordinary employés" or, under "special circumstances," as soldiers. The directive warned, however, that this was "not being a general arming of them [Black men] for military service." For the most part, Sherman used Blacks as laborers. But on occasion, African American men assumed picket duty – a task assigned by military leaders or taken up by the contrabands for their own protection. When Confederate Thomas Black landed on Edisto Island, between thirty and fifty African Americans "armed with guns and pistols and bayonets on sticks" arrested him. The men turned Black over to the USS *Penguin*. Since "he was taken by negroes," however, Flag-Officer Du Pont decided, the southerner was an improper prisoner of war. Du Pont set Black free.[56]

In the wake of these events, President Lincoln tried to distance his administration from concerns over Black armament in December 1861. After reading the annual report of Secretary of War Simon Cameron, the president ordered it rewritten. "War," Cameron had said in his initial draft, "is made to subdue the enemy, and all that belongs to the enemy." Since slaves are the source of the "power of the rebel States" and the federal government "has no power to hold slaves," freed Black individuals must be used to stop the rebellion, including, "when it may become necessary," by arming them. After Lincoln's intervention, the report's advocacy for Black soldiers disappeared. Slaves "constitute a military resource," it now read, and "their labor may be useful to us." Both versions reached newspapers, however, and there was significant political fallout. Moderates cheered and radicals scoffed at the president's action. In January, Lincoln replaced Cameron with Edwin Stanton.[57]

Three months later, General David Hunter took command of the Department of the South (Thomas Sherman's former post). He believed that the War Department instructions on Black soldiers were still in effect and, ignoring the mandate that Black people be used for "ordinary" work rather than soldiering, he started Black recruitment. Hunter even requested distinctive uniforms for them – red pantaloons – no doubt recognizing that the eyecatching image of armed Blacks would demoralize

White southerners. In May, the general accelerated plans and looked to form two Black regiments from contraband laborers then under the auspices of the Treasury Department. He demanded that Treasury officials in Hilton Head turn over "every able-bodied negro between the ages of eighteen and forty-five, capable of bearing arms." In a separate measure, the general declared all slaves free in South Carolina, Georgia, and Florida.[58]

Resistance to Hunter's commands arose from several sites. Treasury leaders, charged with putting the contrabands in fieldwork, fought the loss of manpower. In accord with the American racial hierarchy, they warned the War Department that Black men were "extremely averse to bearing arms in this contest" and that only "great caution and tact" could deliver former slaves from the "unmanliness" of slavery. The Sea Island-based Black men raised a different complaint. In Hunter's conscription, the contrabands saw the slaveholder authoritarianism they thought they had escaped. In June, Congressman Wickliffe ordered an investigation into Hunter's Black troops. He wanted to know if such a regiment had been raised, who authorized it, and whether the War Department had provided "clothing, uniforms, arms, equipments, and so forth, for such a force." In fact, the War Department had refused to recognize Hunter's Black soldiers and, since the general could not pay the men, he was forced to disband the unit in August. Hunter kept one Black company, though, and placed General Rufus Saxton in charge. When Saxton immediately received permission to enroll five thousand more "colored persons of African descent" at "the same pay and rations" as White volunteers, it was clear that it was actually Hunter, not the idea of arming Blacks, that was the real problem.[59]

David Hunter and Abraham Lincoln were acquainted from the general's service as head of White House security after the March 1861 presidential inauguration. Whatever goodwill had been fostered by that relationship was lost, however, when Hunter proclaimed emancipation in three southern states. Treasury Secretary Chase urged the president not to revoke the order, but where Lincoln had been judicious with the Fremont proclamation, he was abrupt with Hunter's. He was less concerned over the politics of the border states where Fremont operated. Hunter's action, by contrast, seemed to hit on the mechanism of American emancipation. In private, Lincoln wrote, "No commanding general shall do such a thing, upon *my* responsibility, without consulting me." His official revocation linked slave emancipation to military necessity only, and provided exclusive power in this realm to the "Commander-in-Chief of the Army and Navy."[60]

Lincoln had come to accept military necessity as the means to access the war powers granted by the Constitution. Yet this concept had deep and deeply troubled roots in the White Western tradition. British common law upheld that there were emergencies – unusual and exceptional moments – that warranted the use of extreme force and authority. A common Latin phrase captured the notion: "Quod enim necessitas cogit defendit" – *that which you know you need, defend.* But the dangers of such thinking have been evident from early on. Necessity depends on perspective, and some have claimed that "necessity" can mean almost anything. John Stuart Mill, the English philosopher, said that "Necessity ... sometimes stands only for Certainty, at other times for Compulsion; sometimes for what *cannot* be prevented."[61]

In the United States, Thomas Jefferson often serves as the authority on military necessity. Observance of the Constitution, he said in 1810, "is doubtless one of the high duties of a good citizen: but it is not the highest. The laws of necessity, of self-preservation, of saving our country when in danger, are of higher obligation." As president, Jefferson had faced the Burr conspiracy, a plot to establish British authority over the western states and Louisiana. To Samuel Brown he wrote, "in an encampment expecting daily attack from a powerful enemy, self-preservation is paramount to all law." Jefferson further explained, "inter arma silent leges" [in war the laws are silent] and that "there are extreme cases ... where the universal resource is a dictator, or martial law."[62]

On July 22, 1862, five days after the Second Confiscation Act sanctioned the president to engage war powers against the Confederacy, Lincoln signaled a readiness to act. He directed Edwin Stanton to issue the sixty-day warning called for by the legislation. He also outlined his position on military necessity, Black soldiers, and widespread emancipation. In a draft to declare slave freedom in Confederate-controlled regions, he set January 1, 1863 as the date on which new guidelines would go into effect. At the same time, Lincoln listened to advice offered by Secretary of State Seward. June and July had been largely inauspicious for Union forces. Confederate General Stonewall Jackson had become legend through his victory in the Shenandoah Valley. On the Virginia peninsula, Robert E. Lee countered a large invasion led by McClellan. Soon, in August, Confederates would wreak a Union military disaster at Second Bull Run. Thus, Seward suggested, it would be better to deliver an emancipation proclamation in the wake of a much-needed military victory – from a position of strength.[63]

September 17, 1862, the deadliest single day of the Civil War, offered Lincoln the chance he was waiting for. By the time night fell on the Antietam battlefield, there were 12,400 Union casualties and 10,300 Confederate. Common regimental and brigade losses reached 50 percent.

A defining moment in a war of attrition, Antietam, said eyewitness reports for the *New-York Daily Tribune,* was a "long, hotly-contested, bloody battle" and "the greatest fight since Waterloo." Union forces bludgeoned the Confederates and drove them from Maryland. This alone led many to score the battle a northern victory. Though McClellan failed to pursue his enemy with vigor (and lost a grand opportunity to finish him), the victory opened the way for a presidential decree on military powers and new military leadership. Pushed by the tenacious authority of White Confederates and the Black refugees' demands for freedom, the president forged ahead with the tools to undermine the Confederate rebellion and American slavery.[64]

Lincoln issued the Preliminary Emancipation Proclamation five days later. It was grounded in two acts of Congress, including the Second Confiscation Act, and laid the groundwork for an emancipation measure based on military necessity – a groundbreaking version of necessity that used state violence for an aim beyond the self-preservation of Whiteness. The president proclaimed that the "object" of the war was to restore "the constitutional relation between the United States and each of the states and people thereof." The method he proposed was gradual, compensated emancipation in the border states and military emancipation in the rebellious ones. Slavery caused the national breech, and Lincoln was forthright in stating that "the Government of the United States, including the military and naval authority thereof, will recognize and maintain the freedom" of former slaves.[65]

Critics in the North and South responded. Two editors, both Democrats, of the *Patriot and Union* in Harrisburg, Pennsylvania, likened the proclamation to a call for unrestrained slave violence. The men said: "Remember that this cold-blooded invitation to insurrection and butchery comes from the Republican President of the United States." Their inflammatory tone caught the attention of a Judge Advocate who advised the secretary of war to arrest them. Confederate leaders in politics and the military agreed with the northern newspapermen. They accused Lincoln of declaring "a war of extermination," a "servile war," and advised the widespread distribution of arms and ammunition to Whites "to meet any outbreak of negroes" that might occur when the proclamation went into effect on January 1. In Arkansas, slaveholders complained that there was nothing they could do to stop the rush of Black individuals to Union gunboats. "The slaves had heard of the President's proclamation."[66]

Jefferson Davis shared these complaints, further protesting the fact that the North had already armed slaves "for a servile war" – indicating General

Saxton's Black soldiers in South Carolina and another group now deployed by General Butler in Louisiana. Davis declared the arming of former slaves a violation of the laws of war and of humanity. He followed recent southern military decisions that singled out Black soldiers as well as the White officers in charge of them. Both groups, he said, would be indicted per Confederate state statutes governing slave rebellion. For Whites this meant a sentence of death; for Blacks, death or enslavement.[67]

Though the final version of the Emancipation Proclamation derived directly from its September predecessor – the first two paragraphs repeat the earlier document – it was a more radical measure. As promised, Lincoln declared that slaves in rebellious states and regions "are, and henceforward shall be, free." The federal government and military were now sworn to "recognize and maintain" this freedom, which undid the course of the nation's history. White enslavers could no longer rely on the United States government. The emancipation order did, however, perpetuate White-held concerns about race when it addressed Black individuals and violence. Lincoln echoed the long-held fear of Black authority and autonomy, professing that freed people should focus on working "faithfully for reasonable wages" and abstain from violent acts. But as much as Black violence should be restrained, Lincoln sanctioned it for "necessary self-defence" and announced that all "suitable" (able) Black persons "will be received into the armed service of the United States."

In the end, the Emancipation Proclamation upheld the notion of individual violence, in self-protection and on behalf of the nation, as a near-universal American right. (Notably, Lincoln would not have granted this license to members of Native communities, such as the Dakota, who were interned in federal military camps during the Civil War.) "Upon this act, sincerely believed to be an act of justice, warranted by the Constitution upon military necessity," Lincoln closed, "I invoke the considerate judgment of mankind and the gracious favor of Almighty God."[68]

————————◆————————

After more than eighty years of existence and two years of Civil War, the nation and its military aligned against the institution of Black enslavement. "Our army is in reality," declared an Ohio newspaperman, "an army of liberation." In Atlanta, a correspondent witnessed "the grand army of liberation, under the command of the sagacious [William T.] Sherman." Yet popular understandings that on January 1, 1863, the "Union army officially became an army of liberation" distract from freedom's violent underpinnings. In this there was no mistake. Owing to the demands for freedom from enslaved communities, the Civil War developed into a mission for slave deliverance that, in turn, rationalized the loss of more than 740,000 men. And embedding state violence in humanitarian ideals would soon prove part of a modern trend.[69]

But Lincoln's Emancipation Proclamation also offered something more. On a legal plane, it was a tool of war – an instrument of violence. On a moral plane, it sought to repair hundreds of years of Black dispossession and degradation by ending enslavement – an act that also allowed for violent Black acts in self-defense and for the recruitment of Black soldiers. Bringing together the proclamation's legal and moral foundations, Republican righteousness – as it had been from the party's start – proved a potent blend of politics and physical force.

Significantly, when Union decisionmakers marked a humanitarian crisis in the Civil War, it was not the crisis suffered by individuals who remained enslaved. Rather, it was the humanitarian crisis experienced by those who had fled enslavement to find shelter behind Union lines. General Butler, for instance, may have struggled with the "political question" of slave fugitives at Fort Monroe (should the slave runaways be freed?), but on the "question of humanity" (should the slave runaways be clothed, sheltered, and fed?), he had "no doubt." The war's Black refugees moved Secretary of the Navy Gideon Welles too. In 1861, Welles stated that a refusal to accept contrabands aboard Union ships would violate "every principle of humanity." The Republican mandate thus offered food and shelter to the combat-displaced population. It did not, however, look to counter the deprivations and traumas of the slave experience or, at the war's start, to level the institution of slavery.[70]

Welles was thus certain that the Emancipation Proclamation could "not be justified on mere humanitarian principles." From a legal basis, his prescription was bleak for those who remained enslaved – and those who would seek to emancipate them. The states had rights, he said, and slave liberation, "a military necessity against Rebel enemies," must be for national "self-defense and for our own [White northern] preservation, the first law of nature." The way to access necessity was through a wartime Constitution. This is where the violent origins of the proclamation are uncovered. Powered by a presidential war decree, emancipation, Welles believed, must be no different than battlefield soldiers firing a gun.[71]

The president agreed with Welles and defended the proclamation as deriving from national need. "I have done no official act in mere deference to my abstract judgment and feeling on slavery," he explained to his naysaying adviser, Albert Gallatin Hodges, a one-time slave-owner from Kentucky.

"My oath to preserve the constitution to the best of my ability, imposed upon me the duty of preserving, by every indispensable means, that government – that nation – of which the constitution was the organic law." Confident that security concerns pushed him to act, Lincoln ignored how the president himself was responsible for defining the meaning of "necessity." Northern Democrats, after all, looked to end the Civil War through a policy, as one article explained, aimed at "every friend of the white race." Their party slogan was "the Union as it was, and the Constitution as it is." But by late 1862, the idea of returning the United States to what it had been was toxic to Republicans. When Lincoln and his supporters mixed their slavery view with the idea of military necessity, emancipation (immediate and war-based) was the result. The White Virginian abolitionist Moncure Conway understood this clearly. "If the demand of the nation were simply that our flag should wave over some forts and custom-houses from which it has been taken down," he said, "the military necessities involved would be very different." Slavery was a legal and military problem only if it was a moral problem too.[72]

Beholden to the Constitution (including the wartime Constitution), the president and his proclamation were thus equally beholden to God. Here, the ethical origins of the Emancipation Proclamation are revealed. In June 1862, before the demands of slave freedom and military necessity coalesced, a Quaker delegation, most of whom were active in Pennsylvania's Underground Railroad, visited the White House. Since "the Constitution cannot now be enforced at the South," said Friend Oliver Johnson to Lincoln, "the abolition of slavery is indispensable to your success." Lincoln, who held several such meetings with Christian leaders, reported that everyone in the room agreed that slavery should end, but not on the means to end it. The conversation had turned to individual prophecy. Throughout his life, the president had fancied himself a divine vessel. In the 1840s, for instance, he declared the marriage of a young couple whom he had introduced to be foreordained: "I believe God made me one of the instruments of bringing your Fanny and you together," he said to Joshua Speed. Some twenty years later, little had changed. "He had sometime thought that perhaps he might be an instrument in God's hands of accomplishing a great work," recorded a member of the Quaker delegation, "and he certainly was not unwilling to be."[73]

Chicago ministers who visited Washington, DC, on September 13, 1862, continued the theological push. "He could not deny that the Bible denounced oppression as one of the highest of crimes," they said; "that our country had been exceedingly guilty in this respect, both at the North and South; that our just punishment has come by a slaveholder's rebellion . . . so that there is the amplest reason for expecting to avert Divine judgments by putting away the sin, and ... by striking at their [the Confederate] cause." Lincoln assured his guests that emancipation was on his mind "by day and night," and promised "Whatever shall appear to be God's will I will do." In the coming days, with the battle at Antietam pending, he therefore "made a vow." A northern military success in Maryland would serve as a spiritual "indication." And by September 22, with the battle won, Lincoln said, "God had indicated this question in favor of the slaves."[74]

The Chicagoan notion that slavery stood as an American transgression – as opposed to a solely southern one – took hold of the president at the very moment he commanded the emancipation process. His God, who demanded violence for national reprimand and rectification, allied more with Old Testament scripture. From this perspective, slave freedom was a great event that portended a national – White – deliverance. Indeed, the moral rectification of which Lincoln spoke was clearly directed at White people, all of whom, in this framing, bore responsibility for the sin of human enslavement. "We know that, by His divine law, nations like individuals are subjected to punishments and chastisements in this world," said Lincoln in March 1863. "May we not justly fear that the awful calamity of civil war ... may be but a punishment, inflicted upon us ... to the needful end of our national reformation as a whole People?"[75]

The idea that slavery, the country's sin, warranted physical reprisal grew to a fevered pitch in the Second Inaugural Address. The Civil War would continue, Lincoln proclaimed, "until all the wealth piled by the bond-man's two hundred and fifty years of unrequited toil shall be sunk, and until every drop of blood drawn with the lash, shall be paid by another drawn with the sword." To deny this truth, Lincoln said, "is to deny that there is a God governing the world."[76]

Fostered by the arming of freed and free Black men, a violent racial justice accompanied the moral and legal logic of the Emancipation Proclamation. Nearly 180,000 African Americans served in the Union Army – a number that, when added to that of Blacks in the navy, accounted for almost 10 percent of all Civil War service members in the United States armed forces. Of these soldiers and sailors, 140,000 had been enslaved at the war's start. "These are palpable facts, about which, as facts, there can be no cavilling," Lincoln said in defense of the proclamation. "We have the men; and we could not have had them without the measure."[77]

The combination of Lincoln's wartime measure and the arming of northern Black soldiers, though, fulfilled White southerners' abiding fear of slave rebellion. On January 12, 1863, Jefferson Davis unveiled his wrath.

He declared that freedom for "several millions of human beings of an inferior race" doomed them to "extermination," and that Lincoln's call for the contrabands "to abstain from violence unless in necessary self-defense" was in truth a call for "a general assassination of their masters." Confederate Congressmen agreed, looking to the precedent of the Haitian Revolution for violent imagery. "President Lincoln has sought to convert the South into a San Domingo [Haiti], by appealing to the cupidity, lusts, ambition, and ferocity of the slave." Southern policy supported the political bluster. "Under the instructions of our President," said General Joseph E. Johnston, "our troops are ordered to bring off all male negroes of military age in danger of falling into the enemy's hands, to keep them out of the Federal Army." What Lincoln and his advisers sought by framing the Emancipation Proclamation as a means of achieving northern defense and southern punishment had quickly come to pass. As Confederate Commander James Waddell observed, Black soldiering "was a new element introduced into the contest, and a very powerful one."[78]

But what was the nature of that power? Some historians have suggested that the movement, the running away, of hundreds of thousands of southern slaves was a slave rebellion – that the enslaved in the South sought their liberation – "a liberation that would be enforced either when they rose to claim it or when Lincoln's soldiers arrived." Undoubtedly, the Black men and women who fled from White slaveholders seized their freedom. But there is more. In a quest for liberation, the contrabands rebelled not only against their southern enslavers, but against the federal government, an institution historically charged to maintain and enforce Black enslavement.[79]

The demands made by Black persons on the national government – for food, shelter, safety, work, and soldiering – began to renovate the United States, a slave society. In turning the violence of the federal state toward the interests of the formerly enslaved, however, the limits of the slave rebellion were soon evident. In Haiti, one-time bondsmen had destroyed a slave system and then assumed political control. In the United States, slavery's fugitives attacked an immediate organ of human enslavement (the Confederacy), but did not look to destroy or control the federal government and its armed forces. Channeled to reform a liberal society from within, Black individuals soon met the shortcomings of such an approach. In the next fifteen years, Black military, political, and cultural power would abut reformulated systems of White supremacy. This was emancipation's fury: freedom from bondage but not freedom from the chains of racism.

The enlistment of Black soldiers in the Union Army forecasted the challenges that lay ahead. Modern studies of Black American soldiering demonstrate how racism often hardens when interracial contact features gross discrepancies in class, education, or work status. In the Civil War, the United States military was a textbook example of the tenacity of racist ideology amid groundbreaking social (and military) policy. Placed in race-segregated units devoid of African American leadership and receiving lower pay than their White counterparts, Black Union military men also faced labor assignments throughout the conflict that were more relentless and rigorous (so much so that the morbidity rate for Black soldiers far exceeded that of Whites). The military conscripted Black bodies with extra abandon too. Allowed to count contraband soldiers from Confederate regions toward their own (White) quota, northern states backed aggressive African American enlistment campaigns. The Union military's racial double standard thus helped perpetuate the hierarchies of race by implementing a specific change – in this case, the acceptance of Black soldiers – and touting it as revolutionary racial progress despite not addressing underlying issues of equity and endemic racism. It was a prime example of how the liberal language of equality ("all men are created equal") can serve as a platform for the creation (and maintenance) of hostile differences and inequity.[80]

White northerners also shared with their southern counterparts a fear of Black men with guns. This anxiety manifested in a need for control. Of Black Americans unattached to the army who "put on the majestic air of soldiers," General William Tecumseh Sherman said, "I have had occasion to punish some of these already." An equally strong northern White distrust existed for sanctioned Black army men. "Discipline is the first requisite for troops of any color," said Virginia Union Governor Francis H. Pierpont. But "these colored troops are new recruits just from bondage" and need to be "under the eye of their [White] officers." To Secretary of War Edwin Stanton, he added, "I know you would not leave your wife and daughters in a community of armed negroes, undisciplined and just liberated from bondage, with no other armed protection."[81]

In varying degrees, such racist thoughts pervaded White northern discourse with evident result. "The bare sight of 50,000 armed and drilled black soldiers upon the banks of the Mississippi," asserted Lincoln to a skeptic in spring 1863, "would end the rebellion at once." "Drilled black soldiers" was euphemism for "black soldiers under White command." And disciplined or drilled soldiers were not insurrectionary ones. In other words, as former slaves transformed into Black Union soldiers, the slave rebellion would come to an end by having brought Black violence under the control of the (White) military.[82]

Leaders of the national military were hardly alone in scrambling to address racial hierarchy in such a revolutionary moment. As the federal government dealt with the demands made by Black communities in the Civil War, certain Whites of all classes in the North and South started to evince a sense of lost entitlement. Some undercut Black autonomy in subtle ways. One Connecticut newspaper noted that Robert Smalls upset theories of racial inferiority by "acting like a white man." Others were more blatant. They were angered that when "the rebel gunboat *J. B. White*" was run out of southern waters and turned over to the US government by White sailors, media coverage all but ignored the event. "On the other hand," said an observer self-identified simply as "WHITE MAN," "look how quickly appreciation and reward follow when negroes are the actors." To the White men and women who felt slighted by federal attention to slaves and free Black individuals, the world had turned upside down. "No special legislation for the benefit of the few [Black people] at the expense of the many [White people]," Mississippi Democrats soon said (ignoring that Blacks outnumbered Whites in their state). "Nigger before, to open the door," demanded WHITE MAN, reflecting the racist idea that Blacks should take the front of the line only to make the way easier for Whites.[83]

Indeed, the world had not changed as much as it may have seemed. In a cruel irony, a war begun over a challenge to the American racial hierarchy soon fostered something other than the justice imagined in the Emancipation Proclamation and the 13th, 14th, and 15th Amendments. A new racial order deeply situated in individual acts of violence and governmental apathy soon appeared.

When Robert Smalls took the *Planter* to Philadelphia for repairs in 1864, he was thrown off a public streetcar. "We don't allow niggers to ride," said the conductor to the war hero. In the South, White individuals intent on the representation of White interests soon banded together. Groups such as the Swamp Fox Rangers, Seymour Knights, Hancock Guards, and the Ku Klux Klan killed thousands of Blacks and Black allies across the South and border states. The Knights of the White Camelia, a secret male-run organization, looked to assert White control in government. Its members pledged to marry only White women. Many such organizations promoted individual and local force as a means of White control. A ban on racial intermixing, which became a central theme of the 1868 presidential election, was upheld by the Democratic vice-presidential candidate. Union General William T. Sherman was no friend of racial equality, but he understood that the ferocity of the White southern response to the changes in federal authority required immediate and serious action. "One thing is certain," he said, "there is a class of people, men, women, and children, who must be killed or banished before you can hope for peace and order."[84]

Over the next three decades, White political leaders and civilians looking out for White interests in the North and South set aside their wartime differences. Now, in the face of what they feared would become a reversal of the racial status quo, they turned toward countering the racial progress and promises that had been made. With a fearsome determination, they worked together across regional and political divides to reformulate the violence of the federal state and the violence of White American individuals to support a race-segregated nation.

PART III

MODERN TRADITIONS

This is not a war between a particular *trade* and *capital*. It is a war between the sons of toil, who represent labor, and their employers who represent *capital*.

Labor activist C. M. Talmage, 1864

If it results in the utter annihilation of these Indians . . . they have been warned . . . I will say nothing and do nothing to restrain our troops from doing what they deem proper on the spot, and will allow no mere vague general charges of cruelty and inhumanity to tie their hands.

Lieutenant General William Tecumseh Sherman, 1868

The men and women in the South who disapprove of lynching and remain silent on the perpetration of such outrages, are particeps criminis, accomplices, accessories before and after the fact, equally guilty with the actual law-breakers who would not persist if they did not know that neither the law nor militia would be employed against them.

Antilynching advocate Ida Bell Wells, 1892

8

TO 1877: AMERICAN CAPITALISM
AND THE GEOGRAPHY OF VIOLENCE

Characterized by horrific violence, including more than 740,000 people dead, the American Civil War lay a foundation for modern America. In this final section, the chapters navigate the passage from slavery to freedom, war capitalism to industrial capitalism, in ways that operated beyond the abolition of human enslavement.

"Slavery" and "freedom" are straightforward terms. The two are often used to signal the organization of society according to opposing values. Indeed, many scholars have found that people define these words in relation to each other. You cannot have freedom, for instance, without having slavery. While the oppositional nature of slavery and freedom is useful to explain how an unrelenting civil war occurred in the United States, it is less useful to describe the dynamics of the post-Civil War age.[1]

Insofar as the Civil War established a national right to sell one's labor, the war was revolutionary. After all, the forced extraction of work from Black bodies was central to American slavery – just as the forced removal of Indigenous bodies from the land was central to colonization. But it is important to note that violent labor extraction and bodily removal represent only one aspect of how human enslavement and settler colonialism shaped life in the United States. Slavery and colonization were economic, social, and political systems. To better understand American violence after the war, we must better understand the changes, continuities, and challenges wrought by a conversion often distilled down to being "from slavery to freedom."

The legal end of slavery arrived through the sudden cataclysm of war. But the shift from war to industrial capitalism that the end of American slavery announced was a fluid, imprecise event that took at least a century to complete. In this time, which comprised the remainder of the nineteenth century, liberal government proved capable of accommodating both economic variations.[2]

Promoted by the abolition of American slavery, the breakdown of war capitalism did not signal a full embrace of just labor practices. Industrial capitalism arrived with labor oppression, hostile differences, and an accelerated Indigenous colonization. These efforts built on previous forms of violence and created new ones. Industrial capitalists would point to employment contracts and the ability of workers to leave their jobs as the antithesis of the labor compulsion that defined slavery. But many workers, especially workers of color who often toiled at the bottom of the industrial wage scale, equated the menial work and unlivable wages of the industrial world to a new kind of enslavement. That poverty limited opportunity and choice in ways akin to slavery is a theme found throughout the industrial age. "We in this country who are poor and at the bottom of the economic ladder, whether we be black or white, are still in slavery," said Hubert T. Delany, the Black lawyer and activist, at a 1938 Emancipation Day celebration in Harlem. "We will continue in bondage as long as we are subject to economic insecurity."[3]

The industrial world and its complex financial arrangements delivered economic insecurity to many in the United States. And, while technological advances in transportation, communication, and weaponry are marked as marvels of the era, they also promoted and supported American violence. For example, the railroad industry required vast amounts of capital, labor, land, natural resources, and national military support. This proved to be a toxic accelerant for labor exploitation, the production of race, and the process of colonization.

Labor discipline, race, guns, and railroads are vital markers for understanding the flows of individual and state violence in the postwar era. Each fostered violence on its own, but together they contributed to an economy of violence across the nation and the world. The public sale of weapons of war, for instance, underwrote a domestic and global distribution of guns by the federal government. And profits made in the gun market assisted the United States in addressing its debt accrued in the Civil War. The retirement of that Civil War debt, often in the form of government-backed bonds, sent investors in search of new opportunities. Many turned to railroad corporations. But a collapse in the United States railroad business in the early 1870s contributed to a worldwide economic breakdown. Here, new forms of economic violence and oppression appeared in the United States while the fiscal collapse impacted national elections and the federal government's ability to uphold the promises encoded in the Emancipation Proclamation. A new racial order, first mediated with the appearance of Black Union soldiers in 1863, soon materialized in the United States.

———————◆———————

On December 9, 1863, Edward B. Smith and Frank Williams approached the watchman at Fort Jackson in Louisiana. Black soldiers in a race-segregated Union regiment, the two worked as musicians, drummers, in the Fourth

Infantry, Corps d'Afrique. They lied to exit the fort. The sergeant of the guard, Smith and Williams said, had given them leave. Once clear of the moat bridge, the men enjoyed hours of personal freedom.[4]

In taking leisure, the soldiers registered a complaint. They were military men, of course, but in this job they traded work for a wage. Lower skilled wage laborers in the Civil War era bore the brunt of a burgeoning industrial order. Here, time to work and time to play were not only distinct, but increasingly controlled by the few – factory owners, railroad tycoons, and commanding officers. In their hiatus from the fort, which was located on the western bank of the Mississippi about thirty miles from the river's end, Smith and Williams retreated from the regimentation of modern life. They may have hunted local game, practiced their drums, or horsed around. Whatever transpired, these young men – Smith was about twenty-five and Williams eighteen – pushed against the demands of their job. This resistance would deeply mark their lives.[5]

When the Union Army first fashioned the Fourth Infantry, Corps d'Afrique, its men derived mostly from units of the Louisiana Native Guard. In spring 1861 in Confederate-controlled New Orleans, property-owning militiamen of color (about 450 of them) formed a regiment that came to be called the Native Guard. Staffed by tradesmen – bricklayers, carpenters, plasterers, cigar-makers, and the like – the Native Guard required members to arm and uniform themselves. Confederate leaders, unable to set aside prejudice despite the militant enthusiasm of the group, often relegated the non-White militiamen to the rear.[6]

In 1862, after the United States gained authority in the region, the Native Guard proved opportunistic and switched sides. By September, General Benjamin Butler had formed the Union's first all-Black regiment from Native Guard recruits. Then, upon assuming control of the men in December, General Nathaniel P. Banks purged the units of Black officers, mixed their ranks – propertied, free men with recently freed slaves – and formed the Corps d'Afrique. Union leaders dispersed the once tight-knit bands of New Orleans fighters northeast to Ship Island off the Mississippi coast, east to Fort Pike and Fort Macomb, south to Fort St. Phillip and Fort Jackson (across the river from one another), and throughout the region's sugar plantations. As it had under Confederate auspices, White management slighted Black fighting fitness and assigned the men to garrison duty.[7]

In 1863, concerns beyond military makeup and duty riddled the former New Orleans militiamen. Wartime society in the Mississippi delta was unstable, the boundaries between freedom and slavery incomplete. Devoid of protective male bodies, families of Black soldiers were targeted for a variety of reasons, including enslavement or re-enslavement. At times, Union Army leaders found it necessary to place "wives and mothers" of Black military members in "the Police Jail and Parish prison for 'safe-keeping.'" As disturbing as this must have been, an inequality in pay stood as the greatest affront to Black troops. The Militia Act of 1862 mandated White soldiers receive $13 per month and Black soldiers $10 per month (with $3 deducted for clothing – effectively $7 monthly). Delayed and missing payments intensified the demand, as one African American group explained, that Black military men "be treated as soldiers" – not with "Perfect equality" in a social sense, but with "the Priviledges [sic], and respect due to a soldier."[8]

From 1863 until June 1864, when pay was equalized, Black soldiers throughout the Union Army protested the military's payment policy. To the freemen of color, the market for soldiering demanded equal pay for equal work. "The colored Troops," said thirteen Black members of a South Carolina regiment, "were enlisted with the promise of the same pay clothing and rations as is accorded to other soldiers in the United States Service." To the recently freed men, the wage labor ideal, a foundation of industrial capitalism, allowed an individual to sell his soldiering and risk of life. This kind of self-ownership around labor and risk was the opposite of working as a slave. Both groups, free and freed Black soldiers, thus upheld a progressive, capitalist approach to the labor market – an exchange they believed the United States should not regulate according to race.[9]

In one of the most important labor confrontations in US history, many northern Black fighters refused their monthly wages while continuing to work as dutiful soldiers. Others opted for a more antagonistic approach. On October 31, 1863, for instance, officers arrested two sergeants of the Fourth Infantry, Corps d'Afrique, for their payday complaints and, on November 19 in South Carolina, Sergeant William Walker encouraged fellow soldiers to stack their arms and refuse to work until the receipt of equal pay. These Black soldiers understood how skin color served as a mark of subordination; their direct challenge was a rational response to White managerial racism. Often categorized as "spontaneous" protest (for taking place without central leadership), Black soldiers' activism responded to local conditions to forge collective action in the army – reflecting the kind of workplace struggle that would become a chronic condition in industrial America.[10]

Tension over the lack of Black leadership, unit composition, and type of duty as well as familial insecurity joined with the dispute over military wages to charge the environment at Fort Jackson in December 1863. In the early evening on the 9th, when Smith and Williams returned to the fort, Lieutenant-Colonel Augustus W. Benedict uncovered their ruse. That it was Benedict and not another officer was unfortunate. Assigned to govern Black troops, Benedict was a sadistic racist. He would punch men in the face or strike them with his sword for minor dress code violations. In July, in Baton Rouge, he had ordered two soldiers of the Corps d'Afrique to be staked to the ground and smothered in molasses. They were kept there from 10 a.m. to 7 p.m. and then the punishment was repeated again the next day. In August at Fort St. Philip, Benedict repeated the torture. Now, at Fort Jackson, he demanded Smith and Williams remove their coats. He struck them with a "mule whip" or "wagon whip" – a corrective tool used on beasts that the army had banned from soldier punishment. "Don't," pleaded Smith. "I won't do it again." Major Nye witnessed "three or four" attacks by the officer. Some reported Benedict hit Williams fifteen to twenty times, while others put the number at "five or six severely."[11]

Half of the fort's five hundred Black men rushed to the scene. "We want to be treated as soldiers," they said. Benedict immediately undercut the professional recognition demanded by the men. "These boys were bad boys," he responded, "and I have treated them as such." Benedict then left for his tent. At 6:30 p.m., an increasing number of the protesters armed themselves and more than a hundred of them started to fire into the air. "Give us Colonel Benedict; we did not come here to be whipped by him," they shouted. "Kill Colonel Benedict, shoot him." One cry in particular later troubled the White officers in charge of the incident investigation: "Kill all the damned Yankees."[12]

Nervous fort leaders requested the service of "one or two gunboats." The shooting had already attracted the *Suffolk*'s captain, who moved his steamer closer to Quarantine Station five miles away. Along with a regiment of troops and a battery of artillery, Commodore Henry H. Bell brought the USS *Pensacola* to the station too. Most of these movements took place in the night. But by 7 p.m., the situation at the fort had already subsided; the next morning, at reveille, every man was "reported to have answered to his name." On December 11, however, fearful that the protest would spread to other Corps d'Afrique outposts, General Banks empowered a military commission "to make thorough investigation of all the facts connected with the affair."[13]

The commissioners interviewed only Fort Jackson's officers. But even the partial story of the mutiny is revealing. Three months before, General Lorenzo Thomas had responded to Benedict's summer cruelties with a public lecture to those in charge at the fort. Thomas had explained "how to treat the men," and he had made the Black men a promise: "If the officers maltreated them in any way or struck them, he would dismiss them." Though colleagues noted that Benedict was not on duty at the time of the visit, he likely learned of the general's words. Indeed, that Benedict offered to resign the day after the December 9 mutiny suggests that he did.

Notably, his resignation was rejected by superiors. They would, however, dismiss him for his cruelty.[14]

General Thomas's speech displayed a preoccupation with race conflict – a tendency reinforced by Benedict in his prejudice and, later, the investigators' emphasis on the shouts about the indiscriminate killing of Whites. General Banks also highlighted this theme when reporting on the commission's findings. They cast no doubt on the "efficiency and reliability of black troops," he said. That the Black soldiers were trustworthy, however, did not alter the general's perception of military and racial order. Banks declared that "the conduct of the soldiers is inexcusable, and must be punished with such severity as to prevent its recurrence." In other words, a protest over race-directed violence by a military officer was to be settled in part by the physical punishment of the Black protesters.[15]

In 1863, a mandate dating back to the Continental Army echoed once more: soldiers must be punished severely to prevent future "misbehavior." And in its reverberation, it sheds light on the origins of industrial labor discipline. While there is excellent evidence that American enslavers provided the framework for worker regulation in the industrial world, that framework is incomplete without an acknowledgement of the contributions made by members of the federal government and national military. In the worker demonstration at Fort Jackson, a battle over the boundaries of race and punishment became part of a negotiation on the boundaries of work under industrial capitalism.[16]

Like the use of punishment against demonstrating soldiers, the use of federal forces against workers in the Civil War skewed such negotiation heavily in the favor of government leaders and industrial capitalists. Even empowered by the war's labor shortage and production demand, workers in search of justice faced unwinnable fights. In Cold Spring, New York, soldiers placed labor leaders in jail without trial and forced them from town after their release. This toppled a strike at the Parrot Shot and Shell Works. Meanwhile, the confiscation of back pay by military leaders – a common legal practice – attacked the economic interests of iron molders on strike at the Brooklyn Navy Yard. Here, managers also stripped protesting dockworkers of earned pay and locked the yard to keep them in. At the federal arsenal in Nashville, workers struck after the government failed to deliver on promises of overtime wages. General Henry Thomas ordered soldiers with bayonets to force them back to work and dismissed two hundred arsenal men he called "untrustworthy." When St. Louis blacksmiths and tailors demanded increased pay, Major-General William Rosecrans declared martial law and arrested strike leaders. He justified the move as vital to protect "private rights and the military power of the nation," sanctioned troops to shield manufacturers from "bad men" (union organizers), and promised to rid the city of workers' unions. The commanding general in Louisville, Kentucky, duplicated Rosecrans's St. Louis design.[17]

In the 1850s, slavery apologist George Fitzhugh had blasted the federal government for its refusal to deploy its might on behalf of industry – especially as it pertained to northern workers. A changed dynamic in the Civil War, a dynamic that now linked industrial leaders to slaveholders, no doubt pleased him. The northern free labor market, even more so than that of southern enslaved labor (which often relied on the interpersonal coercion of enslavers), was being stabilized and ensured by government force.[18]

At Fort Jackson in 1863, thirteen African American soldiers, including Smith and Williams, faced court-martial proceedings in late December. Charged with mutiny, Smith pled innocent. He was found guilty and sentenced "to be imprisoned at hard labor" at a "permanent fortification" for one year. Williams likewise said "not guilty," was found guilty, and, for unexplained reasons, was condemned "to be shot to death with muskets." Seven additional Black mutineers received punishment. The court ordered Private Abraham Victoria to be put to death by firing squad and penalized the others to hard labor for between one month and twenty years.[19]

Benedict's egregious behavior could not be overlooked, however, and Acting Assistant Adjutant-General Lieber immediately suspended the two death sentences for further review. As Williams and Victoria do not appear on the government list that catalogues such executions, they seem to have had their sentences reduced to hard labor. The young men were fortunate. Union officials executed fifty-two Black soldiers in the war. Fourteen of them, including William Walker, were guilty of mutiny. (The most common charge against the condemned Black soldiers was murder – twenty-seven men – followed by mutiny, then rape.)[20]

Lieutenant-Colonel Benedict himself pled "not guilty" to "inflicting cruel and unusual punishment, to the prejudice of good order and military discipline." But his was an easy case. As early as December 17, a little more than a week after the mutiny, army leaders such as General Banks had already declared Benedict's acts "as among the cruel and unusual punishments interdicted by the Constitution." Found guilty, Benedict received the maximum penalty under military code: he was dismissed from service.[21]

The sentencing in the Fort Jackson mutiny was as influenced by race as the actual incident had been. Officers received less stringent punishment, and thus the privileged, White men who filled the ranks of Union officers were the recipients of lesser penalties. Still, racism alone does not account for how the army institutionalized violence to control labor. The military subjected the bodies and minds of Anglo and African American soldiers to great discipline. More than 80 percent of the 179 military executions of White servicemen, for example, took place for desertion. But, as seen in the incident at Fort Jackson, military leaders could and did target Black men because of their skin color and status as common soldiers. Here, at the intersection of race and class, the cruel acts committed by individuals like Benedict could appear (at least momentarily) to meet military norms. Similar constructions of individual and institutional coercion would stand as a central feature of industrial labor operation.[22]

"When the shackles fell from the limbs of those four million blacks," American labor pioneer William H. Sylvis said in 1868, "it did not make them free men; it simply transferred them from one condition of slavery to another; it placed them upon the platform of the white workingmen, and made all slaves together." Evocative of a fantasy where workers stood oppressed collectively with no regard to race, Sylvis's remark nonetheless made a strong point. From a White stance, the Civil War stood more for power and control than liberation. The four years of armed conflict, Sylvis believed, hid the "collision between capital and labor." There is "a social revolution, a war of classes," he explained, forecasting new forms of American violence. And, if efforts "to secure to labor the fruits of its toil . . . produce such a collision," he continued, "let it come."[23]

By positioning workers as the source of a radical effort to overturn the hierarchy of industrial capitalism – what Sylvis calls "a social revolution" – he missed a critical point. The conflict was not a "collision" of workers and capital, it was a campaign waged by industrial capital on workers. And in the 1860s, this campaign was not new. For more than three decades, industrial capitalism had forged significant changes in the lives and communities of countless individuals in the United States. Though business owners and managers suggested that workers were advancing a radical (and thus dangerous) agenda, many working men and women were simply struggling against the revolution that the market and industry brought to their doorsteps. The workers recognized that war capitalism, slavery, and the whip still impacted people's lives even as society pushed such forms of coercion into obsolescence. They recognized, too, the different methods of wage labor discipline, racial inequality, and social hierarchy that were central to the industrial mission.[24]

———◆———

Capitalism is a system of economic and political authority that is integral to the hierarchies of American liberal life. On its most basic level, it is the speculation of money in hope of profit. The profits of speculators have driven the accumulation of great wealth – and, at times, great technological advances – in modern societies. But capitalism's profit and the distribution of profit has frequently relied on local and global exploitation. In the nineteenth century, individuals turned nearly every aspect of existence, from the natural world and human labor to the risk of death, into a commodity. Where many would claim that the market dictates value, it is the market – an abstract and soulless force – that takes the blame when the economy sustains widespread poverty and financial inequity. The decision-makers – people like the owners, corporate board members, and managers who create and maintain the system – often evade responsibility for the conditions they have made.[25]

For many White Americans in the 1860s, especially those in the North, the economic problems of the country were clear. American slavery, they argued, demanded depraved forms of private and state violence to bring about labor discipline. To them, the end of slavery signaled an ethical way forward. Free market capitalism situated in wage labor was the solution. What they failed to realize (or ignored) were the physical, economic, and political forms of restraint and degradation that were central to a "free" market system.

Wage labor (or "free," as in "not enslaved" labor) divorced working people from the raw materials and workplace machines they once owned. Innovation and mechanization replaced technique and artistry, the primary concerns of craftspeople. German thinker Karl Marx understood the great boon and horrific flaw of the new economic order. It separated production from consumption. The world where the artisan and client directly negoti-ated exchange made way for merchants from India to sell Ugandan cotton in Japan and for German cotton industrialists, who sought a more competi-tive product at farms in Togo, to buy advice from former American slaves. Global markets offer promise but enhance the invisibility of workers and economic volatility. When pushed by capitalism's innovative ways, these markets are prone to what Marx called "an epidemic of overproduction." In other words, the ability to produce ever more efficiently in speed, quantity, and cost drives oversupply in capitalist economies as well as wealth accumulation. "Why does over-production cause starvation?" asked an 1877 worker's placard in Chicago. To put it simply, it pushes down prices and negatively effects wages. And in the nineteenth century, wage reductions – as many who witnessed the effect agreed – wrought inhumane results.[26]

The markets of industrial capitalism, however, influenced society far beyond the status of workers and the relationship between labor and capital. Nothing better demonstrates the intricacies of violence and economy after the Civil War than the production and sale of American military goods. Not only would more weapons be distributed into private and public hands, but the market for military weapons also reshaped the postwar economy, which would soon center on railroad development and investment. A rapid postwar demobilization of Union forces started the process.

In the final year of the war, the US military shrank to 77,000 men from more than a million. This brought on a drastic unloading of war equipment by national and state governments. In March 1865, for instance, almost a month before Lee surrendered to Grant at Appomattox, Secretary of War Edwin Stanton started a sale of "war material and ordnance stores." Over the next five years, Stanton and his successors netted $7 million for the US Treasury. Adding more guns to society and helping to dampen domestic market demand, General E. D. Townsend in June 1865 authorized "soldiers honorably mustered out" of Union service to buy "their arms and accouterments." The Ordnance Department sold 158,244 muskets and rifles along with 14,619 sabers and swords – more than 1 million dollars of gear – to its own men. When Confederate weapons and those retrieved from battlefields are included, the number of war arms in private hands may have been as high as half a million (see Fig. 8.1). The Civil War not only educated hundreds of thousands of Americans in the use of industrial-era firearms, it flooded the domestic gun market and made the United States one of the most armed societies in the world.[27]

The gun proliferation catered to a sense of status (and of power and safety) that countless people, especially men, realized through gun ownership – a phenomenon readily seen in prideful poses and armed display in Civil War soldier photography (Fig. 8.2). But the emotional security of gun possession could not prevent the logical outcomes of the postwar gun increases. The first was more intentional gun use, as will be seen later in the battles over racial hierarchy. The second was an increase in the likelihood of gun mishaps. In Cincinnati in 1866, for example, officials credited twenty-two of eighty violent deaths in the city to accidental shootings. A statement by a frustrated reporter in Idaho suggests that this was part of a contemporary trend. "It seems that people will never learn not to sport with firearms by pointing them in jest at other people. Hanging a few would probably deter others from the experiment."[28]

The widespread ownership of industrial-age guns cannot be divorced from the postwar arms glut and continued gun manufacture. Indeed, military leaders fostered arms overproduction by falling prey to innovation. When the Springfield Armory, the federal arsenal that produced more

Fig. 8.1 Artillery captured from rebels, Hartford, CT: Taylor and Huntington, No. 2 State St., 1865. Library of Congress, Prints and Photographs Division. The image above is a common nineteenth-century format called a stereograph. When seen through a stereoscope, the two nearly identical photos would create a single, three-dimensional image.

Fig. 8.2 Unidentified soldier in Union uniform with cavalry saber, pistol carbine, and Colt navy revolver, *c.* 1861–1865. Courtesy of the Library of Congress, Prints and Photographs Division.

than 800,000 guns in the Civil War, developed the "model of 1868," the army purchased 50,000 new ones and "cleaned, repaired, and sold" its cache of the now-obsolete "model of 1866." The navy hired E. Remington and Sons to produce 10,000 breech-loading rifles. But when the weapon did not perfectly meet naval needs, the department sold them – under production and not yet delivered – to a private dealer in Maryland. Military representatives were thrilled. The Ordnance Bureau could keep its "skilled workmen at the factory in employment" to build a replacement. Congress members likewise applauded – not because the navy would be better equipped, but because the sale earned a profit of $27,600, which was the equivalent of 2,000 guns.[29]

The gun market oversupply in the United States reversed the global flow of arms. In 1861 and 1862, American military leaders had bought more than 730,000 guns from foreign dealers. Now, after the war, American gun sellers, public and private, sought to sell to individuals and nations worldwide. The United States government, for instance, peddled arms to South American countries. Turkey secured a 46,000-

gun order from Winchester in 1870. But it was not until hostilities began between France and Prussia that the United States and its citizens began to assert one of their signature modern achievements: command of the global military market.[30]

As a supposedly neutral party to the Franco-Prussian conflict, the United States could not sell weapons to either side. But prices that, a Congressional committee noted, "were largely in excess of the prices obtained before or since," soon overrode diplomatic concerns. The federal government sold more than 865,000 guns – 10 million dollars' worth – between July 1, 1870, and June 30, 1871. According to their later statements, of course, government agents conducted the sales in willful ignorance. "As far as I am individually concerned," explained Ordnance Major S. B. Benét, "I knew nothing in regard to where these stores went."[31]

What the major intended to express through his testimony – that the United States did not directly sell to the French government – was different from what he said: that he had no knowledge of where the arms went. Further Congressional examination revealed how the Ordnance Department maintained its innocence while "nearly all of the arms, though purchased by different parties, ultimately reached the same destination" of France. Many deliveries that took place in New York City, for instance, happened at Hudson River Pier 50, "where the French steamships lie." Here, shipmen marked the boxes of arms with R. F. or F. R. "I heard there, that it meant Republic of France or French Republic," said Hugh Reilly, an American deliveryman. The Ordnance Department thus preserved American neutrality, said Major Silas Crispin, since the guns were "delivered on docks and piers," not directly "to the steamships." Key, too, to this half-baked scheme to avoid responsibility for breaking diplomatic pacts were the private American dealers such as Remington and Sons. In the one-year French–German conflict, Remington served as a French agent. The company manufactured $3 million of guns for the French while buying $11 million of guns and munitions for them. Of these purchases, $1.3 million came straight from the US government.[32]

In the end, the Ordnance Department's activities encouraged lawmakers, who were undeterred from arms dealing by diplomatic affairs or lethal outcomes. Indeed, Congressmen acknowledged that material sold by the "United States to her own merchants and citizens found their way to the theater of war." But since Germany failed to register an "objection to the French government becoming the purchaser of the arms and ordnance sold," American leaders claimed there was no violation of international law.

They refused to acknowledge the situation that they created. Even less troubling to these American decisionmakers was the potential for such powerful weapons to end foreign lives. In a twenty-minute battle in 1877, for instance, Turkish-owned Winchesters killed 2,845 Russians. Only 42 Turks died in the exchange.[33]

Neither global relations nor death could counter profit. Gun sales from 1870–1871 added millions to the United States Treasury. This transnational arms market helped liquidate "in part," said the House committee, the "large public debt of the United States contracted during the [Civil] war." As the money earned by the national government in the gun trade helped to retire United States war bonds, the vehicle for Civil War debt, stakeholders turned to an alternative: the railroads – an industry amid massive growth. And they invested in hope of great profit. What they soon discovered, though, was that they were financing an economy that would prove devastating to many American workers.[34]

When coupled with the telegraph, railroads led a revolution in transportation and communication. A public and private alliance spurred the industry's growth. More than 150 million acres of land – as well as $100 million in loans and bonds – came from the federal government. The companies that advanced postwar railroad construction spent more than $1.7 billion between 1868 and 1873. The number of miles of track doubled to near 71,000.[35]

Railroad expansion continued a relationship that had blossomed in the Civil War. At the dawn of the rail revolution in the 1840s, Prussian military theorist Helmuth von Moltke declared "every new development of railways is a military advantage." In the 1860s, American leaders embraced the Prussian's truism. At the war's start, the federal government worked closely with northern railroads to secure troop and supply transport. Though the power was rarely used, Congress soon authorized the president to nationalize a railroad when "the public safety may require it." In 1862, the United States Military Railroads (USMRR) was created. From several miles of Virginian track, the USMRR grew by capturing and building rails in the South. Just three years later, with 419 engines, 2,100 miles of track, and 6,330 cars, it was the world's largest railroad.[36]

When the war ended, federal support did not. General Sherman wrote to General Grant, "I hope the President and Secretary of War will continue, as hitherto, to befriend these roads as far as the law allows." His hopes were well founded. The military importance of trains in the United States was secure, as modern transportation was the basis of postwar national authority. In "Protection across the Continent," a file submitted to Congress by Secretary of War Stanton, political and military leaders documented how the country would change from a collection of states spread across North America to a national entity policed from Washington, DC. More so than ever, federal force, White land ownership, and agriculture – the central elements of industrial capitalism – would work together. They did so under the aegis of the rails.[37]

In the 1870s, the Pennsylvania Railroad was the nation's largest company. It had 6,600 miles of track, 20,000 employees, and was worth nearly $400 million. Nothing in the American economy came close to the Pennsylvania's scope and scale. Though scholars are hesitant to blame the rail industry for the era's economic swings, its booms and busts matched those of the nation in the postwar era. As railroads affected national economic and political structures, so too did they affect violence throughout the United States. Nowhere was this more evident than in the West, where the industrial order heightened a fast pace of change and intensified conflict.[38]

Federal troops guarded railroad workers and supplies – and the government's reward was almost immediate. "We are in no condition to punish the Indians this year, for our troops are barely able to hold the long thin lines that are travelled by daily stages and small parties of emigrants," General Sherman had observed from the Nebraska Territory in 1866. Luckily for him, the end to the situation was in sight. "By next year the [Union Pacific] railroad will enable us to put a regiment of cavalry at Fort Laramie, which can punish the Indians, who are evidently disposed to contest our right to make roads leading to Montana." The military may have shrunk in size, but its newfound speed and range, which relied on private rail corporations, allowed for rapid deployment and force concentration. This new martial might, as Sherman said, proved important to the settler colonial project.[39]

Railroads sped Indigenous colonization and reinforced White racial convictions, both of which had been underway for centuries. Started by European explorers who asserted the Doctrine of Discovery, White Christian conquering was established as international law. In the United States, White leaders adopted the practice in their dispossession of Native peoples. An 1823 Supreme Court decision laid bare the violence behind the subjugation and who was in control of it: "The title by conquest is acquired and maintained by force," wrote Chief Justice John Marshall, continuing, "the conqueror prescribes its limits."[40]

And yet, the court believed, "a general rule" was that "humanity" and "public opinion" demanded "the conquered shall not be wantonly oppressed, and that their condition shall remain as eligible as is compatible with the objects of the conquest." In an ideal situation, "conquered inhabitants" are "incorporated with the victorious nation, and become subjects or citizens of the government." But the experience of post-Civil War America was far from this supposed ideal. At the time, the government counted roughly 270,000 Indians from 125 distinct communities. Ten of these communities – fewer than 100,000 individuals in total – remained powerful enough to contest the western migration of White Americans in the second half of the nineteenth century. And in 1868, President Grant sent a clear message to the Native peoples in support of his Indian Peace Plan. If they were unwilling to accept reservation life, which was a core component of the plan, they would "find the new administration ready for a sharp and severe war policy," he said. General Sherman agreed, promising that there would be "*peace* within their reservation and war *without*." It was a sentiment echoed with equal clarity by the Commissioner on Indian Affairs: "In case peace could not be obtained by treaty, or should the Indians fail to comply with the stipulations they might make for going on their reservations," he said, "the President might call out four regiments of mounted troops for the purpose of conquering the desired peace."[41]

Notably, the idea that violence cultivated peace stood as a truth for many in the postwar age. Developed in 1872 and treasured by US Army troops, the single-action, .45-caliber six-shooter by Colt was called the "Peacemaker."[42]

Grant, Sherman, and their political and military heirs held true to the goal of occupation and Indian suppression. By 1890, a thousand combat events left two thousand US military members and six thousand Indians dead. The federal frenzy to dictate terms to Indigenous peoples extended to the 1,500-mile pursuit and capture of eight hundred Nez Perce, who fled northwestern ancestral lands for Canadian freedom. However, as the historian Jeffrey Ostler explains, it is important to also include "the destruction of Native economies" as a vital "dimension of warfare" waged by the United States at this time. Such destruction, by and large, did not proceed through official programs. But, as the federal government endorsed the "general process of capitalist development of the West," it ultimately endorsed the damage and draining of resources central to "Indians' economic self-sufficiency."[43]

The restraint placed on Indigenous movement and the loss of Indigenous economies led to a variety of forms of protest and, to counter such protest, countless other horrific physical acts against Native individuals. For example, after meetings in Washington, DC, during which government officials demanded the removal of Utes from Colorado as well as the surrender of Indian leaders involved in recent battles with settlers, state militia, and federal troops, a Ute man named Jack returned home. Jack soon left his reservation and traveled to a Shoshone–Arapahoe enclave in Wyoming where military leaders noted he "failed to comply" with – or submit to – their ultimatums. Not only did Jack refuse to hand over his gun, he shot Sergeant Brady when the soldier demanded the weapon. In response, the men of the Seventh Cavalry fired a mountain howitzer at the tepee into which Jack had fled. They obliterated it and him. Four decades later, in a potent simplification, the soon-to-be authority on hostile difference and human extermination, Adolf Hitler, appreciated how White Americans won the West by having "gunned down the millions of Redskins to a few hundred thousand."[44]

Of course, North American Natives confronted the violence brought by industrialization and colonization in several forms. And even those who adopted modern agricultural practices on individually owned plots of land and attended Christian service could not escape the wrath of White American industrial norms. For as long as White leaders understood alternative customs as a threat, Native ways, even when blended with capitalist and Protestant ideals, stood as a danger. Many Indians learned that moving to reservations was not enough. At times, government officials demanded a complete rejection of tribal traditions. This dynamic was placed in stark relief when federal leaders sanctioned the removal of children to so-called "Indian Schools" in the 1870s. Shipped across the continent, the students were dressed in White-styled clothes, shorn of their long hair, and renamed. Not everyone survived. In 1898, for instance, a brain ailment killed Shoshone, Klamath, and Apache pupils, while the Pennsylvania Railroad struck and killed sixteen-year-old Oneida James Green. Fallen prey to disease, accident, and suicide, the bodies of Native children resting in Carlisle graves bear witness to the violent history of industrial colonization in America.[45]

The railroad boom that brought the West into the national fold and moved Indian children east also disrupted lives in the South. After the Civil War, many Black families in the South sought economic security in private land ownership. The South Carolina freedman Harry McMillan observed, "The people here would rather have the land than work for wages." Often, though, federal government programs created to address the economies of Black areas failed to stabilize African American land ownership. Instead, they promoted the wage labor ideal and protected Whiteness as a political project. In 1866, for instance, the race-based implementation of the Southern Homestead Act, which offered 47 million acres of federal land for development, pushed the freedmen toward the whims of the labor market. Not only was the available land of poor agricultural quality (it was filled with swamps or piney trees), local White officials found ways to block Black applicants. Such practices were widespread. "In the upper part of Charleston District the planters are quietly holding meetings at which they pass resolutions not to sell land to negroes," said journalist Sidney Andrews from South Carolina, and "in Beaufort District they not only refuse to sell land to negroes, but ... many black men have been told that they would be shot if they leased land and undertook to work for themselves."[46]

The barriers to Black land rights and the push to link southern Black economic security to wage labor brought clear results. While postwar White planter elites owned the finest farms that served as a foundation for the continuity of White political power, most freed Black families could not own land. Instead, many lived and worked as share tenants and share-croppers, arrangements that fostered generational cycles of impoverish-ment and debt. A common shift wherein poor Blacks and Whites moved from subsistence farming to farming a single cash crop such as cotton also added to needy southerners' woes. Rather than experiencing the eco-nomic prosperity promised by the ethos of hard work under industrial capitalism, however, these workers joined millions of small farmers, peas-ants, and sharecroppers around the world who provided essential material for industrial enterprises. They took part in the industrial capitalist system but did not enjoy its riches.[47]

Unable to wield land ownership or subsistence agriculture as a shield against racial biases and market instability, many freedmen turned to firearms for personal safety and government-run banks for economic security. As Louis Hoffman, a Mississippi gun-store owner, said in 1864, "when the freedmen being allowed to carry fire-arms, there was not enough guns to be gotten ... every negro wanted a gun." But the sort of protections Black Americans sought proved fleeting and perilous. By 1865, regulation in the Magnolia State – and soon throughout the southern states – promoted Black American disarmament. An African American convention in South Carolina condemned these measures as violations of the Second Amendment and an outrage to those "who have been soldiers, and purchased our muskets from the United States Government when we mustered out of service." Nevertheless, the promise of Black arms and federal support born of the 1863 Emancipation Proclamation remained under siege in the industrial era.[48]

Impoverished (and disarmed) workers in capitalist systems have but one solution to poverty, especially poverty wrought by low pay: work more and harder. An 1820 exchange between noted British economists reflected this capitalist concept. David Ricardo wrote to Thomas Malthus, "I am particularly pleased with your observations on the state of the poor; it cannot be too often stated to them that the most effectual remedy for the inadequacy of their wages is in their own hands." In the American South, the doctrine of hard work justified domination disguised as private property protection: one should not receive land as a government gift; work hard and you will obtain property.[49]

The consensus among White politicians was that former slaves should become diligent wage laborers. But some of the most radical voices sought for the freedmen protections beyond necessity to toil evermore. Building on a legacy of banks that the military had created for "the safekeeping of the pay and bounty moneys ... of colored troops," Congress formed the Freedman's Saving and Trust Company (the Freedmen's Bank) in March 1865. The bank received deposits from freedmen and then invested "the same in the stocks, bonds, treasury notes, or other securities of the United States." In safeguarding the capital of Black laborers – and increasing it through interest payment – the bank offered some defense against economic downturn. Such protective devices, though – especially ones that derive from the same speculative fervor driving American capitalism – have often proved to be less than secure. This was true of the Freedmen's Bank and its charter, the regulatory mechanism that delineated what trustees could and could not do. Faced with limited investment options as the national government reduced its war debt (in part through the sale of military weapons), bank director Henry David Cooke lobbied Congress to amend the charter. A subsequent version from 1870 removed the bank's mandate to participate in the market solely through federal government offerings. Bank directors could now place the earnings of Black men and women in areas of greater promise and risk.[50]

By 1873, the Freedmen's Bank had collected $50 million from about a hundred thousand Black depositors. Bound to Northern Pacific Railroad bonds through Henry Cooke and his financier brother Jay, the bank was set up for failure. At the time, railroad bonded debt was nearing $2.2 billion, a figure slightly greater than the national debt. Then, quite suddenly, the railroad market collapsed – a perfect example of overproduction and unstable capitalization. The first blow arrived in spring, when a crash in the Vienna markets scared European investors. They promptly shifted to conservative assets, pulling money from American railways. The cyclical nature of a United States bound to agriculture then exposed the system's weakest link. Each spring and fall, midwestern farmers financed their planting and harvest. Rural banks, which kept deposits in the East to collect high interest rates, responded in those months by withdrawing large sums. New York financial institutions were the most affected. In September 1873, as cash flowed west to meet seasonal demand, a tight New York money supply triggered banks to call in loans. Overextended railroad speculators could not pay.[51]

On September 8, 1873, the New York Warehouse and Security Company suspended operations. It had financed the Missouri, Kansas and Texas Railroad. Five days later, the principal banking house of Kenyon, Cox and Company, which owed $1.5 million worth of Canada Southern Railroad securities, failed too. And Thursday, September 18, the crisis enveloped Northern Pacific Railroad backer Jay Cooke and Company. Cooke's bankruptcy launched a nationwide economic break-down that "altered the face of society." Owners soon shut down half the nation's iron furnaces and, in New York City, one in four workers went unemployed. Half of the nation's railroads went into receivership. By 1880, the real wage of working-class Americans reached its nadir, stand-ing equivalent to wages in 1860. Until the aftermath of the 1929 crash, Americans used the phrase "the Great Depression" to denote the Panic of 1873.[52]

The Freedmen's Bank struggled to stay solvent up until July 2, 1874, when its remaining tens of thousands of Black account holders lost their savings. Congress faulted the bank's structure. White trustees had no obli-gation to invest their personal monies "as a guarantee for fidelity." But bank directors faced no punishment for their acts. "If adequate penal provisions had been incorporated in the original charter . . . the parties who practically control the operations of the institution would . . . have been subject or liable to criminal prosecution." The original charter had no such provisions. In 1880, when the Senate concluded the third and final Freedmen's Bank investigation, committee members saw no useful remedy. Several of the trustees had died, and those living were "with few exceptions, believed to be insolvent, and a civil suit would be unproductive if instituted against them."[53]

Corporate recklessness and fraud, as well as the economic violence induced by them, have often gone unpunished in America. For the freed people it was, like Black Union military service, a lesson in modern uncer-tainty. Capitalist freedom could mean wealth and a certain measure of autonomy, but so too could it bring deceit, hardship, and oppression – whether it come in the guise of the market or through market-based protection.[54]

The 1873 crash also directed the course of physical violence and race in the South. Since the Emancipation Proclamation, the government had acted as an agent for the freedmen – but when that role mixed with the hierarchies of race, the result was often confusing and unjust. In spring 1866, for example, 700–800 Black Union veterans in Norfolk, Virginia – many of whom had purchased their service weapons – were part of a sizable Black community. In celebration of the passage of the nation's first Civil Rights Act, the city's African Americans paraded and gave public lectures. When malcontented Whites interrupted, however, guns were fired. Captain Stanhope of the Twelfth Infantry ordered a company to investigate. It found one White man dead and, in a move that denotes how the state works to protect Whiteness, quickly disarmed all the Black men in public. That night, gunshots again rang out. This time, one report noted, every Black individual in the streets was fired on, and several were killed. Only the arrival of two hundred soldiers from Fort Monroe stopped the killing.[55]

The next month, a similar scene transpired in Memphis, Tennessee. A group of veterans from the Third Regiment of United States Colored Troops celebrated in honor of the day they had been mustered out. Shots were fired, and White citizens aided the city police "to shoot, beat and arrest every negro in sight." Forty-six African Americans and two Whites died; seventy-five persons were wounded. In addition, White agitators burned ninety-one Black houses and cabins, twelve schools, and four churches. General George Stoneman instituted martial law. (Stoneman, who had delayed his response, soon expressed regret over how violent Whites took advantage of his indecision.) The pattern continued elsewhere. In Texas, White supremacists patrolled several regions. Here, General Joseph Jones Reynolds noted that "the murder of negroes is so common as to render it impossible to keep an accurate account of them." "I have given this matter close attention," he continued, "and am satisfied that a remedy to be effective must be gradually applied and continued with the firm support of the army until these outlaws are punished or dispersed."[56]

What Reynolds did not realize, however, was that the war powers at the heart of the army's "firm support" would run out before White Americans' attachment to racial suppression. Many Whites in the North and South who fully supported the US Army as an occupying agent in the West (a place inhabited in their minds by Indigenous peoples) questioned the appropriateness of a White South governed through continued and explicit displays of national force. The most combative observers worked to undercut the legitimacy and strength of the federal government. Southern White leaders, in particular, targeted the so-called Reconstruction Amendments (the Thirteenth, Fourteenth, and Fifteenth Amendments) that banned enslavement, instituted universal birthright citizenship, and created national male enfranchisement. The amendments suggested the permanence of the shift heralded by the Emancipation Proclamation: federal force in protection of Black citizens. But, in a case centered on the recent change in the use of federal power, the Supreme Court worked against military force. "Was it the purpose of the fourteenth amendment ... to transfer the security and protection of all civil rights ... from the States to the Federal government?" asked Justice Samuel Miller, a Kentucky Republican. In a split 5 to 4 decision, the Court resolved that it was not. A federal attorney gave voice to the defiant spirit he believed would now be bolstered: "We [White men] trample upon these Amendments of the Constitution, and we intend to destroy and defeat them."[57]

Progressive leaders in towns, states, and even in the federal government devised creative solutions to work against such projects to uphold the hierarchy of race in the United States. The Republican governor of South Carolina, for instance, experimented with arming Black men. He secured Springfield muskets from the national government at no cost, used state funds to upgrade them, and then distributed the weapons to Black militiamen. The move was intended to protect Black communities and provide state leadership with a trustworthy force. But in the partisan postwar climate where many southern Whites stood by the Democratic Party, a state-sanctioned Black military body reinforced the thinking of many White Carolinians that Republicans sided only with Black people. When asked whether he would obey an order from the governor to enforce the law, a White militia captain said, "In case of difficulty, I will go with my race." The argument in favor of a comprehensive, race-based armament of citizens to guarantee safety and justice quickly collapsed. Racist decisionmaking – and the White supremacist organizations it spawned – endured.[58]

A brief expansion in national domestic security measures at the start of the 1870s showed the promise and problems (political and economic) of wholehearted civil rights enforcement. President Grant issued several proclamations ordering Ku Klux Klan members to disarm and disband, and he suspended the writ of habeas corpus in South Carolina. He also operated in accord with the Ku Klux Klan Act of 1871, which allowed for the national deployment of troops without state application. Federal leaders also instituted a skillful counterinsurgency against southern groups dedicated to

White supremacy. The efforts of Secret Service and Department of Justice detectives who infiltrated White supremacist societies like the Ku Klux Klan proved most potent. Federal grand juries would offer up more than three thousand indictments as a result of their efforts, with six hundred convictions and hundreds of plea deals. Sixty-five men served between one and five years in a New York federal prison.[59]

These crackdowns directly influenced the 1872 federal election, then the most open and fair in southern history. Yet officials who headed the Klan attack failed in a significant way. By and large, leading Klan members avoided arrest. One problem that federal agents battled was isolation. In distant regions, "the absence of railroads and telegraphs and great length of time required to communicate between remote points," said General Reynolds, facilitated the "devilish purposes" of Whites. Another was that once the government's quest was known, important Klansmen fled. In one instance, United States agents kidnapped a leader who had escaped to Canada. He was returned north amid Canadian protests over its sovereignty.[60]

Thus left behind by their leaders, poor southern Whites bore the brunt of the federal legal action against White supremacist organizations. And their capture and testimony exposed a systemic White-on-White class coercion central to Klan participation. A local official explained, "these men" are "bound together by terrible oaths to acquit each other, and do any kind of false swearing" in court. "I could not get out of it," said North Carolina's William Quackenbush; "if I had tried to, or told anything, I would have been killed." Hugh Lennox Bond, one of the federal judges who presided over the cases, believed there "ought to be another proclamation of emancipation" to sever men like Quackenbush from their wealthy, White overlords.[61]

The federal prosecution of Klansmen highlights important processes: first, the spread of federal force across government agencies and divisions (here the Department of the Treasury, which housed the Secret Service, worked alongside the Department of Justice); second, the tactic of infiltrating White supremacist groups by agents of the national state – measures which would soon be deployed against labor unions and ethnic groups deemed dangerous within the confines of hostile difference in a liberal society; and third, the politics – members of the Democratic Party analyzed the prosecutions not as an attempt at racial justice, but as an abuse of authority. They included in their analyses a criticism of the federal court using African American witnesses and jurors.

To calm Democrats, the planter elite, and those Republicans increasingly fearful of racial equity and a United States governed by federal troops, President Grant initiated a new approach: while government action roused southern Whites, he believed government inaction might quiet them. In 1872, the president replaced his hard-nosed attorney-general, Amos T. Akerman. Former Democrat George Henry Williams now headed a Justice Department that was starved of funding. Before they were shut down in 1873, Klan investigations and trials had nearly consumed the department's whole annual budget. It turned out that federal civil rights enforcement was expensive – and such expense amid an economic depression made it even more troubling to Democratic politicians.[62]

The political upheaval following the 1873 Panic further fated the demise of the Republicans' civil rights protections. Since the Civil War, which first marginalized national Democratic power, Republican leadership wedded the government's moral might to its political will. This eventually proved a precarious formulation. In November 1874, the House Republican majority, which stood at 70 percent, became a 37 percent minority. House Democrats overcame a 110-seat deficit, with 170 seats changing hands. This was the first Democratic House since 1859. Republicans even lost control of the statehouse in Massachusetts, one of the party's progressive strongholds. Blamed for the economic disaster, the Republican Party bore an election called by one of its newspapers "a day of terrible disaster to the country."[63]

The changes in national administration were immediate. Congressional Democrats understood the centrality of the military to their opponents' goals and launched an extended effort to defund national troops and remove soldiers from the South. The Democrats had redoubled their efforts when President Grant resisted, retreating from his appeasement approach to authorize national force against rifle clubs in the month before the 1876 election. He targeted armed White southern men who formed the rifle clubs – groups that used physical intimidation and death to prevent Black men from voting – but to no avail. Even with US soldiers in seventy locations in South Carolina, which assured a better Republican showing in the state, the election was far from peaceful or fair. One estimate supposed that White Democrats killed 150 African Americans in the weeks before the election. Even still, Congressional Democrats continued to lash out. They suggested that the Republicans had created an Indian scare to boost military spending and then used the troops in the South. Based on a platform that targeted federal military spending, the House majority thus took steps to stall funding the armed services. Indeed, at the close of the fiscal cycle on June 30,

1877, army soldiers no longer received pay. It took until November for a military appropriations bill to pass.[64]

Republican President Rutherford B. Hayes was more confident than his predecessor that direct federal involvement in southern civil rights was a mistake. He sought to achieve "safety and prosperity for the colored people" through "peaceful methods" – meaning the elimination of national troops and security forces in the South. Hayes focused not on social equality, which he believed government mandate was unable to deliver, but on uniform male political rights. Situating his approach in the idea of race-sustained interdependence, he believed that political parties representing the whole nation and (in his view) its biracial makeup were the answer – not regional parties segregated by race. "We want a united country," said the Civil War veteran and president.

Toward this end, Hayes put his faith in the Thirteenth, Fourteenth, and Fifteenth Amendments. They "shall be sacredly observed and faithfully enforced according to their true intent and meaning," he promised. But the president's southern plan, said former attorney-general Akerman, battled "lawlessness by letting the lawless have their own way." As Black voter suppression increased, White southern leaders demonstrated how and why federal government force is essential to the modern civil rights that Hayes held dear: by the 1878 midterm election, Hayes judged his "peaceful" effort "a failure."[65]

With southern Democrats once again empowered, President Hayes struggled to deliver on the promises of protection offered by the Emancipation Proclamation and equity by the Reconstruction Amendments. The Republican Party, though, also stood for free labor and industrial capitalism. On this economic front, Hayes found more success. Fearful of disgruntled laborers and the unemployed – groups that were demanding changes in the wake of the economic panic – northern and southern politicians found reason to coalesce. "The whites of the South must do as we do," said Hayes, a White northerner by way of Ohio. "*Forget to drive and learn to lead* the ignorant masses around them."[66]

"The ignorant masses" was a class-based term that included all laborers in the United States. With his words, Hayes thus channeled a longstanding elite paternalism that equated wealth with wisdom and leadership. But even more important, the president demonstrated a key tension within his party in the late nineteenth century. As a booster of minority rights, Republicans focused on Black workers and communities. As a booster of industrial capitalism, Republicans focused on free wage labor and industrial capital. These two political objectives clashed in the constructions of class and race created after the Civil War. In their efforts to protect workers in the United States from earning unsustainably low wages, for example, the Republicans failed to target employers and instead led efforts that fractured the working class along racial lines. They supported legislation that banned Chinese workers, demonized Asian labor, and contributed to horrific waves of anti-Asian violence. And though Republican rhetoric spoke of securing "the largest opportunities and a just share of the mutual profits" for labor and capital – "these two great servants of civilization" – party leaders steeped in elitism readily adopted the views and plans of business owners.[67]

The Republican Party thus cultivated a nationwide system where owners and managers kept wages low, fixed competition on price (not quality), and encouraged unskilled workers through reprimand instead of promotion. Better suited to sustaining hostile difference in American society, this system countered the Republican project of protecting Black rights in the United States. A piece in New York's *Commercial and Financial Chronicle* suggested that this was an economic system that leaders in the South could embrace: southern economic success would materialize now that its "labor is under control for the first season since the war, and next year will be more entirely so."[68]

Whiteness, elitism, property protection, industry defense, and labor discipline – the claims of corporate capital, claims that were national and received bipartisan support – soon supplanted southern civil rights as a rationale for the domestic use of United States force.

9

LAYERING LAW AND RESISTANCE
IN THE GREAT STRIKES

In 1877, a full-blown class crisis erupted in the United States. It was one of several that would mark the late nineteenth century. Beleaguered by a steady stream of wage cuts and losses in job autonomy, American workers wondered about the promises of equality, human dignity, and the protection of individual liberty and property – the promises of a liberal state. They wondered too about the benefits of the great innovations and wealth cultivated in the industrial age. Did the pledges of equality and prosperity apply to them?

How this question led to violent conflict reveals a United States steeped in differences of class and race that supported a particular political and economic hierarchy. A common misconception suggests that workers – often foreign-born – brought extreme ideas about labor to the United States and went to war with American capitalists. Such a view ignores a long American history of worker abuse – abuse that took economic, emotional, and physical forms – as well as the peaceful efforts of American workers to be heard and negotiate. In 1864, for example, an attempt to organize labor in North America developed in Kentucky. Workers proposed "to use every honorable means in our power to adjust difficulties that may arise between employers and workmen" and "to labor assiduously for the development of a plan of action that may be mutually beneficial to both parties." The workers vowed that they would discourage strikes except in exceptional cases. In language that suggested a wish to realize the greater levels of authority accessible to those empowered by a violent, White freedom, they also noted "that self-preservation is the first law of nature."[1]

Yet, while the events of Kentucky certainly model the willingness of many workers to negotiate, their willingness to come to the table was not always reflected in labor conflict. Indeed, more often than not, a political landscape unabashedly in support of industrial capital set the terms of conflict such that violence was nearly inevitable. The following account of the Great Strikes of the nineteenth century tracks the many ways in which leaders crafted workers as dangerous and corporate directors as worthy of the many layers of protection offered by the liberal industrial state.

◆

On Monday, July 16, 1877, when yet another wage cut was to take effect, leaders at the Baltimore and Ohio Railroad stood on alert. Already, B & O workers endured some of the lowest wages in the industry – many earned half their pre-Panic pay. As a result, the industry in North America was under siege. Hundreds of work stoppages, large and small strikes alike, had riddled railroads across the continent since 1873. Now, workers deployed increasingly urgent campaigns. Engineers for the New Jersey Central had recently stopped their locomotives at midnight and, regardless of location, walked away. Grand Trunk Railway workers, whose trains traveled between Montreal and Detroit, deployed the same scheme with equal success. On the 16th at Camden Junction, Baltimore (a central B & O location for trains headed west and south), the tactic resurfaced. A fireman (or stoker) – the person charged with tending fire for the steam-powered train – abandoned his station after his salary had been lowered by 10 percent. Fellow firemen in the yard, whose salaries had been likewise lowered, followed his lead. Earning $1.58 per day, first-class firemen now demanded $2.[2]

Railroad management immediately hired replacement workers. A high unemployment level – a national rate at more than 10 percent – ensured that there were ample qualified candidates. The striking firemen, though, had stayed in the yard to shut down its operation. In response, B & O authorities called on the city's policemen, who soon arrested three demonstrators. These forces then spread out to protect the trains. But, as the police moved beyond their jurisdiction to protect trains outside the city, a county judge recalled them. Railroad President John W. Garrett appealed the decision, countering with an 1860 state statute that allowed him to deploy policemen as company constables. This move ensured that the trains continued to run, but it did little to tame the protest. Soon, about a thousand workers – mostly tin can makers, but also box makers, sawyers, and train engineers – joined in. Hours after the start of the demonstration at Camden Junction, other B & O sites began to witness similar activity. In a few days, half a million laborers across many industries joined some hundred thousand rail workers in a strike that crippled the nation.[3]

This historic episode came to be known as "The Great Strike" (or Strikes) by those largely in sympathy with workers, and "The Great Riots" by those who were not. The earliest chroniclers of the event tended to focus on its singularity. "These events are phenomenal," said J. A. Dacus in his *Annals of the Great Strikes in the United States*. "The world is witness to a spectacle, the like of which has never before been presented." Yet while the scale of the 1877 strikes was exceptional, labor conflict in the United States, especially on the B & O rails, was not. From its start in the 1820s and 1830s, the railroad company had cultivated an environment of lower wages and worker discipline. Its employees, excluded from economic and political decisionmaking, frequently offered a violent retort.[4]

In June 1831, for example, as construction extended lines of the Baltimore and Ohio, contractor Truxton Lyon took the company's money, failed to pay his hired hands, and fled. In negotiations, railroad agents offered the abandoned workers compensation that "was much less than what was due to them from the Contractor." A quarrel soon developed that, for the men, was more about basic survival than economic security. Paid wages acted as subsistence property for unskilled laborers, akin to land for a poor farmer. Safety was an issue too. For not only did the workingmen dress their families in rags and suffer from malnourishment along with their wives and children, they had watched colleagues die on the job – buried alive during excavations and suffering from heat stroke in the southern sun. In response to the railroad's low bid, the men kept to their demands and went on strike.[5]

On the 29th and 30th, the strikers started to destroy the completed work for which they had not been paid. Reports note that rails of wood, iron, stone, and granite were burned, torn up, defaced, or broken in some manner. Two hundred to three hundred demonstrators resisted the county sheriff and his posse, a group of White citizens who served as the city's local armed agents because Baltimore did not have a professional police force until 1857. Railroad management then turned to the governor for help. As the Baltimore militia journeyed twenty-five miles to the location, it was accompanied by "several officers of the US service" who "volunteered their aid." In the early morning of the 31st, these new forces overpowered the workers, some of whom were arrested while "asleep in their cabins." The soldiers captured roughly sixty workingmen. President William Paterson and his directors at the Baltimore and Ohio celebrated their regained ability to use the property that strikers had threatened and destroyed.[6]

To explain their armed response, railroad and local government leaders offered a view of law and order that functioned in favor of corporate property and profit. Since the railroad was "a great public work," Paterson said, the deployment of local and state force in its service was mandated. Indeed, early corporations in the United States were legally bound to fulfill a public service. But, even as later corporate leaders subordinated (and then abandoned) this public function to investor profit, they continued to draw on government forces for support.[7]

The militia captains provided another justification for physically subduing the protesters: that the strike resulted from the influence of only a delinquent few. To ensure the arrest of the so-called "bad apples," they argued, one must arrest some of the good apples too. Brigadier Major Vanwyck of the Baltimore militia, for instance, dismissed the strikers as "deluded" and displayed little concern over whether his forces detained the right individuals. That the militia stormed the scene in the morning when there were no signs of engaged protest, entered workers' homes, and arrested men who were asleep raised no alarm for Vanwyck. "Most of the prisoners," he said, "are believed to have been active and some of them are *known* to have been the principal transgressors in the recent riotous proceedings."[8]

Even the intervention of a local judge, who interviewed the imprisoned workers and immediately released half of them as innocent, did not cause the militiamen to doubt their actions. In response to rail president Paterson's praise, militia leader G. H. Steuart bragged of his units' impartiality, stating on July 7 that his men were "ready to march at a moment's warning in defense of the person or property of the *humblest citizen*." True, perhaps, in a hypothetical sense, it was not true in practice. Vanwyck, Steuart, and their fellow militia officers found no contradiction in ignoring the rights of workers at the same time they pitied the workers' circumstance. Back in Baltimore, the militia appealed for "cloathing, provisions, or money" to effect the "speediest relief" for the "distressed families of the workmen" – families whose wage earners the state forces had just besieged.[9]

Seen through the eyes of the workers, the strike was about livable wages and safe work environments. Violence against property was a means to alleviate laborers' desperate ends. To railroad operators, police chiefs, and militia commanders, though, strikers were unfortunate and unruly.

Ultimately, these protests were about more than the money. An 1857 B & O strike demonstrates how worker autonomy was as important to the trainmen as were wages. To combat theft on freight trains, railroad managers had instituted a new protocol. They required freight train conductors to document the goods in their cars, seal the car doors with wax, and take responsibility for any item lost or stolen. On April 29, the conductors, with the support of other railroad men on the lines of the first and second division, refused to work. With the company's vital link between Baltimore and western Virginia shut down, the railroad took steps to protect its property: it added mail cars to trains (it was a federal crime to hinder mail delivery), hired additional workers, and protected both with armed guards (men gathered by the Baltimore sheriff). One publication said that the company was ready to put trains through to their "destination (Martinsburg) at all hazards, even at the cost of life."[10]

Friday, May 1, saw the greatest conflict. In a ravine near Ellicott's Mills, some three hundred workmen camped in the woods and kept up constant surveillance. When the railroad sent out four freighters, the men leapt on to the moving trains to stop them. Firing muskets, the train guards seriously injured two strikers. "One of the rioters, a young man, received a ball through both thighs, and it is thought he cannot recover," said the *Shepherdstown Register*. "Another was shot in the face ... many more are wounded." Despite the railroad's show of force, however, only one of the trains passed through. The workingmen encumbered the rest by stealing the coupling pins that held the train cars together. But on the next day, the arrival of three militia companies ended the clash. "The strike on the Baltimore and Ohio Railroad has been suppressed by powder and ball, used in the name of the State," reported the *New York Herald*.[11]

In 1857, many in the local media found state force an appropriate reply to the "personal violence" that was "used by the strikers." The staff at the *Spirit of Jefferson* in Charles Town, Virginia, echoed a common refrain: "As a general thing, we are opposed to strikes, and would counsel, if our opinion was consulted, all those who feel aggrieved by the regulations of their employers to stop working peaceably, rather than attempt to do by force that which the organization of society and the laws of the land could not tolerate." American society was, indeed, organized against the interests of working men and women. Yet arguments based in law and order tend to ignore the nature of liberal capitalism. Power and authority are not shared between corporate employers and their most susceptible employees – nor are they shared equitably between the national and local governments, corporations, and workers. With little or no nonviolent recourse to improve work conditions or secure different (let alone better paying) jobs, many workers in the system faced few choices.[12]

The empowerment found in violent acts disrupted this dynamic. Unsurprisingly, though, corporate and government leaders, many of whom sympathized with the indigence of the American working class, refused to accept the disruption. What took place was a brutal cycle of violence learned by generations of workers and business leaders.

In July 1877, the Great Strike that began in Camden Junction on the B & O Railroad was a part of this legacy, featuring the tension between sympathy for workers and the general demand for economic and social order. Once again, reports of violent workingmen devoured the non-working-class public's compassion. By the morning of July 17, strikers had already derailed a train in South Baltimore, critically wounding the engineer and fireman. Martinsburg, West Virginia, which quickly became a hub of early strike activity, saw the first combat injuries later that day. The town's railyards were backlogged with some "75 trains, comprising 1,200 cars, loaded with coal, grain and other freight, including 75 cattle cars, comprising about 600 head of stock."[13]

A B & O vice-president quickly messaged the state for military help. "I will do all I can to preserve the peace and secure safety to your trains and railroad operations," replied Governor Henry M. Mathews. And when seventy-five state militiamen appeared, their commander, Captain Faulkner, deferred to the company leaders. Faulkner ordered his men, for example, to assist in moving a westward-bound train. But just as the freighter started, a twenty-eight-year-old striker named William P. Vandergriff pulled a track switch to stop it. *Der Deutsche Correspondent* reported that John Poisal, "ein Mitglied der Miliz-Compagnie" (a member of the militia), exchanged gunfire with Vandergriff. The shots encouraged the other soldiers on the train to fire as well. Private Poisal, glanced by a bullet to the head, survived; Vandergriff, shot in hand, hip, and arm, suffered a limb amputation and died nine days later. In the aftermath of the exchange, protesters rushed the scene and jeered the military men. Frustrated and outmanned, Faulkner soon disbanded his unit. Notably, many of his soldiers immediately joined with the strikers.[14]

At 3 p.m., a second militia company traveled to Martinsburg. But the Mathews Light Guard from Wheeling, whose members either worked the rails or identified with the rail workers' plight, proved equally susceptible to the will of the working-class crowds. In recognition that his state troops were unreliable in a laborers' revolt, Gov. Mathews requisitioned President Hayes for federal soldiers. "Owing to the unlawful combinations and domestic violence now existing at Martinsburg," he said, "it is impossible with any force at my command to execute the laws of the State." Mathews estimated that two hundred to three hundred military men could end the strike. Hayes, through Secretary of War McCrary, pushed the governor for more detail. "What force can the State raise? How strong are the insurgents?" Mathews relayed that West Virginia had four militia companies. "Two of them," he said, "are at Martinsburg, and in sympathy with the rioters, who are believed to be 800 strong." A third was thirty-eight miles from the nearest railroad. This left the state with "one company of forty-eight men."[15]

On the night of July 18, President Hayes issued a proclamation for the "unlawful and insurrectionary" strikers to "disperse and retire peaceably to their respective abodes on or before 12 o'clock noon of the 19th day of July." On board a special train provided by the B & O company, four hundred national fighters were on their way to Martinsburg. Upon their arrival, they started providing armed escort for trains leaving the town, and they soon overpowered the strike.[16]

Back in Baltimore, Maryland, however, things took a bloodier turn. On July 20, the day after federal soldiers quelled the protests in Martinsburg, militiamen in Baltimore faced continued demonstrations by the city's B & O workers. They openly fired into a raucous crowd. Nine strikers died and about forty were wounded. As a result, fifteen thousand angry protesters descended on the city's B & O depot, where they trapped railroad officials, policemen, militiamen, the mayor, and Governor John Lee Carroll. Carroll, of course, requested federal military assistance. And in the days to come, additional gubernatorial demands reached the White House from Pennsylvania, Indiana, and Illinois – the strikes were spreading.[17]

With the railroads now "practically at a standstill," said a journalist, "the whole country must pay the penalty . . . The East is deprived of its food supplies, and the West of its markets." As the crisis spanned the nation and the nation's industries from Albany, New York, to San Francisco, it halted commerce essential to the overall economy and urban life. "Some of the heaviest manufacturing establishments are compelled to shut down for lack of material," the *New York Times* reported. As metropolitan behemoths like Chicago, Pittsburgh, and New York had but a week's worth of food in reserve, federal force against the "dangerous" workmen, some argued, must be immediate and energetic. "Only a strong Government can grapple promptly with the varied forms of danger that are now strewn thickly over one-third of the Union."[18]

President Hayes agreed that the quick, decisive deployment of public force was best. He sat at the head of a system that could compel the laborers to submit. But he was also a stickler for procedure, which he believed was the foundation of law and order. When state governors failed in their appeals to denote an "insurrection" or "domestic violence" (the terms used in Article IV, Section 4 of the US Constitution), Hayes demanded they reapply. The use of key words had to align with the statute's intent. When Governor James D. Williams asked for authority over national troops stationed in Indianapolis "in view of the threatened domestic violence growing out of the railroad strike," for example, Hayes refused. The president reminded Williams that the Constitution allowed for federal force "in suppressing domestic violence," not the threat of it.[19]

Strict procedural adherence did not restrain the Hayes administration's anti-worker stance, however. The US government had means to arm and reinforce towns and cities beyond state requisition. Despite the disagreement over troops in Indiana, the War Department added national soldiers to its Indianapolis arsenal. At Governor Williams's bidding, these forces were joined by four state militia companies, some 360 men, all of whom were housed and equipped at the nation's expense. A mandate to protect federal property and legal processes further extended this militarization. In places like Illinois, Treasury officials demanded and received soldiers to guard federal warehouses. "You will make such display of your force for moral effect as you may deem expedient," Secretary McCrary ordered his Chicago commander. Meanwhile, United States judges also called on the national military. In St. Louis, a district justice's request led to Colonel Davis taking control of railroad assets, tracks, and yards.[20]

The US Army protected national property, upheld the federal judiciary, and, in the end, dominated strikers. To outsiders, the layers of government force in America appeared brutally efficient. "No serious disturbances" had occurred, said the *Times of India*, "owing to the effective distribution of troops and strong bodies of special constables." To insiders, such force was a partisan ploy. Democrat Durbin Ward condemned political rivals disposed to this use of federal force: "no remedy is found in the Republican brain but the strong arm of government control."[21]

But President Hayes understood his Great Strike troop deployment differently than his detractors. Much like his southern policy, which was grounded in the idea that government soldiers were an impermanent solution, Hayes believed that armed force was insufficient to answer the problems of capital and labor. "The strikes have been put down by *force*," he said in early August 1877, "but now for the real remedy." Still, Hayes was confident that the use of soldiers, militiamen, and policemen presented a neutral, equitable approach to the conflict. He agreed with the consensus of most non-working-class Americans that "resistance to a reduction of wages" sat at the core of strike activity. From this perspective, worker protest ("resistance"), not corporate wage reduction, was the real threat. The president's actions thus echoed what he had done a year before while still the governor of Ohio: then he had used the state militia to safeguard coal company property and the strikebreakers' "right to work."[22]

In 1877, Hayes explained his views on the matters at hand. "Every man has a right to refuse to work, but no man has a right to prevent others from working," he said, once again defending the use of strikebreakers. He spoke similarly on the "question of wages." Ignoring that capitalists set wage scales for large groups of workmen, Hayes came out against the practice of using wage scales when the scales were set by workers' unions and collectives: "Every man has a right to determine for himself the value of his own labor," he said, "but he has no right to determine for other men the value of their labor." While Hayes railed against corporate greed and asked what could be done to sensibly "control the capitalists," he nevertheless consistently blamed workers. "The railroad strikers, as a rule, are good men, sober, intelligent, and industrious," he wrote in his diary. Labor strikes, though, "prevent men willing to work from doing so," "seize and hold the property" of employers, and furnish "opportunity for the dangerous criminal classes to destroy life and property."[23]

Elites in the media and politics agreed with Hayes and helped shift the public narrative during the Great Strikes. Initially, voices from the media reflected sympathy for the workers. "It is hardly to be wondered at that, wrought up to desperation by the scantiness of their pay, especially where they have dependent wives and children," reported the *Wheeling Daily Intelligencer* on July 20, "they strike out in a sort of blind fury against a further decline in their wage." But the notion that the workingmen's violence was an appropriate response to American inequality soon disappeared. Four days later, a California newspaper said, "The situation has been rapidly changing during the last twenty-four hours . . . It is no longer a struggle between classes on both sides, of which there is a good deal to be said, but it is a fundamental one of social order." In New York, editors further explained: "We warn the railroad strikers against allowing themselves and their cause to be overrun by tramps, thieves and the criminal class generally." A new understanding soon spread. "This is no longer a laborers' strike," said the *Cincinnati Gazette*. "It is the rioting of the subterranean elements of society."[24]

The existence of the so-called criminal classes in the United States was, by 1877, common knowledge for social and political leaders. Following a global conversation on criminality, many White elites, among others, believed they could identify lawbreakers by sight. This was the case, for example, when Baltimore police officer J. E. Riley arrested and charged Richard Fedderman simply for "Being a Suspicious Character" on July 21, 1877. The words "tramps," "vagabonds," and "unemployed" were used to characterize the jobless hordes who wandered the country in the aftermath of the 1873 Panic, depicting them as an innately inferior and dangerous caste in American life. Dr. C. W. Chancellor, secretary of state for the Maryland Board of Health, believed tramps to be "willful paupers" and saw poverty as the result of personal laziness. Many commentators joined in the refrain. "The genuine tramp has an intense horror of work, and the very suggestion of it causes him to flee to other parts of the country," said members of New York's General Assembly when investigating an increase in urban crime. Such thoughts pervaded even the minds of those who understood unemployed men and women to be casualties of the economic depression and technological advance ("the improvement of labor-saving machinery"). Tramps, vagabonds, the unemployed: these were "the dangerous classes – the unproductive, the untaught, and unprincipled multitude . . . from which come most of the thieves and paupers." And it was the poor and unemployed, "from motives of envious destructiveness and misanthropy," who are "always ready to inflame and take part in a riot."[25]

The move to interpret Great Strike violence as wanton lawlessness as opposed to a rational response to economic disparity erased the central question of wage increases raised by the rebellious B & O trainmen. "The controversy about wages," said San Francisco's *Daily Bulletin*, "will have to be adjourned until the broader question of order is settled." The violent summer of 1877 was the result of a social breakdown. Impoverished workingmen, once the object of sympathy, quickly developed into a target for national force – and they needed to be punished. "The men who managed this strike – who organized resistance to law, and interference with property – must be held responsible for the crime and disorder that followed," said an observer in Detroit. Chicagoan J. C. McClain had the solution. "There is a battery of artillery here, I believe, and presumably some grape and canister. Let them be used."[26]

In locales where support for the workers registered much lower than in railroad strongholds like Martinsburg, many leaders in the community banded together to do as McClain suggested: use force to thwart the strike. A combination of national, state, local, and civilian services patrolled the streets of Buffalo, New York, for example. Here, three hundred citizens, provided with "navy revolvers and heavy batons" and uniformed with "white silk badges," registered "as special policemen." They "belong to the rich and influential class," reported the *New York Times*. And 1,800 armed Civil War veterans added to Buffalo's civilian-based defense. The city's police, 1,600 state militiamen, and 350 soldiers under the command of a United States marshal also stood guard. By July 25, 1877, these security forces had "arrested several well-known roughs" and disabled "scores of others" with "well-directed cuts from the heavy batons." Ignoring the wounds of the protesting workmen, city officials celebrated "the bold front" that has "over-awed the rioters," proclaiming "that there will be no bloodshed here."[27]

The winning displays of state-backed violence in the Great Strikes validated those who believed in the existence of a natural-born criminal class as well as capitalism's exonerators, the Social Darwinists. "What is meant by 'survival of the fittest?'" asked a Chicago reader. "It is the theory that the strongest – those best adapted to living – survive the weaker in the struggle of life," replied the editor at the *Inter Ocean*. In fact, Social Darwinist adherents promoted the social theories of Herbert Spencer – theories that Charles Darwin, the biologist, never proposed. They upheld the idea that society was a contest, and that the contest took place in an equitable setting. "In this country all men start even in the race," declared the *Clarksville Weekly Chronicle* in Tennessee. From this perspective, it seemed that the results of individualism within a brutal contest – not a system of advantages and unfair conditions – explained the economic, social, and political hierarchies of the United States.[28]

Elitists, it is important to note, were not the only ones to embrace the American crucible of vicious competition. In the South, a Black industrial school leader celebrated life's contest in a comparison of African and Native Americans. Slavery, he said, had served as a school in which Black men and women had adopted lessons of hard work. The problem with Native reservations was that federal handouts made for dependent, deficient individuals and communities. "Let the Indian face the alternative of idleness with hunger, or labor with comfort, and then, not till then, will he work out his salvation." In a revealing statement, the school leader then asserted that Native peoples, not Black Americans, resided at the bottom of the American racial hierarchy. "Many might die," he added, "but the severe training of real life would develop ... a people who would assimilate with us, like the Negro and the Irishman" and "we shall see the survival of the fittest."[29]

Most members of workers' communities – or supporters of them – disputed the validity of such talk. They did not believe that the outcome of struggle, especially that of government force over strikers, justified the current disposition of American life. That "'the fittest survive and move forward in every craft,'" said an Indiana letter writer, "we emphatically deny, for it is paramount to saying that he who is promoted is worthy, and he who is not is not worthy." The writer continued, "Man is more a creature of circumstance than he is successful by will or rule." The circumstance that explained the 1877 strikes, the African American industrial paper *Southern Workman* later explained, was the deployment of federal force – "the abnormal extention of the powers of the national government" – and "a general decay and dissolution of the local communities." The paper asserted that greed – "the new thirst and passion for wealth" – sat at the foundation of the troubles. For it was greedy capitalists and state-backed violence that fostered the Social Darwinists' dream. Life was made "a struggle, not with the powers of nature to obtain the means of subsistence and comfort, which is the normal life for all men, but a struggle of men with each other in which an ever-increasing number must inevitably fail and be crushed."[30]

By the 1870s, workers were familiar with capitalism's crush. Armed citizens, police, private armies, and state and federal soldiers repeatedly delivered it to silence working-class complaint. The democratic impulse of workers, which looked for governments more responsive to the wants and needs of those at the bottom, met the autocratic response of corporate leaders, which looked to control government and retain the privileges of capital for those on top. In New York City in 1874, for instance, only three years before the Great Strikes and just four months into the economic Panic, peaceful protests of the unemployed flourished. With some hundred thousand laborers out of work, city parks served as rallying points. The workers and their families assembled to ask for government-led job opportunities (in the form of public works programs) and a variety of protections like halting wintertime evictions for the unemployed, improving child labor laws, banning convict labor for private businesses, and placing railroads, telegraphs, and canals under national or state control.

As seven thousand men, women, and children prepared to gather in Tompkins Square Park on January 13, however, city leaders decided they had heard enough. On the evening of the 12th, officials revoked the demonstration's permit. The next day, the marchers were therefore declared criminals – not only in the legal sense owing to the event proceeding without proper authorization, but in a social sense: they were poor, and many were immigrants. Arriving at the park fully armed, 1,600 city policemen, without adequate warning, began to beat and arrest them. Mounted units chased workers through the streets. The future labor leader Samuel Gompers, then a twenty-four-year-old cigar maker, called the police action in the park "an orgy of brutality."[31]

New York City Mayor William Frederick Havemeyer, a reporter noted, expressed pity for the conditions of the "poor men who showed that they were willing to work." Yet he "did not approve of their using threatening and intimidating language." Workers' words, then, justified the city's armed response, and the "emergency" – the large collections of workmen in public spaces – required police action "to protect the city against any excesses which some mischievous men among them might be led to commit." In addition, Havemeyer found the protesting workers "crazy," too easily influenced by communist foreigners. "Nothing else could have been done," he said of the police maneuvers. "Nothing better could have happened."[32]

In a speech at the Cooper Institute, the German-American activist Augusta Lilienthal displayed a keen grasp of the situation's dynamic. The city had promoted fiscal concerns in the name of social order and security, but, she wondered, what about democracy? "The constitution afforded them [the workers] the right of free speech, but the police robbed them of the right." Law and order had triumphed over worker protest. This trend extended beyond security tactics and was soon emboldened by new legislation. After an 1876 strike on the Boston and Maine railroad, for instance, Massachusetts lawmakers made the endangerment of business interests by striking a punishable offense. Seven states prohibited train engineers from vacating their position "at any place other than the scheduled" destination. Capitalism, it seemed, demanded safekeeping from laborers and their public remonstrations.[33]

During the turbulent summer of 1877, labor repression continued. In Philadelphia, the mayor banned public protests. In Reading, Pennsylvania, where strikers burned down the Lebanon Valley Bridge on July 22, the state militia fired without warning as it marched from the train depot. The soldiers killed ten demonstrators and wounded forty while delivering gunshot wounds to five policemen. Delaware's *Middletown Transcript* called the trade – a $150,000 railroad bridge for human life and suffering – "A Heartless Butchery." But a dispatch special to the *New York Times* portrayed the event differently. The militia volunteers, it reported, were "assailed by rioters" and defended "themselves with rifles." In a statement that soon proved inaccurate, the *Times* bemoaned that "many policemen" were shot, "but, unfortunately, none of the rioters injured."[34]

The Philadelphia and Reading Railroad offered $15,000 for the arrest of the men who burned the Lebanon bridge. These men, it was presumed, had also incited the militia's subsequent killing spree. Days later, the authorities, including US troops and members of a company police force, arrested four Reading workingmen, the so-called "ringleaders of the riot." By contrast, no militiamen were charged. On July 30, militia commander General Reeder explained why. When he and his soldiers disembarked from the train, he said, they were met by "a large body of men" who hurled "violent gestures, coarse insults, and unspoken threats." He thus stopped and mobilized his regiment, "loading the pieces and moving the musicians to the rear." As to what happened next, Reeder was evasive. "No person ordered me to fire; neither did I fire nor direct another person to fire upon the crowd." Of course, the militia did shoot civilians, but Reeder claimed later that new discoveries vindicated his men: investigators had collected "five cart-loads of stones" at the scene. The "size and weight" of the stones, Reeder said, led him to believe that only working-class men could have thrown them: "it is almost certain strong arms were employed in the work." That rocks are no match for guns was irrelevant. The muscled bodies of laboring men stood as a danger. And working-class danger, as countless elitists of the middle and upper classes proclaimed during the Great Strikes, must be punished. "A standing army" is necessary "even as a police force," wrote one New Yorker, "so long as there is an ignorant rabble with hungry maws and greedy hands."[35]

At the close of the Great Strikes, a Virginia newspaper measured railroad debt against the summertime labor strife: "These bonds are the things that are making the mischief." The collapse in the value of these railroad bonds had helped to create an economic depression that led owners to slash wages and disregard safety, all in the name of profit. The mischief, though, had been in the making for most of the century. At its core was tension and dissent over the limits and boundaries of capitalism. To corporate and political leaders, the working-class crusades appeared to upend a natural order. James Harrison Wilson, who operated the bankrupt St. Louis and Southeastern railroad as its court-ordered receiver, was horrified by worker demands during the strike. "I shall certainly not permit my employees to fix their own wages, nor dictate to me in any manner what my policy shall be." Wilson's vision of political economy, one that thrived through to the 1930s Great Depression, obstructed workers' collectivism, dismissed working-class expression, and denied equal or fair access to capital. Of course, there were many who disagreed. "I don't think that capital should be protected against labor," said Tennessee Republican Thomas B. McElwee. But from West to East and South to North, industry sought to retain American inequality and used physical force to ensure it. "We cannot now stir a step in our life without capital," explained Yale sociology professor and Social Darwinist William Graham Sumner. "Capital is force, human energy stored or accumulated, and very few people ever come to appreciate its importance to civilized life."[36]

———————◆———————

In 1979, historians Philip Ross and Philip Taft stated that "the United States has had the bloodiest and most violent labor history of any industrial nation in the world." Yet many scholars remain puzzled about why this should be. Some suggest that the United States working class lacked the more structured identity found among European laborers and thus took to the streets as an angry, disorganized mess. But American workers between 1890 and 1914 show a level of union membership on par with that found in Germany, France, and, in the later years, Sweden. Though American workers did not reach the high marks of union participation found in Great Britain, they demonstrated a significant level of class awareness and collective action. The experiences of workers in the United States in 1877 supports this conclusion. So the question remains, why was the American industrial experience so catastrophic?[37]

It is tempting to turn to economic inequality for explanation. One scholar notes that the "intensity" of American labor violence resulted from "the intolerability of particular living and working conditions." Here, the argument is that economic inequality leads to violence. And in 1877, the wages and living environments of most American workers were, indeed, unlivable. Unfortunately, however, impoverishment in the lives of American workers was not unique. A global comparison of economic inequality in the late nineteenth century scores Europe far worse in this measure than the United States. In 1870, the wealthiest 10 percent in Europe owned more than 85 percent of their nations' wealth; in the United States, the top 10 percent owned a little more than 70 percent. (Not until after 1960 would the United States take a global lead in inequality.) Economic disparity and conditions undoubtedly made American labor violence a possibility, but inequality itself fails to explain the scope and scale of the violent labor experience in the United States.[38]

The definition of "labor violence" is key. For if "labor violence" indicates the number of workers killed, then the United States is near but not at the top of the list. Estimates of "workers killed in labor disputes, 1872–1914" show Great Britain with seven, Germany with sixteen, France with about thirty-five, the United States with between five hundred and eight hundred, and Russia with some two to five thousand. Figures like these are admittedly difficult to track. The number of workers killed in Pittsburgh on July 21, 1877, for instance, varies between sixteen and twenty depending on the source. And in the United States, such numbers often exclude the Black individuals lynched each year, itself a form of labor control. Nonetheless, the relative scale of the violence that killed workers at the time is clear – and the United States and Russia are murderous outliers.[39]

A broader understanding of "labor violence," which includes violent acts against property and worker repression, renders the United States unique. In 1877 and beyond, protesting American workers targeted the machines and buildings necessary for their work (see Fig. 9.1). Business owners, and the political and police leaders they influenced, often failed to make meaningful distinctions between violence against property and violence against people. They argued, in effect, that the objects of capital were just as valuable as a human life. Such thinking aligned with a greater culture that, in the 1870s and 1880s, upheld corporations as worthy of the same Fourteenth Amendment protections as individuals. By the 1890s, many American courts secured so-called corporate rights with more vigilance than the rights of African Americans, the individuals whose rights the amendment was intended to shield.[40]

Viewed as a more important constitutional charge than protecting individuals, the protection of corporate property wrought a terrifying backlash against laborers. Not only did the American workforce face

Fig. 9.1 Railroad property destroyed by workingmen. S. V. Albee Stereoviews of the Railroad Strike of 1877, AIS. 2019.05, Archives and Special Collections, University of Pittsburgh Library System. Similar to figure 8.2, these two photos are a stereograph.

armed civilians, local police, state militia, and national troops, they confronted professional strikebreakers, labor spies, armies for hire, and corporate arsenals. In 1878, Allan Pinkerton of the Pinkerton National Detective Agency explained that, since the end of the Great Strikes in 1877, his security agents had "been busily employed by great railway, manufacturing and other corporations, for the purpose of bringing the leaders and instigators [union and strike organizers] of the dark deeds of those days to the punishment they so richly deserve." "Hundreds have been punished," Pinkerton exclaimed. "Hundreds more will be punished." Indeed, the deployment of private forces and private arms, common in America but rare in the rest of the industrial world, exacerbated labor conflict and directed conflict resolution toward physical confrontation. By the 1930s when corporate armament peaked, a company such as Republic Steel, which had 52,000 employees, kept on hand 4,000 gas projectiles, 2,700 gas grenades, more than 500 revolvers, 245 shotguns, 143 gas guns, and 64 rifles.[41]

The dominance of corporate capital in industrial America was no accident. Time and again, business and political leaders sought to restrict the right of workers to gather peaceably, picket, form a labor union, or strike. Despite the massive disruption to the railroads in 1877 (and in subsequent years, especially 1886), the federal government failed to develop a process to settle railroad labor disputes until the Erdman Act in 1898. Ten years later, in *Adair v. United States*, Supreme Court justices struck down an Erdman provision that protected railroad worker unionization. Such protection, the court declared, is "an invasion of personal liberty, as well as of the right of property" – for corporations.[42]

Far more than their global peers, working men and women in the United States fought for the existence and viability of their collective actions. Some newspapermen in the wake of the Great Strikes sympathized with the workers' plight. They begged for Congress to stop "legislating in the interests of corporations only" and to defend "the masses" from "any combination of capital whatsoever." Sadly, politicians' refusal to heed these voices ensured that the ascendance of capital and the suppression of labor would deliver cataclysmic results.[43]

Labor repression did not affect United States workers equally. Skilled workers, those with specialized knowledge and abilities unique to their job, more readily resisted wage cuts and challenges to their autonomy. Unskilled or lower-skilled workers stood more vulnerable, especially during an economic depression when the unemployed often proved eager to serve as replacements. The power dynamics of skill was certainly a source of division among the American working classes. But the pervasiveness of the strikes in 1877 across region and industry minimized this tension. By contrast, divisions of race, gender, and ethnicity proved far more problematic.

In 1877, the railroads (and other US businesses) drew from a diverse labor pool. Men and women with Irish, Chinese, Japanese, Native American, Eastern European, Mexican, and African American roots worked as laborers. Meanwhile, leaders in media, politics, and industry often nurtured gender, ethnic, and race-based discord. In July 1877, in Braidwood, Illinois, for example, a coal company imported four hundred southern Black miners during a strike. These men assumed the jobs of the striking miners, who were of European descent. And, if employment competition was not enough to incite violence between the two groups, local newspapers assisted by promoting racist stereotypes. The Black men, it was reported, "obtain the larger part of their provisions by prowling around at night and plundering the gardens, hen-roosts, and pig-pens of the old miners." It was the criminal actions of Black people, the *Ottawa Free Trader* of Illinois explained, not the refusal of the coal mine owner to pay a livable wage, that triggered the violent reaction that soon unfolded. Armed and angry, the strikers drove the Black men and their families from the town – or, as the newspaper said, the strikers "ordered the niggers to leave."[44]

The *Free Trader* highlighted the Whiteness of the strikers, who, despite their three-month strike and armed resistance, were called "sober, industrious, quiet and tractable." Significantly, when light-skinned immigrants arrived in the United States, they entered, as historian Edward Ball explains, "on the top tier of a two-tier caste society." And indeed, as both the European miners' actions and the newspaper coverage of them show, anti-Black violence was one way to align with socially and politically empowered Whites. Nevertheless, the newspaper still trafficked in ethnic caricatures. Of the White miners, the paper noted a "trades-union tyranny" arising from the "ideas that they bring with them from Europe of the necessity of strikes and violence to maintain their 'rights.'" The newspaper coverage of the strike focused on the imaginary degeneracy of all the Braidwood miners – thieving Blacks and radical Europeans. This coverage served to underscore the order and decency of the mine owner. With the help of some twelve hundred state militiamen, the mine company returned the Black men to town, and, obscured from public view as the original cause of the violence, the 56 percent wage reduction ($1.25 per ton of coal to $0.70 per ton) remained in place.[45]

Damaging portrayals of Black male workers abounded in the summer of 1877. When Black men led labor protest, their ability and authority was often questioned. Public accounts negatively portrayed Black initiative, linked Black leaders to chaotic violence, and almost always emphasized the race of the individual or individuals involved. In covering a labor dispute in Greenbriar, Virginia, for example, the *Daily Gazette* did not call the striking Black waiters "strikers" but rather "riotous negroes." In another case, when reporting the arrest of labor organizer C. H. Loder, a New Orleans paper said: "C. H. Loder, the negro who led the lower rabble, was arrested."[46]

One report from the *State Journal* in Missouri covered White and Black workers during the Great Strikes in St. Louis. When White strikers ("a committee of men") at the Laclede Gas Works asked for a reversal of their 25-cent pay cut, the newspaper reported that "the request was immediately granted, and the men returned to work." But when "some 300 negro laborers ... marched up the levee and forced all steamboat companies ... to sign pledges to increase the wages of all classes of steamboat and levee laborers," the *Journal* was shaken: "their demands were of a most extortionary character." Both sets of workers, it must be noted, earned a wage increase from their employers. Yet, in a richly racist representation, the *Sedalia Weekly Bazoo* observed, "The riotous negroes in St. Louis, was one of the dark features of the mob."[47]

Condemnation of Black leadership was common practice in White-authored publications. When construction workers in Galveston, Texas, struck in July 1877, the *Chicago Daily Tribune* was clear. "The strikers are confined entirely to unskilled colored laborers. White mechanics are working as usual." Of the Black men, the paper said: "The movement seems to be without leaders or common purpose, and wherever it has been met with firmness it has accomplished nothing. The negroes appear to be unable to explain why they struck or what they demand." Some newspapers suggested that White outsiders – perhaps some kind of trained or professional labor agitators – were to blame, the implication being that there wasn't even enough Black leadership to get collective action off the ground. In a line that resonated with reporting on the Great Strikes, the *Tribune* offered, "The movement was excited by white demagogues." Similarly, and just a few days later, the *Public Ledger* of Memphis, Tennessee, suggested that Black-led worker resistance had been "instigated by strikers from Northern cities."[48]

The suggestion that White outsiders controlled Black workers was not substantiated by any of the newspapers. Rumors like these simply served to belittle Black-led worker action, Black fortitude, and Black intellect. Unfortunately, however, it proved influential. In his *Annals of the Great Strikes*, journalist J. A. Dacus used the *Chicago Daily Tribune* article nearly word for word to describe the African American labor protest in Galveston:

"The negroes appeared to be unable to explain why they struck, or what they demanded." To state that Black workers did not operate as free and intelligent agents in society was an attempt to undermine Black labor activism. It also opened the way for a more thorough silencing of Black workers and a more violent repression of Black bodies in American streets. As one Dallas newspaper reported: "The brave battalion of the Second Regiment, from Houston, had a trip to Harrisburg, Wednesday night, to quell the riotous negroes who wanted more money for their work."[49]

Race and ethnicity often mixed with gender to further split working-class concerns and mobilization. In August 1877, fifty washerwomen at Marley, Eunson and Company struck in protest when the Newark, New Jersey, shirt factory hired some male washers at a lower rate. As usual, newspapers failed to convey the voices of the female workers. Instead, publications like the *Cincinnati Daily Star* framed the labor demonstration as a battle of the sexes. The newspaper asserted that "nature and custom had allotted" washer work to women and thus called the newly hired workers "male washerwomen." These men, the *Daily Star* claimed, "attempted to oust woman from her sphere." Following sexist conventions, the newspaper upheld women as unyielding protectors of a female domain: "Imagine . . . fifty washerwomen on strike! Behold them with arms and heads awry, laying down the law and gospel to the boss of that shirt factory." The newspapermen applauded the washerwomen's eventual victory not because it was a well-fought labor dispute, but because the result was necessary for maintaining a gendered order. It was an example of what was possible when female workers "judiciously resolved to put their little feet down."[50]

While the newspapermen approved of the women's activism for retaining the washer position as female work, activist women – by virtue of women appearing in public for economic justice – undercut nineteenth-century sexism. A Wisconsin paper thus challenged the celebration of the Newark washerwomen strike (resolved by the firing of the male washers) in a spiteful statement: "Order once more reigns in Warsaw." These words stressed the involvement of Newark's immigrant community in the protest. They also hinted that the arrangement of these "foreign spaces," where workers spoke of "equal pay for equal services for women as well as men," could not endure in the United States.[51]

Akin to coverage of African American and immigrant workers, news media portrayals of women looked to weaken female action and demands. This was particularly noticeable in instances of female violence. During a silk worker strike in Patterson, New Jersey, in June 1877, female workers attacked a male colleague when he "favored returning to work." They tore his coat, threw salt and pepper in his eyes, and, after he drew a revolver (which was not loaded), ran after him for a half mile, captured him, and brought him before a court justice. Many journalists failed to record such bold public acts. In the Dakota Territory, one paper mocked the New Jersey women, who ultimately failed in their quest to reverse the wage reduction. "A recent strike of female silk weavers was quieted by liberal doses of ice cream."[52]

The plight of washerwomen in Galveston, Texas, highlights a struggle unique to Black female domestic work in 1877. As women, these workers faced an array of gender-based biases. As low-status workers, the women faced an array of class-based biases. And as Black persons, the washerwomen faced an array of race-based biases. The newspaper coverage of the Black washerwomen at times highlighted only one of these identities. For example, newspaper editors saw no problem in writing about the women on strike in Galveston and then immediately following up with comments that suggested the "natural" role for women is found in relation to their husbands and children: "There is such a thing as too much self-denial on the part of a wife and mother," said the *Cincinnati Commercial Tribune*. At other times, coverage of the Black washerwomen highlighted several of their identities at once. The *Evansville Journal* noted the race, class, and gender of "the colored washerwomen and scrub women of Galveston Texas" in an article covering an attack by the striking workers on a Black female strikebreaker. The article continued, bringing together a class-based gender racism to frame the violent clash. To the editors of the newspaper the Black washerwomen were "healthy Amazons": exotic, violent Black female workers.[53]

The striking Black washerwomen organized their collective action in a group called the "Ladies of Labor." As the historian Tera W. Hunter notes, their use of this name helped to distinguish the washerwoman protest from the male-led worker strikes then underway in Galveston as part of the Great Strikes. The name also accentuated a claim to a gendered status, "ladies," more commonly deployed to describe upper-class women. At the same time, the "Ladies of Labor" label embraced the radical role of these female workers – women who would take to the streets, occupy public space, and, at times, physically fight against their oppressive labor conditions.[54]

In 1877, as the women struck for a wage of $1.50 per day, they fought resistance from Black and White conservative men, competing businesses that sold the same services at lower prices, and the mainly well-to-do White women whose laundry they cleaned. Nonetheless, the Black washerwomen in Galveston managed unity through a common goal, a wage increase. But when the promise of a better wage was not enough, the strikers used threats and physical force. Large groups of striking washerwomen scared, chased, and, in a few instances, punched, kicked, and clawed at women, Black and White, who sought to cross the picket line. But these were not the only low-status workers with whom the Ladies of Labor would fight. During their strike, the washerwomen often targeted their lower-priced competition found in the city's several Chinese laundries.[55]

In 1877, the Asian laundrymen of Galveston worked in a trade opened to them by one of the first significant waves of Chinese immigration. Best described as migrant laborers, these men had fled places reshaped by global capitalism and imperialism, places where former ways of living had become impossible. Better pay drew many Chinese men to California in the 1849 Gold Rush and most arrived to work as miners. Some worked independently, some for mining companies, and others saw in the mining camps a business opportunity. Laboring in the California mountains, miners sent their clothes for cleaning and pressing to Hawai'i (the Sandwich Islands). When Chinese men opened laundries near these remote camps, miners no longer had to wait months for their washed clothes. By the 1860s, a Chinese man working in a Los Angeles laundry could earn $15 to $20 a month – a significant increase over the monthly wage of $4 to $5 he would gain in rice or tea fields near Guangzhou.[56]

In the 1870s, a later generation of Chinese laundrymen – some of whom turned to laundry as a result of White anti-Asian violence that targeted miners and railroad workers in the United States – filled a different market need. A shortage of laundresses in places like Texas presented a new, profitable prospect. As lower-priced competition for the Black washerwomen, though, the Chinese laundrymen were seen as enemies of the 1877 strikers fighting for a higher wage. Rather than trying to persuade these men to raise prices and wages in solidarity, the Black washerwomen intimidated them to shut down their businesses.

Adding to stark differences already on display as Black working women battled with Chinese working men, the *Dallas Daily Herald* offered harsh anti-Asian journalism when reporting on the Galveston labor situation. The Black washerwomen, the newspaper said, "went for all who worked on cheap, and especially the 'heathen Chinese,' who 'washee Mellican man's clothes so cheapee allee while.'" Phrases such as "Melican malliage" (American marriage), "me no likee," and "muchee talkee" introduced many White Americans to Chinese immigrant communities. Printing in ethnic and racial dialect may have captured speech idiosyncrasies, but there was something more sinister at work as well. The widespread nineteenth-century practice among White publications was to frame foreign subjects as non-White, uneducated, and, all too often, deserving of violence. During the labor strike, the washerwomen summoned an equally violent xenophobia. In August, the Ladies of Labor issued an open letter to the people of Galveston in which they threatened the owner of a Chinese laundry to leave the city or else. "Miss Brooks is ready to sholder her rifle," the washerwomen warned, and "Miss Sillese [is a] sharp shooter."[57]

Galveston's African American washerwomen soon met a more empowered opponent, however. On the strike, one paper reported: "The emergency was met by most of the ladies of the city, who proposed going to the kitchens, rather than burthen their husbands with extra expense." The ability of wealthier White individuals, in this case White women ("ladies"), to assert their privileged status and perform domestic work rather than support wage increases was one clear way to undermine the Black female workers' demands.[58]

The divide between Black and White was never starker, however, than when White men wrought violence against Black laborers. Here, it is important to mark both change and continuity. Many White businessmen, for example, used state and local law as well as personal measures to direct and control Black workers in the late nineteenth century. Indeed, in some parts of the South, modes and treatments developed to control slave labor, such as whippings, remained in place regardless of their legality. "Three parties have been sent before the District Court for whipping two colored men on Mr. Busky's place and two others on Mr. Stewart's place," recorded a Baton Rouge paper in June 1877. But as the arrest of the "three parties" documents, the shift from war to industrial capitalism, slavery to freedom, shifted the forms of legal punishment. In the 1870s, the whipping of free Black workers was not allowed.[59]

What remained more stable, though, was the degree of White answerability for violent actions against Black working men and women. July 1877 offers at least two examples. The first took place when an African American worker aboard the steamboat *Texas* refused instructions to move wood. Instead, the man disembarked and protested his work conditions by sitting on a nearby fence. The mate, a White man, then "ordered him out of his sight." "The negro declined to move," the *Nebraska Advertiser* said, "and was shot ... the murderer was not arrested."[60]

The second example also happened on a boat. Around midnight on July 4, Dr. W. G. Wilson, a White man and an assistant surgeon in the US Navy, started "a drunken frolic" aboard the *N. P. Banks*. The steamer, which had departed from Fortress Monroe, soon resounded with a shot from Wilson's gun. Wilson hit William Brown, a Black man and the intended target, in the wrist. But the bullet traveled through William and struck the sleeping Jennie Brown, a Black woman, in the face. William was wounded,

Jennie struggled for her life. Officials arrested Wilson after the boat docked in Norfolk, Virginia, and the city's mayor remanded the surgeon to jail for ten days while they awaited "the result of the woman's injury."[61]

Ten days later, William Brown recovered and Wilson was released from jail. But on July 26, after more than three weeks, Jennie Brown died. Officials arrested Wilson once again, and the navy removed the surgeon from his post aboard the receiving ship *Franklin*. "This should be a warning," said the *Easton Gazette*, "to young men against carrying fire arms." One must wonder, though, what kind of warning it would be. On October 6, a jury decided the city courts "had no jurisdiction." Wilson was thus released on $3,000 bail, and his case was moved to a Virginia County Court. Three days later, Justice B. T. Tatem "examined" Wilson and cleared him of the charges altogether. "Dr. Wilson, who shot and killed a Negro woman on the steamer *Banks*, discharged," said the Richmond *Daily Dispatch*, though "everybody thought that the jury would visit the full penalty of the law on Dr. Wilson."[62]

Wilson, of course, was cleared by a judge, not a jury, but incidents like this represent the widespread embrace of White supremacy against efforts to build more equitable state and national systems. Just a year earlier, in November 1876, for example, James W. Dixon, a Louisiana cotton planter, accused Percy Smith, a Black employee, of working too slowly. Dixon then shot Smith in the back with "a double-barreled gun loaded with buckshot." Smith died on the spot and the planter fled to Texas. In August 1877, just weeks after Jennie Brown died in Virginia, Francis Nicholls, the Democratic governor of Louisiana, issued a proclamation and $500 reward for Dixon's arrest. It is "important and highly necessary," he said, "that the perpetrator of such crime be brought to justice and dealt with as the law directs." These words, a standard statement from the governor's office, would seem to reflect the notion of an impartial legal system. The reality, however, was more complex.[63]

Nicholls, who in 1860 at the age of twenty-six owned five Black people and in 1862 earned appointment as a brigadier-general in the Confederate Army, was a Conservative Democrat. Since the 1868 enactment of a Louisiana constitution that protected African American civil rights, many so-called conservative White men in the state had been targeting Black voters and their White allies. In Nicholls's ascension to office in 1877, the White supremacists received the change that they had been killing people for. "The government belongs," said a delegate at the convention authoring what would become the new state constitution in 1879, "to the white race ... as an inheritance and birthright." Indeed, with Nicholls in office in 1877, the local courts reflected the return of White structures of power within the state. This was especially true in Louisiana, but the trend could be seen throughout the United States. "Every colored man suing for his wages brings his case before a jury who are prejudiced against him because of his color," explained White Congressman William Henry Harrison Stowell, a Republican from Virginia. "Every colored man tried as a criminal appears before a jury who are inclined to believe him guilty because of his race."[64]

In the end, Nicholls's pledge that the planter Dixon be "dealt with as the law directs" was simply a promise that the planter would be treated in court as a wealthy, White man. And he was. In September, law officers arrested Dixon in Dallas and sent him to jail in New Orleans. The trial on November 10, 1877, took one day. In the morning, twelve White men were impaneled as the jury. Court proceedings started at 12 noon and finished at 6:30 p.m. After thirty minutes of discussion, the jury declared Dixon innocent.[65]

Under the guise of racial impartiality, the White jurors reinforced the long-established hierarchy of White men over Black workmen and Black bodies. Even though Dixon shot Percy Smith in the back, the *Dallas Daily Herald* reported, "the testimony elicited on the trial fully established the fact that the killing was done in self-defense." Dixon's White family, White friends, and White neighbors agreed, filling the courtroom with a "tremendous and spontaneous burst of applause and cheering" to celebrate what they believed to be the "justice and popularity of the verdict."[66]

In stark contrast to such episodes, when Black, marginalized, and poor people committed a crime, they were punished. In June 1877, for instance, Governor Nicholls signed "death warrants in the following cases: Adrien Evegne, colored, for the murder of Richard Jumer, colored . . . . Josquino Florenzo, Chinaman, for the murder of Marie Louise, colored . . . George Morris, colored, for the murder of Sarah Jones, colored . . . The condemned are to be executed in Orleans parish prison yard June 15th." In Arkansas in July, a newspaper recorded the punishment for another African American. "Norman Lindsay, colored, was hanged at Helena, Ark., Friday, for the murder of Rev. Charles Hightower, also colored."[67]

Yet there was a notable exception to this racial dynamic of crime and punishment. When a Black person stood accused of crimes against a White individual, a different code applied altogether. In Arkansas, law officers arrested a Black man suspected of killing a White man. As policemen guarded the prisoner in a wooden building by the train tracks, three armed, masked White men appeared. They moved the police out of the way, opened the door, and shot the Black man dead.[68]

10

WORDS AND ROPES: THE POSTWAR BATTLES OVER RACIAL ORDER

Supporters of the Thirteenth, Fourteenth, and Fifteenth Constitutional Amendments sought to establish a more just legal framework in the United States, which had so recently been a slave society. The amendments guaranteed freedom from enslavement, citizenship to all those "born or naturalized in the United States," and voting rights to all men no matter their "race, color, or previous condition of servitude." These measures challenged the political status quo, and Black men soon openly engaged in politics to an extent "without precedent in the history of this or any other country that abolished slavery in the nineteenth century."[1]

But the democratic revolution delivered by an interracial alliance, mainly channeled through the Republican Party, proved to be short lived. Within two decades of the war's end, White politicians and community members, especially in the South, had used tradition, statute, and brute force to disenfranchise many Black voters. From the Capitol Building to buildings on Main Street, these White men attacked antiracist proposals and the proposals' supporters. The attacks undercut economic and social plans intended to equitably construct race and helped secure institutionalized segregation.

New forms of racial difference and racial violence represent this period in American history, a time when many so-called "ordinary" people took part in cruelties to uphold notions of race, safety, and control in their locales. The production of hostile difference within liberal society served as justification of and incitement for such brutality. Politicians and civilians built the structures of race (and other forms of difference) and contributed to vicious cycles of violent acts (such as lynchings). Where the Reconstruction era marks a burst of African American empowerment and an opportunity to better realize human equality, it also marks violence as an enduring social and political institution in the United States.[2]

From the 1870s to the 1890s, the fight to redefine race after the Civil War was on display in Congress. Twenty-two men, two Senators and twenty Representatives, served as the nation's first Black lawmakers. All came from southern states, places where slavery's legacy left robust African American communities. The presence of Black Congressmen, as White Representative William Stowell noted, was groundbreaking: "He [the Black man] is given equal privileges in Congress now. Instead of being represented by proxy as three-fifths of a man, he now represents in his own person a whole man." This wholeness, though, was often something Black legislators had to defend.[3]

"And I say there is not one gentleman upon this floor," explained White Congressman John Thomas Harris of Virginia, the former slave-owner, "who can honestly say he really believes that the colored man is created his equal."

"I can," answered Alonzo Jacobs Ransier, Black Congressman from South Carolina. Born to a free Black Charleston family with Haitian ties, Ransier proved a formidable foe for White supremacists (see Fig. 10.1).

Fig. 10.1 Hon. Alonzo J. Ransier. Courtesy of Brady-Handy photograph collection, Library of Congress, Prints and Photographs Division.

"Of course you can," Harris said. "But I am speaking to the white men of the House; and, Mr. Speaker, I do not wish to be interrupted again by him." "Now, Mr. Speaker," he continued,

> I know the objection that will occur to the mind of every gentleman on the other side of the House, and of every one here who differs from me on this question. They will say this is prejudice – unjust prejudice. Admit that it is prejudice, yet the fact exists, and you, as members of Congress are bound to respect that prejudice. It was born in the children of the South; born in our ancestors, and born in your ancestors in Massachusetts – that the colored man was inferior to the white.

Ransier did not relent in his challenge of Harris's racist theories. Immediately, he stood up and said, "I deny that."

"I do not allow you to interrupt me. Sit down; I am talking to white men; I am talking to gentlemen," shouted Harris.[4]

That Black men could not represent the schooling, wealth, and social grace of a gentleman was a matter of course for the White Virginian. Like many a proponent of hostile racial difference, Harris framed race as an organic, undeniable condition. "I say, sir, that prejudice may exist, but it is a natural prejudice, a prejudice that God himself placed in the hearts of [White] southern children and the [White] southern people." The North Carolina Representative William McKendree Robbins, who had been born and raised in a slaveholding family, argued in similar fashion regarding the inherent disposition of race. "Not equality, but infinite inequality and variety, is the law of this universe," he said. "Does God, then, repeat? No, sir ... the negro is not a black white man. He is a different man, with different talents, different duties, and different rights."[5]

To politicians like Harris and Robbins, race was inborn – part of a biological and religious ranking that placed White men on top. And a refusal to abide by such rankings had real consequences, in their view. "The penalty that Nature imposes for the violation of her laws," explained the Democrat and one-time slaveholder Congressman John DeWitt Clinton Atkins of Tennessee, is racial "extinction."[6]

The reason for the frank Congressional discussion of race in 1873 and 1874 was a civil rights bill. The bill's supporters sought to ensure equality in public hotels, public transportation, and public schools. "Colored men and women are excluded from our hotels, our common conveyances and places of amusement or resort, and our children from public schools, in almost every State of the Union," Alonzo Ransier testified, "unless ... they submit to unequal and degrading terms." After Congressman Robert Brank Vance, the former Confederate general and slave-owner, said he observed no denial of rights to Blacks in his home state of North Carolina, the African American lawmaker Richard Harvey Cain explained to him why. "Now," said Cain, "[racial discrimination] may not have come under his observation, but it has under mine . . . and the reason why I know and feel more than he does is because my face is painted black and his is painted white. We who have the color – I may say the objectionable color – know and feel all this."[7]

However much Black Congressmen like Ransier and Cain vocalized their experiences of public inequality in the United States, opponents of the proposed legislation disregarded them. Missouri Representative Aylett Hawes Buckner, who once enslaved nine Black people, called the proposal "A bill to create social equality in the late slave-holding States, to consolidate the two races in hostility to each other, and to destroy public schools." New Jersey Democratic Representative Robert Hamilton, agreed: "This bill is a very extraordinary measure; it seeks to efface the natural distinction between black and white; to wipe out all the conventionalities of life." "When we consider what has been done for the colored people in the United States, taken, as they were, from a state of abject bondage . . . and then made absolutely free, made citizens," Hamilton said, "we would naturally conclude that if they [African Americans] had any sense of the principle of gratitude, they would be more gracious than to seek to force themselves into the society and association of the white people." Representative William Smith Herndon, a former enslaver of thirty-eight Black individuals, added, "Eight million whites cannot elevate the four million blacks to their standard by stooping in degradation to their level of superstition, vice, and ignorance. All history has proven that such attempts have resulted in the ruin of the stronger and more refined [White] race."[8]

These declarations of White supremacy unveil slavery's profound influence in Congress nine years after the Civil War's end. But some White Congressmen, like Massachusetts Republican Benjamin Franklin Butler, recognized the failings of their White colleagues' racial machinations. Butler had once believed in a stark racial hierarchy himself. His awakening took place in the 1860s when, as a Union general, he witnessed the valor, honor, and sacrifice of Black soldiers on the battlefield. In an instant, Butler explained, he realized the existence of a shared humanity: "An old-time States-rights democrat became a lover of the negro race."[9]

In 1874, Butler exposed the myth of racial difference. "Was there any objection in the South to consorting with the negro as a slave?" he asked fellow Congressmen. "O, no; your children and your servants' children played together; your children sucked the same mother with your servants' children; had the same nurse; and, unless tradition speaks falsely, had the same father." "You talk about your social prejudices against social equality!" Butler continued. "You once associated with the slave in every relation of life. He has now become a freeman, and now you cannot associate with him ... Why is this?" Butler answered his own question: "It is because the laws of your land, the Constitution of your country, gave all men equal rights in accordance with the fiat of God Almighty which has made some of them your equal in all things, and therefore he is no longer to be associated with or tolerated!" A piercing insight closed Butler's speech: "This is not a prejudice against the negro or any personal objection to him – it is a political idea only."[10]

Representative Butler understood, to use the words of sociologist Dorothy Roberts, that "the very first step of creating race, dividing human beings into these categories, is a political practice." While it is common to hear that race is a social construct, the political construction of race explains how the violence, abuse, and humiliation of race and racism function within a structure of power. Democratic Party critics of the civil rights bill stood ready to deny that power has anything to do with race. The New York Representative Samuel Sullivan Cox, for example, made such an attempt when he offered an amendment to the proposed legislation: "that the penalties of this act shall not be limited to persons of the white race, but that colored or black men who may be in charge of any place of amusement or entertainment, or any other persons hereby affected by this act, who shall discriminate against their white brethren, shall also be held liable to the penalties of this act." Cox's effort to highlight a process of what would today be called "reverse racism" – an effort to reject the idea that power is integral to the function of race in society – quickly unfolded. Representative Butler noted that Black men "are included" as possible offenders in the civil rights bill only "because the bill provides for every natural person, and the negro is a very natural person."[11]

The civil rights debate of the 1870s, in which one side proclaimed human equality and the other human difference, deeply frustrated Representative Cain. He was especially irked by how certain White Congressmen wished to relitigate the recent past. Congress had provided amnesty to most Confederates after the Civil War; these southern men did not face legal consequences or banishment from political office for their role in the rebellion against federal authority. To Cain, the ex-Confederates should be the gracious ones in Congress. "Inasmuch as general amnesty has been proclaimed, I would hardly have expected there would be any objection on this floor to the civil-rights bill, giving to all men the equal rights of citizens," Cain said. "There should be no more contest."[12]

But there Cain sat with his Black colleagues listening to Texas Representative Herndon declaim on federal abuses against slaveholders and Representative Robbins assert the need for White political control. The Thirteenth Amendment overrode states' rights, Herndon declared. "It not only denied the right to protection of slave property," he claimed, "but denied the right to the property itself, seized the four millions of slave property, worth four billions of money to the owners, without compensation, and cut off redress." Though Robbins was willing to let go of what happened in the war ("It is impossible to undo what has been done," he admitted), the former Confederate officer of the Fourth Alabama Regiment was every bit as wedded to hostile difference moving forward. "Sir, slavery had fulfilled its mission, which was to civilize and christianize an originally savage race," he said. "It was God Almighty's school to which he sent the negro to be trained and developed." As Robbins minimized the violence and injustice of enslavement by turning slavery into a divine mission and the whip an educational tool, he had an equally problematic prescription for American politics: "Sir, it is time to recur to the doctrine which is bound up to the salvation of this country – the doctrine that this is a white man's land and ought to be a white man's government."[13]

In the late nineteenth century, whether the racial discussion in Congress centered on African American rights, Asian immigrants, or Indigenous communities, White supremacists agreed that political authority should reside at the intersection of race and gender, placing authority solely in the hands of White men. This cast a particularly ominous shadow over Black women, who represented the inverse of that equation. For the onetime slave-owner Senator James Burnie Beck of Kentucky, the reason to deny all women the right to vote in the United States was, specifically, that there were large numbers of Black women. He explained, "We have been compelled in the last ten years to allow all the colored men of the South to become voters." Already, he suggested, it will take "years and years of care" to turn Black men into "intelligent voters." "Now, it is proposed that all the women of the country shall vote; that all the colored women of the South, who are as much more ignorant than the colored men ... shall vote." Of this, Beck was sure: "Take them [Black women] from their wash-tubs and their household work, and they are absolutely ignorant of the new duties of voting citizens."[14]

The racist presumptions of a flawed Black intellect not only sustained Black political disenfranchisement, it continued to assign Black bodies to labor's lowest rungs. Whether Black labor be coerced, as under slavery, or cut-rate and bullied, as it was after slave emancipation, White supremacists used the economic position of Black communities in the United States as evidence of Black incapacity. To Representative Harris, little had changed in the South now that African American slaves were free: "they [Black people] are still our laborers in the field and our principal dependents in our families and our homes." "The negro was brought to this country, and why was he brought?" asked Representative Robert Milligan McLane of Maryland, "He was brought to labor; he was brought to labor because his labor was cheap." McLane's overall point endured: Black labor resided at the bottom of the national hierarchy.[15]

Much like the analogy drawn between enslavement and attending school, framing enslavement as a cheap source of labor hides the intention, violence, and degradation that sustained the system of human slavery – and the system of Black wage labor after emancipation. Politicians like Beck, Harris, and McLane deployed language that deliberately naturalized a connection between work and race. Saying "Black labor was cheap" is different than saying "Black labor was made cheap." This linguistic turn assigned social and economic disfunction to individuals and communities to explain why Black men and women mostly labored in low-status work. The politicians avoided discussions of political policy, economic organization, and physical terror in their accounts – all part and parcel of the White supremacist playbook in the late nineteenth century.

Of course, this playbook extended beyond the question of Black labor to encompass all non-White workers. In 1882, for example, during a debate on Chinese immigration, Representative John Smythe Richardson, the ex-Confederate and slaveholder, used racialized economics to characterize "the Chinese laborer or cooly." The Chinese worker, Richardson said, "does and can afford to work for one-half the wages which the colored must have in order to get along." At no point in the debate did Richardson question the heartlessness of providing to Chinese workers half the pay of Black workers, a group once acknowledged as the lowest paid in the nation. He opted instead to depict what he saw as an ability to live in extreme poverty as a racial trait distinct to Chinese immigrants.[16]

One function of this race construct was to foster tension among workers, making it more difficult for them to stand in shared protest (as we saw in Chapter 9). But another function was in operation too: to foster the privileges of Whiteness. "The poorest and humblest white person in my district feels and knows that he or she belongs to a superior race morally and intellectually," said Representative Milton Jameson Durham, a Kentuckian who once enslaved a nineteen-year-old African American woman, "and nothing is so revolting to them as social equality with this inferior [Black] race." For the scholar W. E. B. Du Bois, the reason why many poor White workers supported the hierarchy of race was clear. They "were compensated in part by a sort of public and psychological wage," he said. In other words, they received a boost in status and pride for supporting Whiteness.[17]

In the shifting social order of the post-Civil War age, Blacks and Whites and immigrants moved to towns and cities for employment in industry, and this dynamic advanced interracial contact in public and private. These changes challenged the worldview of White supremacists, who made regular speeches in Congress proclaiming a need for White self-defense against the presumed perils of living side by side with racial "Others." The impact of their speechifying was real: it affected federal policy and thus shaped people's lives. But it also served as a deliberate distraction. The truth was that Whites were a comfortable majority in the United States. In the three censuses between 1870 and 1890, the White population represented between 87 and 88 percent of the whole. Paired with this numerical dominance, White people wielded social, economic, and political authority.[18]

Yet claims of White peril abounded. "It is not desirable to have more of them [Chinese immigrants]," said Representative George Douglas Wise, former enslaver of at least eighteen Black men and women, in 1882. "Self-preservation is the first law of nature . . . I hold it to be a duty to provide against that which is dangerous to the existence of our free institutions, to Christian civilization, and to social order." Maine's Thompson Henry Murch agreed. "Are we to ignore the law of self-protection for the sake of that spread-eagle sentiment in which we all love so much to indulge about this being the 'land of refuge to the oppressed and asylum for all nations!'" Born to a slaveholding Virginia family in 1862, Representative Claude Augustus Swanson understood the violent disenfranchisement of Black voters in the 1870s and 1880s to be a "daring" act of White "self-preservation" that "wrested our State government from negro Republican rule and supremacy." Indeed, White supremacy, not "negro misrule," said Swanson in 1893, "is the ark of our covenant . . . it is the corner stone and guaranty of our property and civilization." Fellow Democrat William Henry Denson, born to an Alabama slaveholding family, echoed Swanson. "We [White men] intend to rule that country, and we intend to lynch any man, white or black, that outrages a woman," he said. "We do not intend to resign . . . the means of [White] self-preservation."[19]

Proclamations of this sort obscured the nature of the violence enacted by Whites on Black people in the South. For, if White men acted with "daring," then their violent act becomes one of self-endangerment and self-sacrifice in the face of a legitimate threat. If White men "wrested" authority, they gained control through a legitimate struggle. And if the White men guaranteed the protection of "property and civilization," they acted legitimately and lawfully.

But when Congress started its first investigation into racial conditions in the South in the early 1870s, it uncovered, in many cases through the testimony of Black women, a reign of anti-Black terror. For example, on a May night in 1871, nine members of the Ku Klux Klan arrived at the home of Samuel and Hannah Tutson in Florida. The mob separated the Tutsons from their children, aged nine, five, and ten months old. Five men then took Samuel into the fields and whipped him. Four took Hannah outside, tied her up, stripped her naked, and then whipped and sexually assaulted her. "There were four men whipping me at once," Hannah recorded. As a domestic worker, she knew the assailants. "I have been working and washing for them," she said. "I had not been two weeks from his [one attacker's] mother's house, where I had been washing."[20]

On the night of the violence, the White men also tore down the Tutsons' home. They wanted the land Samuel and Hannah had purchased for $150 a few years earlier. The men did not offer to pay for it; they believed that they could take it. This is a brash example of the relationship emphasized by political scientist Megan Ming Francis between "anti-black violence and the accumulation of capital."[21]

In 1872, Congress published thirteen large volumes documenting extensive economic, sexual, social, and political violence perpetrated by White southerners on Black communities and individuals. The Democratic Party minority, notably, did not believe that White supremacy and the systems of hostile differences it supported had anything to do with these violent acts. Their view was registered in the report by the likes of Samuel Sullivan Cox, who alleged that it was the steps taken to promote racial equality that were to blame. "The atrocious measures by which millions of white people have been put at the mercy of the semi-barbarous negroes of the South," said the White supremacists, caused an outbreak of violence on Black people.[22]

By 1893, thirty years after the Emancipation Proclamation, Representative Charles Henry Grosvenor, a White Ohio Republican, had seen enough. He told White southerners that they had fostered a "mighty cyclone of crime" against African Americans. In Congress, they had done so with words. It was the words of Congressional White supremacists and White supremacists throughout the United States – and, specifically, their constructions of race – that had cultivated hate and violence. The acts of anti-Black violence they cultivated, Grosvenor believed, had cultivated the rationale of human hierarchy alongside words of difference and hate. Grosvenor used a letter he received from a White southerner to make his point. "This whole Southern country is now reaping the crop that they have been sowing for the past twenty-five years," the southerner wrote. "They have educated and trained every young man in the South to become a lawbreaker – to shoot negroes, stuff ballot boxes, and generally disregard law and order." Pennsylvania Representative Josiah Duane Hicks concurred. "For years they [White southerners] have been sowing the wind, and they are now reaping the whirlwind," he said. "Let us look for a moment at the social condition of the South, which is the natural result of the bulldozing, the kukluxism, and white-cap methods of Southern gentlemen," as well as the legal and illegal election measures "as practiced by the Democratic party."[23]

Grosvenor and Hicks were correct: the words of the White supremacist Congressmen revealed how they and many others thought about the world and how they experienced it. Words, as historian Joanna Bourke describes, "tell us what to feel and how to act." Grosvenor and Hicks were wrong, however, that racial violence was mainly a southern affair. While many of the most sensational events took place in the South, incidents of racial violence happened throughout the nation. And wherever they occurred, such violent acts relied on the explicit and implicit support of individuals – those who bore witness in person and in print.[24]

◆

On July 18, 1893, a Black man encountered two White sisters, the McCaddens, in a rural part of Shelby County, Tennessee. What happened next remains in dispute. The "two white women complained that while driving to town, a colored man jumped from a place of concealment and dragged one of the two women from the wagon," said the Black activist and journalist Ida Bell Wells, "but their screams frightened him away." Newspaper accounts across the country reported a different scene. Some claimed the Black man "dragged Miss *Mollie* McCadden from her horse on the public highway and attempted to outrage [rape] her." Others recorded that the Black man assaulted (meaning rape or attempted rape) "Miss *Maggie* McCadden." Several papers took the middle path to report that a Black man attacked "the Misses McCadden." Whichever of the two women was targeted, one newspaper said that the Black individual stripped both of their clothes before one of the sisters "beat the villain off with a heavy stick."[25]

As word of the incident spread, several posses formed to capture the purported assailant. Stories now added an additional charge against the Black man who, while on the run, allegedly raped "a negro girl." This second alleged criminal act led to "the negroes" joining "the white posse." Such coverage suggested that these cases of sexual assault had brought together an angry, armed, interracial band of men. However, while the reported criminal events remained rather unclear, it was even less certain who the criminal was. Newspapers noted the culprit of the assault on the Black victim only as "the negro who attempted to assault the Misses McCadden yesterday."[26]

In this case, the overly broad description cost Charley Martin his life. Martin, a Black man, was shot dead in the back because he did not stop moving quickly enough to satisfy a White posse member. Lee Walker, the man eventually arrested for the McCadden attack, also suffered injustice. In the words of criminologist Margaret Vandiver, the evidence that Walker was the lawbreaker was "exceptionally weak." A sheriff in New Albany, Mississippi, told a constable that "Lee Walker, a rough negro man, who answered the description in every detail, had just passed through town, looking footsore and weary." Neither physical trait (dark skin – the only noted detail of the suspect) nor tiredness reliably linked Walker to the attempted crime. What the sheriff knew, however, was that Walker had been jailed "several times for assaulting different women." So, he arrested Lee Walker.[27]

The consequence of the arrest was immediately clear. Virginia's *Roanoke Times* titled its Walker coverage "A Lynching in Prospect," while the *St. Paul Daily Globe* granted that with Walker in custody "a lynching is probable." It was an open secret that violence policed the hierarchy of race in late nineteenth-century America. Indeed, awareness of this fact may have influenced Walker's decisionmaking when he was being questioned by authorities. For, unless he was indeed "half-demented," as was noted in one source printed two years later, Walker understood the dynamics of race and violence he faced. Walker confessed to a reporter in Memphis that he had attempted to rape the Misses McCadden as well as the other women. Notably, while there is a long history of using coercion to interrogate Black men, particularly in the South, there exists little record of the circumstances surrounding Walker's admission. Nor is there evidence that Walker knew that by confessing he would not be subject to identification by the McCaddens. But what he may have known is that the decision to admit to the crimes may have saved his life, at least for a time. Once he confessed, the suspect was moved from rural Bond Station (where a lynching was highly probable) to a heavily fortified jail in Memphis (where a lynching was less likely). Even then, Judge Scruggs ordered Sheriff A. J. McClendon to ensure Walker's safety.[28]

But it was not enough. Needless to say, starting in the late evening on Friday, July 22, 1893, a mob gathered at the Memphis jail. As the *News-Herald* in Ohio reported, "McLendon ordered his men not to hurt any body," but the sheriff's refusal to deploy force against members of the group seemed to embolden them. "Wild disorder reigned about the jail as the mob gathered to wreak its vengeance," said the *Morning Call*. "The gate of the south wall of the massive structure was forced with a bar of railway iron, used as a battering-ram, on the shoulders of men, and after several attempts squads of men crowded their way within the walls." The use of the rail section to break down the gate helps corroborate an observation made in the *New York Times* that the men most active in the event "were nearly all railway men."[29]

Inside the jail, the men used a chair to knock Sheriff McClendon unconscious and then found their way to Walker's cell. Some reports claim Walker, as he was dragged from the jail, took hold of a glass shard and tried to kill himself with a cut to the neck. Others, including one in the *Los Angeles Times*, noted "his throat was cut" by mob members. Most accounts support that the angry White men stabbed and slashed Walker as they took him outside to the streets of downtown Memphis. "Blood streamed from him in torrents." Two blocks from the jail, near "Williams lumber-yard," the men stripped the seriously wounded Walker of his clothes, put a rope around his neck, and raised him up a telegraph pole. Walker's hands were left untied and "he clutched at the rope when raised to his feet." As his naked body swung, members of the crowd punched and spit at him, dashing him up against the pole. "Then," said the *Hartford Courant*, "a big railroad switchman pulled his legs until his neck cracked. The same man then mutilated the corpse." Brutishly tortured, Walker was now dead.[30]

But, for members of the White throng, the spectacle had in some ways just begun. "Burn him," pleaded voices in the crowd. With lumber from the yard, a "fire was built in the middle of Front street." The murderers tossed Walker's body on it "and the crowd jested and laughed as his flesh blistered and warped under the heat." In the smoldering pyre, Walker's limbs separated from his trunk and his brains and bowels were visible. The sacrilege continued. The *Los Angeles Times* wrote, "the ghastly relic-hunters broke off the teeth, the nails, bits of the skull and pieces of burnt flesh for pocket pieces." Then the White men dragged the charred torso to the courthouse.

They hanged what remained of Walker's body once more – and when it fell "it was again lashed to the pole."[31]

What happened to Lee Walker in 1893 happened to more than three thousand Black men, women, and children between 1883 and 1941 – although American lynching extended beyond both those dates. While the horrific ritual was heavily concentrated in the South, lynchings also occurred throughout the country. The standard definition used for the practice mark it as an extralegal killing committed by three or more persons driven by notions of justice or tradition. In US history, lynchings targeted persons of Hispanic, Native, immigrant, and White origins, but Black individuals were the ones killed in nearly 75 percent of the documented cases. There is no doubt that lynching in America exemplifies, in the words of the historian Hannah Rosen, "the power of violence to articulate (racist) meanings."[32]

Perhaps even more so than the topic of American slavery (and the terrors it encompassed), the torment, killing, and ritualized corpse deface-ment that characterize American lynching often remain a forbidden sub-ject. And the fact that Congress failed to pass any of almost two hundred anti-lynching bills introduced since the late nineteenth century until 2022 testifies to a central predicament. Torture, murder, and corpse mutilation are already illegal. To legislate against lynching, then, acknowledges how these violent acts intersect with the hierarchies of hostile difference. Frederick Douglass called it "lynching black people because they are black" and Ida B. Wells said lynching was used to "keep the race terrorized and 'keep the nigger down.'" In this instance, the use of the "n-word" by a Black person highlights histories of resistance and protest against anti-Black diminishment and hate.[33]

The earliest White men who wrote on lynching failed to critically engage the act as fundamentally about racial violence. Often, this was because the authors themselves accepted the racial order that lynching sustained. In 1887, for instance, the popular historian Hubert Howe Bancroft (and his crew of assistants) asked readers to understand community-based acts of extralegal violence as a central part of "Anglo-American communities." To him, the violence represented a political principle fundamental to the American experience: "the right of the governed [Whites] at all times to instant and arbitrary control of the government." It was, in this sense, part of the liberal social contract: when Whites uncovered "savage" Black men in their midst, they could remove them from society and, in the interest of White self-protection, destroy them. For Bancroft, however, the formation of "popular tribunals" presented a modern paradox. The creation of democracy served to represent the people (the White people), but the people were always authorized, indeed expected, to assume control of the government when they believed government had failed. This assumption of power, he allowed, was "liable at times to the grossest abuse."[34]

Bancroft, though, failed to identify the lynchings of Black people as a gross abuse. "It was unsafe at one time for even a native American to steal in California," he said, "but men of dusky skin indulging in such an offence were almost sure to find, at some historic tree, Apollo's best gift – death." Alongside such romanticized descriptions of murder, Bancroft was also direct: "In autumn of 1851, at Newton, a black man was found guilty of theft and whipped; in the spring of 1852 he was found guilty of theft and hanged." Later in the same book, he described the callous murder of Aaron Bracy with a detached fascination.

> Entering Auburn by a certain road early one morning in February 1858, one might have seen, perhaps with some surprise, a black body pendent from a tall pine about a half mile from the town. The negro's name was Aaron Bracy, and he was placed there, at some moment selected from the silent hours of the night previous, by the citizens of Auburn, who took him from the custody of the law.[35]

The White Yale graduate James Earle Cutler, who wrote what many believe to be the first history of lynching in the United States, was more critical of the practice. Nevertheless, he remained a devotee of racial difference. To Cutler, the illegality of lynching (murder) was a concern, but the fact that it largely targeted Black bodies was not. He wrote against interracial marriage and called Black individuals "shiftless and worthless ... vicious and dangerous." In a passage that seemingly accepts the need for lynching, he said, "The negroes fear nothing so much as force, and should they once get the notion that there is a reasonable hope of escape from punishment, the whites in many parts of the South would be at their mercy." Still, he identified lynching as "our country's national crime" and bemoaned that "lynching is a criminal practice which is peculiar to the United States."[36]

A more complete understanding of lynching acknowledges it as a global practice and recognizes the racial dimensions of its use in America. In human history, lynching persists across time and cultures. Lynch mob members tried to establish normative boundaries of behavior in ancient Greece, republican Rome, early modern Europe, Latin America, Asia, the Middle East, the United States, Africa, and even in some Native American societies. A global tradition of violence found in rural and urban spaces that

255

persists to this day, lynching grounds a community mode of justice in "prerogatives of honor, class, race, ethnicity, gender, and crime control."[37]

Anti-Black violence, some of which can be characterized as lynching, took place throughout the nineteenth century in North America. During the night of Sunday, June 13, 1841, for example, a group of White men approached the home and business of Black grocer Moses Carter in Cobourg, in the Province of Canada. They broke through the front door, destroyed the store's goods, and forced Carter and his wife from their bed. The marriage of the Carters, a Black man and a White woman, was the reason for the attack. Beaten and "shamefully abused" (castrated), Carter was conscious as several men "gagged" and restrained his wife. He watched as at least four men "brutally outraged" (raped) Mrs. Carter. "Warrants were issued against the monsters," a newspaper said, "but all but one had absconded."[38]

The attack on a mixed-race couple was not an isolated incident. Months later, a White mob acted in St. Catharines near the Canadian side of Niagara Falls. Word had spread that a Black man had wed a White woman. Unable to locate the pair, the frustrated group stalked the streets. When it encountered a random Black individual, William Brown, one potential lyncher lobbed "a large stone" at him. The stone "caused almost immediate death."[39]

The connections between anti-Black violence across national borders have often gone unnoticed. A focus on national histories and experiences is in part to blame. So too is the antislavery activist framing of Canada. "We had heard of Canada," said Frederick Douglass, "the real Canaan of the bondmen." But alongside the freedom it offered, the northern nation also served as a site of racial trauma for American slave fugitives and other members of Canadian Black communities.[40]

The issues driving anti-Black violence in Canada were similar to those in the United States: hostile difference structured these settler colonial societies, and certain White people believed it was their duty to uphold the racial hierarchy. To extend the terminology used by scholar Rashad Shabazz to discuss American lynching as a national – not just a southern – phenomenon, there existed an anti-Black "punitive continuity" in North America. One variation, though, can be traced in the response to the violence. In 1841, the *New York Commercial* reported on Cobourg and Moses Carter. The White Canadian community had collected monies "to repair the loss of Carter, so far as it can be repaired by money." Again, in 1852, after the burning and looting of the Black community in St. Catharines, which housed some four hundred people, the city council authorized the mayor to "settle and pay the cost of repairing the damage done in June last to certain houses in that part of the Town known as the Colored Village."[41]

These small acts of restorative justice did nothing to prevent further attacks, however. In 1863, in the Canadian town of Oil Springs near Detroit, for example, the Black community, mainly populated by fugitive slaves from the United States, suffered a similar fate to that in St. Catharines. A White mob burned the houses of Black families and assailed Black persons.[42]

The year 1863, the year of the Emancipation Proclamation, proved similarly terrifying for Black people in the northern United States. As many worked to forge a more equitable racial order, anti-Black violence erupted in US cities like Milwaukee, Detroit, and Newburgh. That urban centers, sites of European immigration and the development of wage labor Whiteness, were central to the trend is clear. In July, the New York City Draft Riots (a name that masks the racial reprisal central to the event) is the most famous example (see Fig. 10.2). Irish and Irish American individuals beat, tortured, and killed Black men and women and burned down a Black orphanage. The mob lynched William Jones, a Black man, who was hanged by the waterfront before his corpse was thrown into a fire. White people in

Fig. 10.2 Illustration of anti-Black violence in New York City in 1863. From *Illustrated London News*, 8 Aug. 1863. Courtesy of the Watkinson Library, Trinity College, Hartford, CT.

New York killed at least 105 Black people over five days. Some estimates push that number to more than a thousand.[43]

The race-based violence in the "free" spaces of North America bridged important political and economic transformations in the nineteenth century. In sites deeply influenced by slave economies, violent acts against Black persons justified and sustained a coercive labor order situated in race. In sites influenced by industrial economies, such violence deprived Black families and communities of capital, intimidated Black men into disenfranchisement, and offered a brutal symbol of low social, economic, and political status. These violent acts indicated both continuity and change.[44]

The cycles of lynching and Black community displacement in the nineteenth century upheld relations of racial power in liberal society, adapted to changes in the political economy, and normalized anti-Black violence in the minds of many Whites. This was reflected, for example, in the callous disregard with which various newspapers printed coverage of the 1893 killing of Lee Walker. In the *Alexandria Gazette*, the article on Walker, titled "Hung to a Telegraph Pole," was printed next to a column reporting the latest food prices – eggs were 11 cents. Readers of Connecticut papers such as the *Waterbury Evening Democrat* or the *Morning Journal and Courier* in New Haven consumed news of Lee Walker ("Lynched and Roasted") in the same column as the baseball scores. (On July 23, the day of Walker's death, the St. Louis Browns split a doubleheader with the Cincinnati Reds.) The normalcy of lynching's racial violence was especially stark in a report from Mississippi: "A negro Lee Walker was hung and afterwards burned at Memphis," said the *Iuka Reporter*, "The same cause as usual."[45]

The same cause as usual. These words conjured up what, by 1893, had become "facts" widely shared in the media: Black people were lawbreakers, Black men were rapists, and the legal system was too slow and too kind to handle Black on White crimes. In an age that saw the end of slavery in the Americas, starting with Haiti in 1804 and ending with Brazil in 1888, the subtext of these messages was that "Black individuals do not deserve to be free."

In newsprint, Lee Walker's lawbreaking was established through declaration. He was described as "the ravisher" and "the villain," "The Negro Rapist," "A Negro Fiend," and "the Negro Rape Fiend." Yet Walker had not been convicted of any crime at the time of his death. Still, to the *Worthington Advance* in Minnesota he was the "negro who assaulted Miss Mollie McCadden" and to the *Times* in Michigan, "a negro who assaulted Miss Mollie McCadden (white)." These assertions of criminal behavior proved their own point. "There is no doubt as to his guilt," said the *Camden Chronicle*.[46]

For those who still doubted, though, newspapers highlighted two additional details. One was the supposed attempt at self-harm. "Walker tried to commit suicide before the lynching by cutting his throat," the *Boston Daily Globe* reported. To the northern newspaper, this was admissible evidence proving Walker's culpability, despite the fact that there was ample reason to think that his throat was cut by members of the White mob. And it was not considered that suicide might be a reasonable action to take if targeted by a lynch mob. To readers, it seemed only to confirm his guilt. And when paired with the second detail, his confession, the suicide bid confirmed the idea of Walker as a man who knew he had committed a terrible wrong. "Walker confessed as soon as he was arrested," the *Ohio Democrat* said, "and he acted as he did because he could not help it."[47]

According to nearly every newspaper report, Lee Walker was among the most prolific rapists in nineteenth-century America. He had attempted four rapes in the past two weeks and two attempts were "successful." Some reports note that he raped "a small colored girl 3 years and 6 months old, who was badly lacerated." Others said that the young Black girl was twelve years old. His other apparent "success" was an assault on "a married woman of his own color." This wild inclination for sexual assault, publications agreed, was not a new behavior. Though the particulars varied, public accounts stated that Walker had been jailed (and released in January 1893) for the rape of Duck Sonders (or Sanders), a Black woman. Whether that crime took place in New Albany, Mississippi, or nearly seven hundred miles away in Milwaukee, Wisconsin, the newspapers could not agree.[48]

Details aside, national and local newspapers stood behind their assertions that Walker was a frenzied rapist. Neighbors in his hometown in northern Mississippi, said the *Camden Chronicle*, heard Walker express "a willingness to die if he could only succeed in his foul designs on certain women." Moreover, many news outlets suggested that all women were in danger from Walker on the ostensible account of his parents confirming that he had sexually attacked between "twenty or thirty women," a string of crimes that started when he was fifteen. In July 1893, though, newspapers could not figure out whether Walker was nineteen years old or twenty-two (his death certificate stated his age as twenty), indicating that he stood accused of having committed an average of between 4 and 7.5 or 2.9 and 4.3 assaults per year.[49]

Such coverage served three purposes. The first was to confirm the alleged uncontrolled sexual appetite of Black men. Reading newspapers in the 1890s, an uncritical reader would learn that there is a Black man hiding behind every rock and tree in hopes of an opportunity to rape.

The second was to confirm Black deviancy regarding White (often male) standards of gender and race. Black men were depicted as being unconcerned or too lazy to protect Black women from sexual assault; on the flip side, depictions of Black women often suggested that they lack sexual restraint. White men, however, were depicted as having the right to govern sexual access to White women, and White women were assumed to be chaste. Within this framework, it was a greater offense for a Black man to rape a White woman than it was for him to rape a Black woman – and, within the logic of hostile racial difference, the rape of Black women by White men was rarely treated as a crime, and when it was, punishment was rarely harsh. Indeed, in the 1890s, the coverage of Lee Walker's case makes part of this construct clear: "Walker assaulted Miss Mollie McCadden, a pretty white girl, and on the same day assaulted a colored girl." Bound to notions of White beauty and purity ("a pretty white girl," as if the assault of an ugly or a non-white one would matter less), this statement further denotes the secondary status of the "colored girl" and her trauma by denying her a name. The historian Crystal Feimster helps to place these dynamics of gender, sexual violence, and race in the post-Civil War South within a broader framework: the "image of the 'black rapist,'" she writes, was "a powerful political tool for violently maintaining white male supremacy, while also denying African Americans their rights as citizens."[50]

The third purpose of the newspaper coverage was for the presumed transgressions of race and gender to open the way for violent acts against Black men. The coverage of Lee Walker that showed him as guilty not only of an attack on the McCaddens, but of many attacks on women, served to verify the notion that his crimes were "the blackest in history." Thus guilty of racial wrongdoing, he was also characterized as a "repulsive black man," guilty therein of both racial *and* gender wrongdoing.[51]

These portrayals of Walker also served to form a basis of consent for his execution. Who could disagree that a man who had tried to rape thirty or so women, one as young as three, deserved punishment? As both Walker's parents and Walker himself confessed that he was a rapist, who could disagree that Walker was not? Moreover, newspapers also offered the sheer number of participants as a gesture of consent. The *Vermont Phoenix* said the lynch mob consisted of "1000 people." The *Camden Chronicle* said the mob numbered 3,000. "There were 5,000 people present," said an article in the *Los Angeles Times*. The *Democratic Northwest* pushed the number even higher: "The cremation was witnessed by fully 10,000 persons." That thousands of people butchered Walker both in their actions and as witnesses offered a broad absolution for the lynching act. For, if the lynching really was a shocking or unjust thing to witness, how could it gather so many viewers?[52]

Some newspapers further emphasized that the mob comprised not only men, but "men, women and children." Others extended the spectrum of approval across the racial divide. This was a theme that started earlier with reports of Walker attacking a Black girl. That attack had supposedly angered the Black community and drew Black men into the hunt for the then fugitive. Building on the theme, papers noted that the lynch mob included "women, blacks and whites." One Missouri weekly said the mob consisted of "men [White men] and negroes, the latter being more demonstrative than the whites, because Walker had outraged four colored girls." Though it is quite possible that some African American individuals supported the murder of Lee Walker, these newspaper accounts read more as attempts to justify the killing through the creation of interracial consent. Notably, these accounts appeared only in a small percentage of publications.[53]

Cultivating notions of consensus by emphasizing crowd participation, however, was a perilous path. For, if everyone in Memphis approved of the killing, then the barbaric, extralegal execution of Walker, a man who had been in legal custody, indicted the population of a major southern city. To be clear, the White person who bore witness to Walker's lynching and did nothing to stop it was just as complicit as the White northerner who read about it and did nothing too. It is likely that this dynamic pushed many editors to shift the blame for the murder on to a subset of the participants. While thousands were in attendance, said the *Detroit Free Press*, "not more than 100 took an active part in the assault and subsequent lynching." Another version said that "not more than forty men took an active part in the lynching and the subsequent barbarities."[54]

To make an individual or a small group of individuals responsible for the killing of Lee Walker showed that his death was perhaps avoidable, that it was an aberrant act, and that the thousands who stood around were otherwise harmless. It also established a clear path forward for resolving the Memphis lynching: since a small number of implicated persons was a seemingly manageable problem, the solution was to arrest those who were involved. It both isolated the event and the culpability for it, and it suggested that the murder was nothing more than a regrettable act committed by a handful of bad people.

But, in an era filled with the lynchings of Black people, there was nothing isolated about Lee Walker's death. As Ida B. Wells understood before she was chased from the city for her antilynching demands, Memphis was a central site for racial terror. In March 1892, a gang of eight White men removed Tom Moss, Calvin McDowell, and Will Stewart, Black co-owners of a grocery that had enticed Black customers away from shopping at a White-owned store, out of the Shelby County Jail – the same facility that would house Walker the following year. The gang fatally shot the three men in a field about a mile away to the north. In August 1894, another such shooting transpired as an officer transported six Black men to the Memphis jail. Dan Hawkins, Warner Williams, John Haynes, Ed Hall, Robert Hayes, and Graham White had been arrested for barn burning. They were shackled, inside a wagon, and defenseless when a White mob descended on them. The gunfire was so relentless that it turned Hawkins's head into "a bloody mass of jelly." Anger over the racial killing resonated as far as Nigeria, where the *Lagos Weekly Record* called it a "revolting case" of "lynching."[55]

When we compare these events with what happened to the officials and the mob leaders in the wake of the Walker killing, a clear picture emerges. A judge suspended Sheriff McClendon, whose failure to secure the Shelby County Jail on two occasions had now cost four Black men their lives. Attorney-General George B. Peters impaneled a grand jury to investigate him. In the end, the grand jury indicted Sheriff McClendon, Deputy Sheriff J. A. Perkins, Jailor Harold, and two police captains, Ohaver and Hackett. Headlines declared these moves a "Warning to Sheriffs" and "Discouraging to Lynchers." But comments on the prosecutions in the *Louisville Times* proved prophetic. "Those indictments against the peace officers of Memphis for their failure to protect Lee Walker, the colored ravisher and murderer of a white girl, from the fury of a mob, are mere legal actions that will never amount to anything." Walker was not accused of murder and his status as a ravisher remains in doubt, but the columnist was otherwise correct. By November 1893, the attorney-general had exhausted "a venire of 500 men without securing a single juror." He "nolle prossed" (dismissed) the cases against the lawmen.[56]

Meanwhile, the police arrested three railway workers: Harry M. Frazer (switchman), Phil Bode (engineer), and Tom Burke (a "one-armed flagman") who were believed to be the principal lynchers. With one other man from the mob, the three were indicted. In their first few days in the Shelby County Jail, some of their friends threatened to break in and take them away. In contrast to what had happened just a week before with Lee Walker, "the governor ordered out the Chickasaw guards and ordered other military companies to hold themselves in readiness." When the White mob stormed the jail on behalf of their White friends, officials beat them back, shooting "one of their number in the leg." Months later, in November, when the charges against the lawmen were dropped, so too did the attorney-general drop the charges against the alleged lynchers. In short order, a Black prisoner had been left unprotected by authorities, tortured, and killed, while the White prisoners responsible for his death were protected by authorities and then legally set free. No one was ever prosecuted for the killing of Lee Walker.[57]

—————————◆—————————

Among an inventory of things for which the United States must be held accountable, wrote the Spanish politician Emilio Castelar, is the "lynching of negroes and the continual insurrection of the Indians and their first disappearance from the surface of the earth." In the 1890s, people around the world took note of American forms of hostile difference, especially those forms clearly linked to human enslavement and settler colonialism. Castelar notwithstanding, most foreigners accepted the logic found in American publications. International accounts of American violence thus often failed to admit that it was part of a systemic approach to a social and political order based on racial hierarchy. In Cape Town, South Africa, for example, the *Cape Times* agreed with the Democratic governor of Alabama, Thomas G. Jones. In defending his state from attacks launched by British antilynching activists, Jones focused on White female fragility and Black male criminality. "The sanctity of [the White] woman," he said, should be protected immediately and stringently even if by a mob. Asian newspapers offered more candid statements. "The lynching evil owes its origins and perpetuation to the presence of the negro race in America," said the *Japan Times*. The *Times of India* explained that "in her free Negro population America has a problem."[58]

The problem, according to White supremacists, was – just as the *Japan Times* said – "the presence of the negro race in America." Even minor attempts at reform, such as allowing African Americans to serve as jurors, irritated advocates of White superiority. To them, having legal courts be fairer to all Americans felt like having ones that were clearly biased against Whites. When this thinking connected with the construction of Black men as rapists – a construction some southern White women used to make "demands of white men" and "achieve a modicum of political power" – fervent calls for anti-Black violence were the result. "If it needs lynching to protect woman's dearest possession from cravening human beasts [Black men]," said women's rights advocate Rebecca Latimer Felton (who would be the first woman to serve in the US Senate), "then I say 'lynch' a thousand times a week if necessary." In reality, Felton said these words in a speech aimed at highlighting the failure of White southern men to protect southern women; however, many readers saw in this excerpt an undeniable call for White supremacy and the use of lynching violence in support of it.[59]

Antilynching activists such as Ida Wells understood the problem differently. They knew, for instance, that White mobs lynched Black people for many reasons beyond the crime of rape – and that most of the rapes were fabricated in the first place. Murder, assault, horse stealing, "testifying for one of his own race," wild talk, consensual interracial sex, labor organizing, scaring a white girl, quitting a job, having a "bad reputation," and "introducing small pox" were just some of the reasons offered by White lynchers for murdering Black individuals. Activists understood, too, that the reasons given for the killings did not make a difference. "The lawless lynchings in the South for alleged crimes against the whites," said Wells, "are in ninety-nine cases out of a hundred simple outrages against our race."[60]

For Wells, lynching sustained a system that degraded Black lives to extract value from them. Of Black people, she wrote, "The labor of one-half of this country has always been, and is still being done by them ... The wealth created by their industry has afforded to the white people of this country the leisure essential to their great progress in education, art, science, industry and invention." Here was the echo of an analysis proposed by progressive African American thinkers and their White advocates since at least the end of the Civil War. "You robbed us for two hundred years," said Congressman Richard Harvey Cain in 1874. "We have raised your cotton, your rice, your corn. We have attended your wives and your children. We have made wealth for your support and your education, while we were slaves, toiling without pay, without the means of education, and hardly of sustenance." The White Virginian (by way of Vermont) Congressman William Stowell echoed Cain's assessment: "He [the Black man] remembers that his labor raised you and your ancestors with all the surroundings of affluence, education and refinement, while poverty, ignorance, and neglect were his lot."[61]

For Wells, Cain, and Stowell, it was important to understand how White people profited socially, economically, and politically from hostile racial difference. They were especially focused on the link between the diminishment of Black people because of skin color and the diminishment of them for the menial work they frequently engaged in. It was the political framing of Black people by race – their diminishment – that opened the way for racial executions such as the lynchings of the nineteenth and twentieth centuries. In their acts of racial murder, White "lynchers implied that the relationship that counted was between blacks and whites," writes the legal scholar David Garland. It was, he continues, "a relationship not of laws . . . but of superiors and subordinates."[62]

This fundamentally unequal relationship cultivated a belief in an "antagonism between the Negroes and white men" – and it was a problem that needed to be solved. One solution was what would become known as the "doctrine of separate but equal," which entailed legal racial segregation in America. Another solution, voiced on Emancipation Day in Charleston, South Carolina, in 1890, was the removal of Black people from the United States. "I believe that the ultimate solution of the so-called problem will be emigration, from necessity if not from choice," said the African American Reverend J. S. Lee. "Amalgamation [racial intermixing] is neither possible nor desirable," he added. "Outrages, such as lynching Negroes, compelling them to ride in smoking cars, refusing them hotel accommodations, are evidences strong and convincing . . . These are shadows of coming events."[63]

Racial segregation and Black emigrationism offered Americans the same fantasy. Since Whites and Blacks could not get along, the races must be separated. At a Colored Convention in Cincinnati, Bishop Henry McNeal Turner advocated that $500 million of the $40 billion that was owed to former slaves for their unpaid labor be set aside "to enable them to begin African emigration." Whether stated by a White segregationist or a Black emigrationist, the idea was essentially the same: once the races lived in isolation, everything would be peaceful and good.[64]

Separation, though, is not racial equity, and when proposed as the answer to racial injustice, it conceals how widespread injustice is the product of longstanding societal machinations, patterns, and structures. The Reverend Lee spoke about the "shadows of coming events." This is what resided in the darkness: when a White mob pulled Lee Walker from the Shelby County Jail, hanged him, mutilated his body, and then dragged his corpse through the Memphis streets, it sent a message throughout the city, nation, and the world about the worth of a Black person in the United States. An American take on a global tradition, lynching violence was not about racial contact (which, in theory, would be solved by racial separation). It was about racial humiliation and terror.

EPILOGUE

Eric Garner, Michael Brown, Tamir Rice, Philando Castile, and George Floyd. Aiyana Mo'Nay Stanley-Jones, Miriam Iris Carey, Tanisha N. Anderson, and Breonna Taylor (#SayHerName). Mya Shawatza Hall. These Black lives lost are recent additions to a list that includes the likes of Lee Walker, Emmett Till, and so many more. This list provides but a partial view of tremendous individual and national loss – a loss of creativity, love, connection, work, and humanity. All Americans pay for the national devotion to the hostile differences, Whiteness, and violence so dear to liberal politics and life.

The names above offer the context in which this book was written. It was a time akin to many other times in the United States when White (often) men killed Black people in the streets, either as agents of the state or in their so-called self-defense. It was a time when a straightforward affirmation, Black Lives Matter, could in response elicit more violence and more hate. In the ten years I spent researching and writing *Born in Blood*, Black activists and their allies inspired me to think more critically about the structures of liberal society, about the nature of inclusion and exclusion, and, of course, about how violence sustains the whole system.

The systemic approach is important. More than fifty years ago, Richard Hofstadter and Michael Wallace published an edited volume titled *American Violence: A Documentary History* (1970). In it, the two scholars collected an array of primary sources in eight categories: Political Violence; Economic Violence; Racial Violence; Religious and Ethnic Violence; Anti-Radical and Police Violence; Personal Violence; Assassinations, Terrorism, Political Murders; and Violence in the Name of Law, Order, and Morality. But even though these categories hint at national systems of physical force and intimidation, the editors refused to subject their categorizations to a greater logic.[1]

Hofstadter's opening, "Reflections on Violence in the United States," remains one of the most influential pieces written on the subject. "The United States," he offered in his opening line, "has a history but not

266

a tradition of domestic violence." Even though violence within the United States (domestic violence) has been "frequent" and "voluminous," Hofstadter argued, "our violence lacks both an ideological and a geographic center." "Second," he added, "we have a remarkable lack of memory where violence is concerned."[2]

In *Born in Blood*, I argue that there is, in fact, a tradition of American violence. It is a process-oriented, ideological tradition centered on slavery and colonization, Whiteness, and hostile difference. Whiteness – or "the racial contract" in the words of Charles W. Mills – "is an exploitation contract that creates global European domination and national white racial privilege." Hostile difference is significant too. That differences exist among individuals and communities is something on which many thinkers agree. However, it is when such difference is understood in antagonism, in hostility, that violence and degradation result.[3]

The frustrating part of Hofstadter's analysis in 1970 is that the information to understand these systems was available. Yet Hofstadter remained wedded to a belief in the neutrality of the liberal state and the (unacknowledged) power of having White skin. He was "impressed that most American violence ... has been initiated with a 'conservative bias.'" "It has been unleashed against abolitionists, Catholics, radicals, workers and labor organizations, Negroes, Orientals, and other ethnic or racial or ideological minorities, and has been used ostensibly to protect the American, the Southern, the White Protestant, or simply the established middle-class way of life and morals." That the establishment of the "American" or the "middle-class way" represents the establishment of a structure of power – and that the establishment of power and hierarchy is essential to understand American violence – eluded the eminent scholar.[4]

Many writers in academic and more public forums subscribe to Hofstadter's notion of violence and forgetfulness. They challenge, however, his use of words such as "our" and "we" – which suggest a widely shared experience – to situate the historical amnesia around violent events in different perspectives. The trauma expert Judith Herman, for example, frames the situation as a "conflict between victim and perpetrator." To forget, "to do nothing," is what the perpetrator asks of society. "The victim demands action, engagement, and remembering." Forgetting is in the interest of the offender, especially an empowered one. In the United States, empowered Whites have "routinely discounted, derided, and dismissed" the views of many Black Americans. In Hofstadter, forgetting violence is part of liberal society; violent acts are ignored because "we" don't wish to engage with difficult subjects. For Herman, forgetting violence must be paired with efforts to remember: it is a battle in which "it is morally impossible to remain neutral."[5]

The story of violence found in this book maps out some of the battles in the American past. Examine enough of these battles and it is soon clear that violence in America is systemic, part of the liberal democratic tradition. This conclusion stems from the evidence presented in the preceding chapters and, in part, from an intellectual dissonance I face whenever reading work that champions the American liberal state. For instance, the scholar James Kloppenberg identifies "prudence, temperance, fortitude, and justice" as liberalism's foundational concepts. The system, for thinkers like Kloppenberg, is sound and just. It is the people historically charged with tending to the system who have failed. Along these lines are those who believe that the trajectory of liberalism thus bends toward justice.[6]

There is no doubt that there have been moments of justice in the American past. The end of bonded servitude in the United States (which took place by the early nineteenth century) and the slow (prudent) abolition of slavery in the North from the 1780s to the 1850s are marks of justice. But how far can these examples go? And how much of this hard-won justice was the result of the system? After all, the existence of bonded servitude and slavery at the nation's founding are terrible marks of injustice. Whether you understand "all men are created equal" as aspirational, an assertion of patriarchy, hypocritical, or a declaration of Whiteness, the statement in 1776 obscured the many forms of unfreedom that persisted in America.

Right now, people from across the political spectrum are examining the values of liberalism. *Born in Blood* offers a historical reckoning that should precede any such reexamination. As a political body, the United States was created as a settler–slave society. Within forty years of its constitutional founding, the nation became one of the greatest slave empires in human history. Should we mark this achievement as temperance, justice, or fortitude?

I do not ask this question in jest. The American liberal state has transformed and continues to change. And it is the liberal state that consolidates and directs violence on governmental and individual levels. Efforts to construct a more equitable nation – and more equitable uses of state and individual force – must then work against the many divisions that have been integral to liberalism and its expressions in the United States.

A challenge of systemic approaches to understanding the American past is clear. In the words of David Graeber and David Wengrow, historians should avoid presentations in which "we are well and truly stuck and there is really no escape from the institutional cages we've made for ourselves."

People build, maintain, and transform the societies and systems in which they live. The inequitable society in which we live, the one that devalues, criminalizes, and punishes many lives – and some lives much more so than others – is a tradition and a choice. I write this with no intent to disparage or defame the nation's past. It is a clear-eyed look into the dynamics of physical force in the United States, many of which are still in operation today.[7]

Acknowledgements

In its earliest forms, *Born in Blood* was linked to Edmund Wilson and the fiftieth anniversary of his classic work on Civil War literature, *Patriotic Gore* (1962). That project, now nearly a decade overdue, transformed into this one. There are several people whose support, care, and questions (unintentionally) pushed me toward what you find in these pages today: Carol Berkin, friend, mentor, and role model; Dan Green, my dear former agent for two non-books; Thomas Slaughter and James Goodman, who found places for my Wilson-based work; and Thomas LeBien and Brian Distelberg.

Two working groups reviewed parts of the manuscript – and their responses, though supportive and kind, made me realize that I had not yet figured the book out. My thanks to the Trinity Institute for Interdisciplinary Studies, directed at the time by Maurice Wade and Meredith Safran, for funding a manuscript workshop in 2016. Cheryl Greenberg, Christina Heatherton, Isaac Kamola, Dan Mrozoswki, John Stauffer, and Evan Turiano served as readers for the workshop – it is a debt I cannot repay. (Actually, in true Trinity fashion the workshop ran $50 over budget and I did pay!) In 2017, the City University of New York Early American Republic Seminar reviewed one of the later book chapters. My thanks to Evan Turiano and David Waldstreicher and the students at my alma mater, the Graduate Center at CUNY: Erin Cully, Alexander Gambacinni, Madeline Lafuse, Miriam Liebman, Cody Nager, Glen Olson, Marcos Reguera, and Helena Yoo.

Over the past decade, I have enjoyed the privilege of leading one of the most prestigious American Studies programs in a liberal arts college in the United States. It has an active faculty that brings in a host of phenomenal guests each year, and some of these guests made contributions that I must acknowledge. I'll add to this list a few job candidates in American Studies (many now well known) whose work and conversations shaped this project too. My thanks to Kandace Chuh, Jorge Cuéllar, Martín Espada, Sarah Fouts, Josh Freeman, Karen Hanna, Walter Johnson, Simeon Man, Marcus Rediker, Gabriella Soto, and Kiara Vigil.

I am also fortunate to work at an institution with robust library collections in my research field. Without the assistance of Christina Bleyer, Eric Johnson-DeBaufre, Jeff Liska, Rick Ring, Eric Stoykovich, Erin Valentino, and the important persons who staff the inter-library loan desk for my many requests, this book would not exist. Beyond Trinity College, several individuals helped locate materials and secure permissions. This includes Shannon Gering (University of Oklahoma Press), Tom Lisanti (New York Public Library), Miriam Meislik (University of Pittsburgh Library), Eisha Neely (Cornell University Library), and Stacey Stachow (Wadsworth Atheneum).

Trinity College is primarily a teaching institution. And while there is an understanding that faculty must produce nationally recognized scholarship, there is no widespread, meaningful faculty support to help achieve it. There is one thing, though, I am grateful for. No research could happen with a five-course teaching load without a regular, one-semester quadrennial leave. Several deans have shepherded my academic leave requests along the way: Rena Fraden, Tim Cresswell, and Sonia Cardenas.

Working at a teaching college means working closely with students. While I thank all the many students who have taken my introductory lecture course, "Born in Blood," there are some who asked key questions or made insightful comments that helped this project take shape. Thank you to Mason Allen, Sawyer Ames, James Barrett, Anna Barry, Abe Bloom, Brandon Campbell, Corey Cheung, Chloe Cyr, Max Dadagian, Dianté Dancy, Sedona Georgescu, Matthew Greene, Byrn Hudson, Devin Iorio, Henry Lucey, Felicia McDevitt, Henry Minot, Katie Moran, Maggie Mori, Devon Mulhaney, Nelson Neo, Silvia Nunez, Shayna Thomas, Day Whaley, and Sophie Wilder. A few teaching assistants for the class deserve applause: Adam Moossmann, Audrey O'Byrne, Evan Turiano (now banned from further mention), and Graham Warnock. Sawyer Ames and Sueann Lee compiled the research for Today in American Violence on my Twitter feed – excellent work! Graduate students deserve love too. Bill Heiden and Sandra Williams, your work and conversations pushed me to rethink some key concepts.

My students have benefited from interaction with activists and public sites. Aswad Thomas, struck by a bullet in Hartford as he was set to play professional basketball in Europe, is VP for the Alliance of Safety and Justice and National Director for Crime Survivors for Safety and Justice. His 2018 Trinity visit changed my students in an instant (thanks to my colleague Sarah Raskin for putting the visit together!). The staff at Old New-Gate Prison and Copper Mine in East Granby, CT, and at the Springfield Armory

National Historic Site in Springfield, MA, have been patient and kind during class visits and whenever I send students to ask them important questions (How can you have a museum about guns and not talk about or commemorate death?). Thank you for your care and attention to these important places.

Imam Mujahid and Sherdil Khan at the non-profit Sound Vision hosted me on several occasions to discuss current events, political violence, and American democracy. I appreciate the opportunity to play the role of a political pundit on Muslim Network TV.

Elena K. Abbott is an extraordinary manuscript guru. I benefited from her demands for clarity, precision, and accessibility – this book would be an unorganized mess without her. Of course, my Cambridge University Press editor is likely wondering as I write exactly what kind of unorganized mess this is going to be. Thank you, Cecilia Cancellaro, for your support and belief in this project. Victoria Phillips at Cambridge was also incredibly helpful in response to my queries along the way. One of the anonymous reviewers of the book manuscript commented on it two times. I know that we understand the past through different lenses, but your careful readings and critiques challenged me to be a more articulate and thorough scholar.

Acts of kindness shall not go unrecognized. As I neared the deadline for this book, Dean John Selders (Trinity) and Kerri Greenidge (Tufts) had nice and supportive things to say. I needed to hear those things in those moments.

Even beyond the pandemic, the past several years have been filled with challenges and challenging loss. I owe this next group for their personal support, professional guidance, and intellectual engagement. The faculty in American Studies at Trinity College is, as I said before, an unmatched group. Their honesty, integrity, and academic rigor is inspiring. Davarian Baldwin, Jordan Camp, Cheryl Greenberg, Amanda Guzman, Chris Hager, Christina Heatherton, Juliet Nebolon, Diana Paulin, Tom Wickman, and Hilary Wyss. Joan Hedrick, now retired, belongs in this group, as does Lou Masur, who has moved on. Each of you has contributed to this work, but, sadly, convention dictates that I am to blame for errors in judgement or interpretation found herein. (Thank you to those who took the time to read and comment: Davarian, Jordan, Cheryl, Chris, Christina, Lou, and Tom. Cheryl and Chris served as my deadline stewards. I thought you were supposed to play good cop, bad cop – it felt like bad cop all the way.)

Nothing has been or would be accomplished in my work life without the assistance of Veronica Zuniga, Gigi St. Peter, Nancy Rossi, Lidija Petrus, Dania Field, Terry Romero, and Sylvia DeMore. The whole ship sinks without you.

As a first-generation college student who became a college professor, I forever struggled to explain my professional life to my parents. They imagined my job to be more like that of a public-school teacher, crafting lesson plans and spending six hours in the classroom each day. To them, my first book was a kind of burnt offering, a thing to be worshipped and revered but not understood. That said, I wanted so badly to hand over a copy of this book to my dad. Edward Gac, though, died in 2018 and since then I've cared for my mom, Maria, ever more caught in dementia's throes. Without the love, care, and support of the staff – a grossly underpaid staff – at the Hearth in Glastonbury and Brookdale Buckingham, I would not have had the time and soundness of mind needed to carry on.

Being part of a wondrous, new family has greatly changed me. Adrian, Dane, and Reece, you are ambitious, talented, kind, and often ridiculous young men. You are awesome and so strong, a strength that pulls you through the trials of a biological parent with an addiction. This stepdad is proud of you every day. To Jill, my love of loves, what else is there to say? Our love is always real, let's make it forever.

Notes

INTRODUCTION: A SYSTEM OF VIOLENCE: LIBERAL SOCIETY IN THE UNITED STATES

1 "From the *Boston Gazette* March 12," *Dublin Mercury* [Philadelphia], May 1, 1770, 1. "London. From the *Boston Gazette*," *General Evening Post* [London], Apr. 24, 1770, 3. Holger Hoock, *Scars of Independence: America's Violent Birth* (New York: Crown, 2017), 5–7, 11. Insults in *The Trial of the British Soldiers, of the 29th Regiment of the Foot* . . . (Boston: William Emmons, 1824), 90.

2 The enslaved status of Attucks is linked to a 1750 runaway slave ad placed by William Brown. See "Ranaway from his Master," *Boston Gazette, or Weekly Journal*, Oct. 2, 1750, 2.

3 Richard Archer, *As If an Enemy's Country: The British Occupation of Boston and the Origins of the Revolution* (New York: Oxford University Press, 2010), 193–197.

4 Ibid., 106.

5 On the global matrix, see Lisa Lowe, *The Intimacies of Four Continents* (Durham: Duke University Press, 2015); Cedric J. Robinson, *Black Marxism: The Making of the Black Radical Tradition* (1983; Chapel Hill: University of North Carolina Press, 2000); Peter Linebaugh and Marcus Rediker, "The Many-Headed Hydra: Sailors, Slaves, and the Atlantic Working Class in the Eighteenth Century," *Journal of Historical Sociology*, 3.3 (1990), 229–232. Frenchmen in *Trial of the British Soldiers*, 97.

6 Warren, Oration at Boston, Mar. 5, 1772, in A Bostonian, *Biographical Sketch of Gen. Joseph Warren* (Boston: Shepard, Clark and Brown, 1857), 30. Taxing in *A Short Narrative of the Horrid Massacre in Boston* (1770; New York: John Doggett, Jr., 1846), 13. Soldier figures in Archer, *As If an Enemy's Country*, xiv. Paine in *Trial of the British Soldiers*, 120.

7 *Account of the Late Unhappy Disturbance at Boston in New England* (London: B. White, 1779), 6. Charles Lloyd to George Grenville, 21 Apr. 1770, American Revolutionary War Manuscripts Collection, Boston Public Library.

8 For problems of nation and difference, see Robinson, *Black Marxism*, 23, 10; Michael Omi and Howard Winant, *Racial Formation in the United States*, 3rd edition (New York: Routledge, 2015), 75–102. On American and Whiteness, see Michel-Rolph Trouillot, *Silencing the Past: Power and the Production of History* (Boston: Beacon Press, 1995), 133; Toni Morrison, *Playing in the Dark: Whiteness and the Literary Imagination* (New York: Random House, 1992), 47. On forgetting violence

274

and invisibility, see Richard Hofstadter and Michael Wallace, eds., *American Violence: A Documentary History* (New York: Vintage, 1971), 3; Michel Foucault, *Discipline and Punish* (New York: Vintage, 1975); W. G. Sebald, *On the Natural History of Destruction*, trans. Anthea Bell (New York: Modern Library, 2004); Judith Herman, *Trauma and Recovery: The Aftermath of Violence – From Domestic Abuse to Political Terror* (1992; New York: Basic Books, 2015), 1–32.

9 *Hobbes's Leviathan: Reprinted from the Edition of 1651* (1909; London: Oxford University Press, 1929), 99. On state and violence, see Max Weber, "Politics as a Vocation" in *The Vocation Lectures*, trans. Rodney Livingstone (Indianapolis: Hackett, 2004), 33; Rudolf von Ihering, *Law as a Means to an End*, trans. Isaac Husik (Boston: Boston Book Company, 1913), 233–325. A recent book more thoroughly positions Hobbes and the state of nature against Indigenous critiques of European society. See David Graeber and David Wengrow, *The Dawn of Everything: A New History of Humanity* (New York: Farrar, Straus and Giroux, 2021).

10 Ascendency in Christopher Tomlins, "Law's Wilderness: The Discourse of English Colonizing, the Violence of Intrusion, and the Failures of American History" in *New World Orders: Violence, Sanction, and Authority in the Colonial Americas*, ed. John Smolenski and Thomas J. Humphrey (Philadelphia: University of Pennsylvania Press, 2005), 22. For the construction of European dominance, see ibid., 22, and Joyce E. Chaplin, *Subject Matter: Technology, the Body, and Science on the Anglo-American Frontier, 1500–1676* (Cambridge: Harvard University Press, 2003).

11 Transfer of violence in Lowe, *Intimacies of Four Continents*, 8. Patrick Wolfe, "Settler Colonialism and the Elimination of the Native," *Journal of Genocide Research*, 8.4 (Dec. 2006), 397–409. Settler societies in Edward L. Ayers, *The Migrations of the American South, 1790–2020* (Baton Rouge: Louisiana State University Press, 2020), 7. On settler slaveholders in Spanish North America, see Andrés Reséndez, *The Other Slavery: The Uncovered Story of Indian Enslavement in America* (New York: Mariner Books, 2016).

12 A notable exception to the basic noting of violent processes is Wendy Warren, *New England Bound: Slavery and Colonization in Early America* (New York: Liveright, 2016). Warren demonstrates how New England involvement in the Atlantic slave economy provided the economic foundation for settler colonization.

13 James Gregory Mumford, *Mumford Memoirs: Being the Story of the New England Mumfords from the Year 1655 to the Present Time* (Boston: Merrymount Press, 1900), 53–54. Assembly order in "Proceedings of the General Assembly held for the Colony of Rhode Island and Providence Plantations, at Newport, 28th day of May, 1707" in *Records of the Colony of Rhode Island and Providence Plantations, in New England, vol. IV*, ed. John Russell Bartlett (Providence: Knowles, Anthony and Co., 1859), 27. The political record notes that the fleeing slave committed suicide by drowning himself in fear of the retribution he faced. This interpretation seems to highlight and serve the power of Rhode Island enslavers as they

note no witnesses to the enslaved man's death. I mark the drowning as an accident in his bid to escape. For additional examples of eighteenth-century slavery and violence in Rhode Island, see Christian M. McBurney, *A History of Kingston, RI, 1700–1900* (Kingston, RI: Pettaquamscutt Historical Society, 2004), 47–48.

14 Metacom in Martha L. Finch, *Dissenting Bodies: Corporealities in Early New England* (New York: Columbia University Press, 2010), 58–59. For slavery profits underwriting colonization, see Warren, *New England Bound.*

15 Sven Beckert, *Empire of Cotton: A Global History* (New York: Vintage, 2014), xvi, 37.

16 Joanne Pope Melish, *Disowning Slavery: Gradual Emancipation and "Race" in New England, 1780–1860* (Ithaca: Cornell University Press, 1998), 14–20. On early American slave economy, see Craig Steven Wilder, *Ebony and Ivy: Race, Slavery, and the Troubled History of America's Universities* (New York: Bloomsbury, 2013). See, too, McBurney, *History of Kingston,* 44–49.

17 Here I diverge slightly from Beckert, believing more in the utility of early governments and their ability to enact violence. There is a palpable difference between government violence in the eighteenth and nineteenth centuries, but I locate those differences more in scale and technological advances. See Beckert, *Empire of Cotton,* xvi.

18 I frame the relationship between the violence of the state and the violence of the individual slightly differently than does Beckert, who sees personal violence as the central mode of war capitalism. See ibid., xvi. See too his distinction between war and industrialism capitalism, 37.

19 John Mack Faragher, "'A Great and Noble Scheme': Thoughts on the Expulsion of the Acadians," *Acadiensis,* 36.1 (Autumn 2006), 82–92. Regulars used in Britain in John Shy, *Toward Lexington: The Role of the British Army in the Coming of the American Revolution* (Princeton: Princeton University Press, 1965), 394–395. For London killing, see Benjamin Franklin, "A Conversation on Slavery, 26 January 1770," in *The Papers of Benjamin Franklin, vol. XVII,* ed. William B. Willcox (New Haven: Yale University Press, 1973), 37–44. On Seider (or Snider), see notes for "February 1770," *The Adams Papers: Diary and Autobiography of John Adams,* ed. L. H. Butterfield et al., 4 vols. (Cambridge: Harvard University Press, 1961), I: 349–350. On state violence and its internal logic, see Allen Feldman, *Formations of Violence: The Narrative of the Body and Political Terror in Northern Ireland* (Chicago: University of Chicago Press, 1991), 21.

20 Adams in *Trial of the British Soldiers,* 102, 117. For Hawkins, see note 23 in "Adams' Notes of Authorities for his Argument for the Defense: October 1770," in *The Adams Papers: Legal Papers of John Adams, vol. III,* ed. L. Kinvin Wroth and Hiller B. Zobel (Cambridge: Harvard University Press, 1965), 81–86.

21 Adams in *Trial of the British Soldiers,* 97, 115, 99.

22 Adams in ibid., 98.

23 Ibid.

24 Fukuyama, "Liberalism and its Discontents: The Challenges from the Left and the Right," *American Purpose*, 5 Oct. 2020, www.americanpurpose.com/articles/liberalism-and-its-discontent/. John Stuart Mill, *Principles of Political Economy* (New York: D. Appleton and Company, 1884), 160. See, too, David Brooks, "The Dark Century," *New York Times*, Feb. 17, 2022, www.nytimes.com/2022/02/17/opinion/liberalism-democracy-russia-ukraine.html.

25 A liberal society sees "individuality and private judgement . . . as essential to well-being and as marks of high civilization," see George H. Sabine, *A History of Political Theory*, 3rd edition (New York: Holt, Rinehart and Winston, 1961), 709. For "prudence, temperance, fortitude, and justice" as central to liberal tradition, see James T. Kloppenberg, *The Virtues of Liberalism* (New York: Oxford University Press, 1998), 5. Convinced, not coerced in Sabine, *History of Political Theory*, 708.

26 Wilkerson, *Caste: The Origins of our Discontents* (New York: Random House, 2020), 387. Levenson, *Adiós Niño: The Gangs of Guatemala City and the Politics of Death* (Durham: Duke University Press, 2013), 2.

27 Du Bois, *Darkwater: Voices from Within the Veil* (New York: Harcourt, Brace, and Hale, 1920). Antagonistic beliefs in Oliver C. Cox, *Caste, Class and Race: A Study in Social Dynamics* (1948; New York: Modern Reader Paperbacks, 1970), 531. Antagonistic differences in Robinson, *Black Marxism*, 10. Liberal state and neutrality in Charles W. Mills, *The Racial Contract* (Ithaca: Cornell University Press, 1997), 83. More recent explorations of difference and its connection to capitalism include Lisa Lowe, *Immigrant Acts: On Asian American Cultural Politics* (Durham: Duke University Press, 1996); David Roediger and Elizabeth D. Esch, *The Production of Difference: Race and the Management of Labor in US History* (New York: Oxford University Press, 2012). Though I align most closely with the critics of liberalism and the structure of difference in society, I also acknowledge in this book the importance of personal responsibility for violent acts, a position more aligned with the traditionalist point of view.

28 Adams in *Trial of the British Soldiers*, 99, 114.

29 Adams in ibid., 114.

30 Adams in ibid., 112–113.

31 Adams in ibid., 116.

32 I borrow from Lisa Beard on James Baldwin. Beard writes, "Violence is attached to black bodies to obscure violence by white people and the state." Beard's impressive piece is "James Baldwin on Violence and Disavowal" in *A Political Companion to James Baldwin*, ed. Susan J. McWilliams (Lexington: University Press of Kentucky, 2017), 356. Trial punishments in Hoock, *Scars of Independence*, 10.

33 Global White supremacy in Mills, *The Racial Contract*, 3; see also, Marilyn Lake and Henry Reynolds, *Drawing the Global Colour Line: White Men's Countries and the International Challenge of Racial Equity* (Cambridge: Cambridge University Press, 2008), 6. On the exceptional terminology, see Robinson, *Black Marxism*, 2. Employer and White supremacy in George Lipsitz, *Possessive Investment in*

Whiteness: How White People Profit from Identity Politics, Twentieth Anniversary Edition (Philadelphia: Temple University Press, 2018), viii. On removal and enslavement, see Cheryl I. Harris, "Whiteness as Property," *Harvard Law Review,* 106.8 (June 1993), 1715–1716. See, too, Omi and Winant, *Racial Formation in the United States,* 106.

34 For examples of earlier framings of American violence, see Frederick Jackson Turner, "The Significance of the Frontier in American History," *Annual Report of the American Historical Association for the Year 1893* (n.p.: American Historical Association, 1893), 190–227; Arthur M. Schlesinger, Jr., "Happiness is a Warm Gun" in *The Crisis of Confidence: Ideas, Power and Violence in America* (Boston: Houghton Mifflin, 1969), 19–24; Richard Hofstadter, "Reflections on Violence in the United States" in *American Violence,* ed. Hofstadter and Wallace, 3–43; Richard Slotkin, *Regeneration through Violence: The Mythology of the American Frontier, 1600–1860* (1973; New York: Harper Perennial, 1996); Christopher Waldrep and Michael Bellesiles, "Introduction" in *Documenting American Violence: A Sourcebook,* ed. Waldrep and Bellesiles (New York: Oxford University Press, 2006), 3–10.

35 Act of May 8, 1792, ch. 33, 1 Stat. 271.

36 Hofstadter, "Reflections on Violence," 3. Hofstadter argues that Americans do not have an ideological bent for violence. Yet slavery and colonization clearly represent such ideological leanings. On the progressive aspect, James C. Scott notes that the "great political reforms of the nineteenth and twentieth centuries have been accompanied by massive episodes of civil disobedience, riot, lawbreaking, the disruption of public order, and, at limit, civil war. Such tumult … was often absolutely instrumental in bringing them about." *Two Cheers for Anarchism: Six Easy Pieces on Autonomy, Dignity, and Meaningful Work and Play* (Princeton: Princeton University Press, 2012), 16. On national force as a positive and negative social influence, see Arthur M. Schlesinger, Jr., "Violence as an American Tradition," in *Crisis of Confidence,* 17. The notion of violence as progressive and conservative reshapes Barrington Moore's conviction that violence is fundamental to great societal reform. Barrington Moore, Jr., *Social Origins of Dictatorship and Democracy: Lord and Peasant in the Making of the Modern World* (Boston: Beacon Press, 1967).

37 Quote in Mayo, *Elements of the Pathology of the Human Mind* (London: Stewart and Murray, 1838), 129. For examples of complexity, see Steven Mintz and John Stauffer, eds., *The Problem of Evil: Slavery, Freedom, and the Ambiguities of American Freedom* (Amherst: University of Massachusetts Press, 2007). Violence as a self-defense tool, see Tim Larkin, *When Violence is the Answer: Learning How to Do What it Takes When your Life is at Stake* (New York: Little, Brown and Company, 2017), 19–20.

38 Emerson in Jared Sparks, *The Writings of George Washington, vol. III* (Boston: Russell, Odiorne, and Metcalf, 1834), 491–492.

39 George Washington to Robert Howe, 22 Jan. 1781, Founders Online, National Archives, https://founders.archives.gov/ (hereafter FONA). Howe to

Washington, 27 Jan. 1781, FONA. Elaine Scarry, *The Body in Pain: The Making and Unmaking of the World* (New York: Oxford University Press, 1985), 12. On violence and nationalism, the Bishop Samuel Seabury said the "popular fury" of American rebels exhibited "the persecuting Spirit of Independency." Papers of the United Society for the Propagation of the Gospel B2 n. 187: Samuel Seabury, May 30, 1775, in Peter W. Walker, "The Church Militant: The American Loyalist Clergy and the Making of the British Counterrevolution, 1701–92" (Ph.D. thesis, Columbia University, 2016), 157. See, too, Hoock, *Scars of Independence*, Maya Jasanoff, *Liberty's Exiles: American Loyalists in the Revolutionary World* (New York: Alfred A. Knopf, 2011).

40 The origins of violent behavior are admittedly complex, addressing a range of biological and social factors. The medical framing of violence as a disease was the first step to understand violent behavior. A conference set up by Surgeon General C. Everett Koop is often seen as the first widespread acknowledgement that violence is a medical issue. *Report: Surgeon General's Workshop on Violence and Public Health, Leesburg, VA, October 27–29* (US Department of Health and Human Services, 1986). A history of or exposure to violent behavior is the primary explanation for how violence perpetuates in society. On violence as learned, see, for example, James Gilligan, *Violence: Reflections on a National Epidemic* (New York: Vintage, 1996). Wake Forest University Baptist Medical Center, "Violence is a Learned Behavior, Say Researchers at Wake Forest University," *ScienceDaily*, www.science daily.com/releases/2000/11/001106061128.htm. On peaceful intervention and de-escalation, see Cure Violence Global, https://cvg.org/.

41 Mintz and Stauffer, eds., *The Problem of Evil*.

42 Workers' language on aggression and enslavement in "The International Industrial Assembly of North America, 1864" in *A Documentary History of American Industrial Society, vol. IX*, ed. John R. Commons and John B. Andrews (Cleveland: Arthur H. Clark, 1910), 123.

43 "Topical Talk," *St. Paul Globe*, 29 Sept. 1889, 4. "Rev. Crane on the Crisis," *Omaha Daily Bee*, 3 July 1893, 2.

44 Lisa Beard offers that Baldwin refused the interviewer's question and alerts readers to Baldwin's awareness of the structures of violence in the United States. See her article "James Baldwin on Violence and Disavowal," 343.

CHAPTER 1: A REVOLUTION RESTRAINED

1 Stats in Bruce D. Porter, *War and the Rise of the State: The Military Foundations of Modern Politics* (New York: Free Press, 1994), 249–250. The best work on violence in the Revolution is Hoock, *Scars of Independence*. On the movement of former slaves and Loyalists, see Jasanoff, *Liberty's Exiles*. Violence as its own phenomenon, see Hannah Arendt, *On Violence* (New York: Harcourt, 1970) and Feldman, *Formations of Violence*.

2 Bailyn, ed., *Pamphlets of the American Revolution, 1750–1776* (Cambridge: Harvard University Press, 1965), 585. Pauline Maier writes of the mob tradition in the colonies as an "established social force" – one guided by principles and reason; *From Resistance to Revolution: Colonial Radicals and the Development of American Opposition to Britain, 1765–1776* (1972; New York: Norton, 1991), 3. The two scholars follow the belief of nineteenth-century Frenchman Alexis de Tocqueville that the United States was made unique "by a love of order and law." Many challenge the assumption of law and order as a guiding principle of the American Revolution. See, for example, Gary B. Nash, *The Unknown American Revolution: The Unruly Birth of Democracy and the Struggle to Create America* (New York: Penguin, 2005); Hoock, *Scars of Independence*; Alan Taylor, *American Revolutions: A Continental History, 1750–1804* (New York: Norton, 2016). On the importance of recognizing violence as a non-derivative factor in society, Feldman, *Formations of Violence*, 21.

3 On egalitarian ideals in Pennsylvania, see Steven Rosswurm, *Arms, Country, and Class: The Philadelphia Militia and the "Lower Sort" during the American Revolution* (New Brunswick: Rutgers University Press, 1987).

4 Fred Anderson, *Crucible of War: The Seven Years' War and the Fate of Empire in British North America, 1754–1763* (New York: Vintage, 2000), 185–201. Wayne to Sharp Delany, 20 Feb. 1777, in Charles J. Stille, *Major-General Wayne and the Pennsylvania Line in the Continental Army* (Port Washington, NY: Kennikat Press, 1893), 49.

5 On militia service, Fred Anderson, *A People's Army* (Chapel Hill: University of North Carolina Press, 1984), 3. Service proclamation in Anderson, *Crucible*, 139.

6 Rufus Putnam, *Journal of Gen. Rufus Putnam Kept in Northern New York during Four Campaigns of the Old French and Indian War*, ed. E. C. Dawes (Albany, NY: Joel Munsell's Sons, 1886), 30, 32, 45.

7 Seth Metcalf, *Diary and Journal (1757–1807)* (Boston: Historical Record Survey, 1939), 7. *Luke Gridley's Diary of 1757* (Hartford: Hartford Press, 1907), 30–31. Wooden horse in Harry M. Ward, *Washington's Enforcers: Policing the Continental Army* (Carbondale: Southern Illinois University Press, 2006), 157; Alice Morse Earle, *Curious Punishments of Bygone Days* (Chicago: Herbert S. Stone and Company, 1896), 128–129.

8 Anderson, *People's Army*, 36–38; "Dual System of Military Justice" in Ward, *Washington's Enforcers*, 3. Despotic in Major-General Charles James Napier, *Remarks on Military Law and the Punishment of Flogging* (London: T. and W. Boone, 1837), 148.

9 Putnam, *Journal*, 9–11, 23.

10 Anderson, *People's Army*, 36–38. Parliament in Colonel H. de Watteville, *The British Soldier* (New York: Putnam, 1955), 121. Also in Ward, *Washington's Enforcers*, 154.

11 Eben Putnam, *A History of the Putnam Family in England and America* (Salem, MA: Salem Press, 1891), 40–47, 80–82. Rufus Putnam, *The Memoirs of Rufus Putnam*,

compiled and annotated by Rowena Buell (Boston: Houghton, Mifflin and Co., 1903), 9–11. Anderson, *People's Army*, 36–38.

12 Putnam, *Journal*, 25, 38–39.

13 Putnam, *Journal*, 75, 35, 39. On Indigenous violence, Claudio Saunt, *West of the Revolution: An Uncommon History of 1776* (New York: Norton, 2014), 67, 85, 156. Political documentation of European–Indian violence, Hoock, *Scars of Independence*, 279.

14 Putnam, *Journal*, 39.

15 Putnam, "Nov. 18," "Feb. 2," *Journal*, 49–52.

16 Putnam, "Feb. 3," Feb. 5," Feb. 6," *Journal*, 52–54. Putnam, *Memoirs*, 21.

17 Putnam, "Feb. 6," "April 10," *Journal*, 54, 61. Putnam, *Memoirs*, 22.

18 Putnam, "Sept. 4," "August 20," "Sept. 27," "Aug. 30," *Journal*, 43, 47, 44.

19 Ward, *Washington's Enforcers*, 1. Anderson, *Crucible*, 582–591, 598–599.

20 Christopher Hibbert, *Redcoats and Rebels: The American Revolution through British Eyes* (New York: W. W. Norton, 1990), xvii–xx. Porter, *War and the Rise of the State*, 249–250. Thomas Bender, *A Nation among Nations: America's Place in World History* (New York: Hill and Wang, 2006), 67. Figures in John Brewer, *The Sinews of Power: War, Money, and the English State, 1688–1783* (Cambridge: Harvard University Press, 1988), 30, 38, 40, 88–91, 114–116.

21 Jamaica and Virginia in Shy, *Toward Lexington*, 24–25. Brewer, *Sinews of Power*, 40. Steve Pincus, *The Heart of the Declaration: The Founders' Case for an Activist Government* (New Haven: Yale University Press, 2016), 11, 19, 52–53. Migration restraint as rebel inducer, Saunt, *West*, 21. Samuel Johnson, *Political Tracts* (London: W. Strahan and T. Cadell, 1776), 161.

22 Richard H. Kohn, *Eagle and the Sword: The Federalists and the Creation of the Military Establishment in America, 1783–1802* (New York: The Free Press, 1975), 4–5. Jasanoff, *Liberty's Exiles*, 36–37. Shy, *Toward Lexington*, 218–220. K. Tsianina Lomawaima points out the similar pattern in taxes and American protest (that protest arose over the reason for taxes more so than tax itself) in "Federalism: Native, Federal, and State Sovereignty" in *Why You Can't Teach United States History without American Indians*, ed. Susan Sleeper-Smith et al. (Chapel Hill: University of North Carolina Press, 2015), 277.

23 On taxes and state violence, Norbert Elias, *The Civilizing Process: Sociogenetic and Psychogenetic Investigations*, trans. Edmund Jephcott, revised edition (1939; Malden, MA: Blackwell, 2000), 268. On taxation, see Sheldon S. Woldin, *Politics and Vision: Continuity and Innovation in Western Political Thought*, expanded edition (Princeton: University of Princeton Press, 2006), 185–186; Marc W. Kruman, *Between Authority and Liberty: State Making in Revolutionary America* (Chapel Hill: University of North Carolina Press, 1997), 92–94; Alexander Keyssar, *The Right to Vote: The Contested History of Democracy in the United States*, revised edition (New York: Basic Books, 2000), 11; Francis Fukuyama, *The Origins of Political Order: From Prehuman Time to the French Revolution* (New York: Farrar, Straus and Giroux, 2010), 351; Michael Mann, *The Sources of Social Power, vol. II: The Rise of Classes and Nation-States, 1760–1914*, new

edition (New York: Cambridge University Press, 2012), 222. On English citizens and representation, Charles Edward Merriam, *A History of American Political Theories* (New York: Macmillan and Co., 1920), 45–46. For virtual representation, see Jack P. Greene, *The Constitutional Origins of the American Revolution* (Cambridge: Cambridge University Press, 2010).

24 29 Oct. 1774, 16 May 1775, in *The Journals of Each Provincial Congress of Massachusetts*, ed. William Lincoln (Boston: Dutton and Wentworth, 1838) [hereafter *JPC*], 42–43, 230.

25 Shy, *Toward Lexington*, 422, 140.

26 Conflict dissolves to violence in ibid., 315. William Pitt on "atoms" in 1766 in *The Parliamentary History of England, vol. XVI: 1765–1771* (London: T. C. Hansard, 1813), 107. Gage in David Hackett Fischer, *Paul Revere's Ride* (New York: Oxford University Press, 1994), 31. Mercy Otis Warren to Catherine Sawbridge Macauly, 29 Dec. 1774, in *Mercy Otis Warren: Selected Letters*, ed. Jeffrey H. Richards and Sharon M. Harris (Athens: University of Georgia Press, 2009), 37. Novanglus [John Adams] to Inhabitants of Massachusetts Bay Colony, in *The Papers of John Adams*, ed. Robert J. Taylor et al., 21 vols. (Cambridge: Harvard University Press, 1977–2022), II: 288–289.

27 English jurist William Blackstone called self-defense "the primary law of nature" that "is not . . . taken away by the law of society." See *Commentaries on the Laws of England, vol. III* (Philadelphia: Bell, 1772), 4. 18 May 1775, in *Journals of the Continental Congress, 1774–1789*, ed. Worthington C. Ford et al., 34 vols. (Washington, DC, 1904–1937) [hereafter *JCC*], II: 55–56. "Resolution of the Continental Congress," May 18, 1775, *JPC*, 706. Benjamin Franklin to Nathaniel Seidel, 2 June 1775, in Paul H. Smith et al., eds., *Letters of Delegates to Congress, 1774–1789*, 25 vols. (Washington, DC: Library of Congress, 1976–2000), I: 433. Zabdiel Adams, *The Grounds of Confidence and Success in War: A Sermon* (Boston: Mill and Hicks, 1775), 5.

28 Committee of Safety to Benedict Arnold, 3 May 1775, *JPC*, 534. Edward Mott to Provincial Congress, 11 May 1775, *JPC*, 697.

29 Woldin, *Politics and Vision*, 197–200. *The Discourses of Niccolò Machiavelli*, trans. Leslie J. Walker (1950; New York: Routledge, 2006), 1.7. "Armed republics make very great progress, whereas mercenary forces do nothing but damage," Machiavelli explained. "Rome and Sparta were for many centuries armed and free. The Swiss are well armed and enjoy great freedom," Niccolò Machiavelli, *The Prince*, trans. Luigi Ricci (1903; London: Oxford University Press, 1921), 48–49.

30 Warren, Oration at Boston, 5 Mar. 1772, 19. Kohn, *Eagle and the Sword*, 5–6. Porter, *War and the Rise of the* State, 250. 26 Oct. 1774, *JPC*, 32–33.

31 Tourists in Paul Lockhart, *The Whites of their Eyes: Bunker Hill, the First American Army, and the Emergence of George Washington* (New York: Harper, 2011), 90. William Windham, *A Plan of Exercise, for the Militia of the Province of the Massachusetts-Bay* (Boston: Draper, 1772), 35. 5 Apr. 1775, *JPC*, 125.

32 All quotes and material from Lockhart, *The Whites of their Eyes*, 80–83.

33 Ward's race order in Joyce Lee Malcom, "Slavery in Massachusetts and the American Revolution," *Journal of the Historical Society*, 10:4 (Dec. 2010), 427. 8 and 16 May 8, 12 June 1775, *JPC*, 208, 230–231, 320.

34 Disarmament in Warren to Preston Committee, Aug. 24, 1774, in Richard Frothingham, *Life and Times of Joseph Warren* (Boston: Little, Brown, and Company, 1865), 346–347. Warren purchased a "Negro boy," Agreement of Joseph Warren with Joshua Green Regarding Payment for an Enslaved Person, 28 June 1770, Collections Online, Massachusetts Historical Society, www .masshist.org/database/viewer.php?item_id=564&br=1. Warren, Oration at Boston, 5 Mar. 1772, and Oration at Boston, 6 Mar. 1775, in A Bostonian, *Gen. Joseph Warren*, 30, 59. Warren to Samuel Adams, 15 June 1774, in Frothingham, *Life and Times*, 317.

35 Slaves in C. B. Alexander, "The Training of Richard Caswell," *North Carolina History Review*, 23.1 (Jan. 1946), 15–16. Richard Caswell to William Caswell, 11 May 1775, *Letters of Delegates*, I: 340–341. "A Schedule of the Taxable Property of Joseph Hewes," 16 Oct. 1777, https://historical.ha.com/itm/autographs/military-figures /signer-joseph-hewes-accounts-for-his-slaves-and-other-property-joseph-hewes-173 0-1779-signer-of-the-declaration-o/a/626-25290. Joseph Hewes to Samuel Johnston, 11 May 1775, *Letters of Delegates*, I: 342.

36 Two slaves, Pompey and Hagar, are listed in "Inventory of the Estate of Mr. Silas Deane Late of Weathersfield decd Represented," Probate, Hartford District, Wethersfield, 1792. Silas Deane to Elizabeth Deane, 7 June 1775, *Letters of Delegates*, I: 436–437.

37 2, 3, 9, and 10 June 1775, *JCC*, II: 78, 79, 84–86.

38 12 Jan. 1775, 5 July 1776, 24 Aug. 1774, *The Revolutionary Records of the State of Georgia, vol. I*, compiled by Allen D. Candler (Atlanta: Franklin-Turner Company, 1908), 41, 152–153, 26.

39 John Adams, "In Congress June and July 1775," in *Adams Papers: Diary and Autobiography*, III: 321. 15 June, 1775, *JCC*, II: 91. Ethan Allen, "Proclamation of Colonels Allen and Easton," 1 June 1775, *JPC*, 716.

40 Slave-ownership and dealings in David John Mays, *Edmund Pendleton, 1721–1803: A Biography*, 2 vols. (Cambridge: Harvard University Press, 1952), I: 107–108, II: 182, 325, 344. Edmund Pendleton to Joseph Chew, 15 June 1775, *Letters of Delegates*, I: 490. Earlier interpretations mark 1 January 1776, as the "birth" of the Continental Army (see Louis Clinton Hatch, *The Administration of the American Revolutionary Army* (New York: Longmans, Green, and Co., 1904), 5); however, Washington's appointment in 1775 set in motion immediate oversight of the Cambridge army by the Continental Congress.

41 Ronald Chernow, *Washington: A Life* (New York: Penguin, 2010), 39–49.

42 Ibid., 39–49. Jon Almon, *An Impartial History of the Late War. Deduced from the Committing of Hostilities in 1749, to the Signing of the Definitive Treaty of Peace in 1763* (London: J. Johnson and J. Curtis, 1763), 63–68. John Barrow, *A New and*

Impartial History of England, From the Invasion of Julius Cæsar, to the Signing of the Preliminaries of Peace, in the Year 1762, vol. IX (London: J. Coote, 1763), 65.

43 George Washington to John Augustine Washington, 18 July 1755, in *The Papers of George Washington: Colonial Series*, ed. W. W. Abbot and Dorothy Twohig, 10 vols. (Charlottesville: University Press of Virginia, 1983–1995), I: 343. Chernow, *Washington*, 61. Washington to John Augustine Washington, 31 May 1754, in *Papers: Colonial Series*, I: 118–119. George II in Horace Walpole, *Memoirs of the Reign of King George the Second, vol. I* (London: Henry Colburn, 1847), 400. *Gazette* in Chernow, *Washington*, 68. "A Short History of the Present War," *Royal Magazine or Gentleman's Monthly Companion*, 1 (London: J. Coote, 1759), 44.

44 Washington to Robert Dinwiddie, 9 Nov. 1756, *Papers: Colonial Series*, IV: 2. Washington, "Orders 6 July 1756," Papers: Colonial Series, III: 238.

45 On how a flogging proceeded, see entry under "punishment" in the Military Dictionary included in Thomas Simes, *The Military Medley*, 2nd edition (London: n.p., 1768). Perry, "Life of David Perry," *Magazine of History*, 35 (1928) in Caroline Cox, *A Proper Sense of Honor: Service and Sacrifice in George Washington's Army* (Chapel Hill: University of North Carolina Press, 2004), 90. Napier, *Remarks*, 163.

46 Flogging stats in James Titus, *The Old Dominion at War: Society, Politics, and Warfare in Late Colonial Virginia* (Charleston: University of South Carolina Press, 1991), 68. Washington advocates for more severe punishment, Cox, *A Proper Sense of Honor*, 92–93.

47 Chernow, *Washington*, 65. Washington, "Orders 25 June 1756," "26 June 1756," *Papers: Colonial Series*, III: 222, 226. Washington to Dinwiddie, 23 May 1756, *Papers: Colonial Series*, III: 171.

48 Newton in Marcus Rediker, *The Slave Ship: A Human History* (New York: Viking, 2007), 157. On whipping Charlotte, see "Whitting to Washington," Jan. 16, 1793, *The Papers of George Washington: Presidential Series*, ed. Dorothy Twohig et al., 21 vols. (Charlottesville: University Press of Virginia, 1987–2020), XII: 5–14. Washington's approval in "Washington to Anthony Whitting," 20 Jan. 1793, ibid., XII: 31–36.

49 Slavery and "disposable" in Patterson, *Slavery and Social Death: A Comparative Study* (Cambridge: Harvard University Press, 1982), 13, 7.

50 Chernow, *Washington*, 183. John Adams to Abigail Adams, 29 May 1775, *The Adams Papers: Adams Family Correspondence*, ed. Lyman H. Butterfield et al., 15 vols. (Cambridge: Harvard University Press, 1963–2022), I: 207–208.

51 Rush in Chernow, *Washington*, 183. Adams to Abigail Adams, 29 May 1775, 207–208.

52 Chernow, *Washington*, 295. Martha Daingerfield Bland to Frances Bland Randolph, 12 May 1777, in *The Papers of George Washington: Revolutionary War Series*, ed. Philander D. Chase et al., 28 vols. to date (Charlottesville: University Press of Virginia, 1985–), IX: 320–323.

53 Abigail Adams to John Adams, 16 July 1775, *Adams Family Correspondence*, I: 245–251. Gilbert Stuart in Chernow, *Washington*, xxi. Christine M. DeLucia, *Memory Lands: King Philip's War and the Place of Violence in the Northeast* (New Haven: Yale University Press, 2018), xi. On the importance of "savage" or "barbarian," see Wayne E. Lee, *Barbarians and Brothers: Anglo-American Warfare, 1500–1865* (New York: Oxford University Press, 2011). Colonial mirror in Michael Taussig, "Culture of Terror – Space of Death: Roger Casement's Putumayo Report and the Explanation of Torture," *Comparative Studies in Society and History*, 26.3 (July 1984), 495.

54 Adams, "In Congress June and July 1775," 321–323. Adams to Elbridge Gerry, 18 June 1775, *Papers of John Adams*, III: 25–27. William M. Fowler, Jr., *Baron of Beacon Hill: A Biography of John Hancock* (New York: Houghton Mifflin, 1980), 78.

55 "Inhabitants of New Hanover County," 19 June 1775, *The Colonial Records of North Carolina, vol. X*, ed. William L. Saunders (Raleigh, NC.: P. M. Hale, 1886), 26. "Proceedings of the Safety Committee in Pitt County," 8 July 1775, in ibid., 87. Colonel John Simpson to Colonel Richard Cogdell, 15 July 1775, in ibid., 94. Kathryn Gehred, "Did George Washington's False Teeth Come from his Slaves? A Look at the Evidence, the Responses to that Evidence, and the Limitations of History," *Washington's Quill*, The Washington Papers, 19 Oct. 2016, http://gwpa pers.virginia.edu/george-washingtons-false-teeth-come-slaves-look-evidence-responses-evidence-limitations-history.

56 Adams, "In Congress June and July 1775," 321. Adams to Gerry, 25–27.

57 Coercion and political leadership, see Kathleen M. Brown, *Good Wives, Nasty Wenches, and Anxious Patriarchs: Gender, Race, and Power in Colonial Virginia* (Chapel Hill: Omohundro Institute, 1996), 372–373. Washington, "Address to the Continental Congress," 16 June 1775, Letter to Martha Washington, 19 June 1775, and Letter to Burwell Bassett, 19 June 1775, *Papers: Revolutionary War Series*, I: 1, 2, 12.

58 "Commission from the Continental Congress" and "Instructions from the Continental Congress," *Papers: Revolutionary War Series*, I: 6, 21. The American state at this point was "*both* place and actor," see Mann, *Sources of Social Power*, 46.

59 Valentine Crawford to George Washington, 24 June 1775, *Papers: Revolutionary War Series*, I: 28. Lund Washington to George Washington, 17 Dec. 1775, ibid., II: 477–482.

60 Washington, "General Orders, 4 July 1775," ibid., I: 54–55.

61 Washington, "General Orders, 6 July 1775," "General Orders, 7 July 1775," "General Orders, 8 July 1775," *Papers: Revolutionary War Series*, I: 67, 71, 75–77.

62 Washington, "General Orders, 6 July 1775," "General Orders, 7 July 1775," "General Orders, 8 July 1775," Letter to John Hancock, 10 July 1775, *Papers: Revolutionary War Series*, I: 67, 71, 75–77, 89. Dave Grossman, *On Killing: The Psychological Cost of Learning to Kill in War and Society*, revised edition (New York: Back Bay Books, 2009).

63 Samuel Osgood to John Adams, 30 Nov. 1775," *Papers of John Adams*, III: 328–330.

64 Adams to Gerry, 18 June 1775, *Papers of John Adams*, III: 25–26. Pay disparity also in Osgood to John Adams, 4 Dec. 1775, ibid., III: 352–353. "Kind" in Osgood to Adams, 30 Nov. 1775.

65 Emerson in Sparks, *The Writings of George Washington, vol. III*, 491–492.

66 On class extremes, see Adams, "I. Fragmentary Notes for 'A Dissertation on the Canon and the Feudal Law,'" May–August 1765, *Papers of John Adams*, I: 106–107. "Dangerous" in Adams to James Sullivan, 26 May 1776, ibid., IV; 208–213. On social movements and masculinity, John Adams to Abigail Adams, 14 Apr. 1776, *Adams Family Correspondence*, I: 381–383.

67 On masculinity, John Adams to Abigail Adams, 14 Apr. 1776.

CHAPTER 2 – LIFE IN THE ARMY OF THE CONTINENT

1 Washington, "Address to the Inhabitants of Canada, 14 September 1775," *Papers: Revolutionary War Series*, I: 461–463.

2 Corbin in Holly A. Mayer, *Belonging to the Army: Camp Followers and Community during the American Revolution* (Charleston: University of South Carolina Press, 1996), 144, 50. Corbin, Bailey, Smith, and Sampson in Carol Berkin, *Revolutionary Mothers: Women in the Struggle for American Independence* (New York: Vintage, 2005), 138–139, 60–61.

3 Deborah Sampson Gannett, *An Address Delivered in 1802 in Various Towns in Massachusetts, Rhode Island and New York* (Boston: H. M. Hight, 1905), 9.

4 NJ recruit in Mayer, *Belonging to the Army*, 20. Nash, *The Unknown American Revolution*, 417–422.

5 Mayer, *Belonging to the Army*, 7. Berkin, *Revolutionary Mothers*, 55. Washington, "General Orders, 23 August 1777" and "General Orders, 27 August 1777" in *Papers: Revolutionary War Series*, XI: 49–51, 73–74. Nash, *The Unknown American Revolution*, 420. Washington, "General Orders, 19 June 1781," Founders Online, National Archives [hereafter FONA], https://founders.archives.gov/.

6 Washington to Stockton, 2 Sept. 1783, FONA. *Warrant for the Execution of Thomas Hickey, at Head-Quarters, New-York, June 28, 1776*, American Archives, Digital Collections and Collaborative Projects, Northern Illinois University Libraries. Washington, "General Orders, 28 June 1776," FONA.

7 On genteel women, Berkin, *Revolutionary Mothers*, 67–68. Chastity and superiority in Brown, *Good Wives*, 368. Washington's class-based views on women are seen in popular military texts, such as Thomas Sims, *The Military Medley*, 2nd edition (London: n.p., 1768), 4–5. Sex workers in armies in Mayer, *Belonging to the Army*, 7–8. Washington to Robert Morris, 29 Jan. 1783, FONA.

8 Jonathan Trenchard, *A Short History of Standing Armies* (London: A. Baldwin, 1698), 7–8.

9 Charles Royster, *A Revolutionary People: The Continental Army and American Character, 1775–1783* (Chapel Hill: University of North Carolina Press, 1979), 25–53. James Kirby Martin and Mark Edward Lender, *A Respectable Army: The Military Origins of the Republic, 1763–1789*, 2nd edition (Wheeling: Harlan Davidson, 2006), 6, 76–77, 110. George Washington to John Hancock, 20–21 Sept. 1776, *Papers: Revolutionary War Series*, VI: 351–354. Washington to John Banister, 21 Apr. 1778, ibid., XIV: 573–579. Small knowledge in Washington to a Continental Congress Camp Committee, 29 Jan. 1778, ibid., XIII: 376–409.

10 Nash, *The Unknown American Revolution*, 187. 29 Mar. 1779, *JCC*, XIII: 388.

11 Paul A. C. Koistinen, *Beating Plowshares into Swords: The Political Economy of American Warfare, 1606–1865* (Lawrence: University Press of Kansas, 1996), 15.

12 Koistinen, *Beating Plowshares into Swords*, 13. Nash, *The Unknown American Revolution*, 218–219. *Laws of the State of Maryland* (1790; Annapolis: Frederick Green, 1905), CCIII: chapter XV, article VII. Virginia, *An Act for Speedily Recruiting the Quota* (Richmond: n.p., 1780), 2. Martin and Lender, *A Respectable Army*, 90–91, 97.

13 "II. Minutes of the Conference, 18–24 October 1775," "General Orders, 31 October 1775," "General Orders, 12 November 1775," Washington, *Papers: Revolutionary War Series*, II: 190–205, 268–270, 353–355. Chernow, *Washington*, 212.

14 Philip D. Morgan and Andrew Jackson O'Shaughnessy, "Arming Slaves in the American Revolution" in *Arming Slaves: From Classical Times to the Modern Age*, ed. Christopher Leslie Brown and Philip D. Morgan (New Haven: Yale University Press, 2006), 189. On Dunmore, Jefferson, and slaves, Jasanoff, *Liberty's Exiles*, 49–50.

15 Washington to John Hancock, 31 Dec. 1775, *Papers: Revolutionary War Series*, II: 622–626. 16 Jan. 1776, *JCC*, IV: 60. Chernow, *Washington*, 212–213.

16 Joseph J. Ellis, *American Creation: Triumphs and Tragedies at the Founding of the Republic* (New York: Alfred A. Knopf, 2007), 35. James Oakes, *The Scorpion's Sting: Antislavery and the Coming of the Civil War* (New York: Norton, 2014), 106. Lockhart, *The Whites of their Eyes*, 104–105.

17 Council of Safety, 8 Jan. 1776, *Revolutionary Records of the State of Georgia*, vol. I: 92. For Black disarmament, see also Morgan and O'Shaughnessy, "Arming Slaves," 192. Committee of Safety, MA, 20 May 1775, *JPC*, 553.

18 John Northrup, James Babcock, Jr., et al., "Protest against Enlisting Slaves to Serve in the Army," *Records of the State of Rhode Island and Providence Plantations in New England*, vol. VIII (Providence: Cooke, Jackson and Co., 1863), 361. James Mitchell Varnum to Washington, 2 Jan. 1778, *Papers: Revolutionary War Series*, XIII: 125. "Proceedings of the General Assembly Held for the State of Rhode Island and Providence Plantations at East Greenwich on the Second Monday in February 1778," *Records of the State of Rhode Island*, VIII: 359. 29 Mar. 1779, *JCC*, XIII: 387–388. See also Nash, *The Unknown American Revolution*, 229.

19 George Washington to James Mease, 21 Jan. 1778, *Papers: Revolutionary War Series*, XIII: 305–307. Washington to Henry Laurens, 3–4 Aug. 1778, ibid., XVI:

236–240. Washington to Ezekiel Cheever, 17 May 1778, ibid., XV: 138. Washington to Brigadier-General William Smallwood, 16 Feb. 1778, ibid., XIII: 563–564.

20 John C. Dann, ed., *The Revolution Remembered: Eyewitness Accounts of the War for Independence* (Chicago: University of Chicago Press, 1980), 17, 30, 412, 228. Joseph Plumb Martin, *Private Yankee Doodle: Being a Narrative of Some of the Adventures, Dangers and Sufferings, of a Revolutionary Soldier*, ed. George F. Scheer (Boston: Little, Brown and Company, 1962), 172.

21 George Washington to Brigadier-General William Maxwell, 10 May 1779, FONA. Washington to Gouverneur Morris, 4 Oct. 1778, *Papers: Revolutionary War Series*, XVII: 253–255.

22 Adams to Gill, 10 June 1775, *Papers of John Adams*, III: 20–22. Erna Risch, *Supplying Washington's Army* (Washington, DC: Center of Military Study, United States Army, 1981), 17–18.

23 Risch, *Supplying Washington's Army*, 17–18. R. Wayne Carp, *To Starve the Army at Pleasure: Continental Army Administration and American Political Culture, 1775–1783* (Chapel Hill: University of North Carolina Press, 1984), 69.

24 Washington to William Livingston, 20 Jan. 1778, Washington to Brigadier-General John Lacey, Jr., 23 Jan. 1778, *Papers: Revolutionary War Series*, XIII: 296–297, 323–324. Chernow, *Washington*, 329.

25 Carp, *To Starve the Army at Pleasure*, 69, 42, 55.

26 Ibid., 55. Official in ibid., 72. Risch, *Supplying Washington's Army*, 18, 20. Washington to Major-General Nathanael Greene, 12 Feb. 1778, *Papers: Revolutionary War Series*, XIII: 514–517.

27 Modern war and allegiance in Joseph J. Ellis, *Revolutionary Summer: The Birth of American Independence* (New York: Knopf, 2013), 134–155. Washington, May 1781, *The Diaries of George Washington*, vol. III, ed. Donald Jackson (Charlottesville: University Press of Virginia, 1978), 356–375. Carp, *To Starve the Army at Pleasure*, 81.

28 Washington, May 1781, *Diaries*, III: 356–375. Carp, *To Starve the Army at Pleasure*, 81. George Washington to Gouverneur Morris, 4 Oct. 1778, 253–255.

29 Washington, "General Orders, 30 August 1776," *Papers: Revolutionary War Series*, VI: 162–164. Nash, *The Unknown American Revolution*, 223. Captain Henry Lee to George Washington, 21 Feb. 1778, *Papers: Revolutionary War Series*, XIII: 632. Washington to Joseph Jones, 10 July 1781, FONA.

30 *State Records of North Carolina, vol. XIV*, ed. Walter Clark (Winston: M. I. and J. C. Stewart, 1896), viii. John Penn, Thomas Burke, and William Sharpe to Richard Caswell, 20 May 1779 and 15 July 1779, *State Records of North Carolina*, 89, 155.

31 Grossman, *On Killing*, 66–72. Twentieth-century leader in ibid., 71. Wayne to Board of War, 3 June 1777, in Stille, *Major-General Wayne*, 64–65.

32 Carl Van Doren, *Mutiny in January* (1943: Clifton, NJ: August M. Kelley, 1973), 20–25. Jonathan Meigs to George Washington, 26 May 1780, FONA. Washington

to Henry Champion, Sr., 26 May 1780, FONA. Washington to Jonathan Trumbull, Sr., 26 May 1780, FONA.

33 Percentage of killers in Grossman, *On Killing,* 177–185. James Thatcher refers to the Massachusetts men who mutinied in early 1780 in his *Military Journal during the American Revolutionary War, from 1775 to 1783* (Hartford: Silus, Andrus and Sons, 1854), 198, 197.

34 Thatcher, *Military Journal,* 197.

35 George Washington to Samuel Huntington, 20 June 1780, FONA. Hardenberg report dated 31 May 1780 enclosed in Goose Van Schaick to Washington, 1 June 1780, FONA.

36 Van Doren, *Mutiny in January,* 21. Joseph Ellis, *His Excellency, George Washington* (New York: Vintage, 2004), 128. James Lovell to John Adams, 2 Jan. 1781, *Papers of John Adams,* XI: 9–10.

37 Wayne to Colonel Johnston, 16 Dec. 1780, in Stille, *Major-General Wayne,* 240–241.

38 Wayne to Washington, 2 Jan. 1781, in Stille, *Major-General Wayne,* 242. Van Doren, *Mutiny in January,* 45.

39 "Enos Reeves: Letterbook Extracts, January 2–17, 1781," in *The American Revolution: Writings from the War of Independence,* ed. John H. Rhodehamel (New York: Library of America, 2001), 630–631.

40 Washington to George Clinton, 4 Jan. 1781, FONA. Van Doren, *Mutiny in January,* 44–49. Washington to John Hancock, 5 Jan. 1781, FONA. Washington to Philip John Schuyler, 10 Jan. 1781, FONA. Clinton's slave-ownership, see Harry B. Yoshpe, "Record of Slave Manumissions in New York during the Colonial and Early National Periods," *Journal of Negro History,* 26.1 (Jan. 1941), 80. For Schuyler's slave-ownership, see Gene Procknow, "Slavery through the Eyes of Revolutionary Generals," *Journal of the American Revolution,* 7 Nov. 2017, https://allthingsliberty.com/2017/11/slavery-eyes-revolutionary-generals/.

41 Wayne to Washington, 2 Jan. 1781, 242. Wayne to General Schuyler, 12 Feb. 1777, in Stille, *Major-General Wayne,* 55. Wayne to Washington, 27 Feb. 1781, in ibid., 262. Thatcher, *Military Journal,* 247.

42 Walter Stewart to George Washington, 4 Jan. 1781, FONA.

43 George Washington to John Stark, 3 Jan. 1781, FONA.

44 Swiss in Fukuyama, *Origins,* 340. George Washington to John Hancock, 5 Jan. 1781, FONA. Anthony Wayne to Washington, 2 Jan. 1781, FONA.

45 John Laurens to George Washington, 7 Jan. 1781, FONA. Arthur St. Clair to Washington, 7 Jan. 1781, FONA. Washington to Wayne, 3 Jan. 1781, FONA.

46 The number of men in the mutiny is perhaps best derived from Wayne's final tally of those discharged and remaining, a total of 2,467; see Wayne to Washington, 29 Jan. 1781, in Stille, *Major-General Wayne,* 260. Washington to Wayne, 8 Jan. 1781. Knox to Washington, 11 Jan. 1781, enclosed in Henry Knox to Washington, 7 Feb. 1781, FONA. For caution, see Washington to Anthony Wayne, 3 Jan. 1781, FONA.

47 Wayne to PA soldiers, 2–4 Jan. 1781, enclosed in Stewart to Washington, 4 Jan. 1781.

48 William Carmichael to Committee on Foreign Affairs, 11 Mar. 1781, in Jared Sparks, ed., *The Diplomatic Correspondence of the American Revolution*, vol. IX (Boston: Nathan Hale and Gray and Bowen, 1829), 68–69. "Revolt of Washington's Army," *St. James's Chronicle or British Evening-Post*, 8–10 Feb. 1781, no. 3112, n.p. 1. Marquis de Lafayette to Madame Lafayette, 2 Feb.1781, *Memoirs, Correspondence and Manuscripts of General Lafayette*, vol. I (London: Saunders and Otley, 1837), 386–387. George Washington to Benjamin Lincoln, 10 Feb. 1781, FONA.

49 George Washington to Philip John Schuyler, 10 Jan. 1781, FONA. Wayne to PA soldiers, 8 Jan. 1781, in Stille, *Major-General Wayne*, 256.

50 Arthur St. Clair to George Washington, 8 Jan. 1781, FONA. Joseph Reed, "Proposals to the Mutineers" and Reed to Mutineers, 8 Jan. 1781, in Stille, *Major-General Wayne*, 258–259. "An Account of the Late Disturbances in the Pennsylvania Line," *Pennsylvania Packet or the General Advertiser*, 27 Jan. 1781, 2.

51 George Washington to Friedrich Wilhelm Ludolf Gerhard Augustin, Baron [von] Steuben, 9 Jan. 1781, FONA. Washington to Nathanael Greene, 9 Jan. 1781, FONA. Washington to Brigadier-General William Maxwell, 10 May 1779, *Papers: Revolutionary War Series*, XX: 428–429. Washington to Arthur St. Clair, 12 Jan. 1781, FONA. Washington to Philip John Schuyler, 10 Jan. 1781, FONA.

52 George Washington to Samuel Huntington, 15 Jan. 1781, FONA. Washington to Jean-Baptiste Donatien de Vimeur, comte de Rochambeau, 20 Jan. 1781, FONA.

53 George Washington to Philip John Schuyler, 6 Feb. 1782, FONA. Seth Warner to Washington, 30 Oct. 1780, FONA.

54 Washington to Continental Congress, 10–11 July 1775, *Papers: Revolutionary War Series*, I: 85–97. Washington to Robert Morris, 30 Dec. 1776, ibid., VII: 489. Chernow, *Washington*, 288–289. Washington to John Hancock, 5 Jan. 1781, FONA.

55 Frelinghuysen's slave-ownership in Deborah Gray White, "Introduction: Scarlet and Black – A Reconciliation" in *Scarlet and Black: Slavery and Dispossession in Rutgers History, Volume I*, ed. Marissa J. Fuentes and Deborah Gray White (New Brunswick: Rutgers University Press, 2016), 1. Frederick Frelinghuysen to George Washington, 23 Jan. 1781, FONA.

56 George Washington to Robert Howe, 15 Jan. 1781, FONA. Washington to Nathanael Greene, 2 Feb. 1781, FONA. Washington to Benjamin Lincoln, 10 Feb. 1781, FONA. Washington to William Livingston, 23 Jan. 1781, FONA.

57 George Washington to Jean-Baptiste Donatien de Vimeur, comte de Rochambeau, 24 Jan. 1781; Washington to Robert Howe, 22 Jan. 1781; Robert Howe to Washington, 29 Jan. 1781, 25 Jan. 1781, 27 Jan. 1781, FONA. Howe's ownership of slaves, see Procknow, "Slavery through the Eyes of Revolutionary Generals."

58 Howe to Washington, 27 Jan. 1781.

59 George Washington to François-Jean de Beauvoir, marquis de Chastellux, 28 Jan. 1781, FONA. Washington to George Clinton, 29 Jan. 1781, FONA.

60 Washington, "General Orders, 30 January 1781," FONA. Washington to Benjamin Lincoln, 10 Feb. 1781, FONA.

61 24 Jan 1781, *JCC*, XIX: 83.

62 I encountered Kandiaronk in the writings of Graeber and Wengrow, *The Dawn of Everything*. Kandiaronk (Adario) in Baron de Lahontan, *New Voyages to North-America*, vol. II (Chicago: A. C. McClurg, 1905), 553–555, 571.

63 Lahontan, *New Voyages*, 555.

64 Ebenezer Denny, *Military Journal of Major Ebenezer Denny* (Philadelphia: J. P. Lippincott, 1859), 34.

65 George Washington to the States, 18 Oct. 1780, FONA. Washington to Abner Nash, 23 Jan. 1781, FONA.

CHAPTER 3 – THE CODE OF AMERICAN VIOLENCE

1 29 Jan. 1781, *Votes and Proceedings of the House of Delegates of the State of Maryland, October Session, 1780* (Annapolis: Frederick Green, 1781), 106. 2 Feb. 1781, *Votes and Proceedings of the Senate of the State of Maryland, October Session, 1780* (Annapolis: Frederick Green, 1781), 49.

2 Articles of Confederation, Art. III, XIII.

3 George Washington to John Mathews, 14 Feb. 1781, FONA. Jurgen Heideking, *The Constitution before the Judgment Seat: The Prehistory and Ratification of the American Constitution, 1787–1791*, ed. John P. Kaminski and Richard Leffler (Charlottesville: University of Virginia Press, 2012), 137. Garrett Epps, *American Epic: Reading the US Constitution* (New York: Oxford University Press, 2013), 24, 28, 31. Akhil Reed Amar, *America's Constitution: A Biography* (New York: Random House, 2005), 25, 141. Patrick Henry observed, "States are the characteristics, and the soul of the confederation," in Heideking, *The Constitution before the Judgment Seat*, 114.

4 Articles of Confederation, Arts. IX, VI, VII.

5 "Resolutions 3 July 1776," *Laws of the State of Maryland*, CCIII: 112.

6 Articles of Confederation, Art. VII. Michael J. Klarman, *The Framer's Coup: The Making of the United States Constitution* (New York: Oxford University Press, 2016), 330. 22 Mar. 1786, 17 May 1786, *JCC*, XXX: 128, 277. 29 Jan. 1781, *Votes and Proceedings of the House of Delegates*, 106.

7 For VA motion, see Francis Corbin on 6 June 1788, in *The Records of the Federal Convention of 1787*, ed. Max Farrand, 3 vols. (New Haven: Yale University Press, 1911), III: 105.

8 On Shays's, see Klarman, *The Framer's Coup*, 11; Pauline Maier, *Ratification: The People Debate the Constitution, 1787–1788* (New York: Simon and Schuster, 2010), 16; George William Van Cleve, *We Have Not a Government: The Articles of Confederation and the Road to the Constitution* (Chicago: University of Chicago Press, 2017), xviii, 226, 262.

9 Lincoln as slaveholder, see Procknow, "Slavery through the Eyes of Revolutionary Generals."

10 David Bernstein, "The Constitutional Convention: Facts and Figures," *The History Teacher*, 21.1 (Nov. 1987), 11–19. Steven Mintz, "Historical Context: The Constitution and Slavery," Gilder Lehrman Institute of American History, History Resources, www.gilderlerman.org.

11 Pinckney, 28 May 1787, in *Records of the Federal Convention of 1787*, III: 47–48. Randolph and Mason in James Madison, *Constitutional Convention: A Narrative History from the Notes of James Madison*, ed. Edward J. Larson and Michael P. Winship (Westminster, MD: Random House, 2005), 14. Ellsworth, 28 Jan. 1783, *JCC*, XXXII: 871.

12 Hamilton on 18 June 1787, in *The Debates in the Several State Conventions on the Adoption of the Federal Constitution*, ed. Jonathan Eliot, 5 vols. (Philadelphia: J. B. Lippincott and Co., 1845), I: 418. Wilson in Madison, *Constitutional Convention*, 31.

13 Mason on 20 June 1787, in *The Debates*, V: 11. Randolph, Martin, Mason, Morris, and Gorham in James Madison's notes, 18 July 1787, *Records of the Federal Convention of 1787*, II: 47–48. See also 18 July 1787, in *The Debates*, V: 332–333.

14 6 Aug. 1787, *The Debates*, V: 381. 30 Aug. 1787, *The Debates*, I: 276.

15 Madison on 14 June 1788, in *The Debates*, III: 408, 410. Dickinson and Dayton on 30 Aug. 1787, in *Records of the Federal Convention of 1787*, II: 466–467. Morris on 17 Aug. 1787, in *Records of the Federal Convention of 1787*, II: 316. Epps, *American Epic*, 107.

16 For Mason and consent, see 14 June 1788, in *The Debates*, III: 378–379.

17 William Symmes to Capt. Peter Osgood, Jr., 15 Nov. 1787, in *The Complete Anti-Federalist*, vol. IV, ed. Herbert Storing (Chicago: University of Chicago Press, 1981), 61. The establishment of national violence in the Constitution was linked to the response to Shays's Rebellion and the Newburgh Conspiracy (but not the mutiny in Washington's army) in a narrative that outlines many of the events mentioned here, in Frederick T. Wilson and Henry C. Corbin, *Federal Aid in Domestic Disturbances, 1787–1903* (Washington, DC: Government Printing Office, 1903), 13–20.

18 James Madison on 14 June 1788 and 16 June 1788, in *The Debates*, III: 378, 414–415. Morris in Madison, *Constitutional Convention*, 113.

19 Mason on 14 June 1788, in *The Debates*, III: 380–381. Pendleton on 16 June 1788, in *The Debates*, III: 440.

20 Nason on 30 Jan. 1788, in *The Debates*, II: 137.

21 MA vote total, *The Debates*, II: 181. Maryland proposed amendment, *The Debates*, II: 553.

22 Lee on 9 June 1788, in *The Debates*, II: 178.

23 Verbs in Epps, *American Epic*, 4–6. Thomas Jefferson to James Madison, 31 July 1788, in *The Papers of James Madison, vol. XI*, ed. Robert A. Rutland and Charles F. Hobson (Charlottesville: University Press of Virginia, 1977), 210–214.

24 For people as basis of the amendment, see Akhil Reed Amar, *Bill of Rights: Creation and Reconstruction* (New Haven: Yale University Press, 1998), 51. Saul Cornell's *A Well Regulated Militia: The Founding Fathers and the Origin of Gun Control in America* (New York: Oxford University Press, 2006) provides one of the clearest explanations of civic duty and individual right in relation to the Second Amendment.

25 Algernon Sidney, *Discourses on Government* (New York: Richard Lee, 1805), II: 196. Cornell, *A Well Regulated Militia*, 11. "The Pennsylvania Committee of Safety: Report to the Pennsylvania Assembly, [29 Sept. 1775]," in *The Papers of Benjamin Franklin, vol. XXII*, ed. William B. Willcox (New Haven: Yale University Press, 1982), 210–213.

26 John Locke, *Two Treatises of Government* (London: Whitmore and Fenn, and C. Brown, 1821), 399, 378. For disarmament in 1768, Cornell, *A Well Regulated Militia*, 14. Allegiance oath in Saul Cornell and Nathan DeNino, "A Well Regulated Right: The Early American Origins of Gun Control," *Fordham Law Review*, 73 (2004), 507.

27 PA statement in Amar, *Bill of Rights*, 47. MA Constitution of 1780 in Oscar Handlin and Mary Handlin, eds., *The Popular Sources of Political Authority* (Cambridge: Harvard University Press, 1966), 466. Response of Northampton and Williamsburgh in ibid., 574, 624. For a more in-depth argument on state constitutions, see Cornell, *A Well Regulated Militia*, 18–25. Michael Waldman, *The Second Amendment: A Biography* (New York: Simon and Schuster, 2014), 32–43. Cornell and DeNino, "A Well Regulated Right," 511.

28 "I. First Draft by Jefferson, [before June 1776]," in *The Papers of Thomas Jefferson*, ed. Julian P. Boyd et al., 45 vols. (Princeton: Princeton University Press, 1950–2021), I: 337–347. Jefferson to Peter Carr, 19 Aug. 1785, *Papers of Thomas Jefferson*, VIII: 405–408. Cesare Beccaria, *An Essay on Crimes and Punishment*, trans. Monsieur de Voltaire (London: J. Almon, 1767), 161.

29 "The Constitution of 1791" in *A Documentary Survey of the French Revolution*, ed. John Hall Stewart (New York: Macmillan, 1951), 232, 236, 238, 259. "Royal Proclamation, 28 Sept. 1791" in ibid., 264.

30 "The Constitution of 1793" in ibid., 458, 456, 467. "The Constitution of the Year III" in ibid., 611.

31 "Title XII: Concerning the Public Force," First Constitution of the State of Guatemala (1825), 134. "Chapter I – Personal Security," Provisional Regulations, Sanctioned by the Sovereign Congress of the United Provinces of South America, for the Government of the State (1817), 682. "Title IV: Of the Elections," Constitution of the State of the Isthmus, 8 June 1841 (1841): 7. "Section 2," Decree No. 76, Declaration of the Rights of the State and of its Inhabitants (1839), 151.

32 "Toussaint Louverture's Constitution, July 1801" in David Geggus, ed. and trans., *The Haitian Revolution: A Documentary History* (Indianapolis: Hackett, 2014), 161, 163.

33 Peter Judson Richards, *Extraordinary Justice: Military Tribunals in Historical and International Context* (New York: New York University Press, 2007), 6–7. Napier, *Remarks*, 9.

34 Laurance to Washington, 5 Feb. 1778, *Papers: Revolutionary War Series*, XIII: 458–460.

35 *The Debates*, IV: 249. *Senate Journal*, 1st Cong., 1st sess. 8 Sept. 1789, 75. Amar, *Bill of Rights*, 50.

36 Hamilton to James McHenry, 3 July 1799, in *Papers of Alexander Hamilton, vol. XXIII*, ed. Harold Syrett (New York: Columbia University Press, 1976), 241–242. "General Orders, 20 July 1799" in ibid., 275–276.

37 Washington, "General Orders, 24 Feb. 1779," *Papers: Revolutionary War Series*, XIX: 250. *The Military Justice System* (Montgomery, AL: Air University, 1962), 69.

38 My take on the Fifth Amendment borrows from Elaine Scarry's classic, *The Body in Pain*, which links society's treatment of human bodies to political processes.

39 Washington to the United States Senate and House of Representatives, 7 Aug. 1789, *Papers: Presidential Series*, III: 398–399. Knox to Washington, 18 Jan. 1790, *Papers: Presidential Series*, V: 10–15. Rutherford in *Senate Journal*, 1st Cong., 2nd sess., 29 Mar. 1792, 418.

40 Act of May 2, 1792, ch. 28, 6 Stat. 264. Act of May 8, 1792, ch. 33, 1 Stat. 271. Whiteness was increasingly a concern for access to federal employment. In 1802, Congress mandated White skin for work in the postal service. Alan Taylor, *The Internal Enemy: Slave and War in Virginia, 1772–1832* (New York: Norton, 2013), 103.

41 Henry Knox to George Washington, 5 Jan. 1791, *Papers: Presidential Series*, VII: 186–188. Beverley Randolph to George Washington, 10 Dec. 1790, ibid., VII: 55–56. John Grenier, *The First Way of War: American War Making on the Frontier* (Cambridge: Cambridge University Press, 2005), 5. 1779 campaign in George Washington to Major-General John Sullivan, 31 May 1779, *Papers: Revolutionary War Series*, XX: 716–719. See also Sarah M. S. Pearsall, "Recentering Indian Women in the American Revolution" in *Why You Can't Teach United States History without American Indians*, ed. Sleeper-Smith et al., 61–62.

42 Fallen Timbers and Knox in William Hogeland, *Autumn of the Black Snake: The Creation of the US Army and the Invasion that Opened the West* (New York: Farrar, Straus and Giroux, 2017), 375, 366.

43 Jefferson to James Madison, 28 Dec. 1794, *Papers of Thomas Jefferson*, XXVIII, 228–230.

44 Mason on 14 June 1788, *The Debates*, III: 380. Mason repeats this argument at the Virginia ratifying convention. See Maier, Ratification, 282. Madison on 16 June 1788, *The Debates*, III: 414. Elihu Marvin, Letter of 21 July 1793, US History Pre-Civil War Collection, Box 1, Folder 7, Watkinson Library, Trinity College, Hartford, Connecticut.

CHAPTER 4 – THE 1850S: A PEOPLE'S GOVERNMENT
AND THE POLITICS OF BELLIGERENCE

1 Beaumont and Tocqueville, *On the Penitentiary System in the United States and its Application in France* (Philadelphia: Carey, Lee and Blanchard, 1833), xivi, 130.

2 Beaumont, *Marie, or Slavery in the United States*, trans. Barbara Chapman (1958; Baltimore: Johns Hopkins University Press, 1999); see, for example, page 216, where he speaks of southern Whites and the "civilizing forces." Alexis de Tocqueville, *Democracy in America*, trans Henry Reeve (New York: J. and H.G. Langley, 1845), 17, 335–336. There is a longstanding debate over the nature of democracy and the hierarchies of race, especially in relation to Tocqueville. See Margaret Kohn, "The Other America: Tocqueville and Beaumont on Race and Slavery," *Polity*, 35.2 (Winter 2002), 169–193.

3 Tocqueville, *Democracy in America*, 335, 2. Beaumont did recognize that Black men were actively excluded from political and civil society. See *Marie*, 190.

4 Tocqueville, *Democracy in America*, 136, 337, 360. For his claims on Natives, see, for example, 364–365. Donald Yacovone notes John H. Van Evrie and Gunnar Myrdal as two other thinkers who note that American democracy is bound to the subordination of Black people. See *Teaching White Supremacy: America's Democratic Ordeal and the Forging of our National Identity* (New York: Pantheon Books, 2022), 295.

5 Masur, *Until Justice Be Done: America's First Civil Rights Movement, From the Revolution to Reconstruction* (New York: W. W. Norton, 2021), 209–210. On global White supremacy as a political system, see Mills, *The Racial Contract.*

6 Edward E. Baptist, *The Half Has Never Been Told: Slavery and the Making of American Capitalism* (New York: Basic Books, 2014), 224–225. See also James Oakes on White suffrage and the silencing of a Black underclass of workers, in *The Ruling Race: A History of American Slaveholders* (1982; New York: W. W. Norton, 1998), 141–142.

7 John Binns, "Some Account of Some of the Bloody Deeds of General Jackson" (Philadelphia?: s.n., 1828). On enlistment lengths, H. W. Brands, *Andrew Jackson: His Life and Times* (New York: Doubleday, 2005), 397–398.

8 On racialization and treatment of Indian populations, see Grenier, *The First Way of War*, 5, 12. Death toll and significance in Brands, *Andrew Jackson*, 217–219. Steven Hahn, *A Nation without Borders: The United States and its World in an Age of Civil Wars, 1830–1910* (New York: Viking, 2016), 228–229.

9 Newspapers in James Parton, *Life of Andrew Jackson, vol. III* (New York: Mason Brothers, 1860), 144–145. Parton uses the newspaper piece on New Orleans as a rejoinder to Jackson's Coffin Handbill critics; I see a larger conversation over violence, Whiteness, and masculinity. See also Brands, *Andrew Jackson*, 400. Keyssar, *The Right to Vote.* David Brion Davis, *Inhuman Bondage: The Rise and Fall of Slavery in the New World* (New York: Oxford University Press, 2006), 279–280. On democracy as a value and institution, see James Crick, *Democracy: A Very Short Introduction* (New York: Oxford University Press, 2002), 3.

10 Here I reject the framing of liberalism as offered by George H. Sabine and others who state that "Liberal political thought developed largely as an elaboration of two fundamental social or moral ideas, that politics is distinctively an art of reaching non-coercive adjustments between antagonistic interests and that democratic procedures are the only effective ways for making such adjustments." See Sabine, *A History of Political Theory*, 755. Tocqueville, *Democracy in America*, 194. Tocqueville was also quite critical of the majority/minority dynamic in American politics. David Grimsted, *American Mobbing, 1828–1861* (New York: Oxford University Press, 1998), 185–190. Editor in ibid., 198. Douglass Hibbs proposes that a "democratic world would not necessarily be a non-violent one." Hibbs's "gamble" is from G. Bingham Powell in David C. Rapoport and Leonard C. Weinberg, "Introduction," *The Democratic Experience and Political Violence*, ed. Rapoport and Weinberg (London: Frank Cass, 2001), 2–3.

11 Keyssar, *The Right to Vote*, 22–23.

12 Dodge in *Congressional Globe*, 32nd Cong., 1st sess. 1118–1119 (1852). S. 22 33rd Cong. (1854).

13 Eric Foner, *Gateway to Freedom: The Hidden History of the Underground Railroad* (New York: W. W. Norton, 2015), 124–125.

14 Newspaper coverage of fugitive slave activity in Samuel J. May, *The Fugitive Slave Law and its Victims* (New York: American Anti-Slavery Society, 1861), 11–12.

15 Newspaper coverage in May, *The Fugitive Slave Law*, 11, 15, 20. Thomas P. Slaughter, *Bloody Dawn: The Christiana Riot and Racial Violence in the Antebellum North* (New York: Oxford University Press, 1991).

16 S. M. Africanus, *The Fugitive Slave Law* (Hartford, CT: n.p., 1850).

17 Act of 9 September 1850, ch. 49, 9 Stat. 446. Baptist, *The Half Has Never Been Told*, 338. Bruce Levine, *The Fall of the House of Dixie: The Civil War and the Social Revolution that Transformed the South* (New York: Random House, 2013), 34. Reséndez, *The Other Slavery*, 257–265.

18 Samuel Ward, Speech of 25 Mar. 1850, and William P. Newman to Frederick Douglass, 1 Oct. 1850, in *The Black Abolitionist Papers, vol. IV: The United States, 1847–1858*, ed. Peter Ripley (Chapel Hill: University of North Carolina Press, 1991), 49, 63.

19 Dodge in *Cong. Globe*, 32nd Cong., 1st sess., 1118–1119 (1852). 14 Dec. 1853, *Journal of the Senate of the United States of America, 1789–1873*, 44. S. 22, 33rd Cong. (1854), 28, 35.

20 Louis Pelzer, *Augustus Caesar Dodge: A Study in American Politics* (Iowa City: State University of Iowa, 1909), 182. Scott Manning Stevens, "American Indians and the Civil War" in *Why You Can't Teach United States History without American Indians*, ed. Sleeper-Smith et al., 146.

21 Oakes, *Ruling Race*, 69–79. On enslaver migration, see also Adam Rothman, *Slave Country: American Expansion and the Origins of the Deep South* (Cambridge: Harvard University Press, 2007). In the history of slavery in the Atlantic world, mobility

and profit commonly mixed. Barbadian enslavers in the 1680s, for instance, reaped great fortunes in anticipation of a slave-free return to England. See Davis, *Inhuman Bondage*, 114–115.

22 Land sales in Gary Gerstle, *Liberty and Coercion: The Paradox of American Government from the Founding to the Present* (Princeton: Princeton University Press, 2015), 28.

23 "Nebraska Territory," *New York Journal of Commerce*, 13 Jan. 1854. "Renewal of the Slavery Agitation – The Nebraska Bill," *New York Times*, 24 Jan. 1854, 4.

24 *Mississippi Free Trader*, 31 Jan. 1854, 4. Fairfax, "Special Correspondence," *Floridian and Journal*, 4 Feb. 1854, 2. *Daily National Era*, 31 Jan. 1854, 2. "Nebraska Meeting in New York," *Sun* [Baltimore], 1 Feb. 1854, 2.

25 There is a strong resonance in Democratic positions in the 1850s to recent, neoliberal developments; see David Harvey, *A Brief History of Neoliberalism* (New York: Oxford University Press, 2005), 2. Douglas in *Cong. Globe*, 33rd Cong., 1st sess. 337 (1854).

26 My thanks for conversations with then Yale graduate student and now Dartmouth Professor Jorge Cuellar who provided me with the language of state abrogation, which sits at the core of my interpretation of popular sovereignty.

27 W. A. Gorman, "Governor's Message," *Daily Pioneer and Democrat* [St. Paul], 10 Jan. 1856, 3. Franklin Pierce, "Proclamation 66 – Law and Order in the Territory of Kansas," Feb. 11, 1856, online in Gerhard Peters and John T. Woolley, *The American Presidency Project*, www.presidency.ucsb.edu. Committee of Vigilance in Harold M. Hyman and William M. Wiecek, *Equal Justice under Law: Constitutional Development, 1835–1875* (New York: Harper Torchbooks, 1982), 5–6. On Kansas–Nebraska Act, see Christopher Childers, "Interpreting Popular Sovereignty: A Historiographical Essay," *Journal of the Civil War Era*, 57.1 (Mar. 2011), 48–70. To understand the role of violence in the 1850s one must recalibrate well-established interpretations of the political situation. Many historians explain the sudden increase in hostility on the collapse of the political center of the slavery debate. Among the four positions available there was, from left to right on the partisan spectrum, antislavery, the Missouri Compromise, popular sovereignty, and proslavery. The Kansas–Nebraska Act annulled the Missouri Compromise. Pandemonium in Kansas, the Dred Scott decision, and Stephen Douglas's 1858 Freeport Doctrine, which claimed that a territory could effectually overturn a proslavery vote through weak police provisions and unfavorable legislation, dispatched popular sovereignty. By the close of the 1850s, Americans contended over slavery from the most extreme outlooks of antislavery and proslavery ideology. The problem with such a reading is that it downplays the role of popular sovereignty in the history of American violence. On historical interpretations, see, for example, David Potter, *The Impending Crisis: America before the Civil War, 1848–1861* (New York: HarperCollins, 1976) and John Ashworth, *Slavery, Capitalism, and Politics in the Antebellum Republic*, vols. I and II (Cambridge: Cambridge University Press, 1995–2007).

28 Grimsted, *American Mobbing*, 187–188. *Report of the Special Committee Appointed to Investigate the Troubles in Kansas, 34 Cong., 1st Sess.* (Washington, DC: Cornelius Wendell, 1856), 2–3, 66–67. Stringfellow and Rees in ibid., 925, 929.

29 *Report of the Special Committee*, 67, 86, 659; proslavery resolutions on 930; antislavery, 89–90. Webb, letter dated 14 Aug. 1854, in ibid., 82–83.

30 Abraham Lincoln, "Speech at Peoria, 16 Oct. 1854" in *Collected Works of Abraham Lincoln*, ed. Roy P. Basler, 8 vols. (New Brunswick: Rutgers University Press, 1953), II: 271–272. For notes on an earlier Lincoln critique of the Kansas–Nebraska Act, see "Speech at Winchester, Illinois, 26 Aug. 1854," ibid., II: 226–227. Martha Nussbaum's observation on the famous Stanford Prison Experiment is apt here: "People who are not individually pathological can behave very badly to others when their situation has been badly designed." *Not for Profit: Why Democracy Needs the Humanities* (Princeton: Princeton University Press, 2010), 43. Of popular sovereignty in Kansas, Robert Christopher Childers asks, "what were the rules?" See his "Popular Sovereignty, Slavery in the Territories, and the South" (PhD thesis, Louisiana State University and Agricultural and Mechanical College, 2010), 311.

31 "Ho! For Kansas!" *Hartford Daily Courant*, 24 Feb. 1857, 3. A Lady [Hannah Anderson Ropes], *Six Months in Kansas* (Boston: John P. Jewett and Co., 1856), 111, 117.

32 *Report of the Special Committee*, 2–3, 57, 66–67, 86, 89–90, 659; resolutions on 930. Webb, letter dated 14 Aug. 1854, in ibid., 82–83.

33 Pierce, "Proclamation," and "Special Message," 24 Jan. 1856, *The American Presidency Project*.

34 Pierce, "Special Message" and "Proclamation 66."

35 Franklin Pierce in *US Senate Journal*, 34th Cong., 1st sess., 24 Jan. 1856, 68. "Introduction," xxviii. "Special Message." The indictments for the antislavery advocates investigated for treason, including John Brown, Jr., were declared a *nolle prosequi*. See *US Senate Journal*, 34th Cong., 1st sess., 24 Aug. 1856, 515. Jefferson Davis to Franklin Pierce, 1 Dec. 1856, in *The Papers of Jefferson Davis, vol. VI*, ed. Lynda Lasswell Crist (Baton Rouge: University of Louisiana Press, 1989), 91.

36 John Stauffer, *The Black Hearts of Men: Radical Abolitionists and the Transformation of Race* (Cambridge: Harvard University Press, 2004). John Stauffer and Zoe Trodd "Introduction," in *The Tribunal: Responses to John Brown and the Harpers Ferry Raid*, ed. John Stauffer and Zoe Trodd (Cambridge: Harvard University Press, 2012), xxvii. David S. Reynolds, *John Brown, Abolitionist* (New York: Alfred A. Knopf, 2005), 135. As one Brown scholar once put it, "John Brown will mean little to those who do not believe God governs the world." Franklin Benjamin Sanborn in Alice Nichols, *Bleeding Kansas* (New York: Oxford University Press, 1954), 283.

37 Allen C. Guelzo, *Fateful Lightning: A New History of the Civil War and Reconstruction* (New York: Oxford University Press, 2012), 80. "The Investigation in Kansas," *Hartford Daily Courant*, 24 May 1856, 2.

38 Superiority and southern rights in Charles Robinson, *The Kansas Conflict* (New York: Harper and Brothers, 1892), 254, 252. Stauffer and Trodd, "Introduction," xxviii. Nichols, *Bleeding Kansas*, 106–107. Reynolds, *John Brown*, 135–136. "Later from Kansas," *New-York Daily Tribune*, 22 May 1856, 5. "War in Kansas," *National Era*, 29 May 1856, 86–87. "Latest from Kansas," *Albany Evening Journal*, 26 May 1856, 2.

39 "Proceedings in Kansas," *Hartford Daily Courant*, 27 May 1856, 2. "Latest from Kansas," *Albany Evening Journal*, 26 May 1856, 2. Brown in Reynolds, *John Brown*, 158.

40 Charles Sumner, *The Crime against Kansas* (New York: New York Tribune, 1856), 3.

41 "The Dismissal of Mr. Crampton ... The Sumner Affair in Congress," *Weekly Herald*, 24 May 1856, 166. Elizabeth Stordeur Pryor, "The Etymology of Nigger: Resistance, Language, and the Politics of Freedom in the Antebellum North," *Journal of the Early Republic*, 36.2 (2016), 203–245.

42 Reynolds, *John Brown*, 163.

43 *Report of the Special Committee*, 105–107.

44 Maury Klein, *Days of Defiance: Sumter, Secession, and the Coming of the Civil War* (New York: Knopf, 1997), 50. "The War in Kansas," *New York Times*, 12 June 1856, 2.

45 *Hartford Daily Courant*, 21 Mar. 1857, 2.

46 Roy Franklin Nichols, *The Disruption of American Democracy* (1948; New York: Collier Books, 1962), 35–36. The estimate from Richard J. Carwardine, *Evangelicals and Politics in Antebellum America* (New Haven: Yale University Press, 1993), 44, as cited in Mark A. Knoll, *The Civil War as a Theological Crisis* (Chapel Hill: University of North Carolina Press, 2006), 12, and in Drew Gilpin Faust, *This Republic of Suffering: Death and the American Civil War* (New York: Vintage, 2008), 172. Andrew Johnson, "Speech on Harper's Ferry Incident, 12 Dec. 1859," in *The Papers of Andrew Johnson, vol. III*, ed. LeRoy P. Graf and Ralph W. Haskins (Knoxville: University of Tennessee, 1972), 329. Daniel P. Braden to Andrew Johnson, 10 Jan. 1860, *Papers of Andrew Johnson*, III: 374. John A. Copeland, Jr., to John A. Copeland, Sr., and Delilah Copeland, 26 Nov. 1859, *The Black Abolitionist Papers, vol. V: The United States, 1859–1865*, ed. C. Peter Ripley (Chapel Hill: University of North Carolina Press, 1992), 45.

47 Shearer Davis Bowman, *At the Precipice: Americans North and South during the Secession Crisis* (Chapel Hill: University of North Carolina Press, 2010), 136, 138, 211. For violence, social order, and territorial expansion, see Ned Blackhawk, *Violence over the Land: Indians and Empires in the Early American West* (Cambridge: Harvard University Press, 2006), 9. William Link, *Roots of Secession: Slavery and Politics in Antebellum Virginia* (Chapel Hill: University of North Carolina Press, 2003), 121. Kenneth Stampp, *And the War Came* (1950; Baton Rouge: Louisiana State University Press, 1970), 5, 147.

48 James Buchanan, "Remarks, January 7 and 11, 1836, On Slavery in the District of Columbia" in *The Works of James Buchanan Comprising his Speeches, State Papers, and*

Private Correspondence, ed. John Bassett Moore, 12 vols. (Philadelphia: J. B. Lippincott Company, 1908–1911), II: 453. Buchanan, "Letter to a Public Meeting," 19 Nov. 1850, in *Works*, VIII: 392–393. Buchanan, Letter to Mr. Mason, 23 Dec. 1853, *Works*, IX: 265. For his consistent anti-abolitionist stance, see also Buchanan, "Remarks, August 18, 1838, On the Abolition of Slavery," IV: 29.

49 Buchanan, "Trial of Judge Peck, 28–29 Jan. 1831," *Works*, II: 113. Buchanan, "Remarks, 3 Jan. 1837," *Works*, III: 146. Buchanan, Letter to Henry Foote, 31 May 1850, *Works*, VI: 386. Buchanan, Letter to the Committee of Notification, 16 June 1856, *Works*, X: 82–83. Buchanan, "Speech, 9 May 1842, on the United States Courts," *Works*, V: 225.

50 Lincoln, "Speech at Springfield, Illinois," 4 Oct. 1854, in *Collected Works*, II: 245. Lincoln to Henry L. Pierce and others, 6 Apr. 1859, *Collected Works*, III: 376. Lincoln, "Speech at Peoria," 265–266.

51 The words on the slave trade are attributed to Henry Clay in Lincoln, "Eulogy on Henry Clay, 6 July 1852," *Collected Works*, II: 132. Many Democrats fought Lincoln's take on universal equality. "Is there an intelligent man throughout the whole country, is there a Senator, when he has stripped himself of all party prejudice, who will come forward and say that he believes Mr. Jefferson, when he penned that paragraph of the Declaration of Independence, intended to embrace the African population?" Andrew Johnson, "Speech on Harper's Ferry," III: 320.

52 Nineteen slaves (five marked as fugitives) are listed for Joshua F. Speed, 1850 US Federal Census, Schedule 2, District No. 2, Jefferson County, Kentucky, 29 Aug. 1850, n.p. Lincoln, Letter to Joshua Speed, 24 Aug. 1855, *Collected Works*, II: 320–321. For some of Lincoln's first thoughts on Kansas–Nebraska, see "Editorial on the Kansas–Nebraska Act, 11 Sept. 1854," *Collected Works*, II: 229–230.

53 This discussion of morality and state structures influenced by discussions in Nussbaum, *Not for Profit*, 23, and Harvey, *Brief History of Neoliberalism*, 2–3.

54 Robert E. May, *The Southern Dream of a Caribbean Empire, 1854–1861* (1973; Gainesville: University of Florida Press, 2002), xiii. Chapter 12 in Walter Johnson, *River of Dark Dreams: Slavery and Empire in the Cotton Kingdom* (Cambridge: Harvard University Press, 2013).

55 Buchanan, "First Annual Message, December 8, 1857," *Works*, IX: 154. Lincoln, "Speech at Springfield, Illinois, 26 June 1857," *Collected Works*, II: 398–399.

CHAPTER 5 – THE UNITED STATES GREETS JOHN BROWN

1 Mills, *The Racial Contract*, 19. Mintz and Stauffer, eds., *The Problem of Evil*.

2 William Whewell, *Grotius on the Rights of War and Peace: An Abridged Version* (Cambridge: John W. Parker, 1853), 91, 195, 281. Locke, akin to Grotius, holds that slavery is a state of war until the relationship of obedience and dominance is set. Locke, *Two Treatises of Government* (London: Whitmore and Fenn, Charing Cross; and C. Brown, 1821), 206–207.

3 The British Somerset case (1772) is often credited with the establishment of freedom as the natural condition of humankind; however, as Stephen C. Neff points out, slavery was singled out as a "local and exceptional matter" as early as the Justinian *Institutes* in the sixth century. Neff, *Justice in Blue and Gray: A Legal History of the Civil War* (Cambridge: Harvard University Press, 2010), 128. Monsieur de Vattel, *The Law of Nations, or, Principles of the Law of Nature* (London: G.G. and J. Robinson, 1797), 389, 356, 421.

4 Adams, "1766. Jany. 2d. Thursday," *Adams Papers: Diary and Autobiography*, I: 282–301. Washington to Bryan Fairfax, 24 Aug. 1774, *Papers: Colonial Series*, X: 154–156. Alan Taylor, *American Colonies: The Settling of North America* (New York: Penguin, 2001), 439. Washington to George William Fairfax, 31 May 1775, *Papers: Colonial Series*, X: 367–368.

5 Jefferson, "I. Comments on Soulés' Histoire, 3 August 1786," *Papers of Thomas Jefferson*, X: 368–377. VA in Edmund S. Morgan, *American Slavery, American Freedom* (New York: Norton, 1975), 309. Wolcott to Alexander Hamilton, 31 Mar. 1797, in *Papers of Alexander Hamilton, vol. XX*, ed. Harold C. Syrett (New York: Columbia University Press, 1974), 569–574. Michael Walton to Jefferson, 14 Dec. 1807, FONA.

6 "Proposals for Conscientious Objectors: Two Drafts, [before 29 Sept. 1775]," in *The Papers of Benjamin Franklin, vol. XXII*, 208–210. Adams to John Randolph, Jr., 1816, FONA.

7 Davis, *Inhuman Bondage*, 169. Sylvanus Bourne to Thomas Jefferson, 8 Sept. 1791, *Papers of Thomas Jefferson*, XXII: 133–134.

8 Washington read reports on the terrifying murder of Whites in Haiti from the likes of proslavery politician Charles Pinckney. See Pinckney to Washington, 20 Sept. 1791, Papers: *Presidential Series*, VIII: 542–546. Washington to Ternant, 2 Oct. 1791, ibid., IX: 50–51. Washington to Ternant, 24 Sept. 1791, ibid., IX: 15–16. Knox to Washington, 22 Sept. 1791, ibid., VIII: 554–555. See notes in ibid.

9 By the late 1790s, Adams was confident that "the french have plundered and wronged Us twice as much as the English." See John Adams to Abigail Adams, 16 Jan. 1797, FONA. Laurent Dubois, *A Colony of Citizens: Revolution and Emancipation in the French Caribbean, 1787–1804* (Chapel Hill: University of North Carolina Press, 2004), 306. Adams to Benjamin Stoddert, 7 June 1799, FONA. Adams to Timothy Pickering, 17 Apr. 1799, FONA. Adams to George Churchman, 24 Jan. 1801, FONA. "Negro Slavery will now I hope be gradually abolished," said Adams to Joseph Ward, 4 Jan. 1811, FONA. Years later, he continued to degrade the revolutionary Black violence of Haiti: "Are they more free?" he asked of the freed Blacks; "Do they live better? Bananas and Water, they Still enjoy, and a whole Regiment would follow a Leader, who should hold a Salt fish to their Noses." Adams to John Taylor, 18 Jan. 1815, FONA.

10 John Quincy Adams to Thomas Boylston Adams, 3 Dec. 1800, FONA.

11 William Johnson to Thomas Jefferson, 10 Dec. 1822, FONA. J. Hamilton, "To the Publick" in *Of the Late Intended Insurrection Among A Portion of the Blacks of the City of Charleston, South Carolina* (Boston: Joseph W. Ingraham, 1822), 2.

12 William Byrd, *The Westover Manuscripts* (Petersburg: Edmund and Julian C. Ruffian, 1841), 112.

13 Elizabeth Brown Pryor, *Reading the Man: A Portrait of Robert E. Lee through his Private Letters* (New York: Penguin, 2007), 278–281. Parks in ibid., 278. For Wise and slaves, see 1860 US Census, Schedule 2, Princess Anne County, Virginia, 25 July 1860, 28. Bullets in Tony Horwitz, *Midnight Rising: John Brown and the Raid that Sparked the Civil War* (New York: Picador, 2011), 149. Governor Henry Wise, "To the Senate and House of Delegates of the General Assembly of the Commonwealth of Virginia," 5 Dec. 1859, in *Journal of the House of Delegates of the State of Virginia for the Session of 1859–1860* (Richmond: William F. Ritchie, 1859), Appendix: 10. Caldwell to Jones, 17 Oct. 1859 and Colonel Lee to Colonel Cooper, Adjutant-General, 19 Oct. 1859, in *Report of the Select Committee of the Senate to Inquire into the Late Invasion and Seizure of Public Property at Harper's Ferry* (Washington, DC: GPO, 1860), 296, 40. Wilson and Corbin, *Federal Aid in Domestic Disturbances*, 100.

14 Horwitz, *Midnight Rising*, 166. Israel Green, "The Capture of John Brown," *North American Review*, 141.349 (Dec. 1885), 563, 568. Wise, "To the Senate and House of Delegates," 10. Sinn in Horwitz, *Midnight Rising*, 170. Pryor, *Reading the Man*, 279. Lee, in *Report . . . at Harper's Ferry*, 41.

15 Lee, in *Report . . . at Harper's Ferry*, 41–42. Lee to John Brown, 18 Oct. 1859, in *Report . . . at Harper's Ferry*, 43–44.

16 Lee, in *Report . . . at Harper's Ferry*, 41–42. Horwitz, *Midnight Rising*, 176–179. Green, "The Capture of John Brown," 566–567.

17 All material and citations in Horwitz, *Midnight Rising*, 153, 159–162, 191, 181–182.

18 "I did not call on the president to protect Virginia, and would not do so," said Henry Wise, "To the Senate and House of Delegates," 22. See ten slave entries for Floyd in 1850 Federal Census, Schedule 2, 6 Dec. 1850, City of Richmond, Henrico County, n.p., and five slave entries for Floyd in 1860 Federal Census, Schedule 2, 26 July 1860, Accomack, St. Georges Parish, Virginia, 33. Garrett to Floyd, 17 Oct. 1859, in Wilson and Corbin, *Federal Aid in Domestic Disturbances*, 296–297.

19 Act of February, 28, 1795, ch. 36, 3 Stat. 424. Wilson and Corbin, *Federal Aid in Domestic Disturbances*, 100–101.

20 Fillmore also read the Militia Act to mandate a proclamation only in situations outside a state request for assistance. Fillmore in *Senate Journal*, 31st Cong., 2nd sess., 21 Feb. 1851, 207. Lee to Cooper, in *Report . . . at Harper's Ferry*, 43. Traditionally Buchanan is marked as obliging in the face of an aggressive Henry Wise to explain why Brown stood trial in Virginia (as opposed to a federal or military court). See, for example, Daniel C. Draper, "Legal

Phases of the Trial of John Brown," *West Virginia History*, Jan. 1940. Current scholars continue to promote the idea that "political needs," meaning a desire to ensure Brown's death, led to Brown's trial in a state court. See William A. Blair, *With Malice toward Some: Treason and Loyalty in the Civil War Era* (Chapel Hill: University of North Carolina Press, 2014), 13. Lee's action as part of a posse comitatus goes much farther to explain the transfer of Brown to state authorities.

21 Wilson and Corbin, *Federal Aid in Domestic Disturbances*, 74–101. For Fugitive Slave Act as a federal responsibility, see Oakes, *Scorpion's Sting*.

22 Wilson and Corbin, *Federal Aid in Domestic Disturbances*, 74–77. Fillmore, 18 Feb. 1851, Appendix, 11 Stat. 1006. Secretary of War Conrad, 17 Feb. 1851, in Wilson and Corbin, *Federal Aid in Domestic Disturbances*, 75.

23 Judge P. Sprague to US Marshal Watson Freeman, Esq., 26 May 1864, in Wilson and Corbin, *Federal Aid in Domestic Disturbances*, 77. Watson Freeman to Commander at Fort Independence in ibid. "Military Barbarity," *Frederick Douglass' Paper*, 16 Mar. 1855. "Our Military Operations," *Frederick Douglass' Paper*, 22 Dec. 1854. John Stauffer, "The Union of Abolitionists and Emancipationists in Civil-War Era Massachusetts" in *Massachusetts and the Civil War: The Commonwealth and National Disunion*, ed. Matthew Mason, Kathryn Viens, and Conrad Edick Wright (Amherst: University of Massachusetts Press, 2015), 19–20. Theodore Parker, "A Sermon Preached at the Music Hall, Boston, June 4th, 1854," *Frederick Douglass' Paper*, 16 June 1854.

24 Charlotte Forten Grimke, *The Journals of Charlotte Forten Grimke*, ed. Brenda Stevenson (New York: Oxford University Press, 1988), 96–97, 66. Many activists were disappointed, too, when a rumored promise that troops would not be used to return Burns to slavery was broken. See, for example, Samuel Joseph May to Thomas Wentworth Higginson, 1854, Antislavery Collection, Boston Public Library. Foner, *Gateway to Freedom*, 148–150. Activists purchased the freedom of Anthony Burns within a year of his re-enslavement.

25 Lee to Cooper, in *Report . . . at Harper's Ferry*, 42–43.

26 Senators Mason, Davis, and Fitch called for legislation to enhance security at federal arsenals in their report, ibid., 19. Henry Wise declared, "A neglected arsenal had been made a positive danger to us," 11. Wise, "To the Senate and House of Delegates," 11, 21, 15–16. See also Horwitz, *Midnight Rising*, 194. Wise to Buchanan, 25 Nov. 1859, John Brown/Boyd B. Stutler Collection, West Virginia Memory Project. W. C. Bruce to C. W. Alexander, 29 Nov. 1859, Brown/Stutler Collection.

27 Lee to Cooper, in *Report . . . at Harper's Ferry*, 43. *The Code of Virginia, Including Legislation to the Year 1860*, second edition (Richmond: Ritchie, Dunnavant and Co., 1860), 809, 783. "Death Warrant of John Brown, November 2, 1859," John Brown Papers, Jefferson County Circuit Clerk's Office, West Virginia Archives.

28 *Provisional Constitution and Ordinances for the People of the United States*, in *Report . . . at Harper's Ferry*, 58.

29 "Death Warrant of John Brown, November 2, 1859."
30 Wise, "To the Senate and House of Delegates," 21–23. The senate report on Brown's attack disagreed with Wise in stating that the event was not covered by Article IV, Section 4, of the US Constitution. It maintained a hardline refusal of Congressional oversight of states (which American enslavers pushed evermore to the forefront of the national political scene) even in cases of attack. *Report . . . at Harper's Ferry*, 18–19.
31 Wilson and Corbin, *Federal Aid in Domestic Disturbances*, 56–57. Holt to Colonel House, 23 Aug. 1831, in ibid., 261–262. House to Adjutant-General Jones, 30 Aug. 1831, in ibid., 262. Jones to House, 26 Aug. 1831, in ibid., 262.
32 Wilson and Corbin, *Federal Aid in Domestic Disturbances*, 56. Jones to House, 6 Sept. 1831, in ibid., 262–263.
33 Capt. Whiting to Jones, 26 Sept. 1831, in Wilson and Corbin, *Federal Aid in Domestic Disturbances*, 263–264.
34 Pierce in *Senate Journal*, 34th Cong., 1st sess., 24 Jan. 1856, 68. "Negro Revolt at Antigua, West Indies," *Weekly Vincennes Gazette*, 21 Apr. 1858.
35 Lee to Cooper, in *Report . . . at Harper's Ferry*, 41–43. A South-Carolinian [Edwin C. Holland], *A Refutation of the Calumnies Circulated against the Southern and Western States Respecting the Institution and Existence of Slavery among Them* (Charleston: A. E. Miller, 1822), 13.
36 Lee to Cooper, in *Report . . . at Harper's Ferry*, 41–43.
37 Wise, "To the Senate and House of Delegates," 6, 16. Horwitz, *Midnight Rising*, 138–139.
38 Wise, "To the Senate and House of Delegates," 3–4. Farmer Charles Conklyn in Horwitz, *Midnight Rising*, 223–224.
39 *Report . . . at Harper's Ferry*, 7.
40 Testimony of Lewis Washington, *Report . . . at Harper's Ferry*, T30, T34–T35. Testimony of John H. Allstadt, *Report . . . at Harper's Ferry*, T42. Horwitz, *Midnight Rising*, 137.
41 Horwitz, *Midnight Rising*, 115–116. Lewis Washington, *Report . . . at Harper's Ferry*, T35–T37.
42 Horwitz, *Midnight Rising*, 221–223. *Herald* in ibid., 222.
43 Allstadt, *Report . . . at Harper's Ferry*, A44. Horwitz, *Midnight Rising*, 124. Copeland letter in ibid., 265. Washington, *Report . . . at Harper's Ferry*, T40.
44 See Testimony of Terence Byrne, for slaveholder query, *Report . . . at Harper's Ferry*, T13.
45 Byrne, 6 Jan. 1860, *Report . . . at Harper's Ferry*, T14. For Brown's men and the distinction between voluntary and involuntary emancipation, see Testimony of Lind F. Currie, 11 Jan. 1860, *Report . . . at Harper's Ferry*, T56.
46 Stauffer and Trodd, "Introduction," in *The Tribunal*, xxxii.
47 Lewis Washington, *Report . . . at Harper's Ferry*, T35–T37. On recognition of the suicidal nature of insurrection: Davis, *Inhuman Bondage*, 306. Stauffer and Trodd, "Introduction," xxxii.

48 On intricacy of Black violence, see Jeff Forret, *Slave against Slave: Plantation Violence in the Old South* (Baton Rouge: Louisiana State University Press, 2015). Madison to William Bradford, 26 Nov. 1774, in *The Papers of James Madison*, ed. William Hutchinson and William M. E. Rachal (Chicago: University of Chicago Press, 1962), 129–131.

49 For a discussion of the legal examination of slaves under the lash (and secrecy), see Winthrop D. Jordan, *Tumult and Silence at Second Creek: An Inquiry into a Civil War Slave Conspiracy*, revised edition (Baton Rouge: Louisiana State University Press, 1995), 92–98. Monroe to Jefferson, 15 Sept. 1800, *Papers of Thomas Jefferson*, XXXII: 144–145. Claiborne to Jefferson, 24 Jan. 1811, *Papers of Thomas Jefferson: Retirement Series, vol. III*, ed. J. Jefferson Looney (Princeton: Princeton University Press, 2006), 325–326. Daniel Rasmussen, author of the most recent, comprehensive work on the 1811 revolt, marks the suppression of knowledge about the event (and scant records) as central to the story; *American Uprising: The Untold Story of America's Largest Slave Revolt* (New York: Harper Perennial, 2012).

50 *Provisional Constitution* in *Report . . . at Harper's Ferry*, 48.

CHAPTER 6 – 1860: THE UNDISPUTED ELECTION
THAT SPARKED DISPUTE

1 Human rights and antislavery man, speech of Thaddeus Stevens in *The Wide-Awake and Central Campaign Club Bulletin* [New York], 5 Oct. 1860 (No. 2), 1–2. Bullies in Almon H. Benedict, *A "Wide Awake" Poem* (Cortland Village, NY: Edward D. Van Slyck, 1860), 11.

2 *The Life and Public Services of Hon. Abraham Lincoln* (Boston: Thayer and Eldridge, 1860), 7.

3 Party platform in *The Wide-Awake and Central Campaign*, 3.

4 *The Wide-Awake and Central Campaign Club Bulletin*, 3. Slave trade in Johnson, *River of Dark Dreams*, 395.

5 William B. Hart, "'I am a Man': Martin Henry Freeman (Middlebury College, 1849) and the Problem of Race, Manhood, and Colonization" in *Slavery and the University: Histories and Legacies*, ed. Leslie M. Harris, James T. Campbell, and Alfred L. Brophy (Athens: University of Georgia Press, 2019), 143.

6 On the function of violence to weed out internal distinction among antislavery and proslavery individuals, see Manisha Sinha, *The Counterrevolution of Slavery: Politics and Ideology in Antebellum South Carolina* (Chapel Hill: University of North Carolina, 2000). Here I refute Jon Grinspan, who offers Republican militarism as the progenitor of unintended consequences. Beating Democrats – a physical and electoral desire – was an intended result. See Grinspan, "'Young Men for War': The Wide Awakes and Lincoln's 1860 Presidential Campaign," *Journal of American History*, 96 (Sept. 2009), 358. Quotations from T. Rail, "The Lincoln Boys" in

The Wide-Awake Vocalist; or, Railsplitters' Song Book (New York: E. A. Daggett, 1860), 64. *Republican Campaign Edition for the Million: Containing the Republican Platform* (Boston: J.P. Jewett and Co., 1856), 5.

7 Backbone in Benedict, *A "Wide Awake" Poem*, 10. Speech of Stevens in *The Wide-Awake and Central Campaign Club Bulletin*, 2. "Hon. John Sherman in Philadelphia," *New York Times*, 15 Sept. 1860. Clarke, "Forward! Forward! Is the Word" in *Wide-Awake Vocalist*, 2. Additional examples are found in *Connecticut Wide-Awake Songster*, ed. John W. Hutchinson and Benjamin Jepson (New York: O. Hutchinson, 1860).

8 On righteousness and violence, see Phyllis Rose, "Tools of Torture," *The Atlantic*, 1 Oct. 1986, 38–39, and Amartya Sen, *Identity and Violence: The Illusion of Destiny* (New York: Random House, 2007). Development of Republican violence in northern places in Grinspan, "'Young Men for War,'" 360–361. Hartford and Clay in uncited 1919 newspaper article "Lincoln Wide-Awakes in 1860" in Folder Campaign – 1860, Wide Awakes, Republican Marching Clubs, Drawer 9, from the files of the Lincoln Financial Foundation Collection.

9 "The Campaign in Connecticut; The Great Demonstration of the Wide-Awakes at Hartford," *New York Times*, 27 July 1860. "Grand Procession of Wide-Awakes at New York on the Evening of October 3, 1860" and "The Wide-Awake Parade" in *Harper's Weekly*, 13 Oct. 1860, 648–650.

10 Herbert Ridgeway Collins, *Political Campaign Torches* (Washington, DC: Smithsonian Institution, 1964). Smell in "The Campaign in Connecticut." "The Wide-Awake Parade," 650. "Emotional appeal" in Allan Nevins, *The Emergence of Lincoln* (New York: Charles Scribner's Sons, 1950), II: 305. "An Attempt to Make Mischief," *New York Times*, 28 Sept. 1860. *Clinton Democrat* in "The Wide-Awakes," *Clearfield Republican* [PA], 14 Nov. 1860, 3. "Our Mass Meeting," *The Democratic Press* [Eaton, Ohio], 20 Sept. 1860, 2.

11 "Fight Between Wide-Awakes and Bell and Everett Men; Torches Destroyed," *New York Times*, 26 Sept. 1860. See also "An Attempt to Make Mischief." Headlines and violent acts in Grinspan, "'Young Men for War,'" 372.

12 "The Wide-Awakes," *Columbia Democrat and Bloomsburg General Advertiser* [Bloomsburg, PA], 6 Oct. 1860, n.p. Lincoln's posse comitatus position ascribed to *New York Herald* in "Rather a Sensible Disunionist," *New York Times*, 21 Sept. 1860.

13 Jefferson Davis, "Address to the National Democracy, 7 May 1860," *Papers of Jefferson Davis*, VI: 290. Douglas R. Egerton, *Year of Meteors: Stephen Douglas, Abraham Lincoln, and the Election that Brought on the Civil War* (New York: Bloomsbury Press, 2010), 69–79, quote on 72.

14 Among the best, recent recountings of the fractious Democratic meeting is in Amanda Foreman, *A World on Fire: Britain's Crucial Role in the American Civil War* (New York: Random House, 2012).

15 Buchanan to C. Comstock, 5 July 1860, and Buchanan to J. B. Baker, 11 Jan. 1858, *Works*, X: 457, 177. James B. Lamb to Andrew Johnson, 21

Dec. 1859, *Papers of Andrew Johnson*, III: 360. Buchanan to J. B. Baker, 5 Sept. 1860, *Works*, XI: 1.

16 "What Shall the South Carolina Legislature Do?" *Charleston Mercury*, 3 Nov. 1860. "Constitutional Union Party Platform of 1860," 9 May 1860, "Democratic Party Platform of 1860," 18 June 1860, and "Democratic Party Platform (Breckinridge Faction) of 1860," 6 Nov. 1860, online in Peters and Woolley, *American Presidency Project*. "The Candidates and Their Characters," *Hartford Daily Courant*, 27 Jun. 1860, 2.

17 "Republican Party Platform of 1860," 17 May 1860, *American Presidency Project*. Lincoln, Speech at New Haven, Connecticut, 6 Mar. 1860, *Collected Works*, IV: 14. "Presidential Election Day," *Hartford Daily Courant*, 6 Nov. 1860, 2.

18 "The Day of Jubilee Has Come!" *Hartford Daily Courant*, 7 Nov. 1860, 2.

19 Lincoln to Nathan Sargent, 23 June 1859, *Collected Works*, III: 388. "Election of 1860," *American Presidency Project*.

20 French newspapers in George G. Blackburn, *French Newspaper Opinion on the American Civil War* (Westport, CT: Greenwood Press, 1997), 29. Haitian paper in "News from Haiti," *New York Times*, 16 Jan. 1861, 6. Marx to Friedrich Engels, 11 Jan. 1860, in *Europe Looks at the Civil War*, ed. Belle Becker Sideman and Lillian Friedman (New York: Orion Press, 1960), 15. Gasparin in ibid., 13.

21 Baron de Stoeckl in ibid., 41. Reclus in ibid., 26.

22 J.C.H. in "What is the Duty of Radical Abolitionists in the Present Campaign," *Douglass' Monthly*, Oct. 1860. Thomas Hamilton, "The Two Great Political Parties," 17 Mar. 1860, in *The Black Abolitionist Papers, vol. V*, 72.

23 H. Ford Douglas, speech delivered on 23 Sept. 1860, in *The Black Abolitionist Papers, vol. V*, 91. Frederick Douglass, "The Chicago Nominations," *Douglass' Monthly*, June 1860. Douglass, "The Late Election," *Douglass' Monthly*, Dec. 1860.

24 Thomas L. Johnson, *Twenty-Eight Years A Slave or The Story of My Life in Three Continents* (Bournemouth: W. Mate and Sons, 1909), 27. In support of such post-emancipation recollections of ex-bondsmen, a Mississippian enslaver noted his slaves were "prophesying freedom for themselves" in October 1860 just before the presidential election; see Oakes, *Ruling Race*, 233.

25 *Crescent*, in Robert S. Harper, *Lincoln in the Press* (New York: McGraw-Hill, 1951), 68. Davis to Rhett, Jr., 10 Nov. 1860, *Papers of Jefferson Davis*, VI: 368. "The Secession Movements at the South," *Baltimore Sun*, 14 Nov. 1860, 1.

26 "Dissolution of the Union?" *Albany Journal*, 1 Nov. 1860, 2. "Address from Gen. Sam Houston to the People of Texas," *New York Herald*, 19 Dec. 1860, 1. "South Carolina," *Hartford Daily Courant*, 8 Nov. 1860, 2. Pontiac, "Sentiment South," *New York Times*, 7 Dec. 1860, 1.

27 Baptist, *The Half Has Never Been Told*, 215–225. Chandra Manning, *What this Cruel War Was Over* (New York: Vintage, 2007), 21. Jefferson Davis, "Speech at Corinth, 21 Sept. 1860," *Papers of Jefferson Davis*, VI: 364. "Democrat District Convention," *Weekly Standard* [Raleigh], 8 June 1859. *Mail* [Montgomery] and SC pamphlet in "The Question of Disunion," *New York Times*, 1 Nov. 1860, 2. Gov. Brown in Jesse

T. Carpenter, *The South as a Conscious Minority: A Study in Political Thought* (1930; Columbia: University of South Carolina Press, 1990), 192.

28 Bates to Republican Committee of Keokuk, Iowa, 15 Sept. 1860, in *Sacramento Daily Union*, 20 Oct. 1860, 6.

29 Minute Men in "Meeting in Houston," *Macon Daily Telegraph*, 4 Dec. 1860, 2. Sixty-nine slaves for Curry marked in 1860 US Census, Schedule 2, Scotts, Perry County, Alabama, 6 July 1860, 32–33. Jabez Lamar Monroe Curry, *The Perils and Duty of the South … Speech Delivered in Talladega, Alabama, November 26, 1860* (Washington, DC: Lemuel Towers, 1860) in *Southern Pamphlets on Secession, November 1860–April 1861*, ed. Jon L. Wakelyn (Chapel Hill: University of North Carolina Press, 1996), 46. Armed resistance in Richmond *Enquirer* in "The Secession Movement," *New York Tribune*, 21 Nov. 1860, 6.

30 Curry, *The Perils and Duty of the South*, 44, 39. Judah P. Benjamin, *The Right of Secession* (Washington, DC: Lemuel Towers, 1861) in *Southern Pamphlets*, 112.

31 Free White men banner in "Ho! Wide-Awakes, Ho!," *Centre Democrat* [Bellafonte, PA], 3 Jan. 1861, n.p. For an excellent account of southern faith in cotton on a global front, see Foreman, *A World on Fire*.

32 John B. Jones, *A Rebel Clerk's Diary at the Confederate States Capital, vol I* (Philadelphia: J. B. Lippincott and Co., 1866), 26. "Attention Wide Awakes," *Centre Democrat*, 3 Jan. 1861, n.p.

33 Buchanan, "Fourth Annual Message, 3 Dec. 1860," *Works*, XI: 7–9.

34 Ibid., 14, 16–17. Neff, *Justice in Blue and Grey*, 8.

35 Buchanan, "Fourth," 9, 17–20. Act of February 28, 1795, ch. 36, 2 Stat. 424. For interpretation of Jeremiah S. Black, see Neff, *Justice in Blue and Grey*, 16.

36 Buchanan, "Fourth," 9, 17–20.

37 Mason in James Madison's notes, 18 July 1787, *Records of the Federal Convention of 1787*, II: 47–48.

38 Buchanan to Mr. Wharton, 16 Dec. 1860, *Works*, XI: 66. Buchanan, "Fourth," 20, 22, 24–25.

39 "The Message," *Constitution* [Washington, DC], 5 Dec. 1860, 2. " President Buchanan's Message," *Sacramento Daily Union*, 21 Dec. 1860, 2. "The President's Message," *Vincennes Gazette*, 8 Dec. 1860. "The President's Message," *Portland Journal*, in *Liberator*, 14 Dec. 1860. Letter from Wm. S. Bailey, 6 Dec. 1860 in *Liberator*, 14 Dec. 1860.

40 "Making Darkness Visible," *Daily True Delta*, 7 Dec. 1860, 1. "The President's Message," *Macon Daily Telegraph*, 7 Dec. 1860, 2.

41 Clingman and Crittenden in *Cong. Globe*, 36th Cong., 2nd sess., 4–5 (4 Dec. 1860). Reuters in "America," *The Times* [London], 17 Dec. 1860, 7.

42 John J. Pettus, "From the United States," *The Times* [London], 19 Dec. 1860, 7. "A Southron Visits Mr. Lincoln," *Easton Gazette*, 8 Dec. 1860, 1. Lincoln, "Remarks Concerning Concessions to Secession [c. Jan. 19–21, 1861]," *Collected Works*, IV: 176. For more alleged Lincoln remarks between his election and the inauguration see, Harper, *Lincoln in the Press*, 70–73.

43 James Oakes makes the case for Seward as a good measure for Republican thinking between the election and inauguration in *Freedom National: The Destruction of Slavery in the United States, 1861–1865* (New York: W. W. Norton, 2013), 64. Seward made popular the concept of a "higher law," but New York Senator Rufus King declared it during the debates over Missouri in 1820. See Davis, *Inhuman Bondage*, 276.

44 "The New Administration – Mr. Seward's Appointment," *New York Times*, 7 Jan. 1861, 4. William Henry Seward, "Democracy the Chief Element of Government" in *Works of William Henry Seward, vol. IV*, ed. George E. Baker (Boston: Houghton, Mifflin and Company, 1884), 326.

45 Oakes, *Freedom National*, 32–33.

46 Burrus Carnahan, *Act of Justice: Lincoln's Emancipation Proclamation and the Law of War* (Lexington: University Press of Kentucky, 2007), 7–9.

47 Adams in William Whiting, *War Powers under the Constitution of the United States*, 10th edition (New York: Little, Brown and Company, 1864), 76–79. Carnahan, *Act of Justice*, 8–9. Oakes, *Freedom National*, 34–41.

48 Johnson, "Speech on Harper's Ferry Incident," 331–332.

49 Stephanie McCurry, *Confederate Reckoning: Power and Politics in the Civil War South* (Cambridge: Harvard University Press, 2010), 60. "The 20th Day of December, in the Year of Our Lord, 1860," *Charleston Mercury*, 21 Dec. 1860. "Federal Rights Violated," 24 Jan. 1861, 1.

50 Klein, *Days of Defiance*, 113, 191–196. "Special Message on the Correspondence with the South Carolina Commissioners," 8 Jan. 1861, Buchanan, *Works*, XI: 96.

51 *National Union* [Kentucky] in Harper, *Lincoln in the Press*, 68. Porter listed as owner of nineteen Black people in 1860 US Federal Census, Schedule 2, Division No. 2, Prince George Parish, June 1860, 52. Wm. D. Porter, *State Sovereignty and the Doctrine of Coercion* (Charleston: Evans and Cogswell's, 1860), 3. McCurry, *Confederate Reckoning*, 53, 60.

52 On British North America, see Amar, *Bill of Rights*, 5.

53 Treaty of Paris in Jasanoff, *Liberty's Exiles*, 319. "Resolutions Adopted by the Kentucky General Assembly," in *Papers of Thomas Jefferson*, XXX: 550–556. A South-Carolinian [Holland], *A Refutation of the Calumnies*, 8, see also 10–11.

54 *Documents, Ordered by the Convention of the People of South Carolina* (Columbia: A. S. Johnston, 1832).

55 Winfield Scott, *Memoirs of Lieut.-General Scott, LLD* (New York: Sheldon and Company, 1864), 16.

56 Joseph Story, *Commentaries on the Conflict of Laws* (Boston: Hilliard, Gray, and Company, 1834), 95. Paul Finkelman, *The Law of Freedom and Bondage: A Casebook* (New York: Oceana., 1986), 73–76.

57 Upshur owned twenty-five individuals in the 1840 US Census, Northampton, Virginia, 10. For Upshur, see the work of Steven Heath Mitton in Davis, *Inhuman Bondage*, 283–284. A Virginian [Abel P. Upshur], *A Brief Enquiry Into the True Nature and Character of Our Federal Government: Being a Review of Judge Story's*

Commentaries on the Constitution of the United States (Petersburg: Edmund and Julian C. Ruffin, 1840), 61, 89.

58 On the Atlantic slave trade reopening, see chapter 14 in Johnson, *River of Dark Dreams*. Lincoln to Messrs. Henry L. Pierce and others, 6 Apr. 1859, *Collected Works*, III: 375. Harvey, *A Brief History of Neoliberalism*, 2–3. Reinhold Niebuhr, *Moral Man and Immoral Society* (1932; New York: Charles Scribner's Sons, 1960), 14. "A man's merit in this country," said one Louisiana planter, "is estimated according to the number of Negroes he works in the field," in Oakes, *Ruling Race*, 123.

59 Davis, *Remarks on the Special Message on Affairs in South Carolina. Jan. 10, 1861* (Baltimore: John Murphy and Co., 1861) in *Southern Pamphlets*, 126. US Const. Art. I, §8, cl.15. US Laws, Statutes, Etc. *An Act to Provide for Calling Forth the Militia to Execute the Laws of the Union* (Philadelphia, 1795). *Speech of Louis T. Wigfall* in Carpenter, *The South as a Conscious Minority*, 212.

60 St. George Tucker, *Blackstone's Commentaries* (Philadelphia: William Young Birch, and Abraham Small, 1803), 367. Chesnut in *Mary Chesnut's Civil War*, ed. C. Vann Woodward (New Haven: Yale University Press, 1981), 241. See also Levine, *The Fall of the House of Dixie*, 38. On Lee, see Benson Bobrick, *Master of War: The Life of General George H. Thomas* (New York: Simon and Schuster, 2009), 20. William Rawle, *A View of the Constitution of the United States of America* (Philadelphia: Philip H. Nicklin, 1829), 296–297.

61 See Lincoln, "Message to Congress in Special Session," 4 July 1861, *Collected Works*, IV: 441.

62 Seward, "Some Thoughts for the President's Consideration," 1 Apr. 1861, in Lincoln's *Collected Works*, IV: 316–318. Foreman, *A World on Fire*, Kindle edition, Kindle locations 2065–2066.

63 Lincoln to William H. Seward, 1 Apr. 1861, in *Collected Works*, IV: 316–318.

64 Grant to Frederick Dent, 19 Apr. 1861, in *The Papers of Ulysses S. Grant*, ed. John Y. Simon et al., 32 vols. (Carbondale: Southern Illinois University Press, 1967–2012), II: 3. Lincoln, "Message to Congress in Special Session," 4 July 1861, *Collected Works*, IV: 426–427, 431–432.

65 Lincoln, "Message to Congress in Special Session," 439. Colonel in "General Butler and the Contraband of War," *New York Times*, 2 June 1861, 1. Lowell, "The Pickens-and-Stealin's Rebellion," *Atlantic Monthly*, 7.44 (June 1861), 762–763. Statistics in James B. McPherson and James K. Hogue, *Ordeal by Fire: The Civil War and Reconstruction*, 4th edition (New York: McGraw Hill, 2009), 28. David Brion Davis estimates 17.2 percent of southern White adults as illiterate compared with a rate of 4.12 percent in free states. Davis, *Inhuman Bondage*, 188. Henry Watson noted from Alabama in 1831, "The people think more of money here than of Education," in Oakes, *Ruling Race*, 72.

66 *House Journal*, 37th Cong., sess. 1, 5 Aug. 1861, 241. Sanford to William H. Seward, 26 Aug. 1862, in *Executive Documents, vol. I* (Washington, DC: GPO, 1863), 665.

67 Brown to Johnson, 2 Feb. 1860, *Papers of Andrew Johnson*, III: 406. Sanford to William H. Seward, 26 Aug. 1862, in *Executive Documents, vol. I*, 664–665.

68 An Act Making Appropriations for Fortifications and Other Purposes, 5 Aug. 1861, ch. 54, 317. An Act to Confiscate Property Used for Insurrectionary Purposes, 6 Aug. 1861, ch. 60, 319.

69 William Todd, *The Seventy-Ninth Highlanders, New York Volunteers, in the War of Rebellion, 1861–1865* (Albany: Bradow, Barton and Co., 1886), 56–65. Confederate surgeon and battlefield recollections in L. P. Yandell to father, 10 Nov. 1861, in *The Rebellion Record: A Diary of American Events*, ed. Frank Moore, 11 vols. (New York: G. P. Putnam, 1861–1868), III: 298–299. Soldier recollections in Michael C. C. Adams, *Living Hell: The Dark Side of the Civil War* (Baltimore: Johns Hopkins University Press, 2014), 71.

70 Yandell slaves in 1850 US Census, Schedule 2, District No. 3, City of Louisville, Jefferson County, Kentucky, 21 Aug. 1850, n.p. Confederate surgeon and battle-field recollections in L. P. Yandell to father, 10 Nov. 1861, in *Rebellion Record*, III: 298–299.

CHAPTER 7 – EMANCIPATION'S FURY

1 Log of Robert Smalls in *Hartford Daily Courant*, 18 June 1862, 3. Interview of Robert Smalls, American Freedmen's Inquiry Commission, 1863, in John W. Blassingame, ed., *Slave Testimony: Two Centuries of Letters, Speeches, Interviews, and Autobiographies* (Baton Rouge: Louisiana State University, 1977), 373. "Report of Maj. Alfred Rhett," in *The War of Rebellion: A Compilation of Official Records of the Union and Confederate Armies*, 4 series (Washington, DC: Government Printing Office, 1880–1901), Series 1: Volume 14, 15 [hereafter cited in the form *OR*, 1:14]. Edward A. Miller, Jr., *Gullah Statesman: Robert Smalls from Slavery to Congress, 1839–1915* (Columbia: University of South Carolina Press, 1995), 8.

2 Orders in "Report of Lieut. F. G. Ravenel," *OR*, 1:14, 14. Miller, *Gullah Statesman*, 2, 8–9.

3 Log of Robert Smalls. "Report of Flag-Officer Du Pont, US Navy," 14 May 1862, *Official Records of the Union and Confederate Navies*, 2 series (Washington, DC: Government Printing Office, 1894–1922), Series I: Volume 12, 821 [hereafter cited in the form *ORN*, 1:12]. "Report of Acting Volunteer Lieutenant Nickels," 13 May 1862, *ORN*, 1:12, 822.

4 "Report of Flag-Officer Du Pont," 821. For northern papers, see, for example, "Gallant Act of Negro Pilot," *Chicago Tribune*, 21 May 1862, 1; "Robert Small," *Burlington Free Press* [Burlington, VT], 23 May 1862; "Notes on Military and Naval Affairs," *Scientific American*, 1006:22 (31 May 1862), 338. Foster to General Joseph G. Totten, 12 Mar. 1861, *OR*, 1:1, 195. A. J. Slemmer to Lieutenant-Colonel L. Thomas, 18 Mar. 1861, *OR*, 2:1, 750.

5 "Report of Flag-Officer Du Pont," 821. James McPherson, *The War that Forged a Nation: Why the Civil War Still Matters* (New York: Oxford University Press, 2015), 81–85.

6 "Gallant Act of a Negro Pilot," *Chicago Tribune*, 21 May 1862, 1. "Heroism of Nine Colored Men," *New York Herald*, 18 May 1862, 1. "Robert Small, a Sable Hero," *Union County Star and Lewisburg Chronicle* [PA], 27 May 1862. "From Port Royal," *Evening Star*, 19 May 1862.

7 On Butler, "contraband," and the limits of a property-based emancipation, see Kate Masur, "'A Rare Phenomenon of Philological Vegetation': The Word 'Contraband' and the Meanings of Emancipation in the United States," *Journal of American History*, 93.4 (Mar. 2007), 1050–1084.

8 "Report of Flag-Officer Du Pont," 821.

9 Chernow, *Washington*, 759. See too Erica Armstrong Dunbar, *Never Caught: The Washingtons' Relentless Pursuit of their Runaway Slave, Ona Judge* (New York: 37 Ink/ Atria Books, 2016). Scott Gac, "Slave or Free? White or Black? The Representation of George Latimer," *New England Quarterly*, 88.1 (Mar. 2015), 73.

10 "Letter of Robert Small," *Hartford Daily Courant*, 4 Sept. 1862, 2. "Letter from the Negro Robert Small," *Chicago Tribune*, 2 Sept. 1862, 2.

11 "His Associates," *New York Daily Tribune*, 3 June 1862, 5. "In Congress, June 2," *Daily Ohio Statesman*, 3 June 1862. *Cong. Globe*, 37th Cong., 2nd sess. 2496 (1862). *Senate Journal*, 37th Cong., 2nd sess., 19 May 1862, 504. *House Journal*, 37th Cong., 2nd sess., 27 May 1862, 763. "General News," *Alexandria Gazette*, 28 May 1862, 2. "An Act for the Benefit of Robert Small[s] and Others," *ORN*, 1:12, 824.

12 Du Pont to Gideon Welles, 29 Aug. 1862, ORN, 1:12, 825.

13 Miller, *Gullah Statesman*, 27. Du Pont to Gideon Welles, 31 May 1862, *ORN*, 1:13, 29. Du Pont to Welles, 21 June 1862, *ORN*, 1:13, 125. A. C. Rhind to S. F. Du Pont, 23 June 1862, *ORN*, 1:13, 126. "The Freedmen of the South," *New York Times*, 15 Sept. 1862, 8.

14 "General News," *New York Times*, 15 Sept. 1862, 8. "The Hero of the Planter," *New York Times*, 3 Oct. 1862, 4, 8. James M. McPherson, "Who Freed the Slaves," *Proceedings of the American Philosophical Society*, 139.1 (Mar. 1995), 1–10. "Did We Miss the Greatest Slave Rebellion in Modern History" in Steven Hahn, *The Political Worlds of Slavery and Freedom* (Cambridge: Harvard University Press, 2009), 55–114.

15 In offering a White position on relationships of bondage, Georg Hegel notes, "it is only through staking one's life that freedom is won." See "Phenomenology of Spirit" in *On Violence: A Reader*, ed. Bruce B. Lawrence and Aisha Karim (Durham: Duke University Press, 2007), 29. "Off Charleston, Steamship Catawba," 20 Dec. 1861, in *Rebellion Record*, III: 506. "Report of Commander Mullany," 28 Apr. 1862, ORN, 1:12, 787. Miller, *Gullah Statesman*, 4, 1–2.

16 "The Prize Planter," *Southern Confederacy* [Atlanta], 27 June 1862, 3.

17 "The Rebel Government; Jeff Davis' Privateers," 22 July 1861, *New York Times*, 1. "The Schooner *S. J. Waring*," *Harpers Weekly*, 3 Aug. 1861, 485. "The Niggers

Again," *Cass County Republican*, 12 June 1862, 2. Untitled article in *Daily Nashville Union*, 27 May 1862. See Tillman/Smalls mentioned also in "The Case of Robert Small," *Chicago Tribune*, 22 May 1862, and "Anthony Trollope on America," *Continental Monthly*, 2.3 (Sept. 1862), 306.

18 J. W. Livingston to Silas H. Stringham, 15 Aug. 1861, *ORN*, 1:6, 85. Drayton to Du Pont, 25 Nov. 1861, *ORN*, 1:12, 322. "Rough Notes of the naval expedition to Roanoke Island," 18 Jan. 1862, *ORN*, 1:6, 583. S. C. Rowan to Lieutenant Commanding R. Werden, 29 Mar. 1862, *ORN*, 1:7, 177. Steedman in "Transcript of the Buell Court of Inquiry," 13 Dec. 1862, *OR*, 1:16, 144.

19 S. H. Stringham to Gideon Welles, 14 Aug. 1861, *ORN*, 1:6, 81. Fulton to Secretary of the Navy, 13 Nov. 1861, *ORN*, 1:12, 293. R. Saxton to M. C. Meigs, 9 Nov. 1861, *OR*, 1:6, 186. Prentiss to Du Pont, 2 July 1862, *ORN*, 1:13, 122. U. S. Grant to H. W. Halleck, 15 Nov. 1862, *OR*, 1:17, 470.

20 Butler to H. W. Halleck, 1 Sept. 1862, *OR*, 1:15, 558. Preston to Du Pont, 11 Oct. 1862, *ORN*, 1:14, 379.

21 "The Case of Robert Small," *Chicago Tribune*, 22 May 1862, 2. Other Smalls satire includes "A Pungent and Forcible Expose of the Scheme to Get up a Vallandigham Party," *Daily Intelligencer*, 1 July 1862, 1.

22 Among the first modern, White historians to engage the question of morality was Arthur Schlesinger, Jr. His 1949 piece "The Causes of the Civil War: A Note on Historical Sentimentalism" is in *The Politics of Hope and the Bitter Heritage* (1963; Princeton: Princeton University Press, 2008). John Ashworth situates the enslaved as central to the abolitionist project and morality in *Slavery, Capitalism, and Politics*. See too Christopher Leslie Brown, *Moral Capital: Foundations of British Abolitionism* (Chapel Hill: University of North Carolina Press, 2006). On prayer, see Robert Smalls, in Blassingame, *Slave Testimony*, 377.

23 Stanton and Sherman interview of colored ministers and church officers in Savannah, 12 Jan. 1865, *OR*, 1:47, 37–39. Nine of the twenty interviewees associated their liberation from enslavement with the Union Army.

24 On gradualism, see Hahn, *Political Worlds*, 50–51. Abolition versus emancipation in David Menschel, "Abolition without Deliverance: The Law of Connecticut Slavery, 1784–1848," *Yale Law Journal*, 111.1 (Oct. 2001), 188.

25 Wilder, *Ebony and Ivory*. Baptist, *The Half Has Never Been Told*. Oakes, *Freedom National*.

26 Oakes, *Freedom National*, 162–163. Butler to Hicks, 23 Apr. 1861, *OR*, 1:2, 593. McClellan, To the Union Men of Western Virginia, 26 May 1861, *Rebellion Record*, II: 1, 753.

27 Harney upheld slaveholder rights in Missouri; see Harney to Thomas T. Grant, 14 May 1861, *OR*, 1:3, 373. Sherman to Colonel Turchin, 15 Oct. 1861, *OR*, 1:4, 307.

28 Dix to Cameron, 8 Aug. 1861, *OR*, 2:1, 763. Dix to Nones, 23 Aug. 1861, *OR*, 2:1, 765. Dix to McClellan, 21 Aug. 1861, *OR*, 2:1, 765. Colored refugees in Amy Murrell Taylor, *Embattled Freedom: Journeys through the Civil War's Slave Refugee Camps* (Chapel Hill: University of North Carolina Press, 2018), 10.

29 Lane to Sturgis, 3 Oct. 1861, *OR*, 2:1, 771–772.

30 Lane to Sturgis, 772. Act of August, 6, 1861, ch. 60, 1 Stat. 319.

31 Fremont, Proclamation, 30 Aug. 1861, *OR*, 2:1, 221–222.

32 Benjamin to Major-General M. Lovell, 23 Dec. 1861, *Rebellion Record*, II: 1, 655. Lincoln to Fremont, 2 Sept. 1861, *OR*, 2:1, 766. Jeff Thompson, Proclamation, 2 Sept. 1861, in *Rebellion Record*, III: 59.

33 Lincoln to Orville H. Browning, 22 Sept. 1861, in *Collected Works*, IV: 532. Lincoln to Fremont, 2 Sept. 1861. Oakes, *Freedom National*, 157–159.

34 Lincoln to Fremont, 2 Sept. 1861. Lincoln to Browning, 532. Menzies, 22 May, in *Cong. Globe*, 37th Cong., 2nd sess. 148 (1862). In July 1863, Lincoln issued orders: one rebel soldier in custody to be put to death for each captured Union soldier executed by the Confederacy. See David Blight, *Frederick Douglass: Prophet of Freedom* (New York: Simon & Schuster, 2018), 405.

35 Fremont, Proclamation, 12 Sept. 1861, *OR*, 2:1, 769–770.

36 McClellan to Asboth, 19 Dec. 1861, *OR*, 2:1, 789. Ross to General Grant, 31 Dec. 1861, *OR*, 2:1, 798. Brown to Townsend, 22 June 1861, *Rebellion Record*, II: 1, 755. Major John Toler to Lieutenant J. L. Palmer, 27 Mar. 1862, *OR*, 2:1, 813.

37 Seward to McClellan, 4 Dec. 1861, *OR*, 2:1, 783. Act of April 16, 1862, ch. 54. 8 Stat. 378.

38 Yancey, Rost, and Mann to Earl Russell, 14 Aug. 1861, *OR*, 2:1, 244. Extracts from the journal of Commander Semmes, 28 Aug. and 30 Aug. 1861, *ORN*, 1:1, 706. Semmes to Mr. Van Lansberge, 30 Aug. 1861, *ORN*, 1:1, 626. Semmes to Hon. J. W. Gefken, 31 Aug. 1861, *ORN*, 1:1, 627. Semmes to R. F. Van Lansberge, 31 Aug. 1861, *ORN*, 1:1, 627. Semmes is listed as owning seven slaves, ages six to thirty-eight. See 1860 US Federal Census, Schedule 2, District No. 1, City of Washington, DC, 1st to the 9th of June 1860, 30.

39 Semmes journal extracts, 10 Sept. and 10 Nov. 1861, 708–709, 719. Oakes, *Freedom National*, 263.

40 This material refers to Confederate national policy as opposed to that of its states. Tennessee, for instance, enacted a near-compulsory conscription of free Blacks in June 1861. See Dudley Taylor Cornish, *The Sable Arm: Black Troops in the Union Army, 1861–1865* (Lawrence: University Press of Kansas, 1987), 15. Magruder to Col. George Deas, 9 Aug. 1861, *OR*, 2:1, 763. Johnston to Major G. B. Cosby, 27 July 1861, *OR*, 1:2, 1004. Commander Daniel Ammen to Samuel Du Pont, 29 Dec. 1861, *ORN*, 1:12, 431. Martin to Lee, 9 Dec. 1861, *OR*, 1:6, 38. Hooker to F. A. Parker, 7 Apr. 1865, *ORN*, 1:5, 546. Colonel Adolph Engelmann to Captain A. Blocki, 7 Apr. 1864, *OR*, 1:34, 721.

41 CSA slave soldiers in Report of Lieut. Col. John G. Parkhurst, 13 July 1862, *OR*, 1:16, Part I, 805.

42 Lincoln, Message to Congress, 6 Mar. 1862, and Letter to Horace Greeley, 24 Mar. 1862, *Collected Works*, V: 145, 169. Hyman and Wiecek, *Equal Justice under Law*, 251–252. Patricia A. Lucie, "Confiscation: Constitutional Crossroads," *Civil War History*, 23 (1977), 304–322. Neff, *Justice in Blue and Gray*, 139.

43 Bones in John Wallace, *Cong. Globe*, 37th Cong., 2nd sess., 2292. Lincoln, "Appeal to Border State Representatives to Favor Compensated Emancipation," *Collected Works*, V: 317–319. Lincoln, "Stay of Execution for Nathaniel Gordon," 4 Feb. 1862, *Collected Works*, V: 128–129.

44 Blair, *With Malice toward Some*, 22 May 1862, *Cong. Globe*, 37th Cong., 2nd sess., 2301. Doolittle, 2 May 1862, *Cong. Globe*, 37th Cong., 2nd sess., 137. Stevens, "Subduing the Rebellion," 22 Jan. 1862, in *Selected Papers of Thaddeus Stevens, vol. I*, ed. Beverly Wilson Palmer and Holly Byers Ochoa (Pittsburgh: University of Pittsburgh, 1997), 241. Skyler Gordon, "Enslaved Soldiers and the Battle of New Orleans," Tennessee Historical Society, https://tennesseehistory.org/battle-of-new-orleans/.

45 Miles to Thaddeus Stevens, 21 Mar. 1862, *Selected Papers, vol. I*, 286. Petition in US *House Journal*, 1861, 37th Cong., 2nd sess., 9 December, 46.

46 "Robert Small," *Raftsman's Journal* [Clearfield, PA], 4 June 1862, 2. "The Prize Planter," *New-York Daily Tribune*, 27 May 1862, 5. "Congressional," *Evening Star*, 24 May 1862, 1. "The Discussion of the African Regiment Bill," *Daily Dispatch*, 7 Feb. 1863, 1.

47 Act of July 17, 1862. ch. 195. Stat. 589–592. Hyman and Wiecek, *Equal Justice under Law*, 248. Neff, *Justice in Blue and Grey*, 135–136.

48 "How to End the War," *Intelligencer*, 31 July 1862, in *Abraham Lincoln: A Press Portrait*, ed. Herbert Mitgang (1956; New York: Fordham University Press, 2000), 298. Chase, 16 Apr. 1862, *The Salmon P. Chase Papers: Journals, 1829–1872, vol. I*, ed. John Niven (Kent: Kent State University Press, 1993), 333. McClellan to Henry W. Halleck, 1 Aug. 1862, *The Civil War Papers of George B. McClellan: Selected Correspondence, 1860–1865*, ed. Stephen W. Sears (New York: Ticknor and Fields, 1989), 381. Karl Marx, "A Criticism of American Affairs," *Die Presse*, 9 Aug. 1862, in *Marx and Engels on the United States*, compiled by Nelly Rumyantseva (Moscow: Progress Publishers, 1979), 149–150.

49 On registry and certificates, see Patricia M. L. Lucie, "Confiscation: Constitutional Crossroads," *Civil War History*, 24.4 (Dec. 1977), 316–321.

50 Arithmetic in William O. Stoddard, *Inside the White House in War Times* (New York: Charles L. Webste, 1890), 179. John Keegan, *The American Civil War: A Military History* (New York: Alfred A. Knopf, 2009), 57, 43. Friction in Lincoln, "Appeal," 318.

51 "To the Friends of Peace," *Christian Recorder*, 16 Feb. 1861. "Negro Slaves as Contraband of War – An Element of Immense Strength to the Government," *New York Herald*, 30 May 1861.

52 Lincoln to Henry J. Raymond, 9 May 1862, *Collected Works*, V: 153.

53 Keegan, *American Civil War*, 45. Mark. R. Wilson, *The Business of Civil War: Military Mobilization and the State, 1861–1865* (Baltimore: Johns Hopkins University Press, 2006), 1. Phillip Shaw Paludan, *A People's Contest: The Union and Civil War, 1861–1865*, 2nd edition (Lawrence: University of Kansas Press, 1996), 22.

54 Mallory, Report of the Secretary of the Navy, 26 Apr. 1861, *ORN*, 2:2, 51–52. Capt. John Rogers, 9 Nov. 1861, *Rebellion Record*, III: 112–113. *New York Herald*

correspondent, 11 Nov. 1861, and office of the *Pawnee*, 11 Nov. 1861, *Rebellion Record*, III: 319–320.

55 Du Pont to Napoleon Collins, 10 Nov. 1861, *ORN*, 1:12, 350. Bankhead's notice in *ORN*, 1:12, 339. "The Black Heroes of the Planter," *Frank Leslie's Illustrated Newspaper*, 21 June 1862, 181.

56 War Department to Sherman, 14 Oct. 1861, *OR*, 1:6, 176. Statement of Thomas Black, *OR*, 1:6, 388.

57 Reports in Edward McPherson, *The Political History of the United States during the Great Rebellion*, 2nd edition (Washington, DC: Philp and Solomons, 1865), 249. Allan Nevins, *The War for the Union, vol. I* (New York: Charles Scribner's Sons, 1959), 402.

58 "Early Recruitment: Lowcountry South Carolina, Georgia, and Florida; Louisiana; and Kansas," in *Freedom: A Documentary History of Emancipation, 1861–1867*, ed. Ira Berlin, Joseph P. Reidy, and Leslie S. Rowland (Cambridge: Cambridge University Press, 1982), Series II, 37–38. Hazard Stevens, "Circular," 11 May 1862, *OR*, 3:2, 54. Hunter to Isaac I. Stevens, 8 May 1862, *OR*, 3:2, 30.

59 Edward Pierce to Salmon P. Chase, 21 May 1862, *OR*, 3:2, 53. "Early Recruitment," 38–39. Hunter to Stanton, 6 June 1862, in *Report of the Military Services of Gen. David Hunter, USA, during the War of the Rebellion* (New York: D. Van Nostrand, 1873), 21. Stanton to Saxton, 25 Aug. 1862, *OR*, 1:14, 377.

60 *Report of the Military Services of Gen. David Hunter*, 7. Neff, *Justice in Blue and Grey*, 138. Lincoln to Chase, 17 May 1862, and Proclamation Revoking General Hunter's Order of Military Emancipation, 19 May 1862, *Collected Works*, V: 221–222.

61 Popular phrase and Mill in Marouf Hasian, Jr., *In the Name of Necessity: Military Tribunals and the Loss of American Civil Liberties* (Tuscaloosa: University of Alabama Press, 2005), 19. John Stuart Mill, *A System of Logic* (London: Longmans, Green, and Co., 1889), 533.

62 Jefferson to John B. Colvin, 20 Sept. 1810, *The Papers of Thomas Jefferson: Retirement Series*, III: 99–102. Jefferson to Samuel Brown, 27 Oct. 1808, FONA. See also Hasian, *In the Name of Necessity*, 23.

63 Lincoln, "Emancipation Proclamation – First Draft" and "Memorandum on Recruiting Negroes," *Collected Works*, V: 337–338. Louis P. Masur, *Lincoln's Hundred Days: The Emancipation Proclamation and the War for the Union* (Cambridge: Harvard University Press, 2012), 80–83. E. B. Long and Barbara Long, *The Civil War Day by Day: An Almanac* (New York: Da Capo Press, 1971), 219–259.

64 Keegan, *American Civil War*, 167–169. McPherson and Hogue, *Ordeal by Fire*, 308–309. A.D.R, "A General View of the Great Battle," and Special Correspondent [George W. Smalley], "The Contest in Maryland," *New-York Daily Tribune*, 20 July 1862, 1, 5.

65 President Proclamation of Sept. 22, 1862. Appendix No. 16 Stat. 1267.

66 Judge Advocate L. C. Turner to Edwin Stanton, 20 Sept. 1862, *OR*, II:4, 585. Confederate Major-General Thomas H. Holmes to Union Major-General Samuel R. Curtis, 11 Oct. 1862, *OR*, 1:13, 727. Jefferson Davis, Proclamation of December 23, 1862, OR, 1:19, 817–821. Arming in preparation in Commander W. W. Hunter, C. S. Navy, 16 Dec. 1862, *OR*, 1:19, 814. Arkansas in Report of Commander Skirk, US Navy, 27 Nov. 1862, *ORN*, 1:23, 509.

67 Davis, Proclamation of December 23, 817–821.

68 *The First Edition of Lincoln's Emancipation Proclamation* (Washington, DC: n.p., 1863) in The Alfred Whital Stern Collection of Lincolniana, Rare Book and Special Collections Division, Library of Congress.

69 Newspaperman untitled editorial in the *Lancaster Gazette* [Ohio], 12 Jan. 1865, 2. W., "Army Sketches No. 7," *Dodgeville Chronicle* [Wisconsin], 22 Sept. 1864, 1–2. McPherson and Hogue, *Ordeal by Fire*, 321. Humanitarian rationale for war, Joanna Bourke, *Deep Violence: Military Violence, War Play, and the Social Life of Weapons* (Berkeley: Counterpoint, 2015), 99–100.

70 Butler to Scott, 27 May 1861, *OR*, 1:2, 53. Welles to S. H. Stringham, 22 July 1861, *ORN*, 1:6, 10.

71 Gideon Welles, 22 Sept. 1862 and 13 Aug. 1863, *Diary of Gideon Welles, vol. I* (Boston: Houghton Mifflin, 1911), 144, 403.

72 Lincoln to Hodges, 4 Apr. 1864, *Collected Works*, VII: 282. Seven slaves are listed for Albert G. Hodges, 1850 US Federal Census, Schedule 2, District No. 1, Franklin County, Kentucky, 25 Sept. 1850, n.p. Moncure D. Conway, *The Golden Hour* (Boston: Ticknor and Fields, 1862), 26. See too James Oakes, "The Only People Who Viewed Emancipation as a Military Necessity Were the People Who Hated Slavery," in *The New York Times 1619 Project and the Racialist Falsification of History: Essays and Interviews*, ed. David North and Thomas Mackaman (Oak Park, MI: Mehring Books, 2021), 102.

73 Lincoln, "Remarks to a Delegation of Progressive Friends," *Collected Works*, V: 279–280. Mary Ellen Snodgrass, *The Underground Railroad: An Encyclopedia of People, Places, and Operations* (New York: Routledge, 2015), 295. Lincoln to Speed, 4 July 1842, *Collected Works*, I: 290.

74 Lincoln, "Reply to Emancipation Memorial Presented by Chicago Christians of All Denominations," *Collected Works*, V: 422–423. Lincoln to cabinet in Gideon Welles, 22 Sept. 1862, *Diary*, 143. In September 1862, Lincoln also penned his "Meditation on the Divine Will," which supports his search for divine indications; see Mark A. Noll, *America's God: From Jonathan Edwards to Abraham Lincoln* (New York: Oxford University Press, 2002), 431.

75 Lincoln, Proclamation of 30 Mar. 1863, *Collected Works*, VI: 157.

76 Lincoln, "Second Inaugural Address," *Collected Works*, VIII: 334. Lincoln to Thurlow Weed, 15 Mar. 1865, *Collected Works*, VIII: 356.

77 "The Black Military Experience" in *Freedom*, Series II, 13–15. Joseph P. Reidy, "Armed Slaves and the Struggles for Republican Liberty in the US Civil War" in *Arming Slaves*, ed. Brown and Morgan, 275. Lincoln to Hodges, 283.

78 General Breckinridge, 14 Aug. 1862, *OR*, 1:15, 551. Davis to the Confederate Congress, 12 Jan. 1863, *OR*, 4:12, 345. Address of Congress to the People of the Confederate States, *OR*, 4:3, 133. Johnston to Charles Clark, 18 Nov. 1863, OR, 1:31, 712. James Iredell Waddell, Notes, 30 Oct. 1864, ORN, 1:3, 808.

79 Liberation in Hahn, *Political Worlds*, 76.

80 For military service and racism, see Gordon W. Allport, *The Nature of Prejudice* (1954; New York: Basic Books, 1979), 277–278. John Cimprich, *Fort Pillow, a Civil War Massacre, and Public Memory* (Baton Rouge: Louisiana State University Press, 2005), 85.

81 Sherman to J. B. McPherson, 1 Sept. 1863, OR, 1:30, 277. F. H. Peirpoint [Pierpont] to Edwin Stanton, 27 Jan. 1864, OR, 1:33, 433.

82 Lincoln to Andrew Johnson, 26 Mar. 1863, OR, 3:3, 103.

83 Editorial in *Hartford Daily Courant*, 28 May 1862, 2. A White Man, "The Difference between White and Black," *Daily Ohio Statesman*, 10 June 1862, 2. "Platform, Adopted by Democratic-Conservative State Convention," *Vicksburg Weekly Herald*, 7 Sept. 1877, 4. Seymour in Miller, *Gullah Statesman*, 21–22. For notion of racial "line cutting," see Arlie Russell Hochschild, *Strangers in their Own Land: Anger and Mourning in the American Right* (New York: Free Press, 2016).

84 Philadelphia and conductor in Miller, *Gullah Statesman*, 22–23. White supremacy in LA in Michael J. Pfeifer, "The Origins of Postbellum Lynching: Collective Violence in Reconstruction Louisiana," *Louisiana History*, 50.2 (Spring 2009), 197. Camelia and Democrat in Nancy Isenberg, *White Trash: The 400-Year Untold History of Class in America* (New York: Viking, 2016), 183. Sherman to Stanton, 21 June 1864, *OR*, 1:39, 132.

CHAPTER 8 – TO 1877: AMERICAN CAPITALISM AND THE GEOGRAPHY OF VIOLENCE

1 For slavery–freedom divide, see, for example, Morgan, *American Slavery, American Freedom*.

2 Beckert, *Empire of Cotton*, 76–78. Beckert directs most of his energy here toward European governments, but a similar dynamic is in effect in the United States.

3 "Emancipation Day Marked in Harlem," *New York Times*, 3 Jan. 1938, 15. Thanks to Molly Simons for bringing this speech to my attention. It is important to layer in a perspectival approach to the transformative nature of the shift from slavery to freedom. W. Fitzhugh Brundage notes the Civil War as revolutionary (which in some respects it was), for example, but misses how many (certainly not all) persons of color found their postwar lives as best understood as a form of enslavement. See *Civilizing Torture: An American Tradition* (Cambridge: Harvard University Press, 2018), 116.

4 Examination of Augustus W. Benedict, 13 Dec. 1864, Mutiny at Fort Jackson, in *OR*, 1:26 (I), 474.

5 Francis Paul Prucha, *A Guide to the Military Posts of the United States, 1789–1895* (Madison: State Historical Society of Wisconsin, 1964), 80. James Fulcher, *Capitalism: A Very Short Introduction* (New York: Oxford University Press, 2004), 8.

6 Noah Andre Trudeau, *Like Men of War: Black Troops in the Civil War, 1862–1865* (New York: Back Bay Books, 1998), 27–34.

7 Ibid., 31, 33–34. Lawrence Lee Hewitt, "An Ironic Route to Glory: Louisiana's Native Guards at Port Hudson" in *Black Soldiers in Blue: African American Troops in the Civil War Era*, ed. John David Smith (Chapel Hill: University of North Carolina Press, 2002), 82. Joseph T. Glatthaar, *Forged in Battle: The Civil War Alliance of Black Soldiers and White Officers* (Baton Rouge: Louisiana State University Press, 1990), 8–9. George Washington Williams, *A History of the Negro Troops in the War of the Rebellion, 1861–1865* (1887; New York: Fordham University Press, 2012), 66–67.

8 Col. Stafford on imprisonment of Black family members in Trudeau, *Like Men of War*, 31. John David Smith, "Let Us All Be Grateful that the Colored Man Will Fight" in *Black Soldiers*, ed. Smith, 49. Capt. J. A. Gla et al. to Gen. Nathaniel P. Banks, 19 Feb. 1863, in *Freedom*, ed. Berlin et al., Series II, 316.

9 Lt.-Col. A. G. Bennett et al. to General Lorenzo Thomas, 21 Nov. 1863, in *Freedom*, 388. For slavery and risk, see Jonathan Levy, *Freaks of Fortune: The Emerging World of Capitalism and Risk in America* (Cambridge: Harvard University Press, 2012), 10, 95–106.

10 Examination of Colonel Charles W. Drew, 9 Dec. 1864, Mutiny at Fort Jackson, 463. Gen. Orders No. 8, HQ Dist. Of Florida, 28 Feb 1864, in *Freedom*, 394. David Montgomery called nineteenth-century labor strife a "chronic battle" in *Workers' Control in America* (Cambridge: Cambridge University Press, 1979), 10.

11 Examinations of Benedict, Capt. James Miller, Second Lieutenant Edward D. Mooney, Major William E. Nye, and First Lieutenant George H. Kimball, Mutiny at Fort Jackson, 474, 467–468, 471, 465, 469. N. P. Banks to H. W. Halleck, 17 Dec. 1863, Mutiny at Fort Jackson, 457. W. Fitzhugh Brundage notes that many officers instituted "capricious punishments" in the Union (and Confederate) militaries; see *Civilizing Torture*, 126.

12 Examinations of Colonel Charles W. Drew, 9 Dec. 1864, Mutiny at Fort Jackson, 460–461. Examination of Benedict, 474.

13 For more on Quarantine Station and the Confederate mutiny at the area's forts, see Michael D. Pierson, *Mutiny at Fort Jackson: The Untold Story of the Fall of New Orleans* (Chapel Hill: University of North Carolina, 2008), 9, 110–113. Banks to Halleck, 456.

14 Mutiny at Fort Jackson, 473. Thomas in examination of James Miller, 468. Banks to Halleck, 456.

15 Banks to Halleck, 17 Dec. 1863, 457.

16 On debate on slavery and punishment as foundation for industrial labor management, see Rob Cooke, "The Denial of Slavery in Management Studies," *Journal of Management Studies*, 40.8 (Dec. 2003), 1895–1918. Interview with James Oakes in North and Mackaman, *The New York Times' 1619 Project*, 96. See,

too, Beckert, *Empire of Cotton*, 116, and Matthew Desmond, "In Order to Understand the Brutality of American Capitalism, You Have to Start on the Plantation," *New York Times Magazine*, 14 Aug. 2019, www.nytimes.com/interactive/2019/08/14/magazine/slavery-capitalism.html.

17 Willful workers in John R. Commons, *Legal Foundations of Capitalism* (1924; Madison: University of Wisconsin Press, 1959), 284. On stagnation and social unrest, Benjamin M. Friedman, *The Moral Consequences of Economic Growth* (New York: Vintage, 2005), 7–8, 120–121. Karl Polanyi, *The Great Transformation; The Political and Economic Origins of our Time* (1944; Boston: Beacon Press, 2001), 155–160. Strike examples in Jonathan P. Grossman, *William Sylvis, Pioneer of American Labor: A Study of the Labor Movement during the Era of the Civil War* (1945; New York: Columbia University Press, 1973), 50–52. Rosecrans, General Order No. 65, 26 Apr. 1864, in Appendix II, Grossman, *Sylvis*, 283–284. St. Louis in Speech of William Sylvis, 9 Jan. 1865, Chicago, in James C. Sylvis, *The Life, Speeches, Labors, and Essays of William H. Sylvis* (Philadelphia: Claxton, Remsen and Haffelfinger, 1872), 135. Nashville and Louisville in Paludan, *A People's Contest*, 196. David Montgomery, *Beyond Equality: Labor and the Radical Republicans, 1862–1872* (1967; Urbana: University of Illinois Press, 1981), 90–134.

18 George Fitzhugh, *Cannibals All! Or, Slaves Without Masters* (Richmond: A. Morris, 1857), chapter 7. On capitalists' turn for help beyond the market to manage worker subordination, Robert J. Steinfeld, *Coercion, Contract, and Free Labor in the Nineteenth Century* (Cambridge: Cambridge University Press, 2001), 8.

19 G. Norman Lieber, General Orders No. 90, 30 Dec. 1863, Mutiny at Fort Jackson, 476–479.

20 Lieber, 479. *List of US Soldiers Executed by United States Military Authorities during the Late War* (n.p, n.d), 8–11. See also *Freedom*, 448.

21 Banks, 17 Dec. 1863, 457. Lieber, 479.

22 About 4 percent of White soldiers executed stood charged with mutiny. The rate was roughly 27 percent for Black soldier executions. *List of US Soldiers*, 2–11. On the importance of looking beyond individual acts of violence, see Harold D. Woodman, "The New History Views the Postbellum South," *Journal of Southern History*, 43.4 (Nov. 1977), 535.

23 Sylvis, Speech at Chicago, 9 Jan. 1865, in *Life*, 130–131. "Let the man who, in this crisis, advocates for the reduction of wages, or the subjugation of labor to the whims and caprices of the wealthy . . . be girdled and encircled with burning fagots," Speech at Sunbury, PA, 16 Sept. 1868, in ibid., 232. Sylvis acknowledged his debt to Judge Frank Tilford, who calmed a Nevada miners' strike in 1864, from whose words he borrowed. See "Frank Tilford," in Oscar T. Schuck, ed., *Representative and Leading Men of the Pacific* (San Francisco: Bacon and Company, 1870), 284–285. With former slaves and feminists, labor radicals explored the unfreedoms in American society; Amy Dru Stanley, *From Bondage or Contract: Wage Labor, Marriage, and the Market in the Age of Slave*

Emancipation (Cambridge: Cambridge University Press, 1998), xi–xii. On control and liberation, see Elliott West, "Reconstructing Race," *Western Historical Quarterly*, 34.1 (Spring 2003), 24, and Carole Emberton, *Beyond Redemption: Race, Violence, and the American South after the Civil War* (Chicago: University of Chicago Press, 2013), 5. On "class struggle," see John Fitch, *The Causes of Industrial Unrest* (New York: Harper and Brothers, 1924), 328–329. Civil warfare, see explanatory note 30, Karl Marx and Friedrich Engels, *The Communist Manifesto, Introduction and Notes by D. Ryazanoff* (1928; Calcutta: Burmon Publishing House, 1944), 103.

24 On capitalism's revolution, see Michael Zakim and Gary J. Kornblith, "Introduction" in *Capitalism Takes Command: The Social Transformation of Nineteenth-Century America* (Chicago: University of Chicago Press, 2012), 6. Charles Sellers, *The Market Revolution: Jacksonian America, 1815–1846* (New York: Oxford University Press, 1994).

25 Fulcher, *Capitalism*, 2. Jonathan Levy, *Ages of American Capitalism: A History of the United States* (New York: Random House, 2021), xiv. Eric Hobsbawm, *The Age of Capital, 1848–1875* (1975; New York: Vintage, 1996), 1. David Montgomery, *Citizen Worker: The Experience of Workers in the United States with Democracy and the Free Market during the Nineteenth Century* (Cambridge: Cambridge University Press, 1993), 10.

26 Fulcher, *Capitalism*, 15. Marx and Engels, *The Communist Manifesto*, 20–22. Beckert, *Empire of Cotton*, 67, 82, 377. Placard in Philip S. Foner, *The Great Labor Uprising of 1877* (New York: Pathfinder, 1977), 190.

27 On demobilization, see Gregory P. Downs, *After Appomattox: Military Occupation and the Ends of the War* (Cambridge: Harvard University Press, 2015), 89–91. Over the six-year period 17 million dollars were earned, and 10 million in 1870–1871. 42nd Cong., 2nd sess., House of Representatives, Report No. 46, "Sales of Ordnance Stores," 15 Apr. 1872, 2. Townsend General Orders No. 101 in General Orders No. 34, 12 June 1865, in *OR*, 1:46 (III), 1273–1274. Exhibit No. 13: Statement Showing the Number and Description of Arms Retained in 42nd Cong., 2nd sess., Senate, Report No. 183, "Sales of Arms by Ordnance Department," 11 May 1872, 167–172. On half a million war arms and armed society, see Pamela Haag, *The Gunning of America: Business and the Making of American Gun Culture* (New York: Basic Books, 2016), 110.

28 Cincinnati in "Latest News," *Evansville Journal*, 8 Jan. 1867, 4. "A Frequent Occurrence," *Idaho World*, 1 Aug. 1872, 1.

29 Testimony of S. V. Benét, Senate Report 183, 150. House No. 46, 4, 10. Michael S. Raber, "Conservative Innovators, Military Small Arms, and Industrial History at Springfield Armory, 1794–1918," *Industrial Archeology*, 14.1 (1988), 14. Troubled state of American arms market after war, Herbert G. Houze, *Arming the West: A Fresh Look at the Guns that were Actually Carried on the Frontier* (Woonsocket: Mowbray, 2008), ix. Joseph G. Bilby, *A Revolution in Arms: A History of the First Repeating Rifle* (2006; Yardley, PA: Westholme, 2015), 223.

30 Guns from foreign dealers in Robert V. Bruce, *Lincoln and the Tools of War* (Indianapolis: Bobbs-Merrill, 1956), 49. Testimony of Silas Crispin, 12 Mar. 1872, House No. 46, 182. Winchester order of 46,000 in Laura Trevelyan, *The Winchester: The Gun that Built an American Dynasty* (New Haven: Yale University Press, 2016), 59. Turkish order noted as 30,000 in Bilby, *Revolution in Arms*, 225.

31 Prices in Committee Report, House No. 46, 10. Gun numbers in Testimony of Secretary of War Belknap, 12 Feb. 1872, House No. 46, 16. Testimony of S. B. Benét, House No. 46, 31. Ephraim L. Acker, Minority Report, 42nd Cong., 2nd sess. House of Representatives, Report No. 46, Part 2, "Sales of Ordnance Stores," 15 Apr. 1872, 2.

32 Testimony of S. B. Benét, House No. 46, 31. Ephraim L. Acker, Minority Report, 42nd Cong., 2nd sess., House of Representatives, Report No. 46, Part 2, "Sales of Ordnance Stores," 15 Apr. 1872, 2. Testimony of Silas Crispin, 11 Mar. 1872, House No. 46, 78. Testimony of Hugh Reilly, 25 Mar. 1872, House No. 46, 162. "The Sale of Arms to France," *New York Tribune*, 9 Apr. 1872, 4. Testimony of W. C. Squire, E. Remington and Sons, House No. 46, 86.

33 House No. 46, 10, 8. Battlefield statistic in Trevelyan, *The Winchester*, 65. A British observer said that in defeat "the Winchester was made use of with deadly effect by the Turkish troops," in Bilby, *Revolution in Arms*, 225–226.

34 House No. 46, 2.

35 Levy, *Freaks of Fortune*, 188. Friedman, *Moral Consequences*, 115. Guelzo, *Fateful Lightning*, 518. Richard White, *Railroaded: The Transcontinentals and the Making of Modern America* (New York: Norton, 2011), 56. O. M. W. Sprague, National Monetary Commission, *History of Crises under the National Banking System*, 61st Cong., 2nd sess., Senate, Doc. No. 538, (Washington, DC: Government Printing Office, 1910), 39–40.

36 Moltke in Guelzo, *Fateful Lightning*, 201. McPherson and Hogue, *Ordeal by Fire*, 401–402. Robert R. Hodges, Jr., *American Civil War Railroad Tactics* (Oxford: Osprey, 2009), 7.

37 Sherman to Grant, 14 May 1866, in 39th Cong., 2nd sess., House of Representatives, "Protection across the Continent," 3 Jan. 1867, Ex Doc. No. 23, 2.

38 Gerald G. Eggert, *Railroad Labor Disputes: The Beginning of Federal Strike Policy* (Ann Arbor: University of Michigan Press, 1967), 4.

39 Sherman to Rawlins, 11 Dec. 1866, in "Protection across the Continent," 4.

40 "Expansion triggered an American racial crisis," see West, "Reconstructing Race," 8. Johnson & Graham's Lessee v. McIntosh, 21 US 589 (1823). Roxanne Dunbar-Ortiz, *An Indigenous Peoples' History of the United States* (Boston: Beacon Press, 2014), 197–201. Robert J. Miller, "The Doctrine of Discovery, Manifest Destiny, and American Indians" in *Why You Can't Teach United States History without American Indians*, ed. Sleeper-Smith et al., 87–100.

41 Statistics in Robert Utley, *Frontier Regulars: The United States Army and the Indian, 1866–1891* (Lincoln: University of Nebraska Press, 1973), 410. Grant in Karl Jacoby, *Shadows at Dawn: An Apache Massacre and the Violence of History*

(New York: Penguin, 2008), 127. Sherman in Utley, *Frontier Regulars*, 139. See also Tim Lehman, *Bloodshed at Little Bighorn: Sitting Bull, Custer, and the Destinies of Nations* (Baltimore: Johns Hopkins University Press, 2010), 64. "Report to the President," 7 Jan. 1868, *Annual Report of the Commissioner of Indian Affairs, 1868* (Washington, DC: GPO, 1868), 27.

42 Colt in Utley, *Frontier Regulars*, 70.

43 Indian population and combat events in Utley, *Frontier Regulars*, 410. John H. Monnett, *Tell Them We are Going Home: The Odyssey of the Northern Cheyenne* (Norman: University of Oklahoma Press, 2001), xiv. Elliott West, *The Last Indian War: The Nez Perce Story* (New York: Oxford University Press, 2009). Jeffrey Ostler, "Indian Warfare in the West, 1861–1890" in *Why You Can't Teach United States History without American Indians*, ed. Sleeper-Smith et al., 156.

44 Jack in M. Wilson Rankin, "The Meeker Massacre from Reminiscences of Frontier Days," *Annals of Wyoming*, 16.2 (July 1944), 135, 143–144. See also Mark E. Miller, *Hollow Victory: The White River Expedition of 1879 and the Battle of Milk Creek* (Niwot: University Press of Colorado, 1997), 158. Hitler in James Q. Whitman, *Hitler's American Model: The United States and the Making of Nazi Race Law* (Princeton: Princeton University Press, 2017), 47.

45 Luther Standing Bear, *My People the Sioux* (Boston: Houghton Mifflin, 1928), 133–150, quote on 138, train ride, 129–132. Colin G. Calloway, ed., *Our Hearts Fell to the Ground: Plains Indian Views of How the West Was Lost* (New York: St. Martin's Press, 1996), 168–171. "Standing Bear, Luther," Carlisle Indian Industrial School, Descriptive and Historical Record of Student, 3019, Student Records, 1879–1918, Department of the Interior, Office of Indian Affairs, Record Group 75: Records of the Bureau of Indian Affairs, 1793–1999, National Archives Building, Washington, DC. Death Record-Register of Pupils, 1890–1900, Carlisle Indian School, RG 75, NA. On railroad as agent of colonization, see James Hedges, "The Colonization Work of the Northern Pacific Railroad," *Mississippi Valley Historical Review*, 13.3 (Dec. 1926), 311–342.

46 McMillan in American Freedmen's Inquiry Interviews, 1863, in Blassingame, *Slave Testimony*, 383. D. W. Menig, *The Shaping of America: A Geographical Perspective on 500 Years of History, vol. III* (New Haven: Yale University Press, 1998), 196–197. Sidney Andrews, *The South since the War: As Shown by Fourteen Weeks of Travel and Observation in Georgia and the Carolinas* (Boston: Ticknor and Fields, 1866), 206. Anonymous letter, 23 Oct. 1870, "Condition of Affairs in the Southern States" in *Index to the Reports of the Senate of the United States for the First Session of the Forty-Second Congress and the Special Session* (Washington, DC: GPO, 1871), lxiii. Dispossession of slaves, who enjoyed forms of property beyond land, and former slaves is one current of the Civil War era. For example, see Dylan Penningroth, "Slavery, Freedom, and Social Claims to Property among African Americans in Liberty County, Georgia, 1850–1880," *Journal of American History*, 84.2 (Sept. 1997), 405–435.

47 Woodman, "The New History Views the Postbellum South," 546. Menig, *Shaping of America*, 196–197. Edward L. Ayers, *Vengeance and Justice: Crime and Punishment in the 19th-Century American South* (New York: Oxford University Press, 1984), 166–167. The term Global South captures the shared experience of such laborers in the postwar era; see its full expression in Beckert, *Empire of Cotton*, 377, 379–426. Roger L. Ransom and Richard Smith, *One Kind of Freedom: The Economic Consequences of Emancipation*, 2nd edition (Cambridge: Cambridge University Press, 2001), 64.

48 *Hoffman in Mississippi in 1875: Report of the Select Committee to Inquire into the Mississippi Election of 1875, vol. I* (Washington, DC: GPO, 1876), liv. Black convention in Emberton, *Beyond Redemption*, 150.

49 *Letters of David Ricardo to Thomas Robert Malthus, 1810–1823*, ed. James Bonar (Oxford: Clarendon Press, 1887), 166.

50 46th Cong., 2nd sess., Senate, Report No. 440, Report of the Select Committee to Investigate the Freedman's Savings and Trust Company, 2 Apr. 1880, i–ii. Levy, *Freaks of Fortune*, 19, 138–143. Charters as risk management, see David A. Moss, *When All Else Fails: Government as the Ultimate Risk Manager* (Cambridge: Harvard University Press, 2002), 94–95.

51 Levy, *Freaks of Fortune*, 106, 131–135, 138–141. National debt in Foner, *Great Labor Uprising*, 16. Nicolas Barreyre, "The Politics of Economic Crises: The Panic of 1873, the End of Reconstruction, and the Realignment of American Politics," *Journal of the Gilded Age and Progressive Era*, 10.4 (Oct. 2011), 408. On agricultural cycles, White, *Railroaded*, 80–81.

52 Sprague, *History of Crises*, 35–37. "Altered the face" in W. E. B. DuBois, *Black Reconstruction in America, 1860–1880* (1935; New York: Free Press, 1998), 595. President Grant opted for inaction when the crisis struck. He did not convene Congress, confident that government interference "would unquestionably extend the panic and increase its violence." Grant to Oliver P. Morton, 19 Sept. 1873, *Papers of Grant*, XXIV: 213. White, *Railroaded*, 50. Eric Foner, *Reconstruction: America's Unfinished Revolution: 1863–1877* (New York: Harper and Row, 1988), 461, 467, 512. Barreyre, "The Politics of Economic Crises," 403, 408–409. Hobsbawm, *The Age of Capital*, 5.

53 Report of the Select Committee to Investigate the Freedman's Savings and Trust Company, ii–iii, v–vi. Levy, *Freaks of Fortune*, 357 note 100. On fraud, see Stephen Mihm, *A Nation of Counterfeiters: Capitalists, Con Men, and the Making of the United States* (Cambridge: Harvard University Press, 2007) and Jane Kamensky, *The Exchange Artist: A Tale of High-Flying Speculation and America's First Banking Collapse* (New York: Penguin, 2008).

54 On freedom, see Ayers, *Vengeance and Justice*, 166. Market as vehicle of exploitation, Woodman, "The New History Views the Postbellum South," 534.

55 Wilson and Corbin, *Federal Aid in Domestic Disturbances*, 108–110.

56 Ibid. Sheridan to Grant, 2 Aug. 1866, in ibid., 141. Reynolds to Adjutant-General, 1 Aug. 1868, in ibid., 127.

57 Downs, *After Appomattox*, 236–241. *Slaughterhouse Cases*. 83 US 77 (1873). Lou Faulkner Williams, *The Great South Carolina Ku Klux Klan Trials, 1871–1872* (Athens: University of Georgia Press, 1996), 132–133. US Attorney Corbin in ibid., 78.

58 Williams, *Ku Klux Klan Trials*, 24–29, militia captain on 23.

59 Williams, *Ku Klux Klan Trials*, 42, 70, 87, 106. McPherson and Hogue, *Ordeal by Fire*, 615–616.

60 Allen W. Trelease, *White Terror: The Ku Klux Klan Conspiracy and Southern Reconstruction* (1971; Baton Rouge: Louisiana State University Press, 1995), 402, 411. Reynolds to Adjutant-General, 1 Aug. 1868, in Wilson and Corbin, *Federal Aid in Domestic Disturbances*, 127. Canada in Williams, *Ku Klux Klan Trials*, 114, 106.

61 Trelease, *White Terror*, 402, 411. Reynolds to Adjutant-General, 1 Aug. 1868, in Wilson and Corbin, *Federal Aid in Domestic Disturbances*, 127. Bond in Williams, *Ku Klux Klan Trials*, 114, 106. J. L. Henry, testimony, 7 Feb. 1871, "Condition of Affairs in the Southern States," 109. Quackenbush, sworn statement, 1 Aug. 1870, in "Condition of Affairs in the Southern States," lviii.

62 *Papers of Grant*, XXII: xiii. Williams, *Ku Klux Klan*, 124. Diary of Hamilton Fish, 22 Oct. and 24 Nov. 1871, in *Papers of Grant*, XXII: 201. Robert W. Flournoy to Grant, May 1871, ibid., XXI: 338.

63 Barreyre, The Politics of Economic Crises," 416–417. Nicolas Lemann, *Redemption: The Last Battle of the Civil War* (New York: Farrar, Straus and Giroux, 2006), 79. "Elections," *National Republican* [Washington, DC], 4 Nov. 1874, 1.

64 Murder estimate in Lemann, *Redemption*, 174. Military defunding in Utley, *Frontier Regulars*, 62, and Ari Hoogenboom, *Rutherford B. Hayes: Warrior and President* (Lawrence: University of Kansas Press, 1995), 305.

65 Brooks D. Simpson, *The Reconstruction Presidents* (Lawrence: University of Kansas Press, 1998), 199. Hayes, 23 Mar. 1877, 25 Feb. 1877, 5 Aug. 1877, in *Diary and Letters of Rutherford Birchand Hayes, vol. III*, ed. Charles Richard Williams (Columbus: Ohio State Archaeological and Historical Society, 1924), 429, 421, 441. Hoogenboom, *Rutherford B. Hayes*, 256–257. Federal force and modern rights is a central theme in Downs, *After Appomattox*. Akerman in Hoogenboom, *Rutherford B. Hayes*, 315. Hayes' failure and southern disregard for Fifteenth Amendment in Williams, *Ku Klux Klan*, 129.

66 Hayes to Guy M. Bryan, 2 Jan. 1875, in *Diary and Letters*, 263. Hoogenboom, *Rutherford B. Hayes*, 255.

67 Wenxian Zhang, "Standing up against Racial Discrimination: Progressive Americans and the Chinese Exclusion Act in the Late Nineteenth Century," *Phylon*, 56.1 (Summer 2019), 13–15. Labor and capital in Republican Party Platform of 1872, see Francis Curtis, *The Republican Party: A History of its Fifty Years' Existence and a Record of its Measures and Leaders, 1854–1904, vol. II* (New York: G. P. Putnam's Sons, 1904), 26.

68 On "low-road capitalism" from which the definitions here are derived, see Erik Olin Wright and Joel Rogers, *American Society: How It Really Works*

(New York: Norton, 2015). *Chronicle* in *Appletons' Annual Cyclopaedia and Register of Important Events for the Year 1877* (New York: D. Appleton and Company, 1882), 231. Philip S. Foner, *History of the Labor Movement in the United States, vol. I* (1947; New York: International Publishers, 1982), 464.

CHAPTER 9 – LAYERING LAW AND RESISTANCE IN THE GREAT STRIKES

1 "The International Industrial Assembly of North America, 1864," 124.

2 Foner, *Great Labor Uprising*, 43–44. *Appletons' Annual for 1877*, 424–425. J. A. Dacus, *Annals of the Great Strikes in the United States* (Chicago: L. T. Palmer and Co., 1877), 27. "Offizieller Bericht der Bahnverwaltung," *Der Deutsche Correspondent* [Baltimore], 17 July 1877, 4. Edward Winslow Martin, *The History of the Great Riots* (Philadelphia: National Publishing Company, 1877), 18.

3 Martin, *History of the Great Riots*, 18. Foner, *Great Labor Uprising*, 31, 45–46.

4 Dacus, *Annals of the Great Strikes*, iii. Philip Dray, *There is Power in Union: The Epic Story of Labor in America* (New York: Anchor Books, 2010), 118.

5 "Melancholy Accident," *Baltimore Patriot and Mercantile Advertiser*, 27 June 1831, 2. Coroner's Inquest from the *Chronicle* in *Baltimore Patriot and Mercantile Advertiser*, 2 June 1831, 2.

6 "Baltimore: Friday, July 1, 1831," *Baltimore Gazette and Daily Advertiser*, 1 July 1831, 2. "The Rail Road Affair," *Baltimore Patriot and Mercantile Advertiser*, 2 July 1831, 2. "Brigade Orders," *Baltimore Gazette and Daily Advertiser*, 5 July 1831, 3. "Easton," *Republican Star and General Advertiser* [Easton, MD], 5 July 1831, 3. US servicemen in "From the Baltimore Gazette and American," *Salem Gazette* [MA], 8 July 1831, 2. Sixty arrests in "Former Riots on the Road," *Democratic Advocate*, 21 July 1877, 3.

7 G. H. Steuart to W. Paterson, 7 July 1831, in "Baltimore, 7th July, 1831," *Baltimore Gazette and Daily Advertiser*, 9 July 1831, 2. On corporations, see William G. Roy, *Socializing Capital: The Rise of the Large Industrial Corporation in America* (Princeton: Princeton University Press, 1997), 71–77. Christopher L. Tomlins, *The State and the Unions: Labor Relations, Law, and the Organized Labor Movement in America, 1880–1960* (Cambridge: Cambridge University Press, 1985), 24.

8 Vanwyck in "From the Baltimore Gazette and American," *Salem Gazette* [MA], 8 July 1831, 2.

9 Steuart to Paterson, 7 July 1831, 2. "From the Baltimore Gazette and American," 2.

10 "Strike on the Baltimore and Ohio Railroad," *Orleans Independent Standard*, 8 May 1857, 2. "Former Riots on the Road," 3. Cost of life in "A Strike and Riot," *Shepherdstown Register*, 9 May 1857, 2.

11 "A Strike and Riot," 2. "The Strike on the Baltimore and Ohio Railroad Suppressed," *New York Herald*, 3 May 1857, 4.

12 Personal violence in "The Railroad Strike at Baltimore," *Belmont Chronicle* [St. Clairsville, OH], 3. "A Strike," *Spirit of Jefferson*, 5 May 1857, 2.

13 Dacus, *Annals of the Great Strikes*, 30–33. Backlog in "Martinsburg, W. Va., July 17, 1877," *Shepherdstown Register*, 21 July 1877, 2.

14 Gov. Mathews to Vice-President King in Martin, *History of the Great Riots*, 20. *Der Deutsche Correspondent*, 20 July 1877, 4. Foner, *Great Labor Uprising*, 47. "The Railroad Strikers," *New Orleans Daily Democrat*, 19 July 1877, 1. "The Strikers," *New North-West* [Deer Lodge, MT], 20 July 1877, 2. "Railroad Strikes," *Spirit of Jefferson* [Charles Town, WV], 24 July 1877, 1.

15 Martin, *History of the Great Riots*, 23–24. Mathews to Hayes, 18 July 1877, in Wilson and Corbin, *Federal Aid in Domestic Disturbances*, 189–190. McCrary to Mathews, 18 July 1877, in Martin, *History of the Great Riots*, 25. Mathews to McCrary, 18 July 1877, in ibid., 25.

16 Hayes, Proclamation, 18 July 1877, in Wilson and Corbin, *Federal Aid in Domestic Disturbances*, 190–191.

17 Martin, *History of the Great Riots*, 27–28. Wilson and Corbin, *Federal Aid in Domestic Disturbances*, 192. Hoogenboom, *Rutherford B. Hayes*, 328.

18 Eggert, *Railroad Labor Disputes*, 9–11. "Political Aspects of the Trouble," *New York Times*, 25 July 1877, 4. New York City to be without meat in "A Conviction that Disturbance in the Metropolis Can Be Checked by the Police," *New Orleans Times*, 26 July 1877, 1. "The Cincinnati Blockade Broken," *New York Times*, 26 July 1877, 1.

19 On use of public force, Hoogenboom, *Rutherford B. Hayes*, 327. Williams to Hayes, 26 July 1877, and McCrary to Williams, 27 July 1877, in Wilson and Corbin, *Federal Aid in Domestic Disturbances*, 200.

20 Williams to Hayes, 26 July 1877, and McCrary to Williams, 27 July 1877. Wilson and Corbin, *Federal Aid in Domestic Disturbances*, 200, 202–203. McCrary to Colonel R. C. Drum, 27 July 1877, in ibid., 202. Foner, *Great Labor Uprising*, 229. David T. Burbank, *Reign of the Rabble: The St. Louis General Strike of 1877* (New York: Augustus M. Kelley, 1996), 91.

21 "The American Railway Strike," *Times of India*, 22 Aug. 1877, 4. "Speech of Durbin Ward," *Cincinnati Daily Gazette*, 11 Sept. 1877, 2.

22 Hayes, 5 Aug. 1877, *Diary and Letters*, 440–441. Resistance in "The B. & O. R. R. Strike," *Stark County Democrat* [Canton, OH], 19 July 1877, 1. Hayes in Ohio, Hoogenboom, *Rutherford B. Hayes*, 327.

23 Hayes, 5 Aug. 1877, *Diary and Letters*, 440–441.

24 "Hardships of the Railroad Business – Difficulties of the Baltimore and Ohio Line," *Wheeling Daily Intelligencer*, 20 July 1877, 1. "Changing Aspect of the Great Strike," *Daily Evening Bulletin* [San Francisco], 24 July 1877, 2. "Strikers and the Mob," *New York Herald*, 24 July 1877, 6. "What the Strike Is," *Cincinnati Gazette* in *Chicago Daily Tribune*, 28 July 1877, 2.

25 Global view of criminality in Ibram X. Kendi, *Stamped from the Beginning: The Definitive History of Racist Ideas in America* (New York: Nation Books, 2016), 257. See also Michael Bellesiles, *1877: America's Year of Living Violently* (New York: New Press, 2012), 113–122, 211–218. Baltimore City Police Department (Criminal

Docket, Middle District), ff. 420–423, covering July 21, 1877 through July 23, 1877, Maryland State Archives C 2109–3 (MSA SC 2221–09–21). Chancellor in *Appletons' Annual for 1877*, 478. Genuine in "Tramps," *Daily Gazette* [Wilmington, DE], 6 June 1877, 1, and "Report of the Select Committee Appointed by the Assembly of 1875 to Investigate the Causes of the Increase of Crime in the City of New York" in *Documents of the Assembly of the State of New York*, volume 6, issue 106 (New York: Jerome B. Parmenter, 1876), 37. "Labor-Strikes," *Appletons' Annual for 1877*, 427.

26 "Changing Aspect of the Great Strike," 2. On violence and social breakdown theory, see Charles Tilly, Louise Tilly, and Richard Tilly, *The Rebellious Century, 1830–1930* (Cambridge:Harvard University Press, 1975), 4–6. *Detroit Tribune* in *True Northerner* [Paw Paw, MI], 27 July 1877, 5. J. C. McLain to Editor, "Is Civilization a Failure?" *Chicago Daily Tribune*, 28 July 1877, 2.

27 "The Mob at Buffalo," *New York Times*, 26 July 1877, 1.

28 D. to Editor, 30 July 1877, "The Weekly Budget of Queries from the Readers," *Inter Ocean* [Chicago], 18 Aug. 1877, 12. "Sober Second Thoughts," *Clarksville Weekly Chronicle* [TN], 4 Aug. 1877, 1.

29 "The Negro and the Irishman," *Southern Workmen and Hampton School Record*, 10.4 (Apr. 1882), 39.

30 Letter to the Editor, "All Are Workingmen," *Indianapolis Sentinel*, 4 Aug. 1877, 7. J. B. Harrison, "Notes on Industrial Conditions" in "A Most Valuable Contribution," *Southern Workman and Hampton School Record*, 15.8 (1 Aug. 1886), 85–86.

31 For Tompkins Square, see Herbert G. Gutman, "The Tompkins Square 'Riot' in New York City on January 13, 1874: A Re-examination of its Causes and its Aftermath," *Labor History*, 6:1 (1965), 44–70. Gompers in Marilynn S. Johnson, *Street Justice: A History of Police Violence in New York City* (Boston: Beacon Press, 2003), 32.

32 Reporter on Havemeyer in "The Workingmen's Demonstrations," *New York Herald*, 9 Jan. 1875, 5. "Mayor Havemeyer and the Laborers," *New Orleans Republican*, 14 Jan. 1874, 1. For more protests, see, for example, "Out of Work," *New York Herald*, 6 Jan. 1874, 5. Havemeyer cited in "The Workingmen Right," *New York Herald*, 15 Jan. 1874, 5.

33 Lilienthal in "Free Speech: German Mass Meeting at the Cooper Institute," *New York Herald*, 31 Jan 1874, 3. Quote on laws in Foner, *Great Labor Uprising*, 33. Eggert, *Railroad Labor Disputes*, 41.

34 Foner, *Great Labor Uprising*, 94. "Riot and Bloodshed at Reading," *Middletown Transcript*, 28 July 1877, 2. "Pennsylvania – Reading," *Chicago Daily Tribune*, 24 July 1877, 1. "Miscellaneous," *Chicago Daily Tribune*, 27 July 1877, 6. "Affairs at Reading," *New York Times*, 28 July 1877, 2.

35 "Reading out of Danger," *New York Times*, 26 July 1877, 2. Frank Reeder to George S. Goodhart, 30 July 1877, in "The Fight with the Reading Mob," *New York Times*, 31 July 1877, 5. "The Mob Fired on at Reading," *New York*

Times, 24 July 1877, 1. Letter to Editor, 25 July 1877, "A Trained Army," *New-York Tribune*, 4 Aug. 1877, 7.

36 "The Late Troubles," *Weekly Register* [Point Pleasant, WV], 9 Aug. 1877, 2. Wilson in Eggert, *Railroad Labor Disputes*, 37. McElwee, "To the Voters of McMinn County," *Athens Post* (TN), 18 Sept. 1874, 2. Sumner, *What the Social Classes Owe to Each Other* (1883; New York: Harper and Brothers, 1910), 62. *What the Social Classes* is Sumner's work that is most often confused with Social Darwinism or the positions of Herbert Spencer; see Robert C. Bannister, *Social Darwinism: Science and Myth in Anglo-American Social Thought* (Philadelphia: Temple University Press, 1979), 99–108. That said, Sumner understood competition and hierarchy as central to American life.

37 Bloodiest in Philip Taft and Philip Ross, "American Labor Violence: Its Causes, Character, and Outcome" in *Violence in America: Historical and Comparative Perspectives*, revised edition, ed. Hugh Davis Graham and Ted Robert Gurr (London: Sage, 1979), 187. Richard Hofstadter argued low union participation and an absence of radical labor ideology make industrial violence in the USA puzzling; see Hofstadter, "Reflections on Violence," 19. Union participation in Michael Mann, *The Sources of Social Power, vol. II: The Rise of Classes and Nation-States, 1760–1916* (1993; Cambridge: Cambridge University Press, 2012), 630–635.

38 Intensity in Robert Justin Goldstein, *Political Repression in Modern America from 1870 to the Present* (Cambridge: Schenkman, 1978), 3. For a more recent example of "inequality = violence," see Walter Scheidel, *Violence and the History of Inequality in History from the Stone-Age to the Twenty-First Century* (Princeton: Princeton University Press, 2017). Figures on inequality in Thomas Piketty, *Capital in the Twenty-First Century* (Cambridge: Harvard University Press, 2014), 349.

39 Statistics from Mann, *Sources of Social Power*, 635. For Pittsburgh figures, see Dacus, *Annals of the Great Strikes*, chapter 10, and Fredrick Kunkle, "Labor Day's Violent Roots: How a Worker Revolt on the B&O Railroad Left 100 People Dead," *Washington Post*, 4 Sept. 2017.

40 Property in Goldstein, *Political Repression*, 3. On corporate personhood, see Adam Winkler, "'Corporations are People' is Built on an Incredible 19th-Century Lie," *Atlantic*, 5 Mar. 2018. Roy, *Socializing Capital*, xiv, 3–5, 41–77.

41 Pinkerton, *Strikers, Communists, Tramps, and Detectives* (New York: G. W. Carelton, 1878), x. On private force unique in USA, see Goldstein, *Political Repression*, 4–5. Republic arsenal in ibid., 12.

42 Hofstadter, "Reflections on Violence," 19. Goldstein, *Political Repression*, xvii. Mann, *Sources of Social Power*, 645. On global comparisons, see Val R. Lorwin, *Private Power and American Democracy* (1970), Stuart Jamieson, *Political Oppositions in Western Democracies* (1968), and H. M. Gitelman, *History of Labor in the United States, vol. I* (1918), quoted in Goldstein, *Political Repression*, 4–5. *Adair v. United States*, 208 US 161 (1908).

43 On Congress, see "The Duty of Congress," *Bismarck Tri-Weekly Tribune*, 7 Sept. 1877, 1.

44 Diverse labor force in Lilia Fernandez, "Recent Histories of Mexican American Men and Women," *Reviews in American History*, 42.3 (Sept. 2014), 481. "Illinois. Braidwood Miners," *Chicago Daily Tribune*, 21 July 1877, 5. "The Braidwood Miners," *Ottawa Free Trader* [IL], 4 Aug. 1877, 4.

45 "The Braidwood Miners," 4. Caste in Edward Ball, *Slaves in the Family* (1998; New York: Farrar, Straus and Giroux, 2014), xiii.

46 "The Riotous Negroes," *Daily Gazette* [Wilmington], 18 Aug. 1877, 1. "The Strike Over," *New Orleans Daily Democrat*, 31 July 1877, 1. The racial dynamic featured here is noted as the "norm of Black devaluation" by Melvin Rogers and "black fungibility" by Stephen Marshall. Rogers, "Introduction: Disposable Lives," *Theory and Event*, 17.3 (2014), muse.jhu.edu/article/559375. Marshall, "The Political Life of Fungibility," *Theory and Event*, 15.3 (2012): muse.jhu.edu/article/484457.

47 "The Strike in St. Louis," *State Journal*, 3 Aug. 1877, 4. "Riotous," *Sedalia Weekly Bazoo*, 7 Aug. 1877, 2.

48 "Another Strike," *Chicago Daily Tribune*, 31 July 1877, 1. "Strikes on the River and Levee," *Public Ledger*, 1 Aug. 1877, 3.

49 Dacus, *Annals of the Great Strikes*, 436. "The State Over," *Dallas Daily Herald*, 5 Aug. 1877, 2. See also "Texas," *New Orleans Daily Democrat*, 12 Aug. 1877, 2.

50 "Serious Strikes," *Cincinnati Daily Star*, 20 Aug. 1877, 2.

51 "'The strikes,'" *Manitowoc Pilot*, 30 Aug. 1877, 3. Gender equality in "Their New Departure," *New York Herald*, 3 Sept. 1877, 10.

52 "A Silk Strike – Pugnacious Women," *New Bloomfield, Pa. Times*, 26 June 1877, 4. "Notes and News," *Bismarck Tri-Weekly Tribune*, 19 Sept. 1877, 2.

53 Roles in "About Women," *Cincinnati Commercial Tribune*, 10 Aug. 1877, 5. Amazon in "About Women," *Evansville Journal*, 12 Aug. 1877, 2.

54 Ladies of Labor in "Texas," *New Orleans Daily Democrat*, 19 Aug. 1877, 2. Tera W. Hunter, *To 'Joy My Freedom': Southern Black Women's Lives and Labors after the Civil War* (Cambridge: Harvard University Press, 1997), 77–80.

55 On Black washerwomen, see ibid., 78–80.

56 On immigration, wages, and laundries, see Scott Zesch, *The Chinatown War: Chinese Los Angeles and the Massacre of 1871* (New York: Oxford University Press, 2012), 6, 17–18; Hunter, *To 'Joy My Freedom,'* 78–79. On capitalism, imperialism, and migrant labor, see Simeon Mann, "Anti-Asian Violence and US Imperialism," *Race and Class*, 62.2 (2020), 26.

57 "The Colored Washerwomen," *Dallas Daily Herald*, 4 Aug. 1877, 2. Terminology in Zesch, *The Chinatown War*, 7. Letter in Hunter, *To 'Joy My Freedom,'* 80–81.

58 "Galveston County," *Dallas Daily Herald*, 5 Aug 1877, 2.

59 Baton Rouge *Grand Era* in the *Donaldson Chief* [LA], 16 June 1877, 1.

60 "A Subscriber Writes," *Nebraska Advertiser*, 12 July 1877, 2.

61 "Surgeon Wilson's Frolic," *New York Herald*, 28 July 1877, 5. "A Woman Shot," *New York Herald*, 6 July 1877, 10. "Sickening Tragedies," *St. Louis Globe-Democrat*, 6 July 1877. "Crimes and Casualties," *Home Journal*, 19 July 1877, 1. Awaiting in "Shooting Affray," *Wheeling Daily Intelligencer*, 6 July 1877, 1.

62 "Telegraphic Summary," *Daily Critic*, 30 July 1877, 1. "Surgeon Wilson's Frolic," 1. "A Woman Shot," 10. "Naval Intelligence," *New York Herald*, 5 Aug. 1877, 9. "Re-Arrested," *Easton Gazette*, 4 Aug. 1877, 3. Jurisdiction in "Latest Morning Dispatches," *North American*, 8 Oct. 1877, 1. "Surgeon Wilson's Case," *New York Herald*, 7 Oct. 1877, 11. Full penalty in "The Fourth-of-July Homicide in Norfolk," *Daily Dispatch*, 10 Oct. 1877, 3.

63 "$500 Reward," *New Orleans Daily Democrat*, 8 Aug. 1877, 4. Buckshot in "A Feliciana Murder," *Donaldson Chief*, 1 Sept. 1877, 2. "The Issue Joined," *Weekly Louisianian*, 29 Sept. 1877, 2.

64 Nicholls owned five Black persons in 1860 Federal Census, Schedule 2, 17 Aug. 1860, Bayou Lafourche Ward 5, Parish of Assumption, Louisiana, 102. *Official Journal of the Constitutional Convention of the State of Louisiana, Held in New Orleans, April 21, 1879* (New Orleans: Jas. H. Cosgrove, 1879), 38. Rep. Stowell, 6 Jan. 1873, 43rd Cong., 1st sess., *Congressional Record* 2, pt. 1: 427.

65 "$500 Reward," 4. "A Feliciana Murder," 2.

66 "Honorably Acquitted," *Dallas Daily Herald*, 22 Nov. 1877, 4. Cheering in "Trial of J. W. Dixon," *Feliciana Sentinel*, 17 Nov. 1877, 3.

67 "Governor Nicholls," *Richmond Beacon*, 9 June 1877, 2. "Telegraphic Summary," *Daily Critic*, 30 July 1877, 1.

68 "Bloody Work," *Memphis Daily Appeal*, 26 June 1877, 1.

CHAPTER 10 – WORDS AND ROPES: THE POSTWAR BATTLES OVER RACIAL ORDER

1 Precedent in Eric Foner, *Reconstruction: America's Unfinished Revolution, 1863–1877* (New York: Harper and Row, 1988), xxv. Foner famously argued political authority as the source of Reconstruction's revolution. See James McPherson, *Abraham Lincoln and the Second American Revolution* (New York: Oxford University Press, 1991), 20.

2 Violence as perpetuating institution, see Feldman, *Formations of Violence*, 21.

3 Stats in "Black-American Members by Congress, 1870–Present," https://history .house.gov/Exhibitions-and-Publications/BAIC/Historical-Data/Black-American-Representatives-and-Senators-by-Congress/ and Foner, *Reconstruction*, 352. Rep. Stowell, 6 Jan. 1874, 43rd Cong., 1st sess., *Congressional Record* 2, pt. 1: 426.

4 Rep. Harris and Rep. Ransier, 5 Jan. 1874, 43rd Cong., 1st sess., *Congressional Record* 2, pt. 1: 377. Three female persons, aged nineteen, fifteen, and five, are marked for John Thomas Harris in 1860. See 1860 Federal Census, Schedule 2, 4 June 1860, Harrisonburg, Rockingham County, Virginia, 2.

5 William's father, Ahi Robbins, is noted as an enslaver in 1850 and 1860. For example, see 1850 Federal Census, Schedule 2, 16 Aug. 1850, Northern Division, Randolph County, North Carolina, n.p.

6 For critique of biological formations of race, see Dorothy Roberts, *Fatal Invention: How Science, Politics, and Big Business Re-Create Race in the Twenty-First Century* (New York: New Press, 2011), 23–25. Rep. Harris, 5 Jan. 1874, 377. Rep. Robbins, 24 Jan. 1874, 43rd Cong., 1st sess., *Congressional Record* 2, pt. 1: 898. Rep. Atkins, 7 Jan. 1874, 43rd Cong., 1st sess., *Congressional Record* 2, pt. 1: 455. Atkins is listed as the owner of twenty-seven persons in the 1860 Federal Census. See 1860 Federal Census, Schedule 2, 6 June 1860, District No. 1, County of Henry, Tennessee, 6–7.

7 Rep. Ransier, 5 Jan. 1874, 43rd Cong., 1st sess., *Congressional Record* 2, pt. 1: 383. Rep. Cain, 6 Jan. 1874, 43rd Cong., 1st sess., *Congressional Record* 2, pt. 1: 565.

8 Rep. Buckner, 6 Jan. 1874, 43rd Cong., 1st sess., *Congressional Record* 2, pt. 1: 427. Buckner's slaveholding in 1860 Federal Census, Schedule 2, 11–12 June 1860, Cuivre Township, Pike County, Missouri, 194. Rep. Hamilton, 17 Jan. 1874, 43rd Cong., 1st sess., *Congressional Record* 2, pt. 1: 740–741. Rep. Herndon, 6 Jan. 1874, 43rd Cong., 1st sess., *Congressional Record* 2, pt. 1: 422. Herndon married into a slaveholding family – and the thirty-eight slaves listed here reside on his father-in-law's estate. See 1860 Federal Census, Schedule 2, 21 July 1860, Beat No. 5, Cherokee County, Texas, 33–34.

9 Rep. Butler, 7 Jan. 1874, 43rd Cong., 1st sess., *Congressional Record* 2, pt. 1: 458.

10 Rep. Butler, 7 Jan. 1874, 457.

11 On social construction of reality, Peter L. Berger and Thomas Luckman, *The Social Construction of Reality: A Treatise in the Sociology of Knowledge* (New York: Anchor Books, 1966). Roberts, *Fatal Invention*, 4. On violence, abuse, and humiliation, see Omi and Winant, *Racial Formation in the United States*, 3. Rep. Cox and Rep. Butler, 19 Dec. 1873, 43rd Cong., 1st sess., *Congressional Record* 2, pt. 1: 341–342.

12 Rep. Cain, 10 Jan. 1874, 43rd Cong., 1st sess., *Congressional Record* 2, pt. 1: 566. See too, Rep. Cain, 24 Jan. 1874, 43rd Cong., 1st sess., *Congressional Record* 2, pt. 1: 901.

13 Rep. Herndon, 6 Jan. 1874, 419. Rep. Robbins, 24 Jan. 1874, 899–900.

14 Two enslaved persons are listed under Beck in the 1860 Federal Census, Schedule 2, 26 July 1860, 3rd Ward City of Lexington, Fayette County, Kentucky, 68. Sen. Beck, 19 Dec. 1881, 47th Cong., 1st sess., *Congressional Record* 13, pt. 1: 188.

15 Rep. Harris, 17 Jan. 1874, 43rd Cong., 1st sess., *Congressional Record* 2, pt. 1: 725. Rep. McLane, 22 Mar. 1882, 47th Cong., 1st sess., *Congressional Record* 13, pt. 3: 2169.

16 Nineteen enslaved persons are listed under Richardson in the 1860 Federal Census, Schedule 2, 6 July 1860, Sumter, South Carolina, 218. Rep. Richardson, 22 Mar. 1882, 47th Cong., 1st sess., *Congressional Record* 13, pt. 3: 2177.

17 For Durham slave-ownership, see entry in 1860 Federal Census, Schedule 2, n.d., Boyle County, Kentucky, 19. Rep. Durham, 6 Jan. 1874, 43rd Cong., 1st sess., *Congressional Record* 2, pt. 1: 406. Du Bois, *Black Reconstruction in America*,

1860–1880 (1935; New York: Free Press, 1998), 700. See also David Roediger, *The Wages of Whiteness: Race and the Making of the American Working Class* (New York: Verso, 2007).

18 Social order in Amy Louise Wood, *Lynching and Spectacle: Witnessing Racial Violence in America, 1890–1940* (Chapel Hill: University of North Carolina Press, 2009), 5–7. Campbell Gibson and Kay Jung, "Historical Census Data Statistics on Population Totals by Race, 1790 to 1990, and by Hispanic Origin, 1970 to 1990, for the United States, Regions, Divisions, and States," Working Paper No. 56, US Census Bureau, 1 Sept. 2002, 19.

19 Rep. Wise, 22 Mar. 1882, 47th Cong., 1st sess., *Congressional Record* 13, pt. 7: 64. See entry for George D. Wise in 1860 Federal Census, Schedule 2, 9 June 1860, St. Georges Parish, Accomack County, Virginia, 1. Rep. Murch, 16 Mar. 1882, 47th Cong., 1st sess., *Congressional Record* 13, pt. 7: 46. See slaves owned entry for John M. Swanson in 1860 Federal Census, Schedule 2, 14–15 July 1860, North District, Pittsylvania County, Virginia, 18–19. Rep. Swanson, 7 Oct. 1893, 47th Cong., 1st sess., *Congressional Record* 25, pt. 3: 213. See slaves owned entry for Augustus R. Denson in 1860 Federal Census, Schedule 2, 5 July 1860, Beat 5, Russell County, Alabama, 36. Rep. Denson, 2 Oct. 1893, 53rd Cong., 1st sess., *Congressional Record* 25, pt. 2: 2037.

20 Samuel Tutson, 10 Nov. 1871, in *Testimony Taken by the Joint Select Committee to Inquire into the Condition of Affairs in the Late insurrectionary States*, vol. XIII (Washington, DC: GPO, 1872), 54. Hannah Tutson, 10 Nov. 1871, *Testimony Taken*, 59–61. See also Hannah Rosen, *Terror in the Heart of Freedom: Citizenship, Sexual Violence, and the Meaning of Race in the Postemancipation South* (Chapel Hill: University of North Carolina Press, 2009).

21 Hannah Tutson, 60. Francis, "Ida B. Wells and the Economics of Racial Violence," *Items: Insights from the Social Sciences*, 24 Jan. 2017, https://items.ssrc.org/reading-racial-conflict/ida-b-wells-and-the-economics-of-racial-violence/.

22 Minority Report in *Report of the Joint Select Committee to Inquire into the Condition of Affairs in the Late insurrectionary States*, vol. I (Washington, DC: GPO, 1872), 289.

23 Letter from "a distinguished citizen of a Southern State" in Representative Grosvenor, 7 Oct. 1893, 53rd Cong., 1st sess., *Congressional Record* 25, pt. 2: 2277. A recent focus on the chicken and the egg question – does the creation of race create violence, or does violence create race? – misses the dialectical relationship in play. For chicken and egg dilemma driven by discriminatory policy, see Kendi, *Stamped from the Beginning*, 9. Rep. Hicks, 6 Oct. 1893, 53rd Cong., 1st sess., *Congressional Record* 25, pt. 2: 2227.

24 I borrow greatly from Bourke in this paragraph. "Words are never neutral: they determine what we think about the world and how we experience it," she writes in *Deep Violence*, 17.

25 Ida B. Wells, *The Reason Why the Colored American is not at the Columbian Exposition* (n.p., 1893), 30. For Mollie [emphasis added], see "A Memphis Lynching," *Roanoke Times*, 25 July 1893, 3. For Maggie [emphasis added], see "Telegraphic

Ticks," *St. Paul Daily Globe,* 19 July 1893, 8. For Misses, see "A Negro Hunt Joined by Negroes," *Sun* [New York], 20 July 1893, 1. Heavy stick in "A Memphis Lynching," 1.

26 "A Negro Hunt Joined by Negroes," 1. "A Lynching in Prospect," *Roanoke Times,* 20 July 1893, 4.

27 The negro and Martin in "A Negro Hunt Joined by Negroes," 1, and "A Lynching in Prospect," 4. Margaret Vandiver, *Lethal Punishment: Lynchings and Legal Executions in the South* (Piscataway: Rutgers University Press, 2005), 62. Arrest material, *Memphis Appeal-Avalanche,* 22 July 1893, 6, in ibid., 62.

28 "A Lynching in Prospect," 4. "Telegraphic Ticks," 8. Demented in *Shelby County's Shame: Story of Big Creek Lynching and Trial* (n.p.: 1895), 7. For a discussion of the legal examination of slaves under coercion, see Jordan, *Tumult and Silence,* 92–98. Vandiver, *Lethal Punishment,* 62–63.

29 Coverage of the killing of Walker was extensive. For each citation covering the event, three or four pieces can be cited. I have opted to name one or two to keep the endnotes manageable. "Vengeance Visited," *Morning Call* [San Francisco], 23 July 1893, 6. "Lee Walker," *News-Herald,* 27 July 1893, 2. "The Negro Walker Lynched," *New York Times,* 24 July 1893, 8.

30 Chair in "The Negro Walker Lynched," 8. Suicide attempt in "Lynched and Cremated," *Boston Daily Globe,* 24 July 1893, 5. "A Ghastly Sight," *Los Angeles Times,* 2. Blood in "Lynched by a Mob," *Detroit Free Press,* 24 July 1893, 1. Lumberyard in "A Ghastly Sight," 2. Hands in "Vengeance Visited," 6. Dashed in "Monstrous," *Los Angeles Times,* 24 July 1893, 1. "Lynching of a Negro," *Hartford Courant,* 24 July 1893, 1.

31 There exists a substantial newspaper record of the event. Examples of forty active men include "Monstrous," 1. Examples of a hundred include "The Negro Walker Lynched," 8, and "Lynched by a Mob," 1. Details of the burning and re-hanging of the body in "Monstrous," 1.

32 Lynching figures and national reach in Charles Seguin and David Rigby, "National Crimes: A New National Data Set of Lynchings in the United States, 1883 to 1941," *Socius: Sociological Research for a Dynamic World,* 5 (Jan. 2019), 2. Lynching definition in ibid., 2, and Lisa Cook, "The Color of Lynching," presented at the American Economic Association Annual Meeting, 6 Jan. 2012, 5. The Equal Justice Initiative has revised lynching numbers significantly higher than those offered by academics. See "Reconstruction in America: EJI Report," Equal Justice Initiative, Aug. 20, 2020, https://eji.org/reports/reconstruction-in -america-overview/. Rosen, *Terror in the Heart of Freedom,* 8.

33 For Congressional bills, see Magdalene Zier, "Crimes of Omission: State-Action Doctrine and Anti-Lynching Legislation in the Jim Crow Era," *Stanford Law Review,* 73 (Mar. 2021), 777. Frederick Douglass, "Lynching Black People Because They Are Black," *Our Day,* 13 (1894), 298–306. Wells, *Crusade for Justice: The Autobiography of Ida B. Wells,* ed. Alfreda M. Duster (Chicago: University of Chicago Press, 1970),

64. For the nuance and complexity of the terminology, see Pryor, "The Etymology of Nigger."

34 Hubert Howe Bancroft, *Works of Hubert Howe Bancroft, volume XXXVI: Popular Tribunals*, vol. I (San Francisco: History Company, 1887), vii. Liberal social contract, see Mills, *The Racial Contract*, 86–87.

35 Bancroft, *Popular*, 521, 562.

36 James Cutler, *Lynch-Law: An Investigation into the History of Lynching in the United States* (New York: Longman's, Green, and Co., 1905), 201, 273–274, 1. W. Fitzhugh Brundage says that for Cutler "Lynching ... was a lamentable but necessary form of justice." Cutler found lynching lamentable, I believe, only in that it subverted the legal process. He did not bemoan that it upheld White supremacy. See Brundage, *Lynching in the New South, Georgia and Virginia, 1880–1930* (Urbana: University of Illinois Press, 1993), 1.

37 Global lynching, see Roberta Senechal de la Roche, "The Sociogenesis of Lynching" in *Under Sentence of Death: Lynching in the South*, ed. W. Fitzhugh Brundage (Chapel Hill: University of North Carolina Press, 1997), 51. Quote in Michael Pfeifer, "At the Hands of Parties Unknown? The State of the Field of Lynching Scholarship," *Journal of American History*, 101.3 (Dec. 2014), 846.

38 The article from the *Cobourg Star*, 30 June 1841, was widely reprinted in the United States. See, for example, "Lynching in Canada," *New York Spectator*, 10 July 1841, 1; "Lynching in Canada," *Atlas*, 10 July 1841, 1; "Lynching in Canada," *North American*, 10 July 1841, 2. Word change from "violated her person" to "brutally outraged" found in "Horrible Outrage in Canada," *New-York Tribune*, 9 July 1841, 2. There is some disagreement whether the event happened on June 13 or June 18. As most articles mark it as a Sunday, I have retained June 13, 1841.

39 Random attack and citations from Brent S. Campney, "'Canadians are not Proficient in the Art of Lynching': Mob Violence, Social Regulation, and National Identity" in *Global Lynching and Collective Violence, vol. II: The Americas and Europe*, ed. Michael J. Pfeifer (Urbana: University of Illinois Press, 2017), 123, 127.

40 On failure to see global lynching connections, see William D. Carrigan and Christopher Waldrep, "Introduction," in *Swift to Wrath: Lynching in Global Historical Perspective*, ed. Carrigan and Waldrep (Charlottesville: University of Virginia Press, 2013), 1–14. Frederick Douglass, *My Bondage, My Freedom* (New York: Miller, Orton and Mulligan, 1855), 281. One of the earliest traumatic examples is Tom Smith. In the 1830s, Smith, an American fugitive slave who opened a Canadian barber shop, married a "not bad-looking Irishwoman." When White lynchers attacked the couple in winter, they rode Smith "upon a rail, and so ill-treated him that he died under their hands." Smith in Susanna Moodie, *Roughing it in the Bush; or, Life in Canada, vol. I* (London: Richard Bentley, 1852), 230–231. Campney mistakenly reports that Moodie recalls the Moses Carter incident when she details what happens to Tom

Smith. It is possible Tom Smith is a pseudonym, but Carter was attacked in summer, not winter, was not killed by the mob, and was not a barber. In November 1841, Sir Richard Jackson, Administrator of the Province of Canada, offered a $400 reward to catch the persons who "committed an assault on Moses Carter" and made no mention of a murder. "Reward," *North American*, 9 Nov. 1841, 3.

41 Rashad Shabazz, *Spacializing Blackness: Architectures of Confinement and Black Masculinity in Chicago* (Urbana: University of Illinois Press, 2015), 22. "Lynching in Canada [from the *NY Commercial*]," *North American*, 10 July 1841, 2. See also "Lynching in Canada," *New York Spectator*, 10 July 1841, 1. "March 14, 1853, St. Catharines Municipal Minutes, 1845–1855," Special Collections, St. Catharines Public Library in Campney, "'Canadians are not Proficient,'" 126. A Black militia attempted to train at the public grounds which sparked the anti-Black backlash in 1852; see "Row at St. Catharines," *Weekly Lancaster Gazette* [OH], 15 July 1852, 4.

42 Oil Springs in Campney, "'Canadians are not Proficient,'"124.

43 Lynching in northern US cities in Michael J. Pfeifer, "The Northern United States and the Genesis of Racial Lynching: The Lynching of African Americans in the Civil War Era," *Journal of American History*, 97.3 (Dec. 2010), 621–635. On NYC Draft Riots, see Leslie M. Harris, *In the Shadow of Slavery: African Americans in New York City, 1626–1863* (Chicago: University of Chicago Press, 2002); Iver Bernstein, *The New York City Draft Riots: Their Significance for American Society and Politics in the Age of the Civil War* (Lincoln: University of Nebraska Press, 2010). W. Fitzhugh Brundage connects southern lynchings to the political economic changes in the Introduction to his *Lynching in the New South*, 1–16.

44 The framework of continuity and change in the exploration of lynching was proposed by Brundage, *Lynching in the New South*, 12–13.

45 "Hung to a Telegraph Pole," *Alexandria Gazette*, 24 July 1893, 2. "Hanged by a Mob" and "The Baseball Scores," *Waterbury Evening Democrat*, 24 July 1893, 2. "Lynched and Roasted" and "On the Ball Field," *Morning Journal and Courier*, 24 July 1893, 3. "General News," *Iuka Reporter*, 27 July 1893, 2. On "ordinariness" in lynching, see David Garland, "Penal Excess and Surplus Meaning: Public Torture Lynchings in Twentieth-Century America," *Law and Society Review*, 39.4 (2005), 794.

46 Ravisher in "Monstrous," 1. Villain in "Lynched the Villain," *St. Paul Daily Globe*, 23 July 1893, 1. Negro rapist in "Lee Walker," *News-Herald* [OH], 27 July 1893, 2. Negro fiend in "A Ghastly Sight," 2. Rape fiend in "Lynched Sunday Morning," *Mexico Weekly Ledger* [MO], 27 July 1893, 2. "In the Latest Style," *Worthington Advance*, 27 July 1893, 2. "Lee Walker," *Times*, 28 July 1893, 6. "State News," *Columbia Herald*, 28 July 1893, 1. "State News Items," *Camden Chronicle* [TN], 28 July 1893, 2. Rayford W. Logan pioneered the approach of analyzing Black representation in print in *The Betrayal of the Negro: From Rutherford B. Hayes to Woodrow Wilson* (1954; New York: Da Capo Press, 1997), 371–395.

47 "Lynched and Cremated," 5. "Lee Walker," *Ohio Democrat*, 29 July 1893, 3.

48 Four attempts and success in "A Negro Lynched," *Salt Lake Herald*, 23 July 1893, 2. Lacerated and married woman in "Vengeance Visited," 6. Twelve years old in "Lynched and Burned," *Indianapolis Journal*, 23 July 1893, 2. For Sonders in Milwaukee, see "Negro Walker Lynched," *New York Times*, 8. For Sanders, see "Lynched by a Mob," 1. Place of previous rape in New Albany, see "A Memphis Lynching," 3.

49 His willingness in "State News Item," 2. Twenty to thirty women, age of nineteen, and comments from parents in an article that ran in many newspapers in, for example, "Lee Walker," *News-Herald* [Hillsboro, OH], 27 July 1893, 2, and "The Bones," *Daily Public Ledger* [Maysville, KY], 24 July 1893, 2. "Negro Walker Lynched," *New York Times*, 8. Twenty-two years old in "Within Memphis' Limits," *Indiana State Sentinel*, 26 July 1893, 2. Death certificate in Vandiver, *Lethal Punishment*, 61.

50 Pretty in "Another Southern Lynching," *Vermont Phoenix*, 28 July 1893, 3. Intersection of race and gender in anti-Black violence in Rosen, *Terror in the Heart of Freedom*, 8. Crystal N. Feimster, *Southern Horrors: Women and the Politics of Rape and Lynching* (Cambridge: Harvard University Press, 2009), 5.

51 Blackest in "A Lynching in Prospect," 4. Repulsive in "Within Memphis' Limits," 2.

52 1,000 in "Another Southern Lynching," 3. 3,000 in "State News Items," 2. 5,000 in "Monstrous," 1. 10,000 in "Hanged and Cremated," *Democratic Northwest* [OH], 27 July 1893, 4. Brundage finds that the "The anonymity offered by the vast crowds who gathered at these lynchings incited participants to acts of almost unlimited sadism." I believe the lack of accountability (which is related to anonymity) and the sanction of large crowds constructed a particularly cruel form of hostile racial difference. See Brundage, *Civilizing Torture*, 225.

53 Children in "Lynched by a Mob," 1. Blacks in "Hanged and Cremated," 4. Negroes in "Lynched Sunday Morning," 2.

54 100 in "Lynched by a Mob," 1. 40 in "Monstrous," 1. The Rev. Alonzo Ames Miner "deplored" southern lynchings, but said that "the North was also barbarous" in a Boston Antilynching Meeting, "Colored People Protest," *Boston Journal*, 30 Aug. 1894, 5.

55 *Shelby County's Shame*, 1–2, 4, 12. Feimster, *Southern Horrors*, 89. "News and Notes," *Lagos Weekly Record*, 13 Oct. 1894, 3.

56 Suspension in "Suspended the Jailor," *Washington Post*, 25 July 1893, 2. Grand jury and arrests in "After the Lynchers," *Atlanta Constitution*, 25 July 1893, 1. "Warning to Sheriffs," *Globe-Republican* [KS], 28 July 1893, 2. "Discouraging to Lynchers," *New York Times*, 25 July 1893, 2. "Officials and Lynchers Indicted," *Roanoke Times*, 6 Aug. 1893, 3. *Louisville Times* in *Hickman Courier*, 18 Aug. 1893, 2.

57 "Troops Ordered," *St. Paul Daily Globe*, 27 July 1893, 1. "The Mob Failed," *Roanoke Times*, 28 July 1893, 3.

58 Castellar [Castelar], 6 Nov. 1897, in "Late Telegrams," *Japan Times*, 3 Dec. 1897, 4. Jones in untitled editorial, *Cape Times*, 26 Oct. 1894, 4. Untitled editorial on lynching, *Japan Times*, 6 Apr. 1898, 2. Untitled editorial on "the Negro question," *Times of India*, 28 May 1892, 4.

59 Felton's address to Georgia Agricultural Society, 11 Aug. 1897, in "Woman's Place on the Farm," *Morning News* [Georgia], 12 Aug. 1897, 8, 3. See also Brundage, *Lynching in the New South*, 198. Quotation from Feimster, *Southern Horrors*, 127–128.

60 For reasons, see Appendix A in Brundage, *Lynching in the New South*, 270–283, and Vandiver, *Lethal Punishment*, 10. Lawless lynchings in "Miss Ida B. Wells, Agitator against Negro Lynching, Speaks," *Pacific Commercial Advertiser* [Hawaiian Islands], 18 Aug. 1894, 2.

61 On degradation and extraction, see Nancy Leong, "Racial Capitalism," *Harvard Law Review*, 126.8 (June 2013), 2152–2154. On value gap (diminishment of Black lives), see Eddie S. Glaude, Jr., *Democracy in Black: How Race Still Enslaves the American Soul* (New York: Broadway Books, 2016). Wells, "Preface," *The Reason Why*, 1. Rep. Cain, 24 Jan. 1874, 43rd Cong., 1st sess., *Congressional Record* 2, pt. 1: 901. Rep. Stowell, 6 Jan. 1874, 47th Cong., 1st sess., *Congressional Record* 2, pt. 1: 427. Oliver C. Cox agreed with this lynching assessment: "By lynching, Negroes are kept in their place, that is to say, kept as a great, easily-exploitable, common-labor reservoir," in "Lynching and the Status Quo," *Journal of Negro Education*, 14.4 (Autumn 1945), 584.

62 Garland, "Penal Excess," 817.

63 Antagonism in "The Two Races of the South," *Richmond Planet*, 8 May 1897, 3. Lee in "Emigration Advocated," *African Repository*, 1 Apr. 1890, 53.

64 Glaude, Jr., uses the term "illusion" instead of fantasy for a more modern (but similar) condition; see *Democracy in Black*, 184. "Colored Convention," *Atchinson Daily Globe*, 29 Nov. 1893, 1.

EPILOGUE

1 Hofstadter and Wallace, eds., *American Violence*, ix–xiv.

2 Hofstadter, "Reflections on Violence," 3.

3 Mills, *The Racial Contract*, 31.

4 Hofstadter, "Reflections on Violence," 11.

5 Herman, *Trauma and Recovery*, 7. Discounted in Ruth J. Simmons, "Slavery and Justice at Brown: A Personal Reflection" in *Slavery and the University: Histories and Legacies*, ed. Leslie M. Harris, James T. Campbell, and Alfred L. Brophy (Athens: University of Georgia Press, 2019), 116.

6 Kloppenberg, *The Virtues of Liberalism*, 5.

7 Graeber and Wengrow, *The Dawn of Everything*, 504.

Index

abolition movement, Kansas-Nebraska Act
and, 104–106
Adams, Abigail, 43, 49
Adams, John, 33–34, 57, 114
Boston Massacre and, 8–9, 11–13
on slave violence, 116
Southern colonies and, 45
on state violence, 8–9
Boston Massacre and, 8–9, 11–13
self-defense arguments for, 9, 11
on Washington, G., as military general,
42–43, 48
Adams, John Quincy, 95, 116–117
on military emancipation of slaves, 148
Adams, Zabdiel, 34
African Americans. *See also* lynching; racial
order; slavery
civil rights for, 244–245, 246–247
in criminal justice system, 241
displacement as result of railroad industry
expansion, 207–208
Freedmen Savings and Trust Company for,
209–210
insolvency of, 210
gun ownership among, 208–209
land rights for, 208–209
on liberalism, 11
removal to Africa, 133
on Republican Party, 140–141
violence against Black working class, 239–241
as wage laborers, 209
Africanus, S, M., 98
Akerman, Amos T., 214, 215
Allen, Ethan, 34–35
alliances and treaties, under Articles of
Confederation, 74–75

Allstadt, John, 128, 129
American Revolution. *See also* American
violence
Continental Congress and
Continental Army formed at, 38–39
Georgia refusal to join, 38–39, 44–45
Massachusetts Provincial Congress and,
36–37
Washington, G., at, 42–46
Massachusetts Provincial Congress, 33,
34–38
Continental Congress and, 36–37
endorsement of physical violence against
British authorities, 37
military setbacks for, 36
Ward and, 36–37
Warren and, 3, 35, 37–38
Washington, G., 42–46
military enrollment and, 24–38
in British Army, 24–30
in colonial provincial armies, 24–30
soldier discipline, 25–27
"no taxation without representation" and,
32–33
Seven Years' War and, 24
violence contextualized within, 23–24
violence during, 71–72
American violence, 13–15. *See also* exemplary
violence
"Bleeding Kansas," 14–15
Brown, J., on, 117
economic opportunity linked with, 28
1860 presidential election as referendum
on, 138
methodological approach to, 15–19
Militia Acts of 1792 and, 13, 85–86

American violence (cont.)
  railroad industry and, 205
    against Indigenous Americans, 205–208
  secessionist movement as influence on,
    149–150
  self-defense arguments for, 13, 34
  self-determination arguments for, 13
American Violence (Hofstadter and Wallace),
  266–267, 278
Anderson, Jeremiah, 120
Anderson, Robert, 149
Anderson, Tanisha, 266
Andrews, Sidney, 207–208
Annals of the Great Strikes in the United States
  (Dacus), 218–219
anti-abolitionist movement, Buchanan
  and, 109
anti-Black violence, 256–257
antislavery movement
  Buchanan on, 109
  Fugitive Slave Act and, 97–98
  Kansas-Nebraska Act and, 104–105
  Quakers in, 115
  Seward in, 147–148
armies. *See* Continental Army; national army
arms sales, to foreign markets, 203–204
Arnold, Benedict, 34
Articles of Confederation
  articles for alliances and treaties, 74–75
  articles for war, 74
  Constitutional Convention as response to, 76
  disintegration of Continental Army, 73
  function and purpose of, 73–74
  political life under, 76
  state violence resolution in, 77
  Virginia House of Delegates and, 75
Asian American workers, 238–239
Attucks, Crispus, 1–4, 12

Bacon, Francis, 9
Bacon's Rebellion, 32
Bailey, Ann, 51
Bailey, William S., 145
Bailyn, Bernard, 23
Baldwin, James, 19, 277, 279
Ball, Edward, 234
Bancroft, Hubert Howe, 254–255

Banks, Nathaniel, 193–194
Barrow, John, 39–40
Bates, Edward, 142
Battle of Antietam, 179–180
Beard, Lisa, 277, 279
Beaumont, Gustave de, 91–92, 295
  on American democracy, 92–93
    during Jackson administration,
      93–96
Beck, James Burnie, 247
Beckert, Sven, 6–7, 276
Benedict, Augustus W., 195, 197–198
Benét, S. B., 203
Benjamin, Judah P., 168
Bill of Rights, 79–80
Black, Jeremiah, 144
Black Americans. *See* African Americans
Black women, labor strikes by, 236–240
Blackstone, William, 282
Bland, Martha Daingerfield, 43
"Bleeding Kansas," 14–15
Bode, Phil, 262–263
Bond, Hugh Lennox, 213
Boston Massacre, 8
  Adams, J., as legal defense after, 8–9, 11–13
  Attucks and, 1–4
  British soldiers and, 1–2
  state violence and, 2–4
Bourke, Joanna, 251
Boyer, Ralph Ludwig, 47
Braddock, Edward (Major General), 40
Braddock, John Augustine, 40
Braden, Daniel P., 107
Bradford, William, 130–131
Breckenridge, John, 137–140
British Army
  Bacon's Rebellion and, 32
  Ethiopian Regiment in, 55
  expenditures during Seven Years' War, 31
  freed slaves in, 55
  funding sources for, 31–32
  Leisler Rebellion and, 32
  relocation of troops, 31–32
Brooks, Preston, 106
Brown, Ezekiel, 54
Brown, John, 3, 134. *See also* Harper's Ferry
  raid

on American violence, 117
Harper's Ferry raid, 107, 117, 118–120
Kansas-Nebraska Act and, 104–105, 108
abolitionist response to, 104–106
violence during, 106–107
Lee, Robert E., and, 118–120
Ossawatomie soldiers and, 137
Provincial Constitution, 131
Radical Abolition Party and, 104–105, 106, 141–142
on state violence, 124
Brown, Joseph E., 141–142
Brown, Mary, 97
Brown, Michael, 266
Brown, Samuel, 179
Brown, William, 239–240
Brundage, W. Fitzhugh, 318
Buchanan, James, 108–112, 121
as anti-abolitionist, 109
antislavery advocates' response to, 109
Compromise of 1850 and, 109
Declaration of Independence and, 110
after 1860 presidential election, 143–147
on disunion/secession of Southern states, 143–147
expansion of Kansas-Nebraska Act and, 109
posse comitatus and, 126
use of federal force by, 126
on White popular sovereignty, 110, 111–112
on White rebellion as domestic violence, 109–110
Buckingham, William, 135
Buckner, Aylett Hawes, 245
Burke, Tom, 262–263
Burns, Anthony, 122–123
Butler, Andrew, 106
Butler, Benjamin Franklin, 166, 245–246
Byrd, William, 117
Byrne, Terence, 129–130

Cain, Richard Harvey, 244–245
Caldwell, James, 1
Calhoun, John C., 96
Cameron, Simon, 177
capitalism. *See also* economic class crisis; Panic of 1873

economic oppression from, 227–229
industrial, 200
merchant, 6–7
racial, 13
state violence and, 13
as system of economic and political authority, 199
war, 6–7, 192
Carey, Miriam Iris, 266
Carmichael, William, 66
Carr, Patrick, 1
Carroll, John Lee, 223
Carter, Moses, 256–257
Cass, Lewis, 125
Castelar, Emilio, 263
Castile, Philando, 266
Caswell, Richard, 37–38
Chase, Salmon P., 147–148, 173–174
Cheney, Asa, 36
Chesnut, James, 152
citizenship
under French Constitution of 1791, 82
for military enrollment, 176
civil rights, for African Americans, congressional debates over, 244–245, 246–247
Civil War, in USA. *See also* racial order; Union Army
Battle of Antietam, 179–180
black soldiers during, 159–160
Confederate States of America, 170–171
re-enslavement of blacks in, 170–171
Congressional arguments for, 156
emancipation of slaves at start of, 164–165
Emancipation Proclamation, 157, 164–165, 180–181
biblical justification for, 183–184
in Confederate States of America, 170–171
critics of, 180–181
as instrument of violence, 181
fall of Fort Sumter and, 153–154, 157–159
First Confiscation Act and, 167, 169–170
gun ownership after, 201–203
Second Confiscation Act and, 173–175
Clarke, J. J., 134–135
Clay, Cassius, 135

Clay, Henry, 150–151
Clingman, Thomas Lanier, 146
Clinton, George, 63, 70
Clinton, Henry, 67
Coleman, James, 61–62
colonization, colonialism and
    conceptual scope of, 5
    confident ascendancy and, 4
    exemplary violence and, 6–7
    Indigenous displacement as result of, 5
    settler, 5
    slavery and, 5–7
    violence as element of, 5
Commentaries on the Conflict of Laws
        (Story), 151
Compromise of 1850
    Buchanan and, 109
    Fugitive Slave Act influenced by, 98–99
    liberal democracy and, 98–99
    slavery under, 98–99
Confederate States of America, 170–171
    re-enslavement of blacks in, 170–171
Confederated States. *See also* United States
    centralized violence of, 74
confident ascendancy, 4
Conrad, Charles Magill, 122
consent. *See* White consent
Constitution, US
    Bill of Rights, 79–80
        North Carolina resolution for, 84
    Black freedom under, 115, 171–172
    Constitutional Convention and
        Articles of Constitution, 77
        drafting of US Constitution, 77
        limits of state violence, 77–78, 80–84
        power of states, 78–79
    Fifth Amendment, 85–86
        slavery under, 171–172
    individual rights in, 80–84
        right to bear arms, 80–84
    Reconstruction Amendments, 212
    war powers under, 178–179
Constitutional Convention, 76–77
    Articles of Confederation and, 76
    Constitution created at
        Articles of, 77
        drafting of, 77

limits of state violence in, 77–78, 80–84
    power of states in, 78–79
delegates to, 76
national army established at, 79–80
slavery and, 76
state violence and
    deployment of, 78
    through militia, 79–80
    in new Constitution, 77–78
Whiteness and, 76
Constitutions, in France
    of 1791, 82
    of 1793, 82
    of 1795, 82
Continental Army
    black slaves in, 56–57
        rejection of, 56
    Continental Congress and, 38–39
        funding through, 57–58
    currency devaluation and, 57–58
    demands for pay and provisions for, 65
    demographics for, 54
    desertion from, 59–60, 62
    disobedience and dissention in, 59–60,
        66–68
    dissolution of, 73
    free Blacks in, 54–57
        Washington, G., response to, 54–55
    military discipline in, 83–84
    mutiny in, 14, 63–65
        Wayne's response to, 66–67, 71–72
    as permanent military force, 54
    supply shortages for, 57–58
        for food, 58–59
    training of, 61–62
    troop morale, 62–63
    Washington, G., and, 39–49
        centralization of, 53
        installation as military general, 42–46
        regional support for, 45
        response to mutiny, 67
        response to participation of Black men
            in, 54–55
    Wayne and, 60, 62–64, 65, 66
        response to military mutiny, 66–67, 71–72
    White consent and, 39
    women in, 51, 52–53

Continental Congress (1775)
Continental Army formed at, 38–39
funding of, 57–58
currency valuation by, 57–58
Georgia refusal to join, 38–39, 44–45
Hancock and, 47, 55, 63, 65, 68
Massachusetts Provincial Congress and,
36–37
Washington, G., at, 42–46
Conway, Moncure, 183
Cooke, Henry David, 209–210
Cooke, Jay, 209–210
Copeland, John A., Jr., 107, 129
Corbin, Margaret, 51
Corps d'Afrique, 193–195
Cox, Oliver C., 11
Cox, Samuel Sullivan, 246
criminal justice system, racism within, 241
Crispin, Silas, 203
Crittenden, John J., 146
Curry, Jabez, 142–143
Cutler, James Earle, 255

Dacus, J. A., 218–219, 235–236
Darwin, Charles, 226
Davis, Jefferson, 96, 104–105, 127–128, 129,
141, 184–185
during 1860 presidential election, 137
Dayton, Jonathan, 77–78
Deane, Silas, 38
Declaration of Independence, 81
Buchanan's interpretation of, 110
Lincoln's interpretation of, 110
Declaration of the Rights of Man, 116
Delany, Hubert T., 192
democracy, in USA. See also specific topics
Beaumont on, 92–93
for Black men, 92–93
during 1850s, 96
Kansas-Nebraska Act, 96
expansion of White male electorate, 93
under Jackson, A., 93–96
Kansas-Nebraska Act, "Bleeding Kansas,"
14–15
Tocqueville on, 92–93
Democracy in America (Tocqueville), 91–92
slavery in, 92–93

Democratic Party, 1860 presidential election
platform, 137–139
Davis, J., and, 137
Douglas, S., as candidate, 137–138
pro-slavery platform, 134
Denny, Ebenezer, 71–72
Denson, William Henry, 249
Dent, Frederick, 154
desertion, from military, from Continental
Army, 59–60, 62
Dickinson, John, 77–78
dissention, in military forces, in Continental
Army, 59–60, 66–68
disunion, of Southern states. See also
secessionist movement
Buchanan address on, 143–147
Republican Party platform against,
132–133
Dix, John A., 166–167
Dixon, James W., 240
Doctrine of Discovery, 205
Dodge, Augustus Caesar, 96–97, 99, 108
"Dodge and Douglas law." See Kansas-
Nebraska Act
Doolittle, J. R., 172
Douglas, H. Ford, 140
Douglas, Stephen, 101, 108, 111, 137,
139–140, 297
Douglass, Frederick, 98–99, 128, 133,
140–141
on lynching of African Americans, 254,
256–257
Doyle, Drury, 106–107
Doyle, James P., 106–107
Doyle, William, 106–107
Dred Scott decision, 111, 132–133, 137–138, 145
Du Bois, W. E. B., 11, 248–249
Du Pont, Samuel Francis, 158–159, 176–177
Durfee, Richard, 57
Durham, Milton Jameson, 248–249

economic class crisis. See also labor abuse;
labor strikes
analysis of, 217
criminal class and, 225–226
gender and, 236
race and, 236

1828 presidential election, in USA
  Adams, J. Q., and, 95
  Jackson, A., as candidate during, 93–95
    "Some Account of Some of the Bloody
      Deed of General Jackson," 93–95
1860 presidential election, in USA
  Buchanan after, 143–147
    on disunion/secession of Southern
      states, 143–147
  Democratic Party platform, 137–139
    Davis, J., and, 137
    Douglas, S., as candidate, 137–138
    pro-slavery platform, 134
  disunion/secession of Southern states
    Buchanan address on, 143–147
    Republican Party platform against,
      132–133
  electoral vote counts in Southern states,
    139–140
  international impact of, 140
  Kansas-Nebraska Act and, 132, 134
  Lincoln victory, 139–140
    White southern response to, 141–142
  "Minute Men" group and, 142
  as referendum on American violence, 138
  Republican Party platform, 132–135
    as antislavery party, 133
    against disunion/secession of Southern
      states, 132–133
    removal of Blacks to Africa, 133
    White southern response to, 141–142
  Wide Awake chapters during, 135–137
    violence between, 136–137
1876 presidential election, in USA,
  214–215
Elements for the Pathology of the Human Mind
  (Mayo), 15
Ellsworth, Oliver, 76–77
emancipation of slaves
  in Confederate States of America, 170–171
  cultural legacy of, 318
  under First Confiscation Act, 167, 169–170
  in New Orleans, 164
  under Second Confiscation Act, 173–175
  self-emancipation and, 160–161
    Planter ship and, 161–163
  at start of Civil War, 164–165

White nationalism and, 163–164
White northerners' response to, 163–164
Emancipation Proclamation, 157, 164–165,
  180–181
  biblical justification for, 183–184
  in Confederate States of America, 170–171
  critics of, 180–181
  ethics of, 183
  as instrument of violence, 181, 182–183
Emerson, William, 48–49
equality, under Declaration of the Rights of
  Man, 116
Erdman Act, USA (1898), 233
Ethiopian Regiment, 55
exemplary violence
  colonization and, 6–7
  merchant capitalism, 6–7
  slavery and, 6–7
  war capitalism and, 6–7
  by Washington, G., 72
    as disciplinary practice, 40–42, 69
  under Washington, G., 40–42

Fedderman, Richard, 225–226
Fifth Amendment, in US Constitution,
  85–86
  slavery under, 171–172
Fillmore, Millard, 98–99, 121, 122
Finch, Graham, 127–128
First Confiscation Act, USA (1861), 167,
  169–170
Fitzhugh, George, 197
Floyd, George, 266
Floyd, John B., 118, 120–121, 149
Fort Sumter, fall of, 153–154, 157–159
Forten, Charlotte, 123
Foster, J. G., 158–159
France
  Constitutions in
    of 1791, 82
    of 1793, 82
    of 1795, 82
  US arms sales to, 203–204
Franklin, Benjamin, 8, 34, 80, 89
Frazer, Harry M., 262–263
Freedmen Savings and Trust Company,
  209–210

freedom. *See also* emancipation of slaves;
  individual freedoms and rights
  for African Americans
    in Continental Army, 54–57
    in US Constitution, 115, 171–172
    as natural condition, 301
    violence and, 114–115
Freeman, Constant, 116
Freeport Doctrine, 297
Frelinghuysen, Frederick, 69
Fremont, John C., 167, 168–169
French, Mansfield, 161
Fugitive Slave Act, USA (1850), 96–100
  antislavery advocates' response to, 97–98
  Breckenridge and, 138–139
  commissions to capture former slaves
    under, 97
  Compromise of 1850 as foundation for,
    98–99
  Dodge and, 96–97, 99
  early fugitive slave laws and, 97
  justification for support of, 96–97, 99
  opposition to, 121–122
  White supremacy and, 99
fugitive slave laws, in USA, 97
Fukuyama, Francis, 10

Gage, Thomas, 33–34
Garner, Eric, 266
Garrett, John W., 120–121, 218
Garrison, Lloyd, 89
Gasparin, Agenor de (Count), 140
Gay, Samuel. *See* Bailey, Ann
gender. *See also* women
  economic class crisis and, 236
  labor abuse and, 236–240
Georgia
  refusal to join Continental Congress,
    38–39, 44–45
  state violence in, 44–45
Gill, Moses, 57
global White supremacy
  active participants in, 13
  passive participants in, 13
  whiteness and, 13
Gordon, Nathaniel, 171–172
Gorman, Willis, 101–102

Gorsuch, Edward, 97–98
Gradual Emancipation Act, USA
    (1784), 165
Graeber, David, 268–269
Grant, Ulysses, 154
Gray, Samuel, 1
Great Strikes of 1877, 14
  beginning of, 221–222
  causes of, 227
  Hayes, Rutherford, response to,
    222–225
  public response to, 225
  railroad debt after, 230
  replacement workers, 218
  state violence during, 226
  strike breakers during, 224–225
Green, Oneida James, 207
Green, Shields, 128
Greene, Christopher, 56
Greene, Nathanael, 21
Grenier, John, 86–87
Grenville, George, 3, 31–32
Grevins, Catherine, 163–164
Grevins, Iris, 163–164
Grimes, James Wilson, 161
Grinspan, Jon, 305–306
Grosvenor, Charles Henry, 250–251
Grotius, Hugo, 113
gun legislation
  in Argentina, 82–83
  in Guatemala, 82–83
  in Panama, 82–83
  in USA, 81–83
gun ownership
  among African Americans, 208–209
  gun market oversupply, 202–203
  in USA, 201–203
gun sales, 204

Haiti, slave revolution in, 83–84, 115–116
Hall, Ed, 261–262
Hall, Mya Shawatza, 266
Hamilton, Alexander, 76–77, 85
Hamilton, Robert, 245
Hamilton, Thomas, 140
Hamlet, James, 97
Hancock, John, 47, 55, 63, 65, 68

Harper's Ferry raid, slave rebellion at, 107,
117, 118–120
capital charges against, 123–124
capture of, 121
death sentence for, 124
federal response to, 118–120
under Militia Acts (1795,1807), 120–122,
144, 302–303
posse comitatus argument, 121–122, 123
Lee, Robert E., and, 118–120, 121, 123
participation of Black slaves in,
126–129
slaveowners' response to, 130–131
political response to, 123–124
Wise on, 124–125
Harris, John Thomas, 243
Hart, William B., 133
Haudenosaunee League, 86–87
Havemeyer, William Frederick, 228
Hawkins, Dan, 261–262
Hawkins, William, 8–9
Hayes, Robert, 261–262
Hayes, Rutherford B., 3, 215–216
Great Strikes of 1877 and, 222–225
Haynes, John, 261–262
Herman, Judith, 267–268
Herndon, William Smith, 245
Hicks, Josiah Duane, 251
Hill, James, 164–165
Hitler, Adolph, 207
Hobbes, Thomas, 4
Hoffman, Louis, 208–209
Hofstadter, Richard, 266–268, 278
Holland, Edwin C., 126–127, 150
Houston, Sam, 141
Howe, Robert (General), 16, 69–70
Hunter, David, 177–178
Hunter, Tera W., 237

Indigenous displacement
through colonization, 5
destruction of native economies through,
206
Doctrine of Discovery and, 205
protests against, 206–207
through railroad industry expansion,
205–208

individual freedoms and rights
in liberal society, 10
right to bear arms, 80–84
Jefferson on, 81
right to revolution and, 81
right to revolution, 81
in national constitutions, 82–83

Jackson, Andrew, 93–96, 125, 172
1828 presidential election, 93–95
"Some Account of Some of the Bloody
Deeds of General Jackson," 93–95
Nullification Crisis and, 150–151
as symbol of White masculinity, 95
Jackson, Stonewall, 179
Jefferson, Thomas, 55, 87, 109, 131
on rebellious slaves, 117
on right to bear arms, 81
on right to revolution, 81
on state violence, 80
on states' rights, 150
on war powers, 179
"John Brown's Body," 117–118
Johnson, Andrew, 148
Johnson, Oliver, 183
Johnson, Samuel, 31–32
Johnson, Thomas L., 141
Johnson, William (Justice), 117
Jones, John B., 143
Jones, Thomas G., 263
Judge, Ona, 160
justice. See military justice

Kandiaronk, 71
Kansas-Nebraska Act, USA (1854), 96, 100–106
abolitionist response to, 104–105
by Brown, J., 104–106
antislavery response to, 104–105
"Bleeding Kansas," 14–15
Brown, J., and, 108
abolitionist response by, 104–106
violence by, 106–107
under Buchanan, 109
Dodge and, 96–97, 99, 108
Douglas, S., and, 101, 108
1860 presidential election and, 132, 134
expansion of, 109

Lincoln on, 103
in newspapers, 100–101
Pierce and, 101, 103–105
popular sovereignty arguments for, 101–102
states' rights arguments for, 101–102
territorial expansion and, 100
violence as result of, 103–106, 107–108, 297
by Brown, J., 106–107
as voter referendum on slavery, 102–105
emigration of transplants to Kansas, 102–105
Killroy, Matthew, 12
King, Rufus, 309
Kloppenberg, James, 268
Knox, Henry, 66, 85–86, 87, 116
Koop, C. Everett, 279
Ku Klux Klan, 250
Ku Klux Klan Act of 1871, USA, 212–213
federal prosecution of Klansmen under, 213

labor abuse
of Asian American workers, 238–239
of freed Blacks, 209
by race, 236–240
White violence and, 239–241
of Union Army soldiers, 196–197
of women, 236–240
labor strikes, 218–230. See also Great Strikes of 1877
of Baltimore and Ohio rail line, 219–221
Black men and, 235–236
by Black women, 236–240
economic oppression as influence on, 227–229
under Erdman Act, 233
from labor repression, 229
Pinkerton and, 233
racism during, 234–235
strike breakers, 224–225
labor violence, 230–233
definition of, 231
destruction of railroad property, 232
Pinkerton and, 233
Lacey, John, Jr., 58
Lahontan, Baron, 71
Lamb, James B., 138

land rights, property rights and, for African Americans, 208–209
Lane, James Henry, 167
Latimer, George, 160–161
Latimer, Rebecca, 263–264
Laurance, John, 84
Laurens, Henry, 56–57
Laurens, John, 65
Leary, Lewis, 129
Lee, Henry, 60
Lee, Richard Henry, 79–80
Lee, Robert E., 3, 152, 179
Harper's Ferry raid and, 118–120, 121, 123
Leeman, William, 120
Leisler Rebellion, 32
Levenson, Deborah T., 10–11
Lewis, Frank, 169
liberal democracy, Compromise of 1850 and, 98–99
liberal society. See also specific topics
black scholarship on, 11
hierarchies in, 19
individual freedoms in, 10
public sphere in, 10
racial capitalism in, 13
state violence in, 9–11
against people of color, 12
tolerance in, 10–11
liberalism, 296
black scholarship on, 11
Lilienthal, Augusta, 228
Lincoln, Abraham, 96, 108. See also Civil War; 1860 presidential election
as antislavery advocate, 132
on arithmetic of Civil War, 174–175
cabinet positions under, 146–148
Seward as Secretary of State, 147–148
compensation to slaveowners, 171–172
on Declaration of Independence, 110
on Douglas, S., 111
in 1860 presidential election
electoral victory, 139–140
White southern response to, 141–142
Emancipation Proclamation, 157, 164–165, 180–181
biblical justification for, 183–184

Lincoln, Abraham (cont.)
  in Confederate States of America, 170–171
  critics of, 180–181
  ethics of, 183
  as instrument of violence under, 181
  on fall of Fort Sumter, 153–154
  First Confiscation Act, 167
  Hunter and, 178
  on Kansas-Nebraska Act, 103
  mobilization of Black men in Union Army, 117–118
  on popular sovereignty policies, 110–111
  posse comitatus and, 137
  righteousness of, 134–135
  Second Confiscation Act, 173–175
  Speed and, 111
  war powers under, 178–179
Lipsitz, George, 13
Livingston, William, 69
Locke, John, 80–81, 113
Lockhart, Paul, 36
Loder, C. H., 234–235
Lovejoy, Owen, 161
Lowell, James Russell, 155
lynching, of African Americans, 251–263, 335–336
  as anti-Black violence, 256–257
  anti-lynching activists, 264–265
  Douglass on, 254, 256–257
  newspaper accounts of, 251–254, 258–259, 260–261
  Wells, Ida B., on, 264–265
  White supremacy and, 263–264

Machiavelli, Niccolo, 35, 80, 282
Madison, James, 77–78, 87–88, 130–131
Magruder, John Bankhead, 170–171
Malthus, Thomas, 209
Marchand, J. B., 161
Marie, or Slavery in the United States (Beaumont), 91–92
Marshall, John (Justice), 205
Martin, Charley, 252
Martin, Joseph Plumb, 57
Martin, Luther, 77
Marvin, Elihu, 87–88

Marx, Karl, 140, 173–174, 199–200
Mason, George, 76, 77, 78, 79, 84, 87–88, 145
Mason, James Murray, 96, 127–128
Massachusetts Provincial Congress, 33, 34–38
  Continental Congress and, 36–37
  endorsement of physical violence against British authorities, 37
  military setbacks for, 36
  Ward and, 36–37
  Warren and, 3, 35, 37–38
  Washington, G., and, 46
  command structure under, 48
Masur, Kate, 93
Maverick, Samuel, 1
Mayo, Thomas, 15
McClain, J. C., 226
McClellan, George B., 166–167
McDowell, Calvin, 261–262
McElwee, Thomas B., 230
McLane, Robert Milligan, 248
McMillan, Harry, 207–208
Mease, James, 56–57
Meigs, Jonathan, 61
Menzies, John, 169
merchant capitalism, 6–7
Metcalf, Seth, 25
Miles, Frederick, 172
military emancipation of slaves, 148
military enrollment. See also Union Army
  during American Revolution, 24–38
  in British Army, 24–30
  in colonial provincial armies, 24–30
  soldier discipline, 25–27
  shrinking of, 200
  US citizenship as result of, 176
military justice, under Fifth Amendment, 85–86
militia. See military enrollment; national militia
Militia Act, USA (1795), 120–122, 144
Militia Act, USA (1807), 120–122, 144, 302–303
Militia Act of 1862, USA, 194
Militia Acts of 1792, USA, 13, 85–86
Mill, John Stuart, 10, 178–179
Miller, Samuel, 212
Mills, Charles W., 113

"Minute Men" group, 142
Missouri Compromise of 1820, 98. *See also*
	Compromise of 1850
Monroe, James, 131
Mormon resistance, in Utah Territory,
	111–112
Moss, Tom, 261–262
Mumford, Abigail, 5–6, 7
Mumford, Thomas, 5–6, 7
Mumford, William Bruce, 174
Murch, Thompson Henry, 249
mutiny, in military forces, in Continental
	Army, 14, 63–65
	Wayne's response to, 66–67

Napier, Charles, 21
Nason, Samuel, 79
national army, Constitutional Convention
	establishment of, 79–80
national militia
	Constitutional Convention, 79–80
	under Militia Acts of 1792, 13, 85–86
	state violence through, 79–80
	Washington, G., on establishment of,
		85–86, 87
nation-states
	as political construct, 4
	as social construct, 4
	USA as, 4–5
	terminology for, 4
nation-states, USA as, 4–5
Native Americans. *See also* Indigenous
	displacement
	in "Indian schools,", 207
nature. *See* state of nature
Neff, Stephen C., 301
*A New and Impartial History of England, from
	Invasion of Julius Cæsar, to the Signing of
	the Preliminaries of Peace, in the Year 1762*
	(Barrow), 39–40
New Orleans, Louisiana
	emancipation of slaves in, 164
	Union Army in, 194
Newby, Dangerfield, 120
Newman, William, 98–99
Nez Perce, 206
Nicholls, Francis, 240–241

Nickels, J. F., 158–159
Niebuhr, Reinhold, 89
"no taxation without representation," 32–33
Nones, Henry, 167
Nullification Crisis, 150–151

Oakes, James, 309
On the Penitentiary System (Beaumont and
	Tocqueville), 91–92
Osgood, Samuel, 48
Ossawatomie soldiers, 137
Ostler, Jeffrey, 206

Paine, Robert Treat, 3
Panic of 1873
	civil rights protections influenced by, 214
	railroad industry during, 210
	White violence during, 210–212
Parker, Theodore, 122–123
Parks, Jim, 118
Peale, Charles Wilson, 42–43
Peloponnesian War, 84
Pendleton, Edmund, 39, 79
Perkins, Joseph, 85, 262
Peters, George B., 262
Pettus, John J., 146–147
Petty, Abiel, 36
Pierce, Franklin, 101, 103–105, 126
Pierpont, Francis H., 186
Pinckney, Charles, 76
Pinkerton, Allan, 233
Pitcher, Zerich, 157–158
Pitt, William, 33–34
Planter (ship), 161–163, 187–188
popular sovereignty
	Buchanan on, 110, 111–112
	Lincoln on, 111–112
	White violence and, 111
Porter, William Dennison, 149–150
posse comitatus
	Buchanan's use of, 126
	Harper's Ferry raid and, 121–122, 123
	Lincoln's use of, 137
presidential elections, in USA *See specific
	elections*
Preston, S. W., 164
Provincial Constitution, of Brown, J., 131

Pryor, Elizabeth Stordeur, 106
public sphere, in liberal society, 10
Putnam, Rufus, 3–4, 25–30

Quackenbush, William, 213
Quakers, in antislavery movement, 115

race, racism and. *See also* African Americans;
    American violence; racial order;
    slavery
  within criminal justice system, 241
  economic class crises by, 236
  within railroad industry, 234–235
  under Southern Homestead Act, 207–208
racial capitalism
  in liberal society, 13
  state violence and, 13
racial differences, 245–246
  new forms of, 242
racial order, in postwar period
  civil rights debates and, 244–245, 246–247
  racial differences and, 245–246
    new forms of, 242
  White peril claims, 249
  White supremacy and, 245–246, 250–251
  White violence as part of, 250–263
racial separation, 265
racism. *See* race
Radical Abolition Party, 104–105, 106,
    141–142. *See also* Harper's Ferry raid
railroad industry. *See also* Great Strikes of
    1877; labor strikes
  American violence and, 205
    against Indigenous Americans, 205–208
  black displacement in South as result of,
    207–208
  under Erdman Act, 233
  expansion of, 204
  during Panic of 1873, 210
  racism within, 234–235
  in South, 207–208
  United States Military Railroads, 204
Randolph, Edmund, 76
Ransier, Alonzo Jacobs, 243–245
Rawle, William, 152
rebellions. *See also* slave rebellions; White
    rebellion

Bacon's Rebellion, 32
Leisler Rebellion, 32
Shays's Rebellion, 75
Reclus, Elisée, 140
Reconstruction Amendments, in USA
    Constitution, 212
Reed, Hiram, 169
Reed, Joseph, 66–67, 68
Reeves, Enos, 63
regeneration through violence, 13
Reilly, Hugh, 203
Relyea, C. J., 157–158
Republican Party
  1860 presidential election platform,
    132–135
    as antislavery party, 133
    against disunion/secession of Southern
      states, 132–133
    removal of Blacks to Africa, 133
    White southern response to, 141–142
  free blacks' response to, 140–141
Ricardo, David, 209
Rice, Tamir, 266
Richardson, John Smyth, 248
Ridley, Luke, 25
right to bear arms, 80–84
  Jefferson on, 81
  right to revolution and, 81
right to revolution, 81
  in national constitutions, 82–83
rights. *See* individual freedoms and rights
Riley, J. E., 225–226
Ripley, Roswell S., 160
Robbins, William McKendree, 244
Roberts, Dorothy, 246
Robinson, Cedric J., 11
Rogers, John, 176
Rogier, Charles, 155–156
Ropes, Hannah, 103
Rosecrans, William, 197
Ross, Philip, 230
Rush, Benjamin, 43
Rutherford, John, 85–86

Sabine, George H., 296
Sampson, Deborah, 51–52
Sanford, Henry S., 155

Saxton, Rufus, 163–164, 178
Scarry, Elaine, 16
Schuyler, Philip John, 63
Scott, Winfield, 122, 150–151
Seabury, Samuel, 278–279
secessionist movement, 149–152
American violence transformed by, 149–150
states' rights argument for, 150–152
in Supreme Court, 151
Treaty of Paris and, 150
Second Confiscation Act, USA (1862), 173–175
Sedgewick, Charles B., 172–173
Seider, Christopher, 8
self-defense
American violence and, 13
white, 13
self-determination
American violence and, 13
white, 13
self-emancipation, by former slaves, 160–161
Planter ship and, 161–163
Semmes, Raphael, 170
settler colonialism, 5
settler colonization, 5
Seven Years' War, 1–2, 24, 31, 39–40
Seward, William Henry, 147–148, 153, 170, 179, 309
Shays, Daniel, 75
Shays's Rebellion, 75
Shepherd, Heyward, 127
Sherman, Thomas, 177
Sherman, William Tecumseh, 106–107, 186, 187–188, 189
A Short History of Standing Armies (Trenchard), 53
Shurtleff, Robert. See Sampson, Deborah
Shy, John, 33
Simons, Molly, 318
Sinn, John, 118
slave rebellions. See also Harper's Ferry raid
Haitian Revolution, 115–116
Washington, G., on, 116
Jefferson on, 117
slave violence, 116. See also Harper's Ferry raid

slaveowners
compensation to, 171–172
justification of violence by, 113
on slaves' participation in Harper's Ferry rebellion, 130–131
slavery, in USA See also Emancipation Proclamation; Fugitive Slave Act; Kansas-Nebraska Act; slave rebellions; slave violence
as biblical transgression, 183–184
colonization and, 5–7
under Compromise of 1850, 98–99
Dred Scott decision and, 111, 132–133, 137–138, 145
Emancipation Proclamation and, 157, 164–165, 180–181
biblical justification for, 183–184
in Confederate States of America, 170–171
critics of, 180–181
ethics of, 183
as instrument of violence under, 181
exemplary violence and, 6–7
expansion of, 96, 100–106, 111
under Fifth Amendment, 171–172
fugitive slave laws, 97
under Kansas-Nebraska Act
emigration of transplants as result of, 102–105
as voter referendum, 102–105
legal end of, 191
under Missouri Compromise of 1820, 98
regional limitations for, 5
violence and, 5–7
exemplary, 6–7
Washington, G., and, 41–42, 55
slaves. See also Emancipation Proclamation; slave rebellions; slave violence
in British Army, 55
rejection of black slaves, 56
in Continental Army, 56–57
Harper's Ferry rebellion participation by, 126–129
slaveowners' response to, 130–131
military emancipation of, 148
self-emancipation by, 160–161
Planter ship and, 161–163
violence by, 114–115

Slemmer, A. J., 158–159

Smalls, Elizabeth Lydia, 157–158

Smalls, Hannah Jones, 157–158

Smalls, Robert, 3–4, 157–160, 164, 172–173
  black-directed violence of, 176–177
  Planter ship and, 161–163, 187–188

Smith, Ann, 51

Smith, Edward B., 193, 197–198

Smith, John, 163–164

Smith, Percy, 240

Smith, Samuel. *See* Smith, Ann

Smith, Silas, 163–164

Snead, Thomas L., 169

"Some Account of Some of the Bloody Deeds
  of General Jackson," 93–95

Southern Homestead Act, USA (1866),
  207–208

sovereignty. *See* popular sovereignty

Speed, Joshua, 111, 183

Spencer, Herbert, 226

St. Clair, Arthur, 65

Stamp Act, UK, 31

Stanley-Jones, Aiyana Mo'Nay, 266

Stanton, Edwin, 177, 179, 186, 200

state of nature, 4
  freedom as, 301
  violence as, 4–5

state violence. *See also* American violence
  Adams, J., on, 8–9
    Boston Massacre and, 8–9, 11–13
    self-defense arguments by, 9, 11
  Boston Massacre and, 2–4
    Adams, J., and, 8–9, 11
    legal guilt for soldiers in, 8–9
  Brown, J., on, 124
  capitalism and, 13
  in Georgia, 44–45
  global White supremacy and, 13
  during Great Strikes of 1877, 226
  as imperial policy, 3
  individual violence as distinct
    from, 276
  Jefferson on, 80
  legal foundations of, 8–9
  in liberal society, 9–11
    against people of color, 12
  racial capitalism and, 13

responsibility for, 8–15
  Washington, G., on, 114

states' rights. *See also* popular sovereignty
  Davis, J., on, 152
  Kansas-Nebraska Act and, 101–102
  as local resistance to national authority,
    151–152
  Nullification Crisis and, 150–151
  secessionist movement and, 150–152
    in Supreme Court, 151
  Treaty of Paris and, 150

Steedman, James Blair, 163

Steuart, G. H., 220

Stevens, Thaddeus, 134–135, 172

Stewart, Will, 261–262

Stockton, Annis Boudinot, 52

Story, Joseph (Justice), 151

Stowell, William Henry Harrison, 241,
  242–243

strikes. *See* labor strikes

Stringfellow, John H., 102–103

Strother, David Hunter, 119

Stuart, Gilbert, 43

Stuart, J. E. B., 118

Sturgis, Samuel Davis, 167

Sugar Act, UK, 31

Sumner, Charles, 106, 147–148, 165

Sumner, William Graham, 230

Swanson, Claude Augustus, 249

Sylvis, William, 198–199

Symmes, William, 78, 292

Taft, Philip, 230

Talmage, C. M., 189

Taussig, Michael, 43–44

Taylor, Breonna, 266

Taylor, James E., 64

Thomas, Henry, 197

Thomas, Lorenzo, 196

Tillman, William, 176–177

Tocqueville, Alexis de, 91–93, 295
  on American democracy, 92–93
    during Jackson administration, 93–96
  racism of, 92
  on slavery in USA, 92–93
  on White supremacy, 92
  on Whiteness in USA, 92–93

Tolbert, Samuel, 63
tolerance, toleration and, in liberal society, 10–11
Townsend, E.D., 200
Townsend Revenue Act, UK, 31
Treaty of Paris, 150
Trenchard, Jonathan, 53
Trumbull, Jonathan, 61
Tucker, St. George, 152
Turner, Henry McNeal, 265
Tutson, Hannah, 250
Tutson, Samuel, 250

UK. *See* United Kingdom
Union Army, Black men in, 159–160, 176–177, 186–187
Corps d'Afrique, 193–195
court-martial of, 197–198
double standards for, 186
formation of regiments, 177–178
labor abuses by, 196–197
Lincoln's mobilization of, 117–118
under Militia Act of 1862, 194
mutiny of, 197–198
in New Orleans, 194
protests of payment policies, 194–195
punishment policies in, 196–197
slave fugitives, 171
United Kingdom (UK)
Seward and, 170
Stamp Act, 31
Sugar Act, 31
Townsend Revenue Act, 31
United States (USA). *See also* African Americans; American Revolution; American violence; Constitution; slavery; *specific topics*
Articles of Confederation for, 76
Compromise of 1850
liberal democracy and, 98–99
slavery under, 98–99
Compromise of 1850 in, Buchanan and, 109
Erdman Act, 233
First Confiscation Act, 167, 169–170
fugitive slave laws in, 97
Gradual Emancipation Act, 165

gun ownership in, 201–203
Ku Klux Klan Act of 1871, 212–213
federal prosecution of Klansmen under, 213
Militia Act (1795), 120–122, 144
Militia Act (1807), 120–122, 144, 302–303
Militia Act of 1792, 13, 85–86
Militia Act of 1862, 194
Missouri Compromise of 1820, 98
Second Confiscation Act, 173–175
Southern Homestead Act, 207–208
United States Military Railroads (USMRR), 204
Upshur, Abel P., 151
USA *See* United States
USMRR. *See* United States Military Railroads
Utah Territory, 111–112

Vance, Robert Brank, 244–245
Vandergriff, William P., 222
Vandiver, Margaret, 252
Vattel, Emmerich, 113–114, 123
Vesey, Denmark, 117
A View of the Constitution of the United States (Rawle), 152
Vining, Richard, 57
violence. *See also* American violence; state violence; White violence
American Revolution and, 23–24, 71–72
anti-Black violence, 256–257
colonization through, 5
of Confederated States, 74
under Emancipation Proclamation, 181
exemplary
colonization and, 6–7
merchant capitalism, 6–7
slavery and, 6–7
freedom and, 114–115
Kansas-Nebraska Act and, 103–106, 107–108, 297
by Brown, J., 106–107
origins of, 279
regeneration through, 13
by slaveowners, 113
slavery and, 5–7
exemplary violence and, 6–7
by slaves, 114–115

violence (cont.)
as state of nature, 4–5
state violence as distinct from individual
violence, 276
transnational flows of, 13
White rebellion as, 109–110
between Wide Awake chapters, 136–137
women and, 236–240

Waddell, James, 184–185
wage labor, 199–200
Walker, Lee, 3–4, 19, 251–254, 258–259,
261–263
Walker, William, 197–198
Wallace, Michael, 266–267, 278
Walton, Michael, 115
war, articles for, under Articles of
Confederation, 74
war capitalism
breakdown of, 192
exemplary violence and, 6–7
war powers, 178–179
Ward, Artemas (General), 36–37, 44
Ward, Durbin, 224
Ward, J. H. Hobart, 136–137
Ward, Samuel, 98–99
Warren, Joseph, 3, 35, 37–38
Warren, Mercy Otis, 33–34
Washington, George. See also Continental Army
Continental Army and, 39–49
centralization of command structure, 53
division between North and South, 45
installation as military general, 42–46, 47
regional support for, 45
response to mutiny, 67
response to participation of Black men
in, 54–55
at Continental Congress, 42–46
demand for pay and provisions by, 65
disciplinary practices under
exemplary violence in, 40–42, 69
slavery and, 42
as enslaver, 41, 44–45, 55
exemplary violence, 72
as disciplinary practice, 40–42, 69
Massachusetts Provincial Congress and, 46
command structure under, 48

military service of, 39–42
on national militia, 85–86, 87
physical presence, 43
on state violence, 114
Washington, Lewis, 128, 129
Washington, Martha, 41–42
Washington, Prophet, 163–164
Wayne, Anthony (General), 60, 62–64, 65,
66, 87
response to military mutiny, 66–67,
71–72
Webb, Thomas, 102–103
Welles, Gideon, 182–183
Wells, Ida Bell, 189, 254, 261–262
as anti-lynching activist, 264–265
Wengrow, David, 268–269
White, Francis, 63
White, Graham, 261–262
White consent, Continental Army and, 39
White peril, claims of, 249
White rebellion, as domestic violence,
109–110
White supremacy, in USA See also global
White supremacy
Fugitive Slave Act and, 99
lynching of African Americans and,
263–264
racial order and, 245–246, 250–251
Tocqueville on, 92
White violence. See also lynching; race; right
to bear arms; slavery
against Black working class, 239–241
through criminal justice system, 241
during 1876 presidential election,
214–215
from Kansas-Nebraska Act, 103–106,
107–108
Brown, J., and, 106–107
during Panic of 1873, 210–212
popular sovereignty and, 111
racial order and, 250–263
whiteness
in criminal justice system, 241
global White supremacy and, 13
as political system, 13
self-defense and, 13
self-determination and, 13

Wickliffe, Charles, 172–173, 178

Wide Awake chapters, during 1860
    presidential election, 135–137
  violence between, 136–137

Wigfall, Louis T., 152

Wilkerson, Isabel, 10–11

Wilkinson, Allen, 106–107

Wilkinson, Louisa Jane, 106–107

Williams, Frank, 193, 197–198

Williams, George Henry, 214

Williams, James D., 223

Williams, Warner, 261–262

Wilson, James, 76–77

Wilson, W. G., 239–240

Wise, George, 134–135, 249

Wise, Henry, 118, 123–125

Wolcott, Oliver, 114–115

women. *See also* Black women
  in Continental Army, 51, 52–53
  economic class crisis for, 236
  violence and, 236–240

Yandell, Lundsford P., 156

Young, Brigham, 111–112